Selective attention in vision

Selective Attention in Vision provides the first integrated account of the most important area of selective attention research. Drawing on twenty years of research experience in the field, Dr Van der Heijden presents a clear and explicit theory of selective attention in vision.

Beginning with an account of the information processing approach, the author goes on to disentangle and define the complex concept of 'selective attention'. The data from four different experimental paradigms are presented and critically discussed, and finally an explicit theory of selective attention in vision is developed.

'A superb analysis and impressive contribution'
Professor C.W. Eriksen, *University of Illinois*

Dr A.H.C. Van der Heijden is Associate Professor at the Unit of Experimental and Theoretical Psychology, Leiden University. He is the author of *Short-Term Visual Information Forgetting* (RKP, 1981).

International Library of Psychology

Selective attention in vision

A.H.C. Van der Heijden

London and New York

First published in 1992
by Routledge
11 New Fetter Lane, London EC4P 4EE

Simultaneously published in the USA and Canada
by Routledge
a division of Routledge, Chapman and Hall Inc.
29 West 35th Street, New York, NY 10001

Typeset by LaserScript Limited, Mitcham, Surrey
Printed and bound in Great Britain by
Mackays of Chatham PLC, Chatham, Kent

British Library Cataloguing in Publication Data

Heijden, A.H.C. Van der
  Selective attention in vision. – (International library of psychology)
  1. Man. Attention
  I. Title II. Series
  153.733

Library of Congress Cataloging in Publication Data

Heijden, A.H.C. Van der.
  Selective attention in vision / A.H.C. Van der Heijden.
  p.   cm. – (International library of psychology)
  Includes bibliographical references and index.
  1. Visual perception. 2. Selectivity (Psychology). 3. Attention.
  I. Title.   II. Series.
  BF241.H43 1991
  153.7'33–dc20   90-24543
                                                                       CIP

ISBN 0–415–06105–9

Hanneke

Aan het roer dien avond stond het hart
en scheepte maan en bossen bij zich in
en zeilend over spiegeling
van al wat het geleden had
voer het met wind en schemering
om boeg en tuig voorbij de laatste stad.

Gerrit Achterberg

Contents

Figures and tables

FIGURES

TABLES

Acknowledgements

The basis of this study is the experimental work done in cooperation with students at the University of Leiden: Alec, Bart, Bert, Cecilia, Diana, Eddy, Erik, Frank, Hanneke, Hans, Hans, Harry, Ineke, Ineke, Jeroen, Jeroen, Marc, Marjan, Martijn, Martin, Miranda, Rino, Ruchama, Sjaak and Wido. They also contributed substantially to the development of the ideas expressed in this work. Drs G. Wolters and W.A. Wagenaar created for me a protected position that made the work possible. Ans Joustra assisted me with writing, and forced me to continue. The Zentrum für Interdisziplinäre Forschung (ZIF) of the University of Bielefeld provided an excellent opportunity to finish the work. Thanks are due to the Canadian Psychological Association (Old Chelsea, Quebec, Canada), Lawrence Erlbaum Associates, Inc. (Hillsdale, New Jersey, USA), Psychonomic Society Publications (Austin, Texas, USA) and Springer-Verlag (Heidelberg, Germany) for permission to draw on and re-use parts of my earlier work.

Chapter 1

The approach

1.0 Introduction

Attention is the main topic of this study. It is not difficult to introduce this topic, because

> Every one knows what attention is. It is the taking possession by the mind, in clear and vivid form, of one out of what seem several simultaneously possible objects or trains of thought. Focalization, concentration, of consciousness are of its essence. It implies withdrawal from some things in order to deal effectively with others, ...

> (James, 1890/1950, pp. 403–4)

Formulated in this way, however, this topic is much too general and broad to be dealt with in a single study. No one really knows what mind, consciousness, thought or attention is and even a concept like 'things' is quite problematic in the study of attention. So, selections and specifications are necessary. In fact, two choices have to be made. The first choice concerns the precise issues to be dealt with, the second how to deal with or approach the selected issues.

As for the issues, the empirical part of the present study is mainly concerned with *central attention* as it operates in detection and recognition tasks in vision. In the next chapter I further delimit and elaborate the concept 'attention' more precisely. To start with, an approximate operational definition suffices. *Attention* shows up as benefits in detection and/or recognition performance in conditions with appropriate selection, emphasis or priority instructions as compared with conditions without such instructions. *Central* attentional effects in vision are demonstrated if these benefits are observed in a situation that excludes directed eye movements.

The approach I wish to follow is a variant of the information processing approach. This approach does not limit itself to operational definitions and the relations between (observable) inputs and (observable) outputs. In general, the information processing approach to perception and cognition tries to infer aspects of the internal structure and functioning of a behaving organism from the overt behaviour of that organism, so that it becomes possible to explain the organism's behaviour in terms of its internal structure and functioning.

It is this *approach* that is the topic of this chapter. More specifically, the present chapter presents a description and justification of the information processing approach *as I practise it* in studying the topic of my concern: central attention in vision (see Palmer and Kimchi, 1986, for an impressive, more general, discussion of the basic assumptions of the information processing approach). Such a description and justification is necessary because *the* scientific method (and *the* philosophy of science) are simply myths. Contemporary philosophy of science does not prescribe how scientists ought to work; it simply describes the successful practices of working scientists (see, e.g., Fodor, 1981a). But one has to be well aware that

> The distance between one's philosophical views ... and everyday psychological investigations is remarkably short. One has but to look at the introductory and concluding sections of reports of straight-forward laboratory observations to see that what experimenters think is being studied and what morals they are prepared to draw from the results is thoroughly conditioned by the stand that they take on the most basic philosophical questions about the nature of mind and of psychological explanation.
>
> (Pylyshyn, 1981, p. 267)

So, to inform the reader about what I think is being studied and what morals I am prepared to draw, I had better first clarify my stand on issues like psychological explanation and the nature of mind.

My first, rather pragmatic, conviction is that basically one can have the psychology one wishes. The only real criterion is that the approach taken works. To show, however, that an approach really works and leads to worthwhile results, it is necessary to isolate it from alternative and competing approaches and to specify what it is trying to accomplish. Only then does it become possible to distinguish between results that are approach-internal and results that are approach-external; to see where modest science ends and borrowing right and left starts. Especially for the information processing approach the borderline between realistic aims and exaggerated claims is extremely thin. Because the approach is surrounded by alternative approaches that advertise important and attractive results, there is a continuous temptation to enter a neighbour's lands.

So, the task that I set myself in the present chapter is to delineate and describe the information processing approach in general, and as I practise it in studying attention in particular, in such a way that my approach can be distinguished from

- alternative approaches within what is nowadays called 'Cognitive Science'. Within the group of sciences concerned with systems that process information the aims and tools of contributors like artificial intelligence, computer science, the neurosciences, linguistics and several branches of philosophy, are clearly different.

- alternative approaches within general experimental psychology. Within contemporary experimental psychology there are not only the influences from previous approaches like Wundt's and Titchener's structural psychologies, gestalt psychology, behaviourism and information transmission psychology; there are also alternative contemporary approaches like ecological psychology, cognitive psychology, and behaviourism, all with different aims and tools.
- alternative variants of the information processing approach. Within the information processing approach in general, various species can be recognized with slightly different aims and tools. These differences are often related to the topics studied: language, thought, imagery, memory, problem solving, etc.

Before turning to my variant of the information processing approach, we first have a brief look at the epistemological viability and the approximate position within psychology of the information processing approach in general.

1.1 A realist theory of science

As stated, the information processing approach to perception and cognition tries to infer aspects of the internal structure and functioning of a behaving organism from the overt behaviour of that organism. Such an endeavour to learn about what is not observed from what is observed is not unique to the information processing approach within experimental psychology but is a characteristic of many more sciences. Einstein and Infeld (1938), for instance, compare a physicist's attempts to understand physical reality with the activities of a man who tries to understand the internal mechanism of a closed watch; he sees the face and the moving hands and even hears the ticks, but he cannot open the watch. If he is inventive and smart, he can develop a model of a possible internal mechanism responsible for what he sees and hears; i.e., he can invent a set of interrelated concepts and principles that can account for what is observed.

Recently, Palmer and Kimchi (1986) also pointed to the successful use of unobservable entities in theorizing in sciences other than psychology.

Examples abound of scientists proposing initially unobservable constructs on the basis of purely "behavioral" research and later having their theories confirmed by more "direct" observation. Biologists such as Mendel proposed the existence of genes that carry hereditary traits on the basis of measured regularities in the characteristics of offspring, and this happened long before DNA was actually observed within cell nuclei. Physicists like Rutherford deduced the internal structure of atoms from measuring the scatter that resulted when they were bombarded by X-rays, again, many years before the existence of these subatomic particles was confirmed more directly. There have also been many important cases in which unobservables were postulated without any presupposition of direct observation, e.g., Newton's hypothesis of gravitational attraction and Darwin's concept of natural selection.

(Palmer and Kimchi, 1986, p. 62)

In an important paper, Manicas and Secord (1983) informed the psychological community about a 'new' philosophy of science for the social sciences that is compatible with, and, in a sense, provides the philosophical basis for exactly this inferential aspect of the information processing approach. They describe a philosophy of science that encourages the search for the internal structure and functioning of a behaving organism, with the overt behaviour of that organism as the only observable given. This philosophy is termed the *realist* theory of science. It is presented as an alternative to the *standard* theory of science. To determine the approximate position of the information processing approach within psychology it is worthwhile to see the essential differences between these two theories. Because the main difference concerns the conception of causality, and therefore of explanation, something about the interpretation of causality in the two views has to be said.

In the standard theory of science the Humean conception of causality is accepted. In a sense, in Hume's view causality is not a phenomenon in the real world. We never observe causes; we only observe (constant) conjunctions of events. It is possible to observe that A is (always) followed by B, but not that B is caused by A. It is the perceivers that add the concept 'cause' to their experiences (see Flanagan, 1984, p. 181). 'On this view, causal relations are regular contingent relations between events. When strict universality is not possible, "reliable regularities between independent and dependent variables" or "probabilistic relationships among complex, interacting variables" may be all that can be achieved' (Manicas and Secord, 1983, p. 400).

Explanation in this theory of science is subsumption under law, or, is deductive–nomothetic. The laws are the observed reliable or probabilistic event–event relationships, expressed in propositions.

> On the deductive–nomothetic account, the explicans [or explanans, i.e., that which explains] contains sentences that represent laws, but these are understood as contingent regularities. In addition, the explicans contains sentences stating specific antecedent conditions. The explicandum [or explanandum, i.e., that which has to be explained], then, "follows from" the explicans as a deduction: The must is logical.
>
> (after Manicas and Secord, 1984, p. 924)

In the realist theory of science a 'natural' conception of causality is accepted. Basic to this conception is the assumption that a world exists independently of cognizing experience and that in this world causality is something real. The 'things' that populate the world have causal properties that reveal themselves under appropriate conditions. Scientific theories try to express the available knowledge about these 'things' and their causal properties. In contrast to the standard theory 'scientific laws in this non-Humean framework are *not* about events or classes of events, regularly or stochastically conjoined, but are about the causal properties of structures that exist and operate in the world' (Manicas and Secord, 1983, p. 402).

Explanation of one or another phenomenon in this theory of science requires that it is shown how the hypothesized, theoretical structures with causal properties, P, in a situation, S, could produce the observed result and not any other result. So, the must of an explanation here is not just logical; the relations sought for are relations of natural necessity (Manicas and Secord, 1984, p. 924).

In summary, the standard and realist theories of science differ with regard to their views of what science and scientists are up to. According to the standard theory, science is in the business of a search for empirical laws or generalizations: statements of regularities between events that are readily available to direct empirical confirmation. A phenomenon is explained if it can be shown to be a particular instance of such a general empirical event–event relation, i.e., a law. According to the realist theory, science is in the business of developing theories that aim to represent what functions in the world. In their theories scientists try to express their knowledge about the causal structures of real things or the causal powers of real things. A phenomenon is explained if it can be shown that, given the state of the hypothesized causal real thing in its real environment, the phenomenon had to occur.

As stated, the information processing approach tries to infer some aspects of the internal structure and functioning of a behaving organism from the overt behaviour of that organism. So, the approach is trying to develop a theory that aims to represent our knowledge about the internal causal properties of that behaving organism. The realist theory of science shows that this approach is at least on sound epistemological grounds: 'a scientist is acting quite appropriately when he or she attempts to infer the nature of the unobserved world from observations of the world's more accessible parts' (Amundsen, 1985, p. 132). As far as philosophy of science is concerned, there is no need to stay on the level of observable event–event relations.

1.2 Against behaviourism

The information processing approach is generally seen as a reaction against behaviourism, the dominating (American) experimental psychology of the first half of this century. As a next step in delimiting the approximate position of the information processing approach it is very informative to see *in what sense* it was a reaction against behaviourism. This is the more so because the reaction as it is generally specified in the literature – a revival of the study of cognitive processes – seems not to have been the true reaction (see Lovie, 1983). So, if the information processing approach was a reaction against behaviourism, what in behaviourism was it reacting against? Equipped with the distinction between the standard and the realist theory of science we are in the position to answer this question.

Behaviourism was founded by J.B. Watson (see, e.g., Watson, 1913; 1919). To understand behaviourism it is essential to see that Watson was advocating two different, logically distinct, theses (see Hebb, 1980; Palmer and Kimchi, 1986).

The first thesis specified the way knowledge should be acquired. So, it concerned the *data* to be used in scientific psychology and the methods used to obtain the data. The point of view was that only observable behaviour could count as data in psychology as a natural science. The validity of introspection as a method of obtaining data was denied because subjective experiences are not scientifically observable. This epistemological thesis is adequately captured by the term *methodological* behaviourism.

The second thesis specified what could count as mental entities. So, it had to do with the *existence* of mental entities. The point of view was that only external observable behaviour is to be counted as mental phenomena. Consequently in a scientific psychology there is no place for internal mental processes and internal mental states. This ontological thesis can be summarized by the term *theoretical* behaviourism.

In the literature now, the reaction of the information processing approach against behaviourism is not construed as a reaction against methodological behaviourism. Information processing psychologists generally agree with the point that only observable behaviour can count as data in a scientific psychology (see also section 1.4). The objectionable consequence of behaviourism emphasized in the literature is that, as a consequence of theoretical behaviourism, it forced scientific psychology to leave out of consideration many topics of importance such as memory, thinking and attention. Behaviourism was very successful in this respect, so the story goes. It was the information processing approach (or cognitive psychology) that rediscovered these important topics. One out of many examples that expressed this view is as follows (see for further examples Lovie, 1983).

> Experimental psychology in America during the first half of the twentieth century was dominated by behaviourism …. Studies of internal mental operations and structures – such as attention, memory and thinking – were laid to rest and remained so for about 50 years.
>
> (Solso, 1979, pp. 11–12)

However, at least for one of these important topics – 'attention' and the closely related concept 'set' – and possibly also for a lot of other topics this story seems to misrepresent the facts. In a lovely paper titled 'Attention and behaviourism – fact and fiction' Lovie (1983) convincingly shows that it is wrong to say that little if any work on attention and related areas was published during the behaviourist's era. Research on attention not only maintained a salient position in the various branches of applied psychology, but also general systematic psychology could not neglect the topic altogether (see, e.g., Paschal, 1941). Moreover, it appears that the concepts 'attention' (Paschal, 1941, p. 386) and 'set' (Gibson, 1941, p. 781) were used even by the (neo-)behaviourists.

On the basis of the results of his literature review, Lovie (1983, p. 305) argues that there was no real reaction against behaviourism. In his view the available data speak for 'a developmental model of historical change where new concepts and approaches become incorporated into the continuing work' instead of for a dramatic and heroic paradigm shift (Kuhn, 1962).

There is, however, reason to seriously doubt this conclusion and to argue, as is traditional in the information processing literature, that there was indeed a paradigm shift. This becomes apparent when we have a closer look at some important studies that appeared in the 1940s, i.e. at the end of the behaviouristic period. Among the most illuminating studies in this context are Gibson's (1941) study of the concept of set in experimental psychology and Hebb's (1949) impressive and innovative study *The Organization of Behavior*.

Gibson (1941) critically reviewed the use of the concept 'set' in experimental psychology. His study clearly supports Lovie's (1983) point of view that topics like attention, set, expectation, and intention were not laid to rest nor remained so for about 50 years. He convincingly shows that the concept of 'set' was at once ubiquitous and ambiguous. It entered the scene disguised as: expectation, hypothesis, foresight, intention, attitude, tension, need, attention, perseveration, preoccupation, etc. The interesting aspect of Gibson's extensive study, however, is that it essentially consists of a long list of experimental facts and observations. No attempt is made to reach any general formulations. Gibson simply declined to attempt any definition of the term 'set' or of the related terms. He formulated problems, drew distinctions and exposed inconsistencies and concluded: 'A survey has been made of experiments ... in the effort to discover a common nucleus of meaning for the term *mental set* and its variants. No common meaning can be discerned, but, instead, a number of ambiguities and contradictions have become evident' (Gibson, 1941, pp. 810–11).

The important question is now: Why did Gibson not attempt to reach a general formulation or definition? Why such a negative conclusion? His study makes clear that it was not because of a lack of relevant *data* as a consequence of theoretical behaviourism, as has been too often suggested by information processing psychologists (see Lovie, 1983). It must have been his philosophy of science that forced him to write about set in the way he did. And indeed, it is not difficult to show that Gibson's study clearly demonstrates that 'what experimenters think is being studied and what morals they are prepared to draw ... is thoroughly conditioned by the stand that they take on the most basic philosophical questions about the nature of mind and of psychological explanation'.

1.3 Toward a realist theory of science

The answer to the question why Gibson (1941) declined to give any general formulations of 'set' and related concepts has to be found in the requirements of the standard philosophy of science, prevailing at that time. The operationalism of those days required that explanations of behaviour were phrased in strictly 'external' terms. All theoretical terms – set, attention, expectation, etc. – had to be eliminated from scientific discourse by translating them into their observational equivalents. Terms referring to internal constructs that could not be directly tied to observations had no place in theorizing and explanation. We see this requirement clearly where Gibson complains:

> A few writers have offered definitions of set, ... But the definitions are always dictionary definitions in the sense that they employ synonyms rather than specify experimentally definable characteristics ...
> Apparently the term *set* denotes a large and heterogeneous body of experimental facts ....
>
> (Gibson, 1941, p. 782)

And just because of the ubiquitous use of the concepts 'set' and 'attention' in a large range of experimental paradigms concerned with, e.g., reaction time, memory, learning, perception, thought, problem-solving, etc., on the level of *experimental facts* or *experimentally definable characteristics* no common meaning could be discerned. In short it was the event–event terminology of the standard philosophy of science, requiring an anchoring of theoretical terms in observational terms, that prevented the emergence of a common meaning. The standard philosophy of science perfectly matched theoretical behaviourism. It was, however, fully inadequate for, what appears to have been, main-stream experimental psychology that simply rejected or neglected theoretical behaviourism (see Hebb, 1980, p. 222).

In his 'The trend in theories of attention', Paschal was very explicit about this presence of data and the adverse effect of the then prevailing philosophy of science in the field of attention.

> The textbooks of the last few years have without exception, we believe, included a treatment of attention. And all of them have treated it, however expressed, as an anticipatory act. As to the character of that act, however, there is some confusion. This is undoubtedly due to the current requirement that such definition shall be in operational terms.
>
> (Paschal, 1941, p. 394)

It was D.O. Hebb (1949), who saw this all clearly and took the consequences. His book – *The Organization of Behavior* – is written in profound disagreement with the positivist, empiricist, programme for psychology. In his view it was impossible to develop an adequate psychology based on a philosophy of science that 'emphasizes a method of correlating observable stimuli with observable response, ..., recognizing that "explanation" is ultimately a statement of relationships between observed phenomena' (Hebb, 1949, p. xiv).

Again, what Hebb (1949) found was not an absence of research on important topics like perception, thought, attention, set, etc., or a shortage of relevant data. What he found was that exactly the presence and the abundance of relevant data created the problem. The available results did not fit within the straitjacket determined by the then prevailing philosophy of science. Theories that conformed to the empiricist, operationalist epistemology did not provide the conceptual apparatus to deal in an effective and elegant way with the available results. Theories became extremely complex and cumbersome, lacked operational clarity and predictive force, and often theorizing was simply avoided (see, e.g., Gibson, 1941). A new epistemology was needed and, in my view, within experimental psychology, Hebb (1949) was the first to clearly recognize this point.

So, Hebb's work was not a reaction against 'research during the behaviourist era'. What he rejected was the standard theory of science. He started theorizing as a devoted proponent of the realist theory of science. He proposed internal structures with causal properties for dealing with phenomena like perception, thought, learning, expectancy, attention, set, etc. ('cell-assembly', 'phase sequence', etc.). As far as its philosophy of science and its general aims are concerned, the information processing approach is clearly the continuation and further elaboration of Hebb's important work (see, e.g., Neisser, 1967; Broadbent, 1958; 1971). So, the information processing approach can also be seen as a real reaction and a paradigm shift with regard to most earlier research (the generally received point of view), but only in as far as the underlying philosophy of science is concerned.

Of course the battle against the standard theory of science was not immediately won and, more surprisingly, is even still going on. Behaviourism and the use of event–event relations is still defended (see, e.g., Skinner, 1977; 1985). In section 1.5 we will see how Skinner's view with regard to experiments is biased as a result of the stand he takes on the question about the nature of psychological explanation. Also the ecological approach, with its preoccupation for 'direct perception', propagates basically the same philosophy of science (see, e.g., Gibson, 1979). An ecological physics has to be developed, and, 'if successful, it will provide a basis for a stimulus response psychology, which otherwise seems to be sinking in the swamp of intervening variables' (Gibson, 1960, p. 701). In this context it is highly illuminating to read *how* Fodor and Pylyshyn (1981) repeat Hebb's arguments in their critical evaluation of Gibson's ecological approach.

1.4 Attention

Not of minor importance is the fact that it was exactly phenomena signified by terms like set and attention – i.e., the topics with which the present study is concerned – that forced Hebb to reject the standard theory of science and led him in the direction of a realist theory of science.

Almost without exception psychologists have recognized the existence of the selective central factor that reinforces now one response, now another. The problem is to carry out to its logical conclusion an incomplete line of thought that starts out preoccupied with stimulus or stimulus configuration as the source and control of action, eventually runs into the facts of attention and so on, and then simply agrees that attention is an important fact, without recognizing that this is inconsistent with one's earlier assumptions. To complete this process, we must go back and make a change in the basis of the theory.

(Hebb, 1949, pp. 4–5)

There are three points here: one is that psychologists have generally recognized the existence of attention or the like; another that they have done so reluctantly and sparingly, and have never recognized the fact in setting up theories. The third point is obvious enough, that we need to find some way of dealing with the facts consistently. Since everyone knows that attention and set exist, we had better get the skeleton out of the closet and see what can be done with it.

(Hebb, 1949, p. 5)

In this 'realist' light, Hebb also evaluated Gibson's (1941) study.

His review needs some clarification in one respect, since he declined to attempt any definition of "set" or any other of the long list of terms with a similar meaning that he gathered together, although he evidently recognized, in classifying them so, that they have something in common .... When one considers the problem in the light of the implicit assumption of a sensory dominance of behavior it becomes clear at once that the notions of set, attention, attitude, expectancy ... have a common element, and only one. That element is the recognition that responses are determined by something else besides the immediately preceding sensory stimulation; it does deny that sensory stimulation is everything in behavior.

(Hebb, 1949, p. 5)

In short, in Hebb's view the study of attention and related phenomena simply requires a realist point of view that allows one to refer to a 'hidden' internal force or entity in one's psychological explanations.

It is very interesting to read how William James (1890/1950) already anticipated this point by exactly noticing what the critical issue was. He started his famous chapter on attention with

Strange to say, so patent a fact as the perpetual presence of selective attention has received hardly any notice from psychologists of the English empiricist school ... in the pages of such writers as Locke, Hume, Hartley, the Mills, and Spencer the word hardly occurs, or if it does so, it is parenthetically and as if by inadvertence. The motive of this ignoring of the phenomenon of attention is obvious enough. These writers are bent on showing how the higher faculties of the mind are pure products of "experience"; and experience is supposed to be of something simply *given*. Attention, implying a degree of reactive spontaneity, would seem to break through the circle of pure receptivity which constitutes "experience" and hence must not be spoken of under penalty of interfering with the smoothness of the tale.

(James, 1890/1950, p. 402; see also his pages 447–8)

And it is also very interesting to read how Neisser (1967) echoed all this in his evaluation of the attempts in the 1950s to apply the mathematical theory of communication, with its quantification of stimulus information in 'bits', to psychology:

> even today many psychologists continue to theorize and to report data in terms of "bits" ... I do not believe, however, that this approach was or is a fruitful one. Attempts to quantify psychological processes in informational terms have usually led, after much effort, to the conclusion that the "bit rate" is not a relevant variable after all. Such promising topics as reaction time, memory span, and language have all failed to sustain early estimates of the usefulness of information measurement. With the advantage of hindsight, we can see why this might have been expected. The "bit" was developed to describe the performance of rather unselective systems: a telephone cannot decide which portions of the incoming message are important ... human beings behave very differently, and are by no means neutral or passive toward the incoming information. Instead, they select some parts for attention at the expense of others, recoding and reformulating them in complex ways.
>
> (Neisser, 1967, p. 7)

The basic reason that the study of attention in particular forces one toward a realist philosophy of science lies in a variant of Amundsen's (1985) principle of epistemological parity. In general the principle states that a theorist in psychology operates under a constraint not found in other sciences, because, in order to deal with all facts consistently, he cannot adopt a view in which the 'knower' or 'a scientist' or 'a subject' as implied by the philosophy of science, is significantly different from 'a subject', 'a scientist' or 'a knower' as described by his substantive psychological theory (see Amundsen, 1985, p. 129). To be consistent, he can only accept psychology/philosophy of science pairs that match; pairs in which the philosophy of science is appropriate to a human being as described by the psychology. (Indeed, Pylyshyn's 'nature of mind' and 'nature of explanation' strongly belong together.) So, if one's psychology only describes a human being properly with statements like 'attention and set exist', 'attention is an important factor', 'responses are determined by something else besides immediately preceding sensory stimulation' (Hebb, 1949), then the principle of epistemological parity forces one in the direction of a philosophy of science that allows one to recognize these facts. The psychological data then simply enforce a realist philosophy of science. (There *are* relevant internal structures and processes. Therefore, explanations have to be framed in terms of internal causal structures and processes.) Only if one manages, in one way or another, to ignore 'so patent a fact as the perpetual presence of selective attention' (James, 1890/1950) does the principle of epistemological parity allow one to adhere to the standard theory of science. (There are *no* relevant internal structures and processes. Therefore, explanations can only be framed in terms of external event–event relations.) Psychology is not capable of ignoring so patent a fact (see, e.g., James,

1890/1950; Hebb, 1949; Neisser, 1967). So, the philosophy of science has to adapt.

So, as far as the topic of our study is concerned, the information processing approach is not only on sound epistemological grounds. The lesson of the (recent) past is that there is no real, viable, alternative.

1.5 Tools: experiments

From the conclusion that the information processing approach is on sound epistemological grounds (section 1.1) and even from the claim that, for phenomena such as attention, set and the like, there is no real, viable, alternative (section 1.4) it does not automatically follow that the realist approach indeed works and leads to sensible results, and that is the only real criterion (see section 1.0).

Skinner simply denies that the approach *can* work. He admits that 'A behavioral account is incomplete, in part because it leaves a great deal to neurology ...' (Skinner, 1985, p. 297; see also his pages 293 and 295), but accuses 'cognitive scientists of speculating about internal processes with respect to which they have no appropriate means of observation' (Skinner, 1985, p. 300). So the important question is: What means do cognitive psychologists and information processing psychologists have? (To a possible difference between 'cognitive psychology' and 'information processing psychology' I return in a later section.)

Skinner (1985, pp. 297–8) discusses four methods for investigating what goes on inside the 'black box': introspection, brain science, simulation and linguistics. And he is not really impressed.

Shevrin & Dickman (1980) argue that "Behaviorism ... must accommodate itself to accepting the importance of what goes on inside the 'black box', especially since we now have methods for investigating its contents" (p. 432). What are those methods?

Introspection is presumably one of them .... But can we actually observe ourselves engaging in mental processes? ... We have no sensory nerves going to the parts of the brain that engage in the "cognitive processes".

Brain science looks into the black box in another way. Cognitive psychologists ... observe causal relations ... and invent mental apparatuses to explain them, but one may doubt that neurologists ... will find anything that resembles them.

Simulation is said to be another source of information about the black box ... are we to understand that the study of computers can tell us what we need to know about human behaviour?

Linguistics is also said to have illuminated the black box, but most of linguistics is itself an offshoot of an earlier cognitive position. Listeners possess a "natural language understanding system" ... and make "a semantic analysis of the message conveyed by the language" .... That is a long way from throwing much light on what speakers and listeners actually do.

(Skinner, 1985, pp. 297–8)

To an information processing psychologist Skinner's list is quite surprising. None of these methods appears essential for the former's scientific work. These are primarily tools used in neighbouring lands. And, even more astonishing, his main (and only) tool, 'experimenting', is completely missing from this list. But information processing psychologists recognize that 'Watson almost singlehandedly transformed psychology into an objective biological science, denying the validity of introspective report and showing by example how to work with behavior instead' (Hebb, 1980, p. 221). Behaviour observed in experiments provides the basic data of the information processing approach (see also Palmer and Kimchi, 1986, pp. 60–1).

Why is it that Skinner (1985) does not even mention the role of experiments? It is not difficult to find an answer to this question. We only have to look again at the main difference between the standard theory of science, which is appropriate to behaviourism, and the realist theory of science, which is appropriate to the information processing approach. We then readily see that the function of experiments is completely different in these two views.

In the standard view, and that is Skinner's view, science is only concerned with observable events. A theory consists of (law) statements summarizing the relations between these events. Therefore the function of experiments and experimenting is primarily to obtain more probable or more reliable empirical regularities between observable events, i.e., between independent, environmental, variables and dependent, behavioural, variables. Experiments have to yield (pseudo) laws summarizing Humean contingent causal relations (see section 1.1). In this context it is highly illuminating to read in the last quotation that, according to Skinner, 'Cognitive psychologists ... *observe* causal relations ...' (italics mine).

In the realist's view, scientists try to represent in theories their knowledge of causal structures in a world that exists independently of their knowledge or theorizing about it. The function of experimenting and experiments is to confront the causal structures, which are not directly observable, with specific and controlled environmental situations. The system of interest is probed and thereby challenged. In this way the system is forced to reveal its causal properties in its observable behaviour.

The difference in views with regard to the function of experiments in science makes for completely different ways of experimenting. Behaviourists, as adherents of the standard view of science, are concerned with finding the most reliable regularities between changes in the environment and resultant behaviour. As observable behaviour, all behaviour, including highly interesting everyday behaviour, can be taken. Also the environment can be the everyday environment (see, e.g., Gibson, 1979, on ecological validity). The only criterion for selecting environment and behaviour to talk about and to experiment with is that reliable relations between external observable events have to be obtained.

Information processing psychologists, as realists, are concerned with establishing the existence and properties of hidden causal mechanisms of real 'things'. The real things they are concerned with are complex, highly structured, things. Their everyday behaviour in a normal environment is the result of a complex causal configuration of different structures and is therefore not directly understandable. In experiments the environment and the behaviour are simplified. A great number of factors are fixed. Only one, or a few, factor(s) are varied. The criterion for selecting the (reduced) environment and the, often terribly boring, (reduced) behaviour is, that the causally efficacious structures and mechanisms of relevance have to reveal themselves in an unambiguous way through their effects.

The foregoing remarks also begin to make clear what 'behaviour' it is that information processing psychology has to explain. Clearly, that is not everyday 'behaviour' in a normal, rich, environment. (Using the then available psychological evidence this was essentially what Hebb, 1949, tried to do.) What has to be explained is behaviour observed in 'simple' experiments, just as in other theoretical sciences.

Unfortunately, in the recent past, adherents of the approach have not been very clear about the basic data that need to be explained (see, e.g., Palmer and Kimchi, 1986). It is often not realized that, just because of the realist's approach,

- it is not the most impressive behaviour which information processing psychologists observe and register, but merely a subject's reactions: 'Yes', 'yes', 'no', ..., or, 'red', 'green', 'red', ...;
- it is not the complete behaviour that is observed and registered, but only some specific, quantifiable, aspects, such as the latency and/or the correctness of the response. Other aspects, e.g., the duration and the detailed execution of the observable behaviour, are simply neglected;
- it is not even the absolute values registered, that serve as basic data, but merely the differences between the values obtained in different experimental conditions. Not the performance as such, but how performance is affected by various experimental conditions, is what is of interest (remember that an Anova or t-test evaluates differences, not absolute values, and that it is tradition in the information processing approach to report only 'significant' results, i.e., reliable differences).

Nevertheless, the endeavour aims to isolate some of the causal structures that, together and in interaction, produce the everyday behaviour. The information processing approach as a branch of 'experimental psychology does not explain everyday behaviour, even though, of course, it is capable of shedding light on the complex mechanisms ... that taken together, underlie the performances by individuals acting in the world' (Manicas and Secord, 1983, p. 407).

So in the information processing approach Skinner's event–event experiments are missing. Nevertheless, experimenting is the tool of the information processing approach. Indeed, Skinner's analysis only demonstrates that, just as in Gibson's (1941) view on theorizing, his view on the function of experiments is thoroughly conditioned by the stand he takes on the nature of mind and of psychological explanation (Pylyshyn, 1981).

1.6 The explicandum: the behaviouristic variant

It is not completely clear whether, either explicitly or implicitly, all information processing psychologists agree with the point of view that it is behaviour, observed in simple experiments, as specified in the foregoing section, that has to be explained. My guess is not, and therefore I introduced this specific view – and this is my view – as a variant of the current information processing approach. Because in the present view it is *observable behaviour*, registered in simple experiments, that has to be explained, the view can be termed the *behaviouristic* variant. In this view theoretical behaviourism is rejected, but methodological behaviourism is maintained, albeit that the function of experiments has changed.

It is necessary to state this point very explicitly because there are information processing psychologists – or are they cognitive psychologists? – suggesting that it is something completely different that has to be explained. They seem to reject both theoretical and methodological behaviourism. In fact, these psychologists suggest that it is 'cognition', or, in general, 'mind', and not 'behaviour', that has to be explained; in one or another way, they are trying to 'solve' the mind–body problem. A few examples follow.

Neisser (1967), in his very influential *Cognitive Psychology*, was one of the first to introduce this – what can be termed – 'cognitive' variant. In his view, the study of 'Visual cognition, then, deals with the processes by which a perceived, remembered, and thought-about world is brought into being from as unpromising a beginning as the retinal patterns' (Neisser, 1967, p. 4). Turvey (1977, p. 81) repeats 'visual information processing, as a methodology and as a philosophy, is devoted to the solution of the following problem: How is the information in the light entering the ocular system mapped onto perceptual experience?' Massaro's (1986) concern is with the computer as a metaphor for explaining perception and action. In his view 'Psychology investigates empirically not only the behavioral and mental worlds, but the relation between the two. If the science succeeds, one outcome will be a solution to the mind–body problem' (Massaro, 1986, p. 73). And Alan Allport states 'Our phenomenal experience may appear structured in terms of "objects", but we should be circumspect in proposing a concept, defined only in phenomenal terms, as a component in a would-be causal account of behavior. To do so would be to risk confusing the explicandum with the explanation' (Allport, 1987, pp. 411–12).

This temptation to regard mind – a perceived and thought-about world, or, our phenomenal experience – or even the mind–body problem, as what has to be explained or understood, does not originate within information processing psychology only. Other sciences often force psychologists in that direction. The neurophysiologist Barlow, for instance, states:

> We now know the sort of thing single neurons *can* do. How might these abilities be organized to enable the brain to perceive? I think this has now become the main question facing perceptual psychology ... there is a very precise map of the visual field in the primary visual cortex ... other areas specialize in particular aspects of the images such as motion or colour. Now this new knowledge of the anatomy and physiology of the brain is profoundly unsatisfactory if it does not start to answer the basic question: "How does visual cortex enable you to see? How does it tell you about your environment?" Those are questions the psychology of perception ought to give one some ideas about, and I think it does.
>
> (Barlow, 1985, p. 140)

And Cummins, a philosopher of science, argues

> The late arrival of cognitive psychology is rather easily accounted for ... by the following fact. Until quite recently, no one had the slightest idea what it would be *like* to scientifically explain a cognitive capacity. In part, no doubt, this was because everyone was mesmerized by the idea that scientific explanation is subsumption under causal law, and cognitive capacities could not possibly be explained that way. Another important factor was that until recently no one had any serious idea – i.e., no scientifically workable idea – how to *describe* cognitive capacities; hence no one had any serious idea what the explanandum was .... There are other fascinating reasons why no one knew until fairly recently what a scientific explanation of a cognitive capacity would be like.
>
> (Cummins, 1983, pp. 52–3)

Neisser (1976) summarizes the information processing view he propagated in 1967, with the flow chart given in figure 1.6.1. He only recognizes technical problems. 'A good deal of psychological and physiological evidence supports this general approach .... It appears, however, that other aspects of perception are more difficult for such models to explain' (Neisser, 1976, p. 17). In my view, however, there is a fundamental problem here. While possibly the goal of

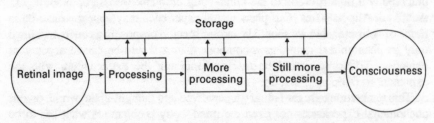

Figure 1.6.1 The explicandum? Cognition as viewed by Neisser (1976).

cognitive psychology, explaining mind – e.g., a perceived world, a mental world, a concept defined in phenomenal terms, a cognitive capacity, etc. – is not the proper topic of information processing psychology. Mind phenomena are (a) not observable, at least not in the regular, scientific, sense (see, e.g., Watson, 1913; 1919; Skinner, 1985, quoted in section 1.5), and (b) certainly not the phenomena observed and registered in the information processing experiments. Therefore, within the information processing approach, mind phenomena are not data that ought to be explained. (In the well-known Bohr–Einstein debate on quantum physics, Bohr defended the point of view that physics had to be concerned with the experimental givens only. Einstein introduced physics-external, 'mind' data with his thesis 'God does not play dice'. Bohr won and Einstein had to 'stop telling God what to do'.)

Moreover, attempts to explain mind phenomena in the way suggested by Neisser (1967; 1976) are like a physicist's attempts to explain from heating a litre of water what it is like for water to boil. Physicists and chemists feel little temptation to indulge in such explanations. The reason is simple. In their scientific world, facts like 'being boiling water' simply do not exist, and certainly do not exist as data to be explained or reckoned with. So they stay at the level of third-person descriptions. Psychologists, however, easily switch positions and often adopt a first-person position. But the fact that for psychologists 'being a human being' is familiar, important, and seems to exist in one or another way (possibly 'insist' is better than 'exist') does not entail that this fact has to enter in their scientific world as a given that needs to be explained. In fact, with overt behaviour as the starting point, it cannot enter in their scientific enterprise as a given in need of an explanation because it is impossible to observe 'being a human being' as overt behaviour.

But even if such facts were observable, then they still are simply not the facts with which information processing psychologists are concerned. The topic of the information processing psychologists is not that which is 'familiar, important, and seems to exist in one or another way'. As with the behaviourists, and as with the physicists, chemists, etc., they have explicitly chosen experimenting as their basic tool. Outcomes of experiments are the data they are concerned with. Those are the data which information processing psychology 'ought to give one some ideas about'.

In texts on information processing psychology one seldom finds a discussion or a further elaboration of this important issue. This is very unfortunate. Because the data are the only real basis of an experimental science, within the information processing approach a thorough reflection about the exact data to be explained (and the relation data–explanation: how do the data constrain kind and detail of explanation) is badly needed. Confusions about *what* it is that has to be explained can only hamper progress from the very beginning. And it is exactly these confusions that obscure the border between realistic aims and exaggerated claims and create the temptation to enter a neighbour's land.

Taken together, in my view the cognitive variant of the information processing approach is a mistaken and impossible variant. It confuses information processing psychology and something like cognitive psychology (a philosopher's toy). Furthermore, up to now, that variant has produced nothing shedding very much light on how a perceived, remembered and thought-about world is brought into being. Within the behaviouristic variant of the information processing approach it is behaviour – more precisely, some aspects of behaviour, and still more precisely, *differences* between some aspects of behaviour – with which theories and explanations have to be concerned. We now turn to these theories and explanations.

1.7 The explicans: the information processor

Judged by its dominant position within psychology, the information processing approach is certainly a successful approach. In general, this success has been achieved because the approach has managed to start the development of a way of thinking that makes it possible to separate a number of scientifically answerable questions about human beings from the general and gloomy questions inherited from the philosophical and psychological past. At the basis of this way of thinking is a general intuition, shared with other sciences, about what kind of causal structures human beings essentially are. This intuition can be expressed in a number of ways (see, e.g., Palmer and Kimchi, 1986; Massaro, 1986). In my view, the essence is approximately the following.

Organisms such as human beings are systems endowed with, or partly consisting of, a complex control system that can perform a diversity of functions all of which serve to keep the organism in a consistent relation with its environment. The control system can perform these functions because in its composition there are

A – structured subsystems whose states and changes of state are determined by the states and changes of state in the organism's environment,
B – structured subsystems whose states and changes of state determine the states and changes of state of the organism in its environment,
C – structured subsystems whose states and changes of state mediate in a modifiable way between the subsystems A and B, or, the subsystems directly related to the sense organs and the effectors.

This complex control system, that causes and controls the organism's overt behaviour, is the causal structure that information processing psychology is interested in. A 'characterization' or 'description' of this causal control structure is the explicans which information processing psychology with its realist philosophy of science is looking for. The appropriate characterization of the system is the appropriate explanation of its behaviour. And a correct explanation of (aspects of) its behaviour is a correct characterization of (aspects of) the system. So, by trying to explain aspects of its behaviour, information processing psychologists are trying to discover aspects of the causal control system.

But lots of sciences are concerned with the same control system (see section 1.0). So, what is the unique feature of the information processing approach and what is at the basis of its success?

There are lots of sciences that seem to be concerned with, what can be called, *absolute* properties of this control system. Neuroanatomists are concerned with its exact, physical, macro- and microstructure. Neurophysiologists try to give an exact description of the biochemical and electrical functioning of the structures distinguished (see, e.g., Kandel and Schwarz, 1985). Ecological psychologists, concerned with visual perception, contribute by specifying precisely how the composition of the world structures the light that reaches the eye, i.e., by providing an exact description of the information contained in light (see, e.g., Gibson, 1979). Workers in the fields of artificial intelligence, and especially computer vision, compute aspects of the environment-determined internal states and changes of states, i.e., generate or construct sequences of internal representations (see, e.g., Marr, 1980). Philosophers try to formulate the essential and absolute properties of information and representation (see, e.g., Fodor, 1981b; Fodor and Pylyshyn, 1981; 1988). Etc., etc.

The unique feature of the information processing approach, the feature that in my view is at the basis of its success, is that, in its present state of development, it is not really concerned with absolute properties of the control system, but with, what I prefer to call, *relative* properties. When information processing psychologists talk about the control system in operation they do not really answer questions of the type 'how does the system operate in situation X?', but questions of the type 'how does the system operate in situation X1, as compared to its operation in situation X2?'. The first question is an absolute one. With the second type of question the absolute properties of the control system are left out of consideration, and only relative properties or differences are considered.

That such a relative-question strategy leads to answerable questions and evades the unanswerable ones is not difficult to see. It is, for instance, extremely difficult to be explicit about the operations within the control system that enable it to see, but it is relatively easy to say something sensible about the differences in operation within the system that entail that it sees better in bright than in dim light. In the former case 'seeing' has to be made explicit, while in the latter case 'seeing' is not the topic and only differences in seeing in bright and in dim light have to be accounted for. To say something sensible about 'seeing' a lot of mind–body philosophy is needed. To say something sensible about differences between seeing in bright and in dim light, a story in terms of differences between rods and cones and differences between their pattern of connections with ganglion cells, etc., etc., suffices.

This unique feature of the approach, the feature that the control system is basically seen as, what can be called, a 'difference generator', is not generally recognized, leading to confusions and misplaced criticisms. For instance, some scientists are embarrassed by the fact that the approach does not even specify, what they see as, its basic concepts or primitives: information (see, e.g., Gibson,

1979; Palmer and Kimchi, 1986; Massaro, 1987), processing (see, e.g., Neisser, 1976; see also figure 1.6.1; Allport, 1980a) and representation (see, e.g., Bieri, 1990). The issue, however, is that these are not the primitives. The real underlying primitives the information processing approach is dealing with are the *differences* in information in situations X1 and X2, the corresponding *differences* in the processing of the information, and the resulting *differences* in observable reactions. (And these differences are appreciably easier to specify than the corresponding absolute values.)

Broadbent (1971) was well aware of this characteristic of the information processing approach. He was very explicit about the essential feature of the concepts 'information' and 'processing' as used in information processing psychology.

> Suppose there are two alternative physical events A and B, such as a square flash of light and a round one. We observe that when A occurs a man produces action I, whereas when B occurs he produces action II. It follows that at every stage of the intervening events within his nervous system there must have been two possible states of the system, one corresponding to A and one to B. It is not essential in any way that there should be an identity in any physical property between A and its corresponding state at any stage in the nervous system; for example, if A occurs it is not necessary that the image on the retina be square. It must merely differ in some way from the image of B. So long as such a difference exists, we may say that the retina transmits information about the occurrence of A and B. Conversely, of course, we do not need to know about the physical nature of the difference to make such a statement ....
> (Broadbent, 1971, p. 7)

But, generally, it is not recognized that the information processing approach is mainly concerned with differences, not with absolute values.

The prime reason that this unique feature of the information processing approach is not generally recognized is, that it is more or less concealed by the actual theoretical practices of information processing psychologists. When they talk about the control system they do not talk about differences only. What they talk about seem to be complete systems with absolute properties. In my view, however, this is illusory. Just as in explaining 'better seeing in bright than in dim light' the word 'seeing' is used but 'seeing' as such is not the topic dealt with in the explanation, so words referring to absolute properties of the information processing system are used in theorizing but their absolute meanings are, in my view, of no importance in explanations in the information processing approach. (But one needs words to formulate issues.)

One important consequence of this feature of the approach is that the control systems, which information processing psychologists talk about, can be hypothetical, or even better, *metaphorical* structured control systems whose exact, i.e., absolute, material constitution or physical instantiation does not really matter. What information processing psychologists really talk about are *models* of the control system, not the real control system itself. What matter in these models are some formal, more or less abstract, properties. It is the properties that can represent the relevant differences in the causal properties of the real control system.

This strategy of the information processing approach makes clear also why it is possible that information processing psychologists talk in a number of completely different ways about the control system and nevertheless understand each other quite well. They characterize aspects of the system in phenomenal or mind terms (e.g., 'see', 'red', etc.), in brain terms (e.g., 'lateral inhibition', 'excitation', etc.), and in several other ways at a level in between (metaphorical, functional, computational, connectionist, etc.). But, in my view, they do not really mean what they say. It is not the language that is used that matters (it is not the control system as such that is characterized), but the differences that can be expressed in that language (what are characterized are the differential causal aspects of the control system). Therefore all languages are to a large extent equivalent if they are capable of capturing the relevant differential causal aspects of the real control system. Even internal horses are allowed:

> The particular theoretical framework that is chosen is arbitrary .... Consider what might appear to be a straightforward question within the context of horse-race models of psychological function. If two horses are in a race, relative to just one, what are the possible consequences? Early experiments showed that detection reaction times (RTs) to the combination of a light and a tone were faster than RTs to either the light or the tone presented alone. ... Raab (1962) observed that the results can be explained by assuming variability in the finishing times of the horses in the race .... The finishing time of the first horse in a two-horse race will, on the average, be faster than the finishing times of the two horses racing separately.
>
> (Massaro, 1986, p. 84)

1.8 Explanation: theory and data

It will be clear by now that the information processing approach as an experimental science, or at least my variant and interpretation of the approach, has managed to find a, in principle reliable and powerful, link between its basic data and its theories.

- What are observed in experiments are basically *differences* between aspects of behaviour in different experimental conditions (see section 1.6).
- The 'information processor' – the model of the control system – is essentially a *difference* generator (see section 1.7).

Exactly this link is exploited by means of experiments. 'The environment is manipulated in an orderly manner, and we see what consequences it has for the subject. From the relationships between the *changes* in the environment and *changes* in behavior, we hope to learn something about the hidden psychological operations involved' (Massaro, 1986, p. 81; italics mine). And, just because of its reliable data–theory link, my information processing approach can afford to be a pure experimental science, in which the data are used to shape and refine the theory and the theory is used to explain the data. The theory asks and requires data, the data move and force the theory. In other words, just because of this reliable data–theory link, my information processing approach is a self-sufficient and independent experimental science. (See Van der Heijden and Stebbins, 1990, for further elaboration.)

In experiments in the information processing approach either one or only a few factors are allowed to vary; the rest of the world is temporarily kept fixed. The varying experimental factors are chosen in such a way that the relevant causal structures are addressed and can reveal their properties and operations in the behaviour that is registered. These factors are varied in such a way that the different levels differentially affect the functioning of the relevant structures. The resulting differences in behaviour are the phenomena of interest. Numerous potential factors addressing the same or different structures are kept fixed to eliminate interfering or obscuring differential effects. Of course, these factors also influence behaviour, but their constant effects are not of interest. In summary, by establishing the right experimental conditions, i.e., by varying and fixing the appropriate factors, it is possible to isolate the differential functioning of the structures of interest, and to keep what is not of interest constant.

Broadbent (1958; 1971) and Massaro (1987), in particular, were clearly aware of, and explicit about, the close and vital, mutually constraining link between theory and data. Moreover, they were both explicit about the underlying methodological logic – the falsification strategy in the scientific enterprise (see Popper, 1959) – that guarantees the theory a start and a gradual development in the correct direction. Basically this strategy consists in generating multiple hypotheses relevant to a particular structure or combination of structures of interest and to eliminate or falsify as many of these hypotheses as possible (see Massaro, 1987, pp. 279–82 for a thoughtful discussion).

Ideally, three stages can be distinguished in this scientific enterprise. (These three stages are also reflected in the structure of the rest of this study.) In the first stage, one has to determine as clearly as possible what function of the total information processor is the function to which one's specific scientific endeavours are directed. For the topic of our concern – selective attention in vision – that function is, of course, 'attention'. But 'attention' is an ambiguous and elusive concept. So first, an unambiguous and acceptable concept of attention, corresponding with a function of the information processor, has to be isolated. Only then can questions with regard to the differential functioning and way of operation of the information processor be formulated that can be answered by experimental evidence. In Chapter 2 we try to isolate a concept of attention that, we presume, cuts nature at its joints.

In the second stage the relevant data have to be gathered. Informative experiments have to be performed and published and the experimental literature has to be scrutinized to find questions and answers to questions pertaining to the function of interest. For the topic of our concern, the relevant evidence consists of the 'benefits': the improvements in detection and recognition performance, observed in experimental conditions with appropriate attentional instructions as compared with conditions without such instructions. In Chapters 3 to 6 the relevant evidence is presented: the benefits and the interpretation of the benefits as reported in the information processing literature.

In the final stage, the empirical discoveries and regularities are translated into a coherent set of hypotheses about the internal structure and functioning of the information processor, i.e., into a model that explains and predicts the information processor's behaviour in terms of its internal structure and functioning. While such a model is phrased in absolute terms, it is only the differences in behaviour for which it accounts that really matter. For the topic of our concern *the differential functioning* of the hypothetical information processor has to account for the *benefits* observed in selective attention tasks. In Chapters 7 and 8 an outline of such an information processor is described.

Benefits only?

1.9 Explanation: underdetermination?

My variant of the information processing approach tries to explain observable behaviour. It deviates from other variants because it takes as a starting point that it is behaviour – in fact, differences between aspects of behaviour – and not mind (perceive, think, etc.) that is explained. That behaviour is 'observed' in experiments, and is available only in a very reduced form as differences in latencies, in percentages correct, in kinds of errors, observed in detection tasks, recognition tasks, selection tasks, etc. This specifies *what* needs explanation.

The aim is to explain the (observed) behaviour in terms of (unobserved) structure and (unobserved) functioning of the information processing system. The 'description' of the information processor is the explanation. In the explanation the level of detail is fixed. While theoretical causal structures can be distinguished at many levels of analysis – quarks, atoms, molecules, cells, modules, organs, etc. – the data–theory (and theory–data) link singles out a unique and appropriate level of analysis for the theory. The level and detail of the data determine the level and detail of the theory. But the precise *language* used to express this level of detail is in principle free (see section 1.7). So, the question remains whether there is a preferred language to characterize structure and to characterize function.

As indicated in section 1.7, it is possible to distinguish three broad groups of languages for theories: (a) mind-languages, or, explanations using phenomenological terms (i.e., see, purpose, want, I, you, consciousness, etc.), (b) model-languages, or, explanations using terms of one or another material system that is already understood (e.g., computer terms like input, buffer, central processor, etc.), and (c) brain-languages, or, explanations in terms of (groups of) neurons and their connections (i.e., retina, occipital lobe, on-centre–off-surround cell, lateral inhibition, etc.). See Palmer and Kimchi (1986), Massaro (1986) and Bieri (1984, in Massaro, 1986) for a similar distinction. Dennett (1978) uses a related distinction of intentional stance, design stance and physical stance.

Explanations in contemporary information processing psychology are mainly in model-terms, and often the computer (see, e.g., Massaro, 1986) or the computer program (see, e.g., Neisser, 1967; Palmer and Kimchi, 1986) are used as metaphors. However, the exact choice of metaphors is not essential (for the topic of our prime interest, attention, often a 'search light' or a 'zoom lens' is used as a metaphor). The issue to be raised is whether for the information processing approach this model or metaphor language has to be preferred over the mind and the brain language.

My answer to this question is affirmative. In my view the information processing, or model-level language, is the preferred one. The basic reason is that the concepts or primitives in a model language can be chosen in such a way that they are maximally compatible with the level of detail of the data to be explained. (In my view, exactly this compatibility explains in large part the attractive power of the computer program metaphor; see Massaro, 1986, and Palmer and Kimchi, 1986.) Explanations in mind terms suggest far too much; the global connotations accompanying mind terms suggest a completeness and richness of explanation not warranted by the data. Moreover, introspection and phenomenology have not yet been capable of offering a set of primitives that can be used in effective, causal, explanations. Explanations that are really phrased in brain terms offer much too much; the absoluteness and level of detail of brain terms induce a precision of explanation not required by the data. Moreover, also neurophysiology and neuroanatomy have not yet been capable of offering a set of primitives that can be used in effective, causal, explanations. (As we will see in the next section, a brain-inspired *model language* comes close to doing a good job.)

So, one or another model language seems to be the appropriate one. There are, however, critics within and outside psychology. Massaro (1986; 1987) has adequately dealt with most of these criticisms. One, however, merits a further discussion: the criticism that information processing theories using model terms are severely underdetermined by the data, i.e., the criticism that an infinity of such information processing models is consistent with the data (see, e.g., Flanagan, 1984, p. 191). Because it is interesting to hear this criticism from an outsider, we quote Rose, a biologist.

The systems approach sees organisms essentially as sophisticated computers possessing particular functional components to achieve specified outputs, the products of an arbitrary number of internal black boxes and their interconnections. The research task is to separate observed behaviours into component units, for instance goal-directed functions employing various strategies towards desiderata such as satiety, orgasm or whatever. The black boxes can be modelled to generate predictions as well as *post hoc* accounts.

However, the problem with this type of abstract function-box modelling is that, whilst it may pass a theory test, it is likely to fail a reality test; an infinite number of models is always possible for any outcome, and failures can always be "adjusted" by modifying parameters without changing basic design elements.

(Rose, 1980, p. i)

If we neglect the biological colouring, the message is clear: there are far too many possibilities; constraining knowledge of the hardware, the brain, is essential.

For my variant of the information processing approach, however, the problem of underdetermination is not really a problem. In fact, by interpreting the control system as a difference generator described in model terms, underdetermination is brought in deliberately. This can be done, however, because my information processing approach does not aim to solve all (scientific) problems with regard to human beings. The approach is only a member of the total cognitive science group, and of course, the ambition of the group as a whole is much larger.

For each member of the cognitive science group, the first responsibility is to be as clear as possible about its aims and tools and possible contribution. Only then is a real cooperation possible. As far as, in my view, the information processing approach is concerned, its first and primary problem is the explanation of some aspects of observed behaviour. Hypotheses about aspects of structure and function of the internal information processor are only used and needed in so far as they serve a function in this explanation of behaviour. The internal reality test of an information processing model is in its confrontation with the aspects of behaviour it aims to explain, not in its confrontation with the neuroanatomical and the neurophysiological reality as Rose suggests. And as far as the information processing approach is concerned, all models that pass this test are equally real. Scope, elegance, simplicity and beauty are the criteria to base a choice upon.

However, knowledge of the structure and functioning of the central nervous system and of many things more is indeed essential for a *more complete* understanding of the human information processor. It is, for instance, impossible for any variant of the information processing approach to infer the hardware structure and neurophysiological functioning of a behaving organism from the overt behaviour of that organism. If overt behaviour is the only given, then such an endeavour is like solving one equation (with observed behaviour as the outcome) in two unknowns (structure and functioning). Such an equation allows for an infinity of solutions, and therefore, agreement will never be reached (this is essentially Rose's criticism). Only with a second equation in two unknowns can a definitive solution be obtained. The neurosciences and the other members of the cognitive science group have to provide this additional information.

In summary, my view is that, starting with observed behaviour, human visual information processing and central attention in vision can be adequately modelled by the information processing approach. However, to arrive at a more complete understanding a cooperation with other members of the cognitive science group, especially neuroanatomy and neurophysiology, is needed. To anticipate such a cooperation, for the moment, it is only wise to stay as much as possible within the constraints set by the anatomical and physiological nature of the control system, and to try to make the hypothetical constructs of such a kind that they are compatible with neurophysiological information or can readily be attached to neurophysiological information when that knowledge becomes available (see, e.g., Hebb, 1949; Broadbent, 1958).

In the next section we briefly describe two of these constraints: the modular organization of the (visual) cortex and the structure and functioning of neurons. We there also introduce 'new connectionism' as a hardware-inspired model language that perfectly suits the information processing approach. It is up to the reader to decide whether to read, skim or skip that section.

1.10 Modularity, neurons and connectionism

The current view among neuroscientists is that the various attributes of the visual world are analysed separately within the brain. The primary visual cortex (V1) can be regarded as a topographically organized centre for the detection of the complete range of stimulus properties, such as colour, movement, orientation, etc. V1, or area 17, distributes its information over a surprisingly large number of higher order, topographically less precise, visual areas, in front of the primary visual cortex: the secondary visual areas (V2, V3, V3A, V4, MT, etc., in areas 18 and 19). These 'modules' appear to be specialized in the analysis of limited aspects of the retinal image, often only one single parameter, such as retinal disparity, (orientation of) contours, (direction of) movement, size, shape, colour, etc. (See, e.g., Szentagothai, 1975; Zeki, 1978; Cowey, 1979; 1981; Van Essen, 1979; Barlow, 1981; 1985; Stone and Dreher, 1982; Van Essen and Maunsell, 1983; DeYoe and Van Essen, 1988; Livingstone and Hubel, 1988; Zeki and Shipp, 1988.) Cells in these modules, in turn, provide convergent input to cells in the inferotemporal cortex. Here the cells have very large receptive fields and need very specific and complex trigger features for their activation. This non-retinotopic representation and subsequent stages (e.g., the substantia innominata) possibly have to do with recognition, the learned significance of stimuli, learned behavioural responses, etc. (See, e.g., Cowey, 1981, p. 405; Allport, 1987.) Figure 1.10.1 gives an outline of the modular visual system.

So, in this multiplicity of visual areas, one can identify a separation between (pre-striate) cortical areas, apparently driven by 'simple' properties of the visual input such as colour, form, etc., in which spatial relations are preserved, albeit often lacking exact retinotopy and showing various topological transformations (Barlow, 1985; Creutzfeldt, 1985) and (temporal) cortical areas, apparently driven by complex visual properties, independent of and insensitive to the location of these properties, mediating object identification (see, e.g., Styles and Allport, 1986, for further details).

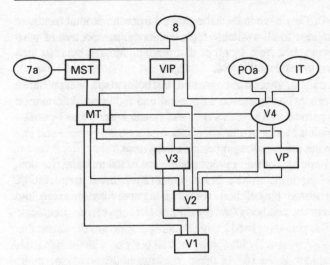

Figure 1.10.1 Visual modules in the brain of the macaque monkey.

Besides neurophysiological evidence there is other evidence suggesting that the visual image is coded in several distinct areas. For instance, there is evidence that damage, artificially restricted to one visual area, produces selective disturbances in visual processing (Cowey, 1981, p. 408). Human psychophysics and neuropsychology also offer clear evidence. In psychophysical demonstrations the trick is to isolate a particular source of information and to show that a specific function is still performed. Julesz's (1971) demonstrations of stereopsis without monocular cues is the prime example (see Brady, 1981, p. 4). Neuropsychological data – often showing specific and isolated breakdown patterns – also strongly support the modularity hypothesis (see, e.g., Marshall, 1984, pp. 225–6).

> Occasionally people with strokes suffer surprisingly specific visual losses – for example, loss of color discrimination without impairment of form perception, loss of motion perception without loss of color or form perception, or loss of face recognition without loss of the ability to recognize most other categories of objects or loss of color or depth perception.
>
> (Livingstone and Hubel, 1988, p. 740)

Taken together, the present view of visual analysis in the brain is that modules, relatively isolated networks of neurons, decompose the complex, multidimensional, visual input. In the brain, the visual input is taken apart.

Fodor (1983; 1985; see also Marshall, 1984) coined the term 'vertical faculties' for these modules. They are individuated in terms of the specific content domains with which they deal (e.g., depth, form or colour). Some further properties of vertical faculties are: input driven, mandatory, encapsulated from much of the organism's background knowledge (i.e., quite stupid), largely organized around bottom-to-top information flow and largely innately specified (see Fodor, 1985, p. 4). They have to be distinguished from 'horizontal faculties' that apply their operations to all available representations, irrespective of what those representations are, i.e., from faculties that are individuated by what they do, not what they do it to (Marshall, 1984, p. 213).

Modularity is not only an important constraint, but holds also a great promise for the information processing approach in general and for visual information processing theory in particular. These modules can function as, not too global – not too detailed, building blocks of the information processing system and can really help to explain the information processor's behaviour.

The neuron is the basic unit of the nervous system and of the modules. In total, there are about 10^{11} neurons in the brain. Generally, three parts can be distinguished in each neuron: the cell body (or soma), a nerve fibre (or axon), and a group of extensions of the cell body (the dendrites). Neurons can communicate with other neurons. The pathways used in this communication are the axons that form terminal junctions (synapses) either with the cell body or with the dendrites of other neurons. There are about 10^{14} of these pathways in the brain; so, on the average, each neuron has about a thousand incoming pathways.

The language used in communication consists of electrical impulses (or spikes), generated in the cell body. The maximum frequency of generating impulses for a cell is about 1000 per second. These electrical impulses are propagated along the axon, which can be regarded as a kind of insulated conductor. At the synapses a chemical transmitter substance is released in the small gap between axon of emitter and receptor location (of cell body or dendrite) of receiver. This transmitter substance influences the state of the receiving neuron in one of two ways. Either it increases the likelihood that the receiving cell will generate impulses. This happens when the synaptic junction is excitatory. Or it decreases the likelihood that the receiving cell will generate impulses. This is the case when the synapse is inhibitory.

It will be clear that 10^{11} neurons and 10^{14} pathways are quite a lot of wheels and pawls. To serve a role as a language in psychological explanations this complexity has to be reduced in one way or another. In fact, what is needed is a *model* of this system, that retains its essential properties in a less complex form. The terms used for concepts and hypotheses of that model can then function as a language in psychological explanations.

The use of a simplified language to talk about neurons, their connections, networks, the functions performed by networks, etc., in explanations in psychology – even explanations involving attention – has a long history. James (1890/1950), for instance, after having set out his views on attention, continues with

The natural way of conceiving all this is under the symbolic form of a brain-cell played upon from two directions. Whilst the object excites it from without, other brain-cells or perhaps spiritual forces, arouse it from within. The latter influence is the "adaptation of the attention". *The plenary energy of the brain-cell demands the co-operation of both factors:* not when merely present, but when both present and attended to, is the object fully perceived.

(James 1890/1950, p. 441)

And Hebb (1966) distinguishes two mechanisms, set and attention, and presents schematic diagrams of possible mechanisms.

Diagram of a possible mechanism of a set [to add]. The excitation from the prior stimulus ["add"] is held in a reverberatory loop. The second stimulus ... is connected with two motor paths ...; but the reverberatory activity supports only one of these ... (Figure 41).

Schematic diagram of a mechanism of attention in which a central process, C1, supports one sensory input (from A), C2 supports another (B). Event A will be responded to if C1 is active, event B if C2 is active (Figure 42).

It is worthwhile to distinguish three ways to use this neuron-pathway language to talk about and model the functioning of the human information processor, i.e., three ways to use this language in explanations.

First, this language can be used in a rather informal way to formulate simple general principles, more or less in the way James (1890/1950), just quoted, did. In Lindsay and Norman (1977) a great number of simple and elegant examples can be found. The formalism used in these examples is quite simple. Neural cells, modelled as nodes, are represented by circles (O). Inputs to nodes can be excitatory ($\rightarrow$;+) and inhibitory (–o ;–). Each input connection is characterized by two numbers: (a) its rate of firing or level of activation ($X \geq 0$) and (b) its amplification or gain ($-1 \leq g \leq 1$; the gain is positive if the input is excitatory and negative if inhibitory). The output of a node equals the algebraic sum of its inputs, $\Sigma\, g.X$, plus its background rate. Figure 1.10.2 gives an example.

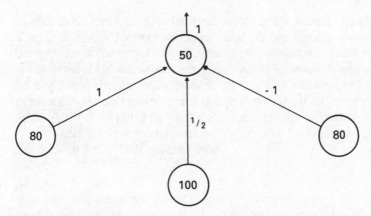

Figure 1.10.2 Basic building block of a connectionist network. The ouput of the upper node equals its background rate (50) plus the weighted sum of its inputs (1 x 80) + (1/2 x 100) + (–1 x 80), which is 100.

Secondly, this language can be used in a much more sophisticated way. This is done in, what is called, the new connectionism, or, the connectionist approach (see, e.g., Hinton and Anderson, 1981; Rumelhart and McClelland, 1986; McClelland and Rumelhart, 1986; see Dennett, 1984, for a general discussion). Within this approach, the basic principles are essentially the same as described above, but the use of computers makes it possible to simulate and study the behaviour of rather complex, interactive, pseudo-neural networks. Most of this work up to now has been concerned with associative memory. McClelland and Rumelhart's (1981) model is concerned with word reading. Phaf, Van der Heijden and Hudson's (1990) model that we describe in Chapter 8 performs selective attention tasks.

Thirdly, it is possible to use this language in a global way to indicate or outline complex mechanisms. The requirement then is not that the mechanism is actually modelled and implemented as in connectionist models. The requirement is that it is not impossible to model the mechanism in a connectionist manner. The knowledge about neurons and their communication then functions as an important background constraint. This is essentially the approach used by Hebb (1949). Connectionist-inspired global outlines can perform the functions which unspecified (i.e., empty) functional components serve in most contemporary information processing models.

Equipped with such components, information processing models are no longer susceptible to Allport's (1980a) criticism that 'psychologists' theories (that is, theories expressed in words rather than in explicit processes ...) have succeeded in doing justice to the richness and complexity of human cognition in simply being so general and underspecified, in process terms, as to mean almost anything' (Allport, 1980a, p. 30). Furthermore this style of theorizing exactly yields the type of theories information processing psychologists are ultimately looking for.

> By designing systems to learn, [connectionists] have reentered the domain on which the associationist and the behaviorist concentrated. However, there is an obvious difference between the [connectionist's] approach to learning and that of the associationist or behaviorist – the [connectionist] is interested in describing the *structure* in which the learned information is stored and the procedures by which the system is able to learn, whereas the associationist or behaviorist settled for *laws* characterizing learning behavior. It is this which links the [connectionists] with the [information processing] tradition.
>
> (After Bechtel, 1985, p. 59; italics mine)

Chapter 2

The topic

2.0 Introduction

The empirical part of this study – Chapters 3 to 6 – is mainly concerned with central attention in detection and recognition tasks in vision. For these tasks attention can be operationally defined as the benefits in detection and/or recognition performance as a result of appropriate selection, emphasis or priority instructions as compared with conditions without such instructions. Central attentional effects are demonstrated if such benefits are observed in a situation that excluded directed eye movements.

The information processing approach, however, is not willing to limit itself to operational definitions and/or a listing of the exact experimental situations and the corresponding observed behaviour. Ultimately, the approach wishes to come up with a set of related hypotheses about the internal structure and functioning of an information processor, i.e., with a model, that makes it possible to explain and predict aspects of the information processor's behaviour in terms of its internal structure and functioning.

The aspects of behaviour my variant of the information processing approach wishes to explain and predict are basically differences in performances observed under different experimental conditions (see Chapter 1). For research on attention these differences are the benefits, i.e., the improvements in detection and recognition performance, observed in conditions with appropriate attentional instructions as compared with conditions without such instructions. So, ultimately, the approach has to come up with a model that can account for and can even predict these benefits. In short the aim is to explain attention as benefits in terms of attention as an internal mechanism. To avoid ambiguity from now on we use the word attention to indicate that internal mechanism.

To arrive at such a model two steps seem essential. First, an acceptable concept of attention has to be isolated so that questions with regard to the function and way of operation of attention can be formulated that can be answered by experimental evidence. Second, the relevant experimental literature has to be reviewed to find the answers to these questions. The present chapter is mainly concerned with the concept of attention and with some of the relevant questions; the next four chapters with the relevant experimental literature.

Isolating such a concept of attention is necessary because, in the past 'the word "attention" quickly came to be associated ... with a diversity of meanings that have the appearance of being more chaotic even than those of the term "intelligence"' so that 'To the question, "What is attention?" there is not only no generally recognized answer, but the different attempts at a solution even diverge in the most disturbing manner' (Spearman, 1937, p. 133, and Groos, 1896, p. 210, in Berlyne, 1974, p. 123). Moreover, the concept of attention was often very broadly construed. For James attention was something like 'anticipatory thinking' (James, 1890/1950, p. 439), and for Hebb it was some 'sort of process that is not fully controlled by environmental stimulation' (Hebb, 1949, p. xvi). For Titchener the concept was so comprehensive that he could state 'the doctrine of attention is the nerve of the whole psychological system' (Titchener, 1908, p. 173).

Current information processing psychology has not yet really solved this definition problem. Attention is still an ambiguous and elusive concept. (No one knows what attention is.) 'The notion of "attention" ... is generally left undefined, or defined by reference to subjective experience. ("Every one knows what attention is".) In practice, the *observable* criterion for successful "attention" to (or awareness of) an environmental event invariably turns on the ability of the subject to *act* voluntarily, or, arbitrarily, in response to that event ...' (Allport, 1987, p. 408). It is very likely that in the term attention a number of notions, in shifting compositions, is involved: 'Attention is not a single concept, but the name of a complex field of study' (Posner, 1975). So, what notions are involved and which notion deserves most of all the name 'attention'?

To find an unambiguous and acceptable concept of attention we first briefly review some of the literature from the early introspective and experimental psychology. Starting there has the advantage that we encounter a number of notions and concepts, described in an absolute way, that can shape our intuitions about what distinctions have to be made and what is really essential in the study of attention. Next, we briefly introduce the initial theoretical apparatus of information processing psychology as concerned with the study of attention and look at what notions survived, what concepts disappeared and what new ideas were added. Finally, we indicate the topics, questions and issues with which the empirical part of our study will be concerned.

2.1 Von Helmholtz

The intuition that one can 'look' out of the corner of the eyes, i.e., the recognition of the possibility of shifting attention, independent of eye movements, to a position other than the line of sight, was a common one in the days of early introspective psychology (see, e.g., James, 1890/1950, p. 437; Wundt, 1912, p. 20; Von Helmholtz, 1924, p. 455). But the opinions about what actually happened then strongly differed. In particular, the difference between the views of Von Helmholtz and James is highly interesting. In this section we introduce Von Helmholtz's view. In the next section we have a closer look at James's theorizing.

In his *Handbuch der physiologischen Optik* (section 28), Von Helmholtz described a series of experiments which he regarded as of great importance. Von Helmholtz (1894) summarizes this research as follows.

> I refer now to the experiments ... with a momentary illumination of a previously completely darkened field on which was spread a page with large printed letters. Prior to the electric discharge the observer saw nothing but a slightly illuminated pinhole in the paper. He fixed his gaze rigidly upon it, and it served for an appropriate orientation of directions in the dark field. The electric discharge illuminated the printed page for an indivisible instant during which its image became visible and remained for a very short while as a positive after-image. Thus, the duration of the perceptibility of the picture was limited to the duration of the after-image. Eye movements of a measurable magnitude could not be executed within the duration of the spark, and movements during the brief duration of the after-image could no longer change its position on the retina. Regardless of this I found it possible to decide in advance which part of the dark field surrounding the continuously fixated pinhole of light I wanted to perceive, and then actually recognized upon the electric illumination single groups of letters in that region of the field, though usually with intervening gaps that remained empty. After strong flashes, as a rule, I read more letters than with weak ones. On the other hand, the letters of by far the largest part of the field were not perceived, not even in the vicinity of the fixation point. With a subsequent electric discharge I could direct my perception to another section of the field, while always fixating on the pinhole, and then read a group of letters there.
>
> These observations demonstrated, so it seems to me, that by a voluntary kind of intention, even without eye movements, and without changes of accommodation, one can concentrate attention on the sensation from a particular part of our peripheral nervous system and at the same time exclude attention from all other parts.

Location

> (Von Helmholtz, 1894; Warren and Warren, 1968, translators)

Von Helmholtz (1871) referred to the same series of experiments and stated that he considered the observations of great importance because they showed that there 'is a change in our nervous system, independent of the motions of the external movable parts of the body, whereby the excited state of certain fibres is preferentially transmitted to consciousness' (Von Helmholtz, 1871; Warren and Warren, 1968, translators). And in relation to similar observations he stated 'In this respect, then, our attention is quite independent of the position and accommodation of the eyes, and of any known alteration in these organs; and free to direct itself by a conscious and voluntary effort upon any selected portion of a dark and undifferenced field of view. This is one of the most important observations for a future theory of attention' (Von Helmholtz, *Physiologische Optik*, p. 741, quoted in James, 1890/1950, p. 438).

In Von Helmholtz's description of what happens when one 'looks out of the corner of the eyes' four statements are of crucial importance.

– According to Von Helmholtz 'one can concentrate attention', or attention 'is free to direct itself'. Attention is something as such, one or another kind of 'force' or 'inner activity'. (Also Wundt, 1874, described attention as an 'inner activity' determining the degree of presence of ideas in consciousness.)

– This force or inner activity operates on 'a particular part of our peripheral nervous system', i.e., intervenes relatively early, and brings it about that 'the excited state of certain fibres is preferentially transmitted to consciousness'.

– As a result, the corresponding part, portion, sector or region of the visual field is perceived: the letters in that region are read or recognized. So, attention is concerned with a region in space.

– Without that force or inner activity 'the letters of by far the largest part of the field were not perceived, not even in the vicinity of the fixation point'. So, attention as a force is seen as essential for visual perception.

An important problem in this view is, of course, how attention is controlled and directed. As stated, this is done by a conscious and voluntary effort. However,

> The natural tendency of attention when left to itself is to wander to ever new things; and so soon as the interest of its object is over, so soon as nothing new is to be noticed there, it passes, in spite of our will, to something else. If we wish to keep it upon one and the same object, we must seek constantly to find out something new about the latter, especially if other powerful impressions are attracting us away.
>
> ...we can set ourselves new questions about the object, so that a new interest in it arises, and then the attention will remain riveted. The relation of attention to will is, then, less one of immediate than of mediate control.
>
> (Von Helmholtz, *Physiologische Optik*, par. 32, in James 1890/1950, pp. 422–3)

So, against a natural tendency of (involuntary, passive, or 'automatic') attention to move from news to news, attention can be directed voluntarily to different regions in the visual field and can be maintained there by one or another kind of (voluntary, active, or 'controlled') interrogation. (It is interesting to note that in the two quotations above the word 'new' is used five times.)

2.2 James

James (1890/1950) was familiar with at least some of Von Helmholtz's observations but doubted the correctness of the interpretation. Moreover, he was not too impressed with the observation that one can attend to objects in the periphery of the visual field without making the appropriate eye movements. For him 'The accommodation or adjustment of the sensory organs', i.e., peripheral adjustments, were essential in this type of sensory or perceptual attention. Nevertheless he knows and admits that

> It has been said, ..., that we may attend to an object on the periphery of the visual field and yet not accommodate the eye for it. Teachers thus notice the acts of children in the school-room at whom they appear not to be looking. Women in general train their peripheral visual attention more than men .... Practice, ..., enables us, *with effort*, to attend to a marginal object whilst keeping the eyes immovable. The object under these circumstances never becomes perfectly distinct – the place of its image on the retina makes distinctness impossible – but (as anyone can satisfy himself by trying) we become more vividly conscious of it than we were before the effort was made.
>
> (James, 1890/1950, p. 437)

But he did not really believe that one can 'look out of the corner of the eyes' in the way Von Helmholtz suggested. To support his view he quotes Hering, who remarked

> Whilst attending to the marginal object we must always attend at the same time to the object directly fixated. If even for a single instant we let the latter slip out of our mind, our eye moves towards the former .... The case is then less properly to be called one of translocation, than one of unusually wide dispersion, of the attention, in which dispersion the largest share still falls upon the thing directly looked at.
>
> (Hering, in James, 1890/1950, p. 438)

(It is interesting to see that this dispersed, distributed, or shared attention view is not consistent with Von Helmholtz's remarks that 'the letters of by far the largest part of the field were not perceived, not even in the vicinity of the fixation point' (Von Helmholtz, 1894; Warren and Warren, 1968, translators) or that 'an impression only from [attended] parts of the picture is received' (Von Helmholtz in James, 1890/1950, p. 438).)

James was much more impressed by another set of experiments and observations.

> Still more interesting reaction-time observations have been made by Münsterberg ... reaction-time is shorter when one concentrates his attention on the expected movement than when one concentrates it on the expected signal. Herr Münsterberg found that this is equally the case when the reaction is no simple reflex, but can take place only after an intellectual operation. In a series of experiments the five fingers were used to react with, and the reacter had to use a different finger according as the signal was of one sort or another. Thus when a word in the nominative case was called out he used the thumb, for the dative he used another finger; similarly adjectives, substantives,

pronouns, numerals, etc., or, again, towns, rivers, beasts, plants, elements; ....
In a second series of experiments the reaction consisted in the utterance of a
word in answer to a question, such as "name an edible fish", etc.; or "name the
first drama of Schiller", etc.; ... Even in this series of reactions *the time was
much quicker when the reacter turned his attention in advance towards the
answer than when he turned it towards the question* .... To understand such
results, one must bear in mind that in these experiments the reacter always
knew in advance in a general way the *kind* of question which he was to receive,
and consequently the *sphere within which* his possible answer lay. In turning
his attention, therefore, from the outset towards the answer, those brain-
processes in him which were connected with this entire "sphere" were kept
sub-excited, and the question could then discharge with a minimum amount of
lost time that particular answer out of the "sphere" which belonged especially
to it.... It is a beautiful example of the summation of stimulations, and of the
way in which expectant attention, even when not very strongly focalized, will
prepare the motor centres, and shorten the work which a stimulus has to
perform on them, in order to produce a given effect when it comes.

(James, 1890/1950, pp. 432–4)

On the basis of these and similar observations, James recognizes – besides eye
movements as a peripheral mechanism for selective attention ('The accommodation or adjustment of the sensory organs'; James, 1890/1950, p. 434) – as the
one and only mechanism for central attention 'The anticipatory preparation from
within of the ideational centres concerned with the object to which the attention
is paid' (James, 1890/1950, p. 434).

In search of means to express this notion, James used terms like 'reinforcing
imagination', 'inward reproduction', 'ideational preparation', 'anticipatory
thinking', 'premonitory imagination', 'anticipatory imagination', 'creation of an
imaginary duplicate of the object in the mind', 'ideal construction of the object',
'mental duplicate', and 'reproduction of the sensation from within'. In his view,
'preperception' seemed the best possible designation for this central attentional
process (p. 439). 'The image in the mind *is* the attention; the *preperception* ... is
half of the perception of the looked-for thing' (James, 1890/1950, p. 442).

In James's account of what happens when one attends to one or another object,
four statements are of crucial importance.

– According to James 'The image in the mind *is* the attention' and 'The idea is
   to come to the help of the sensation and make it more distinct'. So, in this view
   attention is not an entity in its own right, such as an inner force or inner
   activity. Paying attention is a resultant; it is the result of a succesful
   preperception or a correct expectation or anticipation (see also, however,
   James, 1890/1950, pp. 447–54, on attention as a resultant or a force).
– This attending occurs within spheres of knowledge or in ideational centres
   where the brain processes are kept sub-excited, i.e., this expectant attention
   contributes centrally, or relatively late. (In summarizing his view, James

emphasizes 'high' level or 'late' expectations. It is, however, worthwhile to notice that in his text he recognizes expectations on many different levels: from 'reproduction of the sensation from within' via 'anticipatory thinking' to 'preparation of the motor centres'.)

- As a result one becomes more vividly conscious of an object and the object becomes more distinct. (Eye movements that bring the object in focus are needed to make it really distinct(!).)
- Without this 'anticipatory imagination' the objects are still perceived, but not fully perceived. There is great perceptual uncertainty about unattended objects, especially as far as temporal aspects are concerned (James, 1890/ 1950, pp. 409–16).

In James's view expectation, imagination, anticipation, or in general, 'thought', *is* the attention. So, there is no problem of the control of attention; the problem of the control of attention is reduced to the problem of the control of thought. Consciousness is central and it is an essential characteristic of consciousness that it selects. The principle of selection, according to James, is 'relevance'. Consciousness selects so that thought tends to run in logical grooves (Boring, 1957, p. 514). As a result of this 'active and voluntary' attention 'each of us literally *chooses*, by his ways of attending to things, what sort of a universe he shall appear to himself to inhabit' (James, 1890/1950, p. 424).

But of course, if this is the whole story, then the world has few possibilities to report itself. James was well aware of this problem. Besides this 'active and voluntary' attention he also recognized 'passive, reflex, non-voluntary, effortless' attention.

In *passive immediate sensorial attention* the stimulus is a sense-impression, either very intense, voluminous, or sudden – in which case it makes no difference what its nature may be, whether sight, sound, smell, blow, or inner pain – or else it is an *instinctive* stimulus, a perception which, by reason of its nature rather than its mere force, appeals to some one of our normal congenital impulses and has a directly exciting quality ... we shall see how these stimuli differ from one animal to another, and what most of them are in man: strange things, moving things, wild animals, bright things, pretty things, metallic things, words, blows, blood, etc., etc.

(James, 1890/1950, pp. 416–17)

For James this kind of attention is also not a force but an effect. 'We don't bestow it, the object draws it from us. The object has the initiative, not the mind' (James, 1890/1950, pp. 448–9, but see also pp. 447–54!).

2.3 Attention, expectation and intention

Let us have a brief look at the main differences between the two views of active, voluntary, central attention. Von Helmholtz's central attention is characterized in terms of 'the where', i.e., in terms of position or spatial location, and not in terms of 'the what', i.e., the identity. Moreover, for Von Helmholtz, central attention intervenes early and has primarily to do with 'to see'. Voluntary attention is a force or inner activity that directs and determines the perception. It determines what part of the world is perceived. James's central attention is mainly defined in terms of 'the what', i.e., the identity or meaning, and not in terms of 'the where', i.e., spatial position. For James central attention intervenes relatively late and is close to 'to know'. Voluntary attention consists of the reinforcement of ideas and impressions by the preexisting contents of the mind. It makes what is attended to more vividly conscious.

It will be clear that Von Helmholtz's and James's main views with regard to voluntary central attention are completely different. There is a huge gap between the view of attention as an original force determining from *where* in visual space something, it does not matter what, is perceived and the view of attention as an effect or resultant of other inner activities – imagination, preperception, expectation – determining *what* and *how* something, it does not matter where, is perceived. We need words to characterize the essence of these two views. Von Helmholtz's view seems closest to what is nowadays generally meant by the term attention. James's not very strongly focalized expectant attention is much closer to what is generally indicated by the term expectation. Let us therefore use the words 'attention' and 'expectation' to designate the relevant inner activities in Von Helmholtz's and James's views respectively.

The first important problem now to be considered is whether these two views are mutually exclusive or complementary. Is there only one inner activity in attentive acts or are attention and expectation nearly always occurring together?

For Von Helmholtz the two views are not really mutually exclusive. He admits that 'imagination' and 'expectation' also play a role (see James, 1890/1950, p. 441). In relation to observations with stereoscopic pictures illuminated by an electric spark he remarks:

> These experiments are interesting as regards the part which attention plays in the matter of double images .... For in pictures so simple that it is relatively difficult for me to see them double, I can succeed in seeing them double, even when the illumination is only instantaneous, the moment I strive to *imagine* in a lively way how they ought then to look. The influence of attention is here pure; for all eye movements are shut out.
>
> (Von Helmholtz, *Physiologische Optik*, p. 741, in James, 1890/1950, p. 441; italics mine)

So, in fact, Von Helmholtz recognizes two different 'attentions': attention as a force determining from where something is perceived (see section 2.1), and attention as a resultant determining what is seen there or how something is seen there.

Also for James the two views are not really incompatible. As stated, he recognized a second attentional mechanism, albeit not a central one. In James's theory 'the accommodation or adjustment of the sensory organs' plays the role of

Von Helmholtz's attention. In vision this mechanism determines which part of the visual field is clearly perceived. So, it is Von Helmholtz's force in disguise. So, also, James recognizes two 'attentions': attention as a resultant of other inner activities determining what becomes vividly conscious (see section 2.2), and attention as an early selection mechanism for choosing parts of the visual field.

It is not really necessary to further elaborate what the remaining differences and correspondences between Von Helmholtz's view and James's view are. At this moment it is only of real importance to notice that both recognize two 'types' of attention, one concerned with the 'where' and one concerned with the 'what', this, however, without any beginning of an attempt to present an integrated view, spelling out how the two 'types' of attention are related. This observation is of importance because it leads to the question how it was possible that two such eminent scientists as James and Von Helmholtz came to emphasize only one, and a completely different, 'aspect' of attention, mentioning the other only in the passing (Von Helmholtz) or in disguise (James).

One quite boring and not very fruitful answer to this question is the standard answer that this is simply another demonstration of the unreliability of introspection. In my view, the real answer to this question has to be found in the type of experiments that were regarded as providing the crucial information with regard to the question of what the function of attention really is. Let us therefore have a closer look at these experiments and see what factors were varied and what factors were fixed.

In his experiments, Von Helmholtz used a page with letters and decided in advance which *part* of the field he wanted to perceive. So, what he did, was to vary position (left, right, up, down) while keeping material or content fixed (letters and letters again). As a result, he differentially taxed, what we called attention, and kept, what we called expectation, fixed. Of course, expectation was not eliminated. Von Helmholtz certainly expected a flash of light and visible letters on each trial!

In the experiments of Münsterberg to which James referred, on each trial a single word or sentence was presented and the subject was instructed to answer as fast as possible. In these experiments the material or content was varied (towns, rivers, boats, plants) while position was kept fixed (one question and one question again). As a result, expectation was differentially taxed while attention was kept fixed. Of course, attention was not eliminated. The subjects certainly attended to the question on each trial.

So, the crucial experiments were orthogonal in what was varied and what was fixed. Of course, such experiments easily lead to the conviction that what is varied, just because it is varied and shows differential effects, exists and is important, and that what is fixed and therefore shows no differential effects, does not really exist or is of no importance.

From the foregoing it will be clear that the lessons to be learned from the early introspective psychology are, that

- in nearly all attentive acts at least two factors can be recognized: attention and expectation
- it is terribly easy to overlook this point because in most experiments only one factor is varied while other factors are kept fixed.

The last lesson hints at an intriguing possibility. Just because one easily overlooks the effects of factors that were not varied it is possible that there are even more 'attentional' factors, whose existence was not noticed, because the appropriate manipulations were not applied.

Indeed, Gibson (1941) has shown how easy it is to overlook that in experimental tasks yet a third 'attentional' factor is working. Gibson critically reviewed the usage of the concept 'set' in experimental psychology (see also section 1.2). Originally, as introduced by Watt and Ach of the Würzburg school, the concept 'set' was used to describe a task attitude (Einstellung) induced by instructions (Aufgabe) and involving a more specific selective agent (determinierende Tendenz) that determined when and how one or another task was going to be performed ('The *Aufgabe* may ... be thought of as setting up in the subject an *Einstellung* or "set"; and the subject, in accepting an *Aufgabe*, as becoming *eingestellt*' (Boring, 1957, p. 404)).

Gibson now, clearly and convincingly, shows that in this general concept of set at least two (attentional?) factors have to be distinguished: expectation (i.e., James's 'reproduction of the sensation from within' or 'anticipatory imagination'); and intention, an advance preparation with regard to whether to react and if so, how, with what class of responses, to react (something like James's 'prepa[ration] of the motor centres').

The term *set* has been found to be correlated with different things. The following examples may be given in summary:
(1) a prearoused expectation of stimulus objects, qualities, or relations (perception experiments);
(2) ....
(3) an expectation of stimulus relationships either prearoused or acquired during repeated stimulation (conditioning experiments);
(4) an intention to react by making a specific movement, or not so to react (reaction-time and conditioning experiments);
(5) an intention to perform a familiar mental operation (multiplying, memorizing, giving an opposite word);
(6) ....

(Gibson, 1941, p. 811)

Gibson also shows that it is possible to vary the intention to react while keeping the expectation of stimulus objects fixed (see, e.g., Hilgard and Humphreys, 1938), and also that it is possible to vary the expectation of stimulus objects while keeping the intention to react fixed (see, e.g., Mowrer, Rayman and Bliss, 1940). It is more than likely that, just because the intention to react was not manipulated independently of attention and expectation in Von Helmholtz's and James's crucial experiments, they simply overlooked the importance of this factor.

Taken all together, it seems that three different 'attentional' factors, capable of producing benefits given appropriate instructions, can be distinguished: attention, expectation, and intention. What we now have to look for is whether, and if so how, something like attention, expectation, and intention entered the more abstract and stilted model language of the information processing approach.

2.4 Broadbent

For our purposes it is not important to consider research on attention during the behaviourist era. Chapter 1 showed that attention did not so completely disappear from the scene as is often suggested (see also, Lovie, 1983). But it is also true that the way in which the relevant issues were formulated is so remote from the languages used by the earlier introspective psychology and by contemporary information processing psychology, that not very much sense can be made of it. Only in the 1950s did interesting attentional research and important theoretical work start appearing again that makes it possible to refer back in an intelligible way to the early years of modern experimental psychology (Von Helmholtz, Wundt, James, Titchener). Unfortunately, this referring back was not often done, however. Attentional research seemed to start from scratch again and most issues were newly detected for the second time (see Neumann, in prep.).

Moray (1969) lists some developments connected with this 'renaissance of attention'. Firstly, the use of an operational definition of attention in stimulus–response language which allowed private introspection to be replaced by 'external' experimenting. (See Chapter 1 for a somewhat different interpretation of exactly this development!) Secondly, important problems introduced by communication systems, control centres, etc., for which applied psychologists had to find answers. Thirdly, 'the development of new kinds of apparatus and techniques ... in the field of auditory research it is impossible to overestimate the importance of the tape-recorder ...' (Moray, 1969, p. 5). And indeed, nearly all initial information processing research was concerned with audition, not with vision.

This early auditory information processing research resulted in a number of large-scale models or theories, i.e., sets of related principles or hypotheses characterizing aspects of structure and functioning of the human information processor. For a number of reasons it is worthwhile to consider briefly some of these auditory information processing theories. Firstly, a description of these models at least indicates what was new in the information processing approach as opposed to the earlier introspection approach. Secondly, these early theories have strongly influenced all subsequent, so also contemporary, theorizing in information processing research.

The first theory to be considered is Broadbent's (1958) 'filter theory of attention'. In this theory, Broadbent tries to capture the results of his own research and that of many others (e.g., Cherry's, 1953, well-known shadowing experiments). In his own research Broadbent used a modification of the familiar memory-span experiment, the split memory-span experiment.

Normally one presents a series of six or eight digits, rather like a telephone number, and asks the subject to repeat them back immediately. In the experiment we are now considering the listener was given a pair of head-phones in which each ear was connected to a separate channel, and two lists of digits were presented simultaneously. Thus one ear might receive 7 2 3 while the other ear simultaneously received 9 4 5. The listener was asked to reproduce all six digits in any order he chose: and surprisingly enough was often able to do so. When he could, the order of reproduction was in the vast majority of cases either 7 2 3 9 4 5, or else 9 4 5 7 2 3. That is, all the information from one channel appeared in response before any of the information from the other channel. A response of the type 7 9 2 4 3 5, alternating channels, was never obtained. The experiment was also performed with deliberate instructions to the subjects to alternate channels and so give the digits in the order in which they actually reached the ears. This was virtually impossible: although some subjects did achieve it to a limited extent, it seems likely that it was done by a preliminary response to the information in some order followed by a transposition of this order into the required one before the digits were reproduced publicly .... Before drawing any far-reaching conclusions from these results ... it is necessary to be sure that they are not due to some peculiarity of the relation between the two ears .... Another set of experiments ... made sure that this was not the case. They were similar to the split memory-span experiment already mentioned, but instead of using the two ears they used the eye and ear simultaneously. In another variation different frequency regions were stimulated, by mixing two tape recordings each containing three digits, but passing one of the recordings (before mixing) through a filter rejecting low frequencies. In both these cases results generally similar to the binaural case were found, being most clear-cut with the eye and ear, and less frequent when two voices of different spectra were employed. In the eye and ear case it was especially striking that half the individuals studied reproduced the auditory information first and then the visual second, so that the effect cannot be due to some persistent auditory after-effect absent from other senses.

(Broadbent, 1958, pp. 212–13)

(It is worthwhile noticing how the words 'channel' and 'filter' are used in this quotation. They clearly refer to the experimental apparatus.)

The information processing theory based on these and similar observations is summarized in figure 2.4.1. Information enters the system in parallel and is temporarily stored in a short-term store (the S-system). Further on in the system is a limited capacity channel, the P-system. Its capacity is very much smaller than the capacity of the S-system. A 'filter' is postulated that has to regulate the

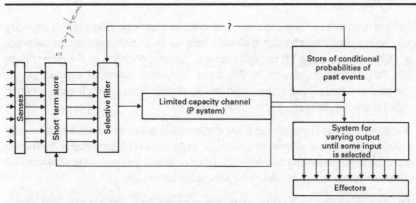

Figure 2.4.1 Broadbent's (1958) information processing and selective attention model (after Broadbent, 1958, p. 299).

information-traffic between the S-system and the P-system. This filter has the ability to select a sensory 'channel' in the S-system – e.g., information from the left or from the right, or with a certain pitch or loudness – and to allow all information with this property access to the limited capacity channel. The P-system is responsible for 'further processing', i.e., categorizing or recognizing the information. (It is worthwhile to notice how the words 'channel' and 'filter' are used in this theory. They clearly refer to 'components' of the hypothetical information processor.)

In Broadbent's account of what happens in split-span and related auditory selective attention tasks, four features, or properties of hypothetical components, are of crucial importance.

- There is a special central mechanism, the filter, that is uniquely devoted to the selection of information. This mechanism or component accounts for the 'selectivity of attention'.
- The filter selects one of the sensory channels in the S-system, so it operates relatively early in the stream of information processing ('a filter at the entrance of the nervous system which will pass some classes of stimuli but not others' (Broadbent, 1958, p. 42)).
- The non-rejected or non-suppressed information enters the limited capacity channel (P system). This channel accounts for the limited capacity and unitarity of attention. ('It is quite possible to say ... that our limited capacity single channel is to be equated with the unitary attention of the introspectionists. Indeed, the writer believes that the one is simply a more exact version of the other' (Broadbent, 1958, p. 300).) This limited capacity channel processes, i.e., identifies or categorizes, the information, or, allocates responses to the stimuli. Phrased otherwise, 'The P system might, in some usages of the term "perception", be regarded as a perceptual mechanism' (Broadbent, 1971, p. 135). So, only what passes the P system is really perceived, i.e., identified or recognized.

- Information not passing the filter and therefore not enjoying the full capacity of the P system resides for a short while in an initial stage of the nervous system that can store all the information simultaneously: the S system. Here the information is stored in the form of simple physical characteristics (sensation): exactly the characteristics used by the filter to single out a channel (see Neumann, in prep., for a detailed analysis).

Because it is the filter, or the filter setting, that determines what information is transferred from the S system into the P system, it is of importance to further specify the rules according to which the filter operates. Broadbent is very explicit about these rules. In his summary of principles he writes:

(B) The selection is not completely random, and the probability of a particular class of events being selected is increased by certain properties of the events and by certain states of the organism.
(D) Properties of the events which increase the probability of the information, conveyed by them, passing the limited capacity channel include the following: physical intensity, time since the last information from that class of events entered the limited capacity channel, high frequency of sounds as opposed to low (in man), sounds as opposed to visual stimuli or touch as opposed to heat (in dogs).
(E) States of the organism which increase the probability of selection of classes of events are those normally described by animal psychologists as 'drives'. When an organism is in a drive state it is more likely to select those events which are usually described as primary reinforcements for that drive.
(Broadbent, 1958, pp. 297–8)

It is quite surprising to note that these are exactly the factors James (1890/1950) classified under passive immediate sensorial attention (see section 2.2). So, according to Broadbent's principles, voluntary attention does not play any role. But his subjects were capable, after appropriate verbal instructions, of performing in split-span and related selective attention tasks! So voluntary attention must have been involved.

2.5 Deutsch and Deutsch

The second theory to be considered is Deutsch and Deutsch's (1963) 'response selection theory of attention'. Deutsch and Deutsch rejected Broadbent's assumption of a limited capacity categorizing channel and the protective filter. The basic reason was that, in their view, the information processing capacities required from the filter were so complex that the filter had to be as complicated as the limited capacity P system it had to protect.

It seems that selection of wanted from unwanted speech can be performed on the basis of highly complex characteristics. For instance, Peters (1954) found that if an unwanted message is similar in content to the wanted one, it

produces more interference with the adequate reception of the latter than if it is dissimilar to it. This shows that the content of the two messages is analysed prior to the acceptance of one and rejection of the other. Gray and Wedderburn (1960) have also found that when speech was delivered to subjects in both ears simultaneously, such that a meaningful sequence could be formed by choosing syllables or words alternately from each ear, the subjects reported back the meaningful sequence rather than the series of words or syllables presented to one ear or the other. Treisman (1960) presented two messages, one to each ear, and subjects were asked to repeat what they heard on one ear. The messages were switched from one ear to the other in the middle and it was found that subjects tended to repeat words from the wrong ear just after the switch. "The higher the transition probabilitites in the passage the more likely they were to do this" (Treisman, 1960).
Other evidence, indicating that complex discriminations would be required of the filter, has been produced by experiments concerning the selection of novel stimuli …. Sharpless and Jasper (1956), studying habituation to auditory stimuli in cats, found that habituation, …, was specific not only to the frequency of sound presented, but also to the pattern in which a combination of frequencies was presented. Evidence for human subjects is presented by Sokolov (1960) and Voronin and Sokolov (1960), who report that when habituation has been established to a group of words similar in meaning but different in sound, then arousal occurred to words with a different meaning …. Such evidence as the above would require us, on filter theory, to postulate an additional discriminative system below or at the level of the filter, perhaps as complex as that of the central mechanism, to which information was assumed to be filtered.

(Deutsch and Deutsch, 1963, pp. 81–2)

They therefore reject the hypothesized filter and limited capacity system and assume that all sensory messages which impinge upon the organism are perceptually analysed at the highest level (Deutsch and Deutsch, 1963, p. 85). Instead of the limited capacity channel they postulate a system containing a large number of 'central structures' or 'classifying mechanisms'. In this theory a message will reach the same perceptual and classifying mechanisms whether attention is paid to it or not. The information is grouped or segregated and identified or categorized by these perceptual and discriminating mechanisms (Deutsch and Deutsch, 1963, p. 83).

Each central structure also has a preset weighting of importance. This importance, or relevance, determines what is selected, when something is selected. Among the structures receiving an information input, the one with the highest weighting of importance can '… switch in further processes, such as motor output, memory storage, and whatever else it may be that leads to awareness …' (Deutsch and Deutsch, 1963, p. 84). Whether or not this will happen depends upon the state of general arousal of the system. Only when this

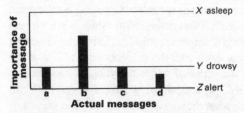

Figure 2.5.1 Diagram illustrating Deutsch and Deutsch's (1963) selection model.

general state is not too low, will the system operate as just described. In relation to figure 2.5.1, Deutsch and Deutsch remark:

> Any given message will only be heeded if the horizontal line (Y) representing the degree of general arousal meets or crosses the vertical line, the height of which represents the "importance" of the message. Whether or not alerting will take place then depends both on the level of general arousal and on the importance of the message. Attention will not be paid to message b though it is the most important of all incoming signals, when the level of general arousal is low (Position X). When the level of general arousal is at Z, which is very high, attention could be paid to all the signals a, b, c, d, and e. In fact, attention is paid only to b ...
>
> (Deutsch and Deutsch, 1963, p. 85)

because b has the highest weighting of importance.

In Deutsch and Deutsch's account of what happens in selective attention tasks, four hypotheses or properties of the information processor are of crucial importance.

- Not attention as such but the weightings of importance have a causal role. What is presented is 'the outline of a system which will display the type of behavior we associate with attention' (Deutsch and Deutsch, 1963, p. 84). Attentional effects are a resultant of importance or relevance interacting with the information. (In the latter part of their paper Deutsch and Deutsch are not too clear about attention as a resultant or attention as an independent force.)
- This interaction occurs centrally (in a system containing 'central structures' or 'classifying mechanisms' that segregate and identify the information), or, relatively late.
- Attention as a resultant is needed for actions and for awareness, i.e., for the 'further processes, such as motor output, memory storage and whatever else it may be that leads to awareness .... Only the most important signals coming in will be acted on or remembered' (Deutsch and Deutsch, 1963, p. 84).
- 'Attention' is not needed for perception. 'One of the salient features of the system as proposed is that it assumes that all sensory messages which impinge

upon the organism are perceptually analyzed at the highest level' (Deutsch and Deutsch, 1963, p. 85), or, perception as such can do without attention (how this squares with 'leads to awareness' is not clear).

Because, with adequate general arousal, it is the weightings of importance that determine whether a message is selected or not, it is of fundamental importance to know what determines, in its turn, these weightings of importance. Deutsch and Deutsch are not very clear about this. In very general terms, it is assumed that the central structures are linked together by connections established by experience and with 'resistances' determined by past learning. Excitation, spreading via these connections, determines both a structure's threshold (leading to an increased readiness to perceive a stimulus whether it is there or not) and its weighting of importance (Deutsch and Deutsch, 1963, p. 85).

The system as proposed allows the world to report itself, because 'more important signals than those present at an immediately preceding time will be able to break in, for these will raise the height of the level [of general arousal] and so displace the previously most important signals as the highest' (Deutsch and Deutsch, 1963, p. 84).

2.6 Early, late and later

At this point it is worthwhile to relate Broadbent's (1958) and Deutsch and Deutsch's (1963) theories to Von Helmholtz's and James's views described in the foregoing sections. It will be clear that Broadbent's view is much closer to Von Helmholtz's view than to James's conceptualization. In Broadbent's model there is a dedicated component, positioned relatively early, with selection as its only function. Again 'the where' (together with some other simple physical characteristics) is of uttermost importance. Furthermore, Broadbent's selection has primarily 'to perceive' as a result. What is not selected is not really perceived. (It is the *perceptual* mechanism that is thought to be of limited capacity; see, e.g., Broadbent, 1971, p. 133.) While Broadbent recognizes the facilitating role of 'anticipation' (see, e.g., Broadbent, 1958, pp. 282–7; p. 300), this factor does not play any real role in his final theorizing. (It is remarkable that Broadbent, 1958, never mentions Von Helmholtz!)

It will also be clear that Deutsch and Deutsch's model is much closer to James's view than to Von Helmholtz's view. The operation of the weightings of importance and the way in which they originate (contextual importance or relevance) show much resemblance to the operation of expectations (preperception) in James's theory. The weightings of importance produce attentional phenomena as a result. They function as a kind of central attention (i.e., selection) primarily defined in terms of 'the what' and not in terms of 'the where'. They influence the stream of information processing relatively late, i.e., in 'central structures' or 'classifying mechanisms' (remember that James recognized effects of expectation on many different levels). What is not so attended is still perceived, but without awareness (?). Location or spatial position does not play any role in Deutsch and Deutsch's theory. (Deutsch and Deutsch, 1963, never refer to James!)

The two models lead, of course, to the information processing variant of the question raised in section 2.3: How is it possible that, based on data obtained in, at first sight, rather similar auditory information processing tasks, two so completely different models are proposed? What was it that led Broadbent to the conclusion that only an early operating, meaning-independent selection mechanism could adequately account for the data? And what was it that forced Deutsch and Deutsch to the conclusion that only a late operating, meaning-dependent selective process could adequately handle the results? In my view the answer to this question has again to be found in the type of experiments that were regarded as providing the crucial information about selection in auditory information processing, i.e., in the experimental factors that were varied and the factors that were fixed. To see this the terms 'attention' and 'expectation', used in relation to Von Helmholtz's and James's research, are very useful.

In Broadbent's (1958) split-span experiments two series of digits in two separate 'channels' were presented on each trial, and the subjects had to repeat these digits in any order they chose. So, what Broadbent did was to vary channels (left vs right, eye vs ear, etc.), while keeping material or content fixed (digits and digits again). By presenting only digits, expectation was fixed and no differential effect of expectation was observed. (Of course, expectation was not eliminated. Subjects certainly expected digits on each trial.) It appeared that the subjects reported the digits by 'channel' ('ear'–'ear'; 'eye'–'ear'; 'high-frequency'–'low-frequency', etc.). So, by fixing expectation and by varying channels, Broadbent created an experimental condition that could show relatively pure effects of Von Helmholtz's attention. And Broadbent rediscovered Von Helmholtz's attention.

In the experiments referred to by Deutsch and Deutsch (1963) a second variation was introduced: something like 'meaning' also varied ('similar content'–'dissimilar content'; 'meaningful sequence'–'random sequence'; 'high transition probability'–'low transition probability'; 'similar in meaning'–'different in meaning', etc.). In this way, experimental conditions were created in which effects of James's expectation could also show up. And Deutsch and Deutsch rediscovered James's expectation. (Of course, attention was not eliminated. Deutsch and Deutsch simply neglected the attentional effects.)

So, again, the crucial experiments were close to orthogonal in what was varied and what was fixed. And again the experiments led to the conviction that what is varied, just because it is varied and shows differential effects, exists and is important, while what is fixed and therefore shows no differential effects, does not really exist or is of no importance.

It will be clear that the lessons to be learned from early auditory information processing psychology are exactly the same as those to be learned from the early introspective psychology (see section 2.3):

- in nearly all attentive acts at least two factors can be recognized: attention and expectation
- it is terribly easy to overlook this point because in most experiments only one factor is varied while other factors are kept fixed.

An early information processing theory in accordance with this analysis is Treisman's theory (see, e.g., Treisman, 1960; 1964). Treisman's theory combines both Broadbent's (1958) theory and Deutsch and Deutsch's (1963) theory. The theory became well-known in 1971, when Broadbent (said he) adopted it in his *Decision and Stress*.

Figure 2.6.1 presents one of the versions of Treisman's theory. As in Broadbent's model there is a selective filter with about the same properties as Broadbent's filter, except that it does not completely block the unwanted messages but merely attenuates them. The weakened and unweakened messages pass further into the system. As in Deutsch and Deutsch's (1963) model, the kernel of the system consists of a large number of central structures: 'dictionary units'. One important property of these units is that they have variable thresholds: importance or relevance, conveyed by explicit instructions or context, is reflected in lower thresholds and therefore in a higher probability of a unit's being triggered, even by a weakened input. In summary, Treisman (1960; 1964) proposed an information processing model with two, simultaneously operating, mechanisms:

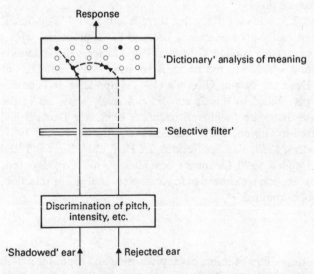

Figure 2.6.1 Treisman's (1960) information processing and selective attention model (after Broadbent, 1971, p. 148).

1. An attenuation-filter that passes relevant messages unweakened but attenuates unwanted mesages. This is quite close to what we called attention.
2. Internal anticipatory preparation in a dictionary with units with variable thresholds. This is quite close to what we called expectation. (As with Deutsch and Deutsch's model, Treisman's proposal deviates from James's theoretical view in postulating only 'high' level expectations.)

Nevertheless, Treisman's theory involving two simultaneously operating selection mechanisms was never as seriously considered and investigated as the other two pioneer information processing models. It is, for example, interesting to read in Keele (1973, p. 151) that Broadbent's (1958) and Deutsch and Deutsch's (1963) theories and the available data leave us with a gap in our knowledge or with an unresolved dilemma. With regard to auditory information processing he remarks: 'if selectivity occurs at the level of physical character-istics of the message, why does the meaning of the ignored message affect response to the selected message? If, on the other hand, selectivity occurs at the level of activated memory, why do physical characteristics of the sound, namely direction and frequency, affect selection?'

Treisman's theory has no problems with this dilemma: the attenuation filter selects on the basis of physical characteristics, and low threshold settings entail that attenuated messages can still affect responding. (Keele, 1973, p. 150, mentions explicitly only the filter mechanism in Treisman's theory.)

The prime reason for not seriously considering Treisman's alternative was that it was regarded as redundant. Two, simultaneously operating, selection mechan-isms seemed too much. The search for parsimony meant that most investigators preferred a one mechanism theory.

As stated in section 2.3, it is very likely that there is still a third 'attentional' factor whose existence easily goes unnoticed because the appropriate experi-mental manipulations are rarely applied: Gibson's (1941) factor, called intention (an advance preparation whether to react and, if so, how, with what class of responses, to react). However, despite Gibson's (1941) impressive and convin-cing analysis, concepts related to this factor did not really show up in the information processing literature (neither Broadbent, 1958, nor Deutsch and Deutsch, 1963, referred to Gibson, 1941; see, however, Allport, 1980a; 1987; Neumann, 1987; Sanders, 1983; Van der Heijden, La Heij, Phaf, Buys and Van Vliet, 1988; Van der Heijden, 1990, for some recent attempts to revive aspects of this factor). In the next section we show that in a complete analysis of selection, this third factor cannot be omitted.

2.7 Selections

Most subsequent theories of human information processing and central selective attention disagreed with regard to two basic issues: (a) the limited capacity (LC) vs unlimited capacity (UC) processing issue, and (b) the early (or precategorical) vs late (or postcategorical) selection issue. These issues were not regarded as independent issues, but sold as combinations; a stand with regard to issue (a) implied a stand with regard to issue (b).

In fact, two selecting–processing combinations were proposed and strongly defended. The first is the LC-processing–early-selection combination. (LC processing required early selection.) The prototypical model is Broadbent's (1958) filter model (see section 2.4). Basically similar or closely related models have been proposed among others by Sperling (1963), Estes and Taylor (1964; 1966), Neisser (1967), Rumelhart (1970), Coltheart (1972; 1975), and Kahneman (1973); see also Broadbent (1982). The second is the UC-processing–late-selection combination. (UC processing seemed to imply late selection.) Deutsch and Deutsch's (1963) model is the prototypical model (see section 2.5). Similar or closely related models have been proposed among others by Norman (1968), Morton (1969), Keele (1973), Posner and Snyder (1975), and Posner (1978).

It is of importance to know, however, that points of view with regard to the capacity issue and points of view with regard to the level at which selection occurs are in principle independent (see, e.g., Kahneman and Treisman, 1984; Allport, 1987; Van der Heijden, 1981; 1987; Van der Heijden, Hagenaar and Bloem, 1984). In this study I will treat them independently. In section 2.9 I briefly discuss some aspects of the capacity issue with regard to vision. In the rest of this section I have a closer look at the selection issue.

With regard to the selection issue, two views have dominated the literature. The first maintains that a selection mechanism operating in a stage prior to the stages concerned with categorizing the information, i.e., a mechanism that operates on a level containing unidentified information, has to be postulated to account for central selective attention. This is the early or precategorical selection view originally proposed by Von Helmholtz and re-introduced by Broadbent (1958; see, e.g., Pashler, 1984, Van der Heijden, 1981, 1984, 1987, and Chow, 1986, for recent formulations of this view for visual information processing). The second view suggests that a selection mechanism operating in a stage containing identified information adequately characterizes this selection aspect. This is the late or postcategorical selection view originally formulated by James and re-introduced by Deutsch and Deutsch (1963; see also Norman, 1968; see, e.g., Mewhort, Campbell, Marchetti and Campbell, 1981, and Coltheart, 1984, for recent reformulations and variations of this view for visual information processing).

While Treisman (1960; 1964) had already shown that a satisfying marriage and a fruitful merging of the two views is possible, nearly all investigators neglected or rejected her proposals as unparsimonious (see section 2.6). So, subsequently, most leading theorists strongly suggested that in nearly all experimental tasks one of these selection mechanisms sufficed. The well-known debates concerning 'early selection or late selection', 'precategorical selection or postcategorical selection', 'input selection or output selection' and 'stimulus set or response set' reflect this basic conviction. (Note that all these dichotomies concern the level at which the selection mechanism operates, not the mechanism of selection.)

'But Occam's razor, though a very good rule of method, is certainly no law of nature' (James, 1890/1950, p. 453). And it is 'laws of nature' and not parsimony that the information processing approach seeks. And, as already suggested in sections 2.3 and 2.6, it might be true that one mechanism is never sufficient and that – if attention, expectation and intention are regarded as distinct selection mechanisms – in all tasks more, simultaneously operating, mechanisms are involved. Let us briefly consider 'stimulus set' (i.e., early, precategorical, input selection) and 'response set' (i.e., late, postcategorical, output selection) before we leave the auditory domain. Is it 'stimulus set' *or* 'response set' or is it 'stimulus set' *and* 'response set'?

According to Broadbent (1970; 1971) subjects may use either of two processes for selecting material: 'stimulus set' and 'response set'.

> In concrete terms, stimulus set is obtained by the instruction "Listen to this voice and repeat whatever it says, regardless of any other sounds you hear". Response set is obtained by the instruction "Listen to this medley of voices and repeat any digits you may hear" The first instruction controls the source of the stimuli controlling response, but not the vocabulary used in response; the second controls the vocabulary of responses but not the source of stimuli.
>
> (Broadbent, 1971, p. 177)

Broadbent's analysis is incomplete, however. Firstly, the 'stimulus set' instruction is not a pure instruction. Indeed, the instruction makes one source of stimuli important or relevant, but it *not only* controls the source of stimuli. It also controls at least two other potential sources of variation because the instruction includes an 'action set' part and a 'response set' part. Firstly, subjects are not asked to push buttons, point with their fingers or kick with their feet. Subjects are asked *to speak*. So, the instruction also induces an 'action set' consisting of (a) an intention to act, and (b) to act in a specified way. Secondly, subjects are not asked to report wordlength, word-class, pitch, etc. They have to repeat what the voice *says*. And that excludes vocabularies or 'spheres of knowledge'. And if the voice tells a real story, context information during repetition still further restricts what are appropriate responses. So, lots of 'response sets' are excluded and, as a result, a unique, albeit very large, 'response set' is induced.

Secondly, the 'response set' instruction is not a pure instruction either. Indeed, the instruction makes one category of words, digits, important or relevant for response, but *not only* controls the vocabulary of responses. At least two other potential sources of variation are controlled because the instruction includes a 'stimulus set' part and an 'action set' part. Firstly, subjects have to *listen*, not to look at the tape recorder, the wall, the experimenter, etc. Moreover, subjects have to listen to this medley of voices, not to the ticking of the clock, the traffic noise outside, the noises of the tape recorder, or, the frequency of the breathing of the experimenter. So, lots of 'stimulus sets' are excluded and only one specific 'stimulus set' is induced. Secondly, subjects have to *repeat* the digits, not to count the digits, add, subtract, or multiply them or try to remember them. So, also a lot of 'action sets' are excluded and only one intention (a) to act, (b) in a specific way is induced.

So, with both instructions there is a 'stimulus set' part, a 'response set' part and an 'action set' part. Of course, 'stimulus set' is simply another word for attention (Von Helmholtz; Broadbent), 'response set' for expectation (James; Deutsch and Deutsch) and 'action set' for intention (Gibson). So it follows that under both instructions, the 'stimulus set' instruction and the 'response set' instruction, three attentional factors are involved: attention, expectation and intention. (It will be clear that Broadbent's, 1971, analysis is also completely inconsistent with Treisman's two-factor model, which he says he adopts.)

To further see, whether for visual information processing one mechanism ever suffices, it is worthwhile to have a closer look at the most important, at least most often used, experimental tasks in vision. The distinction between 'input' (Treisman, 1969) or 'unit' (Kahneman, 1973) selection tasks, and 'dimension' (Treisman, 1969) or 'attribute' (Kahneman, 1973) selection tasks is in this context most relevant, and we restrict our discussion to these two groups of tasks. The question we have to face is: Is it 'input selection' *or* 'attribute selection' or 'input selection' *and* 'attribute selection'?

For visual information processing the partial-report task (see, e.g., Sperling, 1960) and the partial-report bar-probe task (see, e.g., Averbach and Coriell, 1961) were regarded as prototypical input selection tasks. In a partial-report bar-probe task a row of letters is briefly presented. The row is followed by an arrow or a bar, pointing at one of the letter positions. The subject has to name the letter that was in that position. So that letter is the 'input' or 'unit' to be selected. (Accuracy is the dependent variable.) According to the traditional analysis 'selective attention to inputs' is the mechanism operative in these tasks, where 'selective attention to inputs is the allocation of capacity to the processing of certain perceptual units in preference to others' (Kahneman, 1973, p. 135; see also Treisman, 1969, and neglect the capacity issue).

The Stroop task (see, e.g., Stroop, 1935) was regarded as a prototypical attribute selection task. In the orthodox Stroop task subjects see a card with rows of coloured colour words. The words are printed in incongruent colours, e.g., the word red in green, the word green in blue, etc. Subjects have to name the colours of the words in reading order. So, colour is the attribute or dimension to be selected. (Time is the dependent variable.) In the traditional analysis, 'attention to attributes' is the mechanism operative in this task: 'Attention to attributes affects the post-perceptual stage of response selection' (Kahneman, 1973, p. 111). It is worthwhile to note the dichotomy between early (selection for processing) and late (response selection) in these definitions.

More recent theoretical analyses have indicated, however, that, while the distinction between inputs or objects and attributes or dimensions is vital (see, e.g., Kahneman and Treisman, 1984, p. 45) the distinction between input selection *tasks* and attribute selection *tasks* is not as obvious as was initially thought (see, e.g., Neumann, 1980, pp. 357–63; Van der Heijden, 1981, pp. 85–110; Van der Heijden et al., 1988; Phaf et al., 1990). In fact, it is not difficult to show that all input selection tasks always involve some forms of attribute selection and that all attribute selection tasks always involve one or another form of input selection. The tasks seem mainly to differ in what is emphasized in the instructions. Let us consider the partial-report bar-probe task and the Stroop task in more detail.

In partial-report bar-probe tasks the subjects are instructed to name the letter. So, selection of an object, i.e., the letter on the indicated position, is required. However, input selection is not sufficient for task performance. Without any specification there is in this task not only an ambiguity with regard to the position of the object to be responded to (i.e., with regard to the where). There is also uncertainty with regard to the property or attribute of the object to be responded to (i.e., with regard to the what). Given letter naming as the task, only one dimension of the object is relevant for responding and has to be selected. That dimension is the shape of the letter. Shape and only shape determines what response has to be given. All other attributes of the selected object (position, size, colour, etc.) are irrelevant for responding. That 'shape selection' is not emphasized in the instructions to the subject results from the fact that it is generally agreed that letters are objects that have to be read. (But one can ask the subject to name the position, size, or colour of the indicated letter.) So, letter reading in the partial-report bar-probe task requires, besides input selection, also (shape) attribute selection.

In the orthodox Stroop task, subjects are instructed to name the colours. So, selection of an attribute, i.e., the colour, is required. However, this attribute selection is not sufficient for task performance. Without any specification there is in this task not only an ambiguity with regard to the attribute to be responded to (i.e., with regard to the what). There is also uncertainty with regard to the position of the object to whose property one has to respond (i.e., with regard to the where). Position and only position determines the object carrying the relevant property at a certain position in the response sequence. That 'input selection' is not made very explicit in the instructions to the subject results from the fact that it is generally agreed that the colours of the words have to be named in reading order. (But one can instruct the subject to name the colours in a completely different order.) So, colour naming in the Stroop task requires, besides (colour) attribute selection, also input selection.

So, both the 'input selection task' and the 'attribute selection task' are simultaneously input selection tasks (the where has to be specified) and attribute selection tasks (the what has to be specified). In the partial-report bar-probe task the instruction emphasizes position, but the subject has also to select a dimension. In the Stroop task the instruction emphasizes colour, but the subject has also to select a position. In other words, in both tasks, and in nearly all experimental tasks, 'two distinct functions... are controlled by different aspects of the information presented...: Stimulus choice, the segregation of relevant items from irrelevant ones, must be guided by some identifying property...: Response choice,..., is controlled by other properties ...' (Kahneman and Treisman, 1984, p. 31).

However, even the specification of the 'where' and the 'what' is not sufficient to ensure the desired task performance. First, subjects have to react overtly and are not expected to remain silent. More specifically, in both tasks under discussion subjects have to speak; not to write, to push buttons, etc. Second, subjects have to respond with letter names and colour names; they can, however, also categorize the letters as 'vowel' or 'consonant' and the colours as 'bright' or 'dark'. So, still a third factor, an 'action set', is involved, consisting of (a) an intention to act, and (b) to act in a specified way. Just because all experiments in the information processing tradition require (simple) overt actions of a specified type, the existence and importance of this selective factor is virtually never recognized.

This analysis of selection in vision again suggests the conclusion that in (nearly) all (experimental) tasks more attentional factors or selective processes have to be distinguished: one process concerned with the 'where' (i.e., controlling the source of stimuli to be responded to), a second concerned with the 'what' (i.e., controlling what aspect of the stimulus is of importance) and a third concerned with 'what to do' (i.e., controlling whether, and if so, how, to react). These processes are very close to the processes already suggested by Von Helmholtz, James, and Gibson, respectively: attention, expectation, and intention.

2.8 Attention, acuity and eye movements

The analysis presented in the foregoing sections strongly suggests that there are (at least) three central processes that can produce benefits under appropriate selection, emphasis or priority instructions: Von Helmholtz's attention (see also Broadbent), James's expectation (see also Deutsch and Deutsch) and Gibson's intention. Of course, this outcome introduces a whole bunch of questions. Are they independent processes? If not, how do they interact and/or inform each other? If so, how are they related? etc. etc. However, these questions need not concern us now. In Chapter 8 we will return to these and similar questions. The purpose of the foregoing sections was not to find answers to such questions. The reason that we introduced these topics was only to sharpen intuitions so that an unambiguous and acceptable concept of attention could be isolated.

We are now in a position to specify in an unambiguous way the central process we are primarily interested in. Indeed, it is Von Helmholtz's type of attention: attention in visual perception, presumably concerned with position, location, or the 'where' – a central process producing benefits in situations where expectations and intentions are experimentally fixed. What we first of all want to know is whether this type of attention really exists (remember that James and Deutsch and Deutsch simply denied its existence). If its existence is firmly established it is worthwhile asking further questions. Is it an independent force or is it a resultant of other processes? What exactly is it concerned with? Indeed positions, or objects, or even dimensions of objects? What is its function? What are its temporal and spatial characteristics?

Not all experiments that claim to have demonstrated the existence of 'attentional' effects in vision, however, really demonstrated the existence of central attentional effects in vision. The basic reason is that in a great number of studies there is a confounding between possible central attentional effects and a very influential peripheral and structural effect: the effect resulting from differential retinal acuity. Let us have a brief look at this latter effect.

It is well known that the human eye is markedly inhomogeneous with regard to its capacity for resolving detail. This capacity, i.e., the retinal acuity, is defined in terms of the minimal separation that the eye can resolve. As a measure, the reciprocal of the visual angle (in minutes of arc) subtended by a just-resolvable stimulus is used. In the human daylight or cone visual system, acuity is highest in the fovea and declines progressively from there to the periphery of the retina (see, e.g., Haber and Hershenson, 1974, p. 51). This fall-off in acuity also shows up in recognition latencies. Eriksen and Schultz (1977) showed that the time to name a letter increases by about 100 ms as the letter is moved 3 deg from the fovea (see also Lefton and Haber, 1974). Also brightness judgements (see, e.g., Shulman, Wilson and Sheehy, 1985) and dot-detection latencies (Van der Heijden, Wolters and Enkeling, 1988) reflect the retinal inhomogeneity in a similar way.

It is very difficult to appreciate how small the high acuity window of the retina really is. Acuity is down to half its maximum value at an eccentricity between 0.5 and 1.5 deg of arc, the exact value depending upon the kind of measurement instrument used (see Anstis, 1974). Figure 2.8.1 gives an impression of this rapid acuity fall-off. The figure was developed by Anstis (1974). He determined recognition threshold sizes for letters presented in isolation on different retinal positions. For the figure presented, each letter was made 10 times its threshold height. Each letter should be equally readable when the centre of the figure is fixated. According to Sperling (1984), who used similar displays, the size of these characters matches the information processing capacity of the retinal area on which they are imaged.

It is generally agreed that acuity is best explained in terms of hardware, i.e., neurons and their connections. Firstly, in the centre of the fovea the receptors of the daylight visual system – the cones – are packed very tightly together. Their number falls off very rapidly towards the periphery of the retina. Secondly, from the bundle of axons of retinal ganglion cells that leave the eye most are devoted to the transmission of information from the foveal region that has the highest receptor density. Thirdly, also in the striate cortex (V1) the amount of neural tissue representing each degree of visual field declines monotonically with eccentricity from the fovea (the cortical magnification factor: see, e.g., Cowey, 1981). So, the visual information processing system is built in such a way that

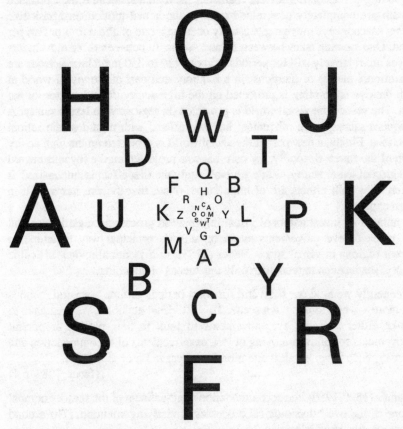

Figure 2.8.1 A chart demonstrating variations in acuity with retinal position.
(From Anstis, 1974.)

most of its computing power is devoted to a small portion of the visual field: the portion projected on the fovea.

The visual system is provided with means that make it possible to enlarge the area of acute or foveal vision over time. The direction in which the eyes are pointing can be changed. These eye movements are controlled by six muscles, that act as three antagonistic pairs. One pair is responsible for up and down movements of the eyes, one pair for side to side movements and one pair for a rotational movement. A number of neural centres are involved in instructing and coordinating these muscles.

For most visual information processing tasks the saccadic eye movements are of prime importance. These (saccadic) eye movements serve the function of allotting the visual system's processing power to different regions of the visual world in turn. Saccadic eye movements are very fast movements with speeds up

to 1000 deg per second. They are 'ballistic' movements, because their distance
and path are completely determined prior to the actual motion. In a task like
reading, saccadic eye movements usually occur at a rate of about four or five per
second. One saccade takes between 30 and 40 ms. In between these movements
the eyes are relatively still for periods of about 150 to 350 ms. These periods are
the fixational pauses or fixations. In a fixation, that part of the visual world at
which the eye is pointing is projected on the high acuity, foveal, region of the
retina. The rest of the visual world is projected on regions with lesser acuity. A
subsequent saccadic eye movement has two effects with regard to the retinal
projections. Firstly, a new part of the visual world is projected on the high acuity
region of the fovea. Secondly, the part that was projected on the fovea is moved
to a region of lesser acuity. While generally only the first effect is emphasized, it
is likely that both effects are of importance. (Note that the eye has a built-in
limited capacity!)

A number of investigators of visual information processing regard these and
other types of eye movements as an organism's principal way to attend to
different regions in visual space. Haber (1983), in his critical review of iconic
memory, seems even to recognize only this means of attending.

> Frequently we hold our head still for short periods of time – several seconds
> or more – while looking at a scene. To shift visual attention, we then have to
> make either saccadic eye movements to look in new places, or pursuit
> movements to follow a moving object, or movements of accommodation and
> convergence when we shift attention from near to far or vice versa.
>
> (Haber, 1983, p.4)

For James (1890/1950) 'the accommodation or adjustment of the sensory organs'
was one of the two 'physiological processes' underlying attention. (The second
process we discussed in section 2.2.)

In the study of *central* attention, for obvious reasons, (saccadic) eye movements to, or in the direction of, the to-be-attended target have to be precluded.
Appropriate eye movements that bring the projection of a location or region of
the visual field onto the high acuity region of the retina can also produce benefits
in accuracy and latency. But those benefits are not brought about by central
attention. So, by allowing appropriate eye movements to occur, possible benefits
brought by central attention are completely confounded with benefits resulting
from peripheral adjustments. But then not even the existence of central attention
can be really established, let alone its properties when it exists. Central attention
has to be varied, but acuity (just as expectation and intention) has to be fixed. (In
James's analysis, both peripheral and central factors were allowed to vary. As a
result, James did not know what central attention is.)

In the literature a number of different attempts to meet this condition can be
found. The simplest method is to instruct the subjects not to move their eyes in
the direction of the target. The problem with this method is that it is far from clear
whether subjects can really obey such an instruction. Colegate, Hoffman and

Eriksen (1973) report an experiment involving eye movement recording that clearly showed that naive subjects could not. The same observation under identical instructions was reported by Engel (1976).

A somewhat more complicated method is to instruct subjects not to move the eyes, and to record any eye movements made. The analysis can then be restricted to those trials in which no eye movements were recorded. The problem with this method is that most eye movement registration equipment presently in use is not very sensitive. Often, movements of up to 1 or 2 deg are not detected (see, e.g., Hughes, 1984; Shulman, Wilson and Sheehy, 1985; Shulman, 1984). Given the observation that there are often small saccades (Engel, 1976, p. 52) and slow drift movements (see Posner, 1980, p. 19), this method cannot really be recommended. The best method seems to be to use exposure durations that are too short to allow directed eye movements during stimulus exposure.

Recently, Rayner, Slowiaczek, Clifton and Bertera (1983) provided relevant information with regard to this issue. They attempted to assess the average minimum saccadic latency under a number of different conditions. Their estimates ranged between 175 and 200 ms. These estimates appeared well in line with earlier ones. 'Most estimates of the average minimum latency of an eye movement have ranged between 150 and 250 ms, with the typical estimate slightly less than 200 ms' (Rayner et al., 1983, p. 912). It is worthwhile to note that these figures are averages of latency distributions. So there are shorter and longer latencies. This all leads to the conclusion that (saccadic) eye movements are only effectively precluded if total exposure durations are used that are appreciably below the average minimum latency; even below 150 ms. We therefore only consider experiments with very short exposure durations.

2.9 Unlimited capacity in vision?

It is common practice in theorizing about information processing and central attention to use and to mix up indiscriminately data obtained in the visual and auditory domains (see, e.g., Keele and Neill, 1978; Allport, 1980a, b; Broadbent, 1982; Kahneman and Treisman, 1984; Johnston and Dark, 1982; 1986). Especially strong has been the tendency to use data obtained in auditory tasks such as split-span experiments and dichotic listening tasks to also settle fundamental theoretical issues concerning information processing and central attention in vision. Moreover, the general idea is that models of auditory information processing are equally applicable to visual information processing tasks.

Such global theorizing not only leads to 'small' errors in the interpretation of data (for example, auditory information processing specialists often simply neglect the retinal acuity gradient in a theoretical synthesis). Such theorizing might also neglect more fundamental differences between vision and audition, differences that can have far reaching consequences for the resulting theories. One of these fundamental differences might be a difference in 'capacity'.

In sections 2.4 and 2.5 we briefly described the pioneer auditory information processing models. These models not only differed on selection issues, but also, on what can be called 'the capacity issue'. Broadbent's first and most fundamental principle was that 'A nervous system acts to some extent as a single communication channel, so that it is meaningful to regard it as having a limited capacity' (Broadbent, 1958, p. 297). Deutsch and Deutsch (1963) start their theoretical considerations with 'the probable conclusion that a message will reach the same perceptual and discriminatory mechanisms whether attention is paid to it or not ...' (Deutsch and Deutsch, 1963, p. 83). Here we have the origin of one of the most heavily debated, and, in my view, one of the least productive issues in information processing research: the limited vs unlimited capacity issue. (See Allport, 1980a, b; 1987; Neumann, 1980; 1987; Van der Heijden, 1990, for critical discussions.)

Basically the issue is quite simple. After Deutsch and Deutsch (1963) one view holds that all information registered is processed in parallel up to the stage of memory activation, or that all possible identification is also actually done. This is the UC-processing assumption (see, e.g., Norman, 1968; Morton, 1969; Shiffrin and Schneider, 1977). After Broadbent (1958) the other view holds that only a limited amount of the information that can be identified is actually identified. This is the LC-processing assumption (see, e.g., Sperling, 1963; Estes and Taylor, 1964; 1966; Rumelhart, 1970; Kahneman, 1973). And that is all.

Most investigators are proponents of one or another limited capacity view. At first sight, that seems reasonable. The eye, for instance, has certainly limitations, and there are also only a limited number of axons connecting eye and brain (see section 2.8). Things become appreciably less reasonable, however, if one sees how the limited capacity notion is worked out and used in theories (see, e.g., Allport, 1987, and Neumann, 1987, for critical reviews).

What all theories have in common is the view that the limitations are *central* limitations: limitations that have nothing to do with the sense organs or with the effectors. (The observation that human beings cannot do everything and certainly not everything at the same time is simply translated into the theoretical assumption that they have central limitations.) For the rest, the theories diverge in a bewildering way. Some theorists construe the limitation in terms of the brain's capacity to transmit or handle information. Selective attention, e.g., a filter, has to take care that the capacity is optimally used (see, e.g., Broadbent, 1958; Moray, 1967). Others describe the limitations in terms of limits of 'focal attention' (see, e.g., Neisser, 1967), or of one or another type of 'mental energy' that functions as attention (see, e.g., Kahneman, 1973). Still others account for the limitation in terms of limited 'resources' (see, e.g., Norman and Bobrow, 1975; Navon and Gopher, 1980). Neumann (1985; 1987) gives an intriguing description of the twists and turns of the limited central capacity notion.

Recently, Neumann, Van der Heijden and Allport (1986) suggested that too global theorizing, and in particular the indiscriminate use of data from auditory and visual information processing research in this theorizing, might have had the result that 'to the question "How is capacity limited?" there is not only no generally recognized answer, but the different attempts at a solution even diverge in the most disturbing manner' (after Groos, 1896, p. 210, in Berlyne, 1974, p. 123). In their attempt to separate fiction from fact, they pointed to a number of fundamental differences in the character of information processing in vision and audition. For present purposes the discussion of one of these differences suffices. It concerns the radically different information-carrying properties of light and sound, the corresponding (obvious) structural differences between the eye and the ear and the resulting differences in the 'further processing' requirements in the visual and auditory perceptual systems.

There is an essential difference between light and sound. Reflected light from different surfaces (and emitted light from different sources) can converge at points in space essentially without interaction or interference. Sound waves from different sources, on the contrary, interact; they summate and form a complex wave form.

Just because light does not interact it is possible to recover directly the immanent spatial structure of the light by using a lens. The external eye has two of these lenses: the cornea and the lens. They allow light from spatially separate surfaces or sources to be projected onto spatially separate regions of the receptor surface of the eye, the retina. Just because sound waves interact, such external means for separating auditory information are not available for the ears. Spatially separate regions of the receptor surface in the ear, the basilar membrane, are used to code frequency information, not spatial information. So 'visual information is already spatially sorted out on the retina; in the ear, sound is not. Visual information processing is intrinsically spatial; spatial direction is merely one of the computable properties of auditory information' (Neumann et al., 1986, p. 185).

Given this state of affairs, it is not unlikely that attentional mechanisms also differ between these two modalities. In audition, selection of information coming from a particular source involves a complex process of disentangling – this, because all simultaneous information is contained in one, single, acoustical pattern. In a sense, the wanted information has to be undone from unwanted information coming from other sources. The main problem here is one of signal–noise separation. One way of solving this problem is by getting rid of the noise (filtering out the signal). Possibly this is the solution chosen by evolution for attentional selection in audition. The apparently serial nature and limited capacity, often brought forward to characterize auditory information processing, seem to support this hypothesis.

In vision, the potential objects of attention have well-defined locations and can be selected by selecting this location. There is no disentangling problem, there is no need to get rid of the noise. The main problem is here a problem of choice among parallel events over the entire visual field. The choice of one event can leave all other events undisturbed. Possibly this is the solution chosen by evolution for attentional selection in vision. Then, however, there is no need to postulate that visual information processing is also serial and of limited capacity.

Possibly visual information processing is much better characterized by parallel processing and unlimited central capacity.

Taken all together, there is no a-priori reason to assume that one or another kind of limited central capacity system is simply built into the visual information processing system and, consequently, has to be used as an explanatory concept. Borrowing reasons from auditory information processing research, as has been common practice up to now, only obscures matters and delays progress. The best strategy seems to be to investigate what problems the human visual information processing system solves and how it does so (see, e.g., Van der Heijden, 1990). In the course of such a study it will become apparent whether a capacity-concept is needed to explain the observed facts.

2.10 Simple versus complex

In general, it seems that simple experimental tasks, with few variables, are best suited for investigating human performances and functions. In fact, Galileo and Newton learned much about our physical world by studying the simplest kinds of pendulums and weights, mirrors and prisms; also, contemporary biologists devote more attention to tiny germs and viruses than to magnificent lions and tigers (Minsky, 1985). Contemporary information processing psychology often uses such simple tasks. However, the information processing approach started with and still often uses quite complicated experimental tasks that are very difficult to interpret.

One reason for this state of affairs has already been hinted at in section 2.4. The problems information processing psychologists were mainly concerned with – the capacity of the human information processor and the role of attention in information processing – had their roots in applied problems. Moray (1969) aptly described this origin.

> Towards the end of the Second World War a number of important problems arose for which answers were required from applied psychologists .... Communication systems in ships, planes and air traffic control centres all produced situations in which there was a high flow of information, and in which the human operator might be required to do two things at once .... Furthermore the growing number of semi-automatic control processes, in which the human operator was required to perform rather little physical exertion, but had to handle great quantities of information displayed on dials and other forms of information readout, again drew attention to the need for a study of how observers handle simultaneously received signals, and how fast they can switch from one task to another.

> (Moray, 1969, pp. 4–5)

Another reason seems to be inherent in the information processing approach as originally conceived. The main aim of this approach was to infer the internal structure and functioning of a behaving organism from the overt behaviour of that organism, so that it became possible to explain the organism's behaviour in terms of its internal structure and functions. This goal invited the formulation of broad theories providing an approximate sketch of the whole information processor (see, e.g., Broadbent, 1958; Deutsch and Deutsch, 1963; Treisman, 1960; 1964). Because theorists are also only human beings, often further experimentation did not really have the function of a critical test of their theory; rather, the main function of further research was in the defence of the theory. (See, e.g., section 2.7 on 'stimulus set' and 'response set' and on 'input selection' and 'attribute selection'.) This function was better served by complex tasks with many obscuring variables than by simple tasks. The more complex the experimental situation, the easier it is to show that at least some aspects of the results are compatible with at least some aspects of one's a-priori theoretical views. Making complex tasks still more complex, is what is often observed.

To get real insight into human information processing and performance, both simple tasks and complex tasks have to be analysed. The basic reason is that simple tasks can reveal properties and mechanisms that can shed light on performance in complex tasks, but that, of course, this matter also needs investigation. For at least two reasons it is not a-priori known whether, and, if so, how, performance in simple tasks and in complex tasks is related.

Firstly, as Kahneman and Treisman (1984) suggest, there is no assurance that the same mechanisms of processing and selecting information are relevant in simple tasks and in complex tasks.

Secondly, even if the same mechanisms of processing and selecting of information are relevant in simple tasks and in complex tasks, we must see how each of the simple mechanisms relates to all the other mechanisms. (Knowledge about the brain may serve as an example. Even if we understood how each of the billions of brain cells works separately, this would not tell us how the brain works as an agency. See Minsky, 1985.)

But just because the information processing approach has recently provided some fundamental insights into human information processing by using simple tasks, the time has come to investigate whether, and, if so, how, these insights can be used to explain performance in more complex tasks. Therefore in the empirical part of our study we start with simple tasks and only then move on to more complex tasks. Consequently, the following four empirical chapters are devoted to

- single-item detection and recognition tasks with accuracy as the dependent variable,
- single-item detection and recognition tasks with latency as the dependent variable,
- multiple-item detection and recognition tasks with accuracy as the dependent variable,
- multiple-item detection and recognition tasks with latency as the dependent variable.

Chapter 3

Single-item detection and recognition tasks with accuracy as the dependent variable

3.0 The start

In the research of the recent past, attentional issues – especially the early vs late selection issue – and processing issues – especially the limited capacity vs unlimited capacity issue – were inextricably interwoven (see section 2.7). In the most influential views early attentional selection and limited capacity were unbreakably conjoined. In Broadbent's (1958; 1971) filter model, there are attentional effects just because there is a limited information processing capacity (see section 2.4). Selective attention functions by rejecting or suppressing the unwanted information. In subsequent models attention itself was regarded as a limited commodity. Processing one 'unit' or 'object' was not a problem for attention, but with 'too much' information attention itself imposed the limitation. In these models selective attention functions by selecting and processing only the desired information (see, e.g., Neisser, 1967; Kahneman, 1973). With both these early selection views, attentional effects are only to be expected when distractors are present in sufficient numbers so that the capacity of the system is exceeded.

It was exactly this theoretical context that made single-item studies of fundamental importance. In single-item studies, a minimum of information is presented: a single dot, a single letter, etc. So, there is no information overload for a hypothetical information processing channel, or alternatively, attention is in no way pushed to its limits. If, nevertheless, attentional effects show up, then these effects have nothing to do with capacity limits of either a processing channel or of attention itself, and a capacity-independent account has to be sought. Moreover, in single-item studies there are no noise items or irrelevant visual signals to suppress or to inhibit. So, if attentional effects show up, another conception of the operation of attention than 'filtering' or 'attenuation' of irrelevant material has to be developed. So, the important issues for single-item studies are (a) can attentional effects be demonstrated, and (b) if so, how are they brought about? In this chapter we look at single-item studies with percentage correct as the dependent variable. The next chapter is devoted to single-item studies with latency as the dependent variable.

In the research on the effect of 'attention' with single-item displays, i.e., with 'empty' visual fields, and with percentage correct as the dependent variable, two types of tasks can be distinguished: *detection* tasks and *recognition* tasks. There are two variants of the detection task. Either a single item, e.g., a faint dot or a weak flash of light, is presented on only some of the trials and subjects have to indicate whether there was a stimulus or not. Or a stimulus is presented on each trial and subjects have to indicate where the stimulus was. In a recognition task a stimulus, e.g., a letter or a form in 1 out of *n* orientations, is presented on each trial and subjects have to indicate what the stimulus was. With both types of tasks it is investigated whether foreknowledge of the position where the item is going to appear enhances performance relative to a condition where no foreknowledge of position is given, i.e., whether foreknowledge of position produces 'benefits'.

This single-item research had a very peculiar and intriguing start. There are two 'older' papers that are often referred to and that both reported a null-effect. There were no positive effects of foreknowledge of position, was the suggestion. The first 'unsuccessful' study was reported by Mertens (1956). His task was a detection task. He presented his subjects with very weak flashes of light. The subjects indicated the detection of a flash by pressing a button. Conditions were blocked. In some blocks of trials – the no foreknowledge blocks – the flashes could appear in any of four positions around a fixation point. In the fore-knowledge blocks the flashes occurred at only one of these positions. (The subjects were instructed to maintain fixation on a central fixation mark.)

From his results, to which we return further on, Mertens concludes

> If the eye is fixed, the probability of observation is practically independent of whether the attention is fixed upon the light source or not. Furthermore, [directing attention] has the disadvantage that it fatigues the observer more than [not directing attention], because in the first case he has to stress himself continually not to look in the direction of attention.
>
> (Mertens, 1956, p. 1070)

(Remember Hering's observations on attention and eye movements referred to in section 2.2!)

Mertens's interpretation of his data is terribly strange, however. The values upon which he bases his conclusion are intensity ratios, I_N/I_F, where I_N is the flash intensity needed to have a proportion *p* correct in the no foreknowledge condition and I_F the intensity required for the same proportion correct in the foreknowledge condition. The values found for proportions *p* of 0.25, 0.50 and 0.75 were 1.02, 1.11 and 1.18. So, all values are larger than 1, indicating that a more intense light was needed in the no foreknowledge condition than in the foreknowledge condition!

So, there was a clear effect of foreknowledge of position. Not so for Mertens, however. He argues that only the value obtained at *p* = 0.25 is useful! This value is only 1.02, so 'practically no influence of the attention upon the probability of observation was found' (p. 1070). But in this way, experiments can be used to prove any point whatsoever. Simply include one condition producing the wanted (null) effect and talk the rest away.

The second unsuccessful study was reported by Grindley and Townsend (1968). The task they used was a recognition plus detection task. Subjects had to say where (in which of four positions) which single target (a T in one out of four orientations) was presented. They compared a foreknowledge of position condition with a no foreknowledge of position condition. No positive effect with foreknowledge was found. (The same negative results were obtained with simultaneous position cueing in a second acuity task and in a luminance discrimination task.) Grindley and Townsend conclude that with single-item displays, instructions to attend to part of the visual field have no effect on perception.

There are, however, strong reasons to doubt Grindley and Townsend's conclusion. The most important one is that their experiments fail to meet the basic methodological standards. In the first experiment, 10 subjects participated. Each subject received only 8 trials in the foreknowledge condition and 8 in the no foreknowledge condition, or, in total, in each condition only 80 judgements were collected. This total number is less than the number of observations one subject receives in one session in contemporary experiments. But sheer quantity is not the important point. What is important is that with 80 judgements, only very dramatic improvements in recognition accuracy can be observed. Subtle improvements remain unnoticed because of random effects. An example can illustrate this point. With a 50% correct exposure duration in the no fore-knowledge condition, as Grindley and Townsend used (i.e., with a total of about 40 correct judgements), a 2.5%, 5% and 10% improvement will result in an expected additional number of correct responses of 1, 2 and 4 in the fore-knowledge condition (i.e., in a total of 41, 42 and 44 correct judgements). So, even with a 10% improvement, on the average for only 4 out of 10 subjects is one additional correct response to be expected. Of course it is more than highly likely that such effects go completely unnoticed.

Grindley and Townsend (1968) were familiar with Mertens's work. 'There is ... an experiment by Mertens (1956) which indicates that in the case of *single* stimuli ... foreknowledge of position had no significance' (Grindley and Townsend, 1968, p. 18). And because Grindley and Townsend's publication became well known, since then, it has been lore and tradition in the information processing literature to repeat and repeat: Neither Grindley and Townsend nor Mertens found any effect of foreknowledge of position in single-item tasks (see, e.g., Bashinski and Bacharach, 1980; Egly and Homa, 1984; Posner, 1980; Sperling, 1984).

In summary, this type of single-item research had a bad start. Crazy data handling, silly experiments and sloppy reading led to the conviction that no effects of foreknowledge of position have to be expected with this type of task.

3.1 A better start

Despite the unfortunate start, some investigators tried again to demonstrate positive effects of foreknowledge of position in single-item detection and recognition tasks with accuracy as the dependent variable. In this section we briefly describe the further developments for detection tasks and recognition tasks.

Detection tasks

Van der Heijden and Eerland (1973) were the first to demonstrate a positive effect of (fore)knowledge of position in a single-item signal detection task (is there a capital O or not?). They presented their subjects stimulus cards, 50% of which contained a grey, rather vague, O in one of the four quadrants. Of these Os 50% were surrounded by a small black rectangle that served as a cue indicating the quadrant where the O could appear. (It is reasonable to assume that the black rectangle was faster perceived than the grey O, and that the simultaneous cue therefore effectively was a pre-cue giving foreknowledge of position.) The other 50% of the Os were surrounded by a big rectangle encompassing all four quadrants, i.e., the whole field. This big rectangle served as an advance neutral cue, giving no foreknowledge of position. Of the blank cards 50% contained a

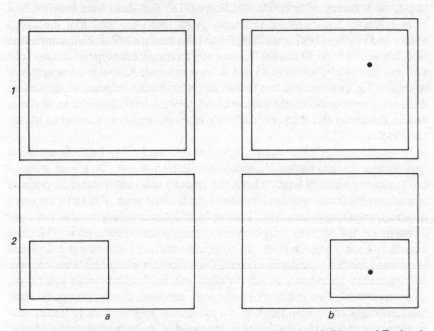

Figure 3.1.1 Examples of stimulus cards used by Van der Heijden and Eerland (1973). 1a and 1b: Big rectangle without and with 0 (no foreknowledge condition); 2a and 2b: Small rectangle without and with 0 (foreknowledge condition).

small rectangle, the other 50% a big one. Figure 3.1.1 shows some examples of the stimulus cards.

It appeared that, with exposure durations yielding performance exceeding chance level, the cue (i.e., the small rectangle) indeed resulted in higher detection accuracy. So, similar results as reported by Mertens (1956) were obtained. Now, however, the outcome was reported as a success, not as a failure.

Bashinski and Bacharach (1980) replicated and extended this result in a more elaborate study. The target was again an O appearing either on the right or on the left of a central fixation point. Targets were presented on 50% of the trials. As cues, they used a + sign and a right or left pointing arrow. The neutral plus sign indicated that the target, if it occurred, was equally probable on the right and on the left. The arrow indicated that the target, if it occurred, could occur in the direction of the arrow approximately 80% of the time and in the other direction 20% of the time (i.e., the cue was 'valid', or informative, on 80% of the trials and 'invalid', or misleading, on 20% of the trials; in the next chapter we return to this experimental manipulation). The cues were presented 180 ms prior to a 100 ms target presentation (so the trial duration was 280 ms; dangerously long). Subjects had to indicate whether there was a signal (detection), and if so, where the signal was (localization).

The results indicated that if the arrow correctly indicated the position of the target, the accuracy of detection was highest, i.e., that there were benefits. In a more elaborate replication of this study (with much too long trial durations) Müller and Findlay (1987, exp. 2) replicated this result, albeit that a much smaller benefit was observed. In this study, however, a very peculiar type of (double) cue and very low cue validities (0.43 and 0.29) were used. As will become apparent in section 4.2, exactly these two factors might have been responsible for the fact that only a very small benefit was observed. (For the analysis of the localization data in Bashinski and Bacharach's, 1980, study the reader is referred to Müller and Findlay, 1987.)

In an important experiment, Egly and Homa (1984, Exp. 2) provided approximate foreknowledge of position in a detection task. On a trial, subjects had to identify a central fixation letter (the primary task) and to name the position of a second letter that was displaced from the fixation point. (So, in fact it was a two-item, not a single-item task.) The displaced letter could appear at any of eight locations on any of three imaginary rings around the fixation letter. The rings were at 1, 2 and 3 deg. On foreknowledge trials the ring containing the displaced letter was specified verbally in advance. On no foreknowledge trials the ring was only specified afterwards. Foreknowledge and no foreknowledge trials were randomly mixed. Two important results were obtained. Firstly, the approximate foreknowledge of position resulted in a substantial improvement in localization performance. Secondly, the benefits increased with increasing ring distance: 3.1%, 9% and 11.1% for the rings at distance 1, 2 and 3 deg, respectively. So, exact foreknowledge of position seems not to be necessary in this type of task (see also Egly and Homa, 1984, Exp. 3).

Recognition tasks

Shaw and Shaw (1977) were the first to report improved accuracy with approximate foreknowledge of position in a single-item recognition task. One out of three target letters was presented at one out of eight positions in a circular array. Two probability distributions were used for choosing the target position. In the baseline or no foreknowledge condition all eight positions were equally probable (8 × 0.125). In the experimental or approximate foreknowledge condition the positions varied in the probability with which a target would occur (2 × 0.25; 2 × 0.05; 4 × 0.10). Per experimental session only one of the distributions was used. Average identification accuracy was about 67% and 72% in the baseline and the experimental condition. So, the benefit observed was about 5%. (See Posner, Snyder and Davidson, 1980, p. 169, for a discussion of how this benefit might have been brought about. See, however, also Egly and Homa, 1984, p. 778.)

Also Egly and Homa (1984, Exp. 1) reported improved performance with approximate foreknowledge of position in a 'single-item' recognition task with accuracy as the dependent variable. In fact, exactly the same stimuli and procedure were used as in the detection task described earlier, except that subjects had now to name the identity of the peripheral letter instead of its position. In a 'random' presentation condition, as used in the detection task, a clear benefit brought by advance ring cueing was obtained. The benefits were 3.4%, 2.8% and 5.9% for the rings at distance 1, 2 and 3 deg, respectively.

Van der Heijden, Schreuder and Wolters (1985) were the first to report improved performance with exact, instead of approximate, foreknowledge of position. In their experiment, single letters were presented on one out of five positions on an imaginary circle around a fixation point. On foreknowledge trials the position of the target was specified in advance by presenting one dot at a corresponding position on the circumference of a similar, but slightly larger, imaginary circle. On no foreknowledge trials 5 dots were presented in advance on positions corresponding to all possible target positions. The average target duration was 10 ms, and the dots preceded the target by 50 or 100 ms. Foreknowledge (one dot) and no foreknowledge (five dots) trials were randomized. Under the experimental conditions used the identification performance for no foreknowledge and foreknowledge trials equalled 73.2% and 76.4%. The benefit brought by advance position cueing of 3.2% was highly significant because all subjects showed the effect. In a number of studies using essentially the same exposure conditions we have reliably replicated this phenomenon (see, e.g., Van der Heijden, Wolters, Groep and Hagenaar, 1987; Van der Heijden, Neerincx and Wolters, 1989). Moreover, using this advance dot procedure, the ring cueing or approximate foreknowledge effect reported by Egly and Homa (1984) was also replicated (Van der Heijden et al., 1987).

Taking all together, it will be clear that, after the initial failures, there is now sufficient evidence indicating that single-item detection and single-item recognition benefit from foreknowledge of (approximate) position. The important issue is of course how these benefits are brought about.

3.2 Attention?

The term 'attention' is very often used and nearly as often misused in the experimental psychology literature. In general, it seems that the unwritten rule is that, where an explanation in terms of whatever explicit mechanism is not readily conceivable, it makes good science to invoke the concept attention to do the job. This also applies to the results described in the previous section. It is quite difficult to conceive of an explicit mechanism responsible for the benefits. So, in accordance with the rule, in the literature generally the concept 'attention', and not very much more, is used to explain these results. However, before embarking upon such an attentional explanation, it is necessary to investigate whether other explanations, not in terms of one or another attentional mechanism, are also adequate. 'There is substantial intuitive appeal ... in the idea ... that, when an input from a particular point of space is highly probable, attention is preferentially allocated to that point .... But serious efforts must be directed towards disentangling this from a simple bias, in the sense of requiring little evidence for an expected input' (Duncan, 1980, p. 93).

In 'requiring little evidence for an expected input', however, two possible sources of bias are conflated: one based on 'requiring little evidence', the other on 'an expected input'. The first has to do with the willingness to react or not to react, or with, what we called, 'intention'. The second has to do with the anticipation of 'the what' that has to be reacted to, or with, what we called, 'expectation' (see sections 2.3 and 2.6). So, two viable 'simple bias' explanations have to be excluded: explanations in terms of differential 'intentions' to react or not to react in the foreknowledge and no foreknowledge conditions, and explanations in terms of differential 'expectations' in the foreknowledge and no foreknowledge conditions. (Because of the exposure conditions used, a third possible source of bias, i.e., the bias stemming from differential retinal acuity, has been effectively excluded.)

In the literature an alternative explanation for the results reported, not invoking the concept attention, but emphasizing a differential involvement of intention, is sometimes suggested. Strictly speaking, this alternative explanation only applies to the yes–no threshold detection tasks of Van der Heijden and Eerland (1973), Bashinski and Bacharach (1980) and Müller and Findlay (1987, exp. 2) but is also often used in connection with the other types of tasks discussed in this chapter (see, e.g., Duncan, 1980; Posner, 1980). This explanation is derived from signal-detection theory that uses an 'ideal observer' as the norm. The concept 'criterion shifts' – and corresponding shifts in willingness to respond with 'yes, target present' – is essential in this account (see, e.g., Sperling, 1984; Posner, 1980; Posner, Snyder and Davidson, 1980; Possamai, 1986). This explanation simply states that foreknowledge of position does not mediate any change in the 'internal evidence' or 'internal representation' of the target. What happens, according to this view, is that subjects lower their criterion, i.e., require less evidence for responding 'yes' at a cued position, and/or raise their criterion, i.e., require more evidence for responding 'yes' at uncued positions (see, e.g., Duncan, 1980; Sperling, 1984). It can be shown that, given some further assumptions, this is an optimal strategy (see, e.g., Sperling, 1984).

For a number of reasons, however, this criterion shift explanation seems not to be the correct explanation for the results presented in the previous section.

- Firstly, contrary to Mertens (1956) and Grindley and Townsend (1968), Van der Heijden and Eerland (1973), Bashinski and Bacharach (1980) and Müller and Findlay (1987) did not simply determine the proportions of correct detections for which such an explanation possibly applies. In all three studies there were target-present trials and target-absent trials in both the foreknowledge and the no foreknowledge condition. Therefore the appropriate measures from signal detection theory could be used. In all three experiments an increased detection sensitivity, (d'), was demonstrated. So, the results cannot simply be accounted for in terms of a greater willingness to say 'yes' in the foreknowledge condition. (For the, very complicated, analysis of the data of joint detection-plus-localization tasks the reader is referred to Müller and Findlay, 1987.)
- Secondly, in Egly and Homa's (1984) position detection task subjects had to respond by naming 1 out of 8 positions on a ring on each trial. It is very difficult to see how a criterion shift for 8 positions simultaneously can improve the choice of one of these positions.
- Thirdly, also in the forced-choice recognition tasks as used by Shaw and Shaw (1977), Egly and Homa (1984) and Van der Heijden and associates (1985; 1987; 1989) criterion shifts cannot improve performance. Subjects had to respond with a letter name on each trial and 'requiring less evidence' or 'a greater willingness to respond' cannot produce more accurate recognition performance on foreknowledge trials than on no foreknowledge trials. (In fact, with less evidence worse performance has to be expected!)

Taken all together, an explanation in terms of differential intentions in the foreknowledge and the no foreknowledge conditions seems not to be the appropriate explanation for the results presented in section 3.1.

As far as we know, explanations in terms of differential 'expectations' – something like James's 'preperception', Deutsch and Deutsch's 'importance', or Treisman's 'lowering of central thresholds' (see Chapter 2) – have never been seriously considered for the results under discussion. Remember, these 'expectations' are generally regarded as independent from position, or, regarded to apply to all positions equally (see Chapter 2). Therefore it is very difficult to see how such a kind of expectation can be more adequate and therefore improve accuracy in the foreknowledge condition as compared with the no foreknowledge condition. In the detection tasks and in the recognition tasks the experimental procedures effectively preclude the existence or development of a differential adequacy of particular target expectations in the foreknowledge and no fore-knowledge conditions. If 'The idea is to come to the help of the sensation and make it more distinct' (James, 1890/1950) or if high 'weightings of importance' lead to an increased readiness to perceive a stimulus whether it is there or not (Deutsch and Deutsch, 1963), then this occurs in the foreknowledge and no foreknowledge condition equally. So, there is no differential higher order expectation; there are only differences in (fore)knowledge of position. Therefore an explanation of the results described in section 3.1 in terms of a differential adequacy of expectations in the foreknowledge condition and the no fore-knowledge condition has also to be rejected.

Taking the point of view that there are three central 'mechanisms', capable of producing benefits – attention, expectation and intention (Chapter 2) – and given that two of these have to be excluded as incapable of accounting for the data – expectation and intention (this section) – forces us to the conclusion that it is indeed 'attention' (or 'expectation restricted to spatial position', but let us call that 'attention') that produces the benefits in the present type of tasks. The fact that the critical manipulation in these tasks is concerned with position, i.e., with the 'where', considerably strengthens this conclusion. So, it is worthwhile to find out what attention does.

3.3 An empirical regularity

Until very recently information processing psychologists had not very much to tell about *how* the benefits brought by foreknowledge of position are affected by attention. Egly and Homa (1984, p. 792) state 'The best explanation to account for the benefits on cued trials was probably the one offered by most subjects: They reported afterward that it was reasonably easy to "set" themselves for seeing information on the cued ring and that the displaced letter was simply seen more clearly as a result'. According to other authors something like 'perceptual tuning' or 'very early selective control' (Bashinski and Bacharach, 1980), or 'increasing efficiency of search' (Van der Heijden and Eerland, 1973) must be at the basis of this result.

Nowadays somewhat more can be said, however, about how benefits in recognition accuracy are brought about in one type of task: the dot cueing paradigm with exact advance position information used by Van der Heijden and associates. In these experiments a short-duration visual cue, close to the position of the impending target, was used. This 'exact' cue always indicated the target position correctly, or, was 100% valid. The insight in what was happening in this single-item recognition task came in a number of steps. Because of the far-reaching theoretical consequences – but also because it can serve as an illustration of the way of working within the information processing approach – we analyse in some detail what is going on in this type of task. This section and the next three sections are devoted to this endeavour.

It takes some time to see that there is an obvious, but often neglected, methodological peculiarity that at least partly explains why it is so difficult to demonstrate benefits in the type of task we are concerned with and why benefits, if found, are so small. That methodological peculiarity is the available room for improvement in this type of experiment. To assess benefits, performance in the foreknowledge condition has to be compared with a baseline performance in a no foreknowledge, or no cue, condition. For the no foreknowledge condition an exposure duration is chosen in such a way that a baseline recognition performance of I_{nc} results (a typical value of I_{nc} is 0.75). So, with foreknowledge of position no improvement is possible on the proportion, I_{nc}, of the trials that already resulted in correct responding without foreknowledge of position. In other words, there is only room for improvement of a proportion $(1 - I_{nc})$ of the trials; benefits larger than $(1 - I_{nc})$ are simply impossible.

To see whether $(1 - I_{nc})$, i.e., the relatively small room for improvement, was indeed the factor that makes it difficult for benefits to show up, Van der Heijden et al. (1987) reanalysed the Van der Heijden et al. (1985) data and the results obtained in three similar unpublished single-item recognition experiments. In all these experiments effective exposure duration was manipulated in order to obtain for each subject a baseline performance, I_{nc}, of 0.75, or, a room for improvement, $(1 - I_{nc})$, of 0.25. Such a procedure is, however, never completely successful in that some subjects show a somewhat higher, others a somewhat lower baseline performance. The analysis capitalized on these individual differences. Linear functions relating benefits (or costs) per subject, delta I, to their individual room for improvement, $(1 - I_{nc})$, were determined. For all four experiments the same reliable empirical relation was consistently obtained, namely

$$\text{delta } I = a(1 - I_{nc}) - b \tag{3.3.1}$$

and generally the correlation between delta I and $(1 - I_{nc})$ was substantial. This function indeed suggests that it is the room for improvement that determines the benefits observed: subjects with below average baseline performance show larger benefits and subjects with above average baseline performance show smaller benefits of advance position information.

As stated, the analysis capitalized on small, accidental, between-subject variations in baseline performance $(1 - I_{nc})$. To see whether the relation held over a broader range of exposure conditions two further studies were performed. Van der Heijden et al. (1987) deliberately increased the within-subjects and between-subjects variations in baseline performance by positioning the targets on one of three rings, just as Egly and Homa (1984) did. Of course, due to the decreasing retinal acuity, baseline performance decreases with ring eccentricity (see section 2.8). Van der Heijden et al. (1989) varied baseline performances by using different exposure durations. Of course, baseline performance decreases with decreasing exposure duration. In both studies again the same relation was observed. So it seems that equation (3.3.1) really captures an empirical regularity that can reliably be observed under a broad range of exposure conditions.

Equation (3.3.1), however, is only an empirical regularity found in the data. It can be used to predict aspects of performance, not to explain them. It is a kind of 'reliable regularity', sufficient in the standard view of science tradition, but it does not as yet reveal 'causal properties' as searched for in the realist tradition. To function as an explanatory model satisfying the information processing approach, at least a sensible interpretation of the equation has to be found that tells us something about how the difference, delta I, is generated by the information processor (see Chapter 1).

The first interpretation that comes to mind is, of course, that delta I is a proportion of the available room for improvement (and that makes sense), minus a constant (and that makes little sense). In fact, this interpretation of the equation leads to unacceptable consequences. A simple rewriting of the equation makes this readily apparent:

$$\text{delta } I = a\{(1 - b/a) - I_{nc}\}. \tag{3.3.2}$$

In this form it is clear that delta $I = 0$, not for $I_{nc} = 1$, but for $I_{nc} = 1 - b/a$. If actual values obtained in experiments are used it invariantly appears that $1 - b/a < 1.00$. But then equation (3.3.1) or (3.3.2), interpreted as a model, suggests that for values of $I_{nc} > (1 - b/a)$ the effect of correct foreknowledge of position is negative! Theoretically this is a very unattractive outcome. Furthermore, such a result is not apparent in any of our data and therefore this interpretation of equation (3.3.1) or (3.3.2) as a model is simply wrong. So, we have to look for an alternative interpretation that removes this theoretical inconsistency and empirical inadequacy.

Fortunately, equation (3.3.2) suggests a direction in which that search has to go. The equation says that benefits are not a fraction of the total room for improvement, $(1 - I_{nc})$, but a fraction of only a part of the available room for improvement, $\{(1 - b/a) - I_{nc}\}$. Another simple rewriting of equation (3.3.1) shows this even more clearly:

$$\text{delta } I = a\{1 - (I_{nc} + b/a)\}.$$

So, the question to be answered is: What part of the total room for improvement is at the basis of the benefits in our recognition tasks?

3.4 A tentative model

To find a theoretically consistent and empirically adequate alternative interpretation of the empirical relation expressed in equation (3.3.1), two pieces of experimental evidence are essential. That evidence was reported by Egly and Homa (1984). We already mentioned Egly and Homa's letter naming task and position naming tasks in section 3.1. To really appreciate the relevant experimental evidence it is essential to know that in their position naming task the exposure durations were rather similar to those used in the letter naming task, and that nevertheless quite a lot of location errors were made. So, it appears that under the exposure conditions used in the letter naming task, subjects not only often have no identity information but also no position information.

The first important observation is that in the no foreknowledge conditions performance in the position naming task – albeit far from perfect – was better than performance in the letter naming task. In terms of complements, the room for improvement was smaller in the position naming task than in the letter naming task.

The second important observation is that, even with this smaller room for improvement, the improvement as a result of approximate foreknowledge of position was substantially larger in the position naming task (about 8% averaged over rings) than in the letter naming task (about 4%).

These two points together suggest the possibility that the room for improvement for *position* information is the part of the total room for improvement we are looking for. The room for improvement is smaller for position information than for identity information (observation one) and the identity benefits can be expressed as a fraction of the room for improvement for position information (observation two). In other words, these results suggest that it is improved position information that is, in one or another way, at the basis of the cueing effect. More specifically, Egly and Homa's (1984) results are consistent with the hypothesis that for their task

delta $I = g(P_c - P_{nc})$

where P_c is the proportion of trials where position information is available with *approximate* foreknowledge of position and P_{nc} is the proportion of trials where position information is available in the no foreknowledge condition. In other words, their results are consistent with the hypothesis that the recognition benefits brought by approximate cueing are a fraction, g, of the localization benefits brought by cueing.

For our dot-cueing tasks with *exact* location information in the foreknowledge condition, this result suggests that the benefits, brought by cueing, are a fraction of the room for improvement, not in terms of identity information, I_{nc}, but in terms of position information, P_{nc}, i.e., that

delta $I = g(1 - P_{nc})$ (3.4.1)

where P_{nc} is the proportion of trials where position information is available in the no foreknowledge condition. This equation is based on the assumption that in these dot cueing tasks, where the cue was exact and always valid, cueing results in perfect position information. So, $P_c = 1$ and $(P_c - P_{nc})$ reduces to $(1 - P_{nc})$. And, just because the cue was exact and always valid, $(1 - P_{nc})$ equals not only the room for improvement for position naming but also the benefit in position information brought by cueing. So, equation (3.4.1) also states that the identity benefit is a fraction, g, of this position benefit.

It will be clear that equation (3.4.1) does not suffer from the drawback of equations (3.3.1) and (3.3.2). If $P_{nc} = 1$, its maximum value, than delta $I = 0$.

Theoretically this makes sense: there is no further increase in identification performance by location cueing given already-perfect localization performance in the no foreknowledge condition. Moreover, this feature of the relation is not in contradiction with any of our data. So, equation (3.4.1) can possibly serve as a starting point for a model.

To serve as a model for performance in the dot cueing tasks, it is of course essential that equation (3.4.1) is consistent with the empirical regularity embodied in equation (3.3.1). Fortunately, this is not difficult to show (see also Van der Heijden et al., 1989). If we assume that only a fraction, $s < 1$, of the localized items are correctly recognized, i.e., that

$$I_{nc} = sP_{nc}, s < 1 \tag{3.4.2}$$

and therefore that

$$(1/s)I_{nc} = P_{nc}$$

equation (3.4.1) can be rewritten as

$$\text{delta } I = g\{1 - (1/s)I_{nc}\}.$$

Because

$$\text{delta } I = g - g(1/s) I_{nc} + g(1/s) - g(1/s)$$

it follows that

$$\text{delta } I = g(1/s) (1 - I_{nc}) + g(1 - 1/s). \tag{3.4.3}$$

Because g and s are constants, it appears that equation (3.4.3) is indeed of the form

$$\text{delta } I = a(1 - I_{nc}) - b$$

with $a = g(1/s)$ and $-b = g(1 - 1/s)$.

The next important question concerns, of course, the viability of equation (3.4.1) as a model. Are the data indeed compatible with the suggestion that it is improved position information that is at the basis of the identity benefits? Fortunately, equation (3.3.1) with the observed I_{nc}s provides a means to test in a preliminary way equation (3.4.1) with its nonobserved P_{nc}s. And if the foregoing analysis is indeed on the right track, a number of interesting theoretical predictions should be substantiated. We mention some of these predictions and investigate their correctness by examining the parameters obtained for the empirical relation describing the data reported by Van der Heijden et al. (1985). For that experiment the empirical relation, i.e., equation (3.3.1), was

$$\text{delta } I = 0.178(1 - I_{nc}) - 0.016 \ (r = 0.783).$$

First, from equations (3.3.1) and (3.4.3) it follows that

$$a + b = g(1/s) + g(1 - 1/s) = g.$$

Because in equation (3.4.1) g stands for a positive fraction, i.e., $0 \le g \le 1$, also the sum of the parameters of the empirical relation has to be a positive fraction. The value obtained equals $0.178 - 0.016 = 0.162$, and is indeed a positive fraction. Confronted with the data, the model expressed with equation (3.4.1) says, that of the localization benefit brought by cueing, a fraction of 0.162 shows up as identification benefit.

Secondly, with g now given and with the knowledge that $a = g(1/s)$ (or $b = g(1 - 1/s)$), it is easy to find s. Because we assumed that $I_{nc} = sP_{nc}$ (i.e., that the proportion correctly identified is a fraction, s, of the proportion correctly localized) the parameter s has to be smaller than 1 for the model to be correct. For Van der Heijden et al.'s data s equals 0.910, a value consistent with the starting assumption (see equation 3.4.2). The outcome of the analysis says that in the no foreknowledge condition 0.910 of the correctly localized items are correctly identified.

Thirdly, with $1/s$ given now and with I_{nc} ($= 0.732$) as data it is not difficult to estimate the not directly observed, hypothetical or theoretical, localization performance, P_{nc}, by means of equation (3.4.2). Because P_{nc} stands for the proportion of trials with correct localization of the letter in the no foreknowledge condition, the value obtained has to be smaller than 1, i.e., $P_{nc} < 1$. The estimate obtained for Van der Heijden et al.'s data equals 0.810, a value well in line with the theoretical assumption. Moreover $(1 - P_{nc}) = 0.190$ and is indeed smaller than $(1 - I_{nc}) = 0.268$, an outcome consistent with the point of view that the room for improvement for position information is the part of the total room for improvement we were looking for.

The three predictions and the obtained values show that the model given by equation (3.4.1) is at least qualitatively consistent with the data. The uninterpretable, inconsistent and inadequate empirical relation describing Van der Heijden et al.'s (1985) results

delta $I = 0.178(1 - I_{nc}) - 0.016$ (with $I_{nc} = 0.732$)

can be replaced by the readily interpretable theoretical relation

delta $I = 0.162(1 - P_{nc})$ (with $P_{nc} = 0.810$)

that gives exactly the same result (for I_{nc} and P_{nc} delta $I = 0.031$). Also for other sets of data we consistently found that the three predictions just tested were not violated (see, e.g., Van der Heijden et al., 1989). So, the analysis seems indeed on the right track.

The analysis presented is, however, only a preliminary analysis. Quantitatively, there remains something to be wished. The main problem with the present analysis is that, for a number of reasons, the parameters we started with need not be the correct parameters.

Firstly, in the type of task under discussion it is very likely that guessing is involved. It is far from clear how guessing affects performance and especially how it affects the parameters estimated with equation (3.3.1).

Secondly, to estimate the model parameters the empirical relation summarizing the data reported by Van der Heijden et al. (1985) was used. To obtain this relation, delta I was determined as a function of $(1 - I_{nc})$. Theoretically, however, there is no reason to prefer this relation over $(1 - I_{nc})$ as a function of delta I. (Both $(1 - I_{nc})$ and delta I are, in a sense, 'dependent variables'.) The two regression equations lead to different estimates of the parameters. At present the best way to obtain the parameters is unknown.

Last, we do not really know whether cueing in the dot-cueing task results in perfect position information, i.e., we do not really know whether the assumption that $P_c = 1$ is correct. It is true that in the dot-cueing task the *cue* is exact, always valid and easily visible. So, nominally there is perfect position information. It is not clear, however, whether this entails that the *letter* is also always correctly localized, i.e., whether there is also effective letter location information. In section 3.6 we return to this issue and show that this assumption is almost correct.

For all these reasons it is better to leave this analysis based on curve fitting and to turn to a more detailed analysis of identification and localization performance.

3.5 A detailed analysis

The analysis of the data of the letter naming task just presented, strongly suggests that location information plays an essential role in producing identification benefits. A naming task, however, only provides information about identification; not about localization. So all conclusions about localization performance are only theoretical speculations. To find out what exactly happens in our type of task additional data are needed. Of course, localization tasks as reported by Egly and Homa (1984; see section 3.1) provide some of the relevant information. But an identity plus location naming task provides much better opportunities for further analysis because this task produces all data needed simultaneously and in the interesting combinations. Because such a task involves both identity naming (the 'what') and position naming (the 'where'), the responses can be categorized into four classes: both dimensions correct $(P+I+)$, position correct and identity incorrect $(P+I-)$, position incorrect and identity correct $(P-I+)$ and both dimensions incorrect $(P-I-)$.

Van der Heijden, Wolters, Fleur and Hommels (in prep.) performed such an experiment. In the experiment eight different letters and five possible target positions were used. In the foreknowledge condition one dot and in the no foreknowledge condition five dots were presented before target presentation (see section 3.1). The dot cues were presented for 25 ms and the letter was presented immediately after presentation of the dot(s), i.e., the stimulus onset asynchrony was 25 ms. Table 3.5.1 presents the data for cued (i.e., foreknowledge) and neutral (i.e., no foreknowledge) trials separately.

The model we use for a first analysis of these data has as a basic assumption that the probability of each type of response can be expressed as a multiplicative combination of the probability that position information is available ($P = Pc$

Table 3.5.1 Proportions of answers for the four possible response categories in the single-item localization-plus-recognition task. (From Van der Heijden et al., in prep.)

	P+I+	P–I+	P+I–	P–I–
cue	0.6514	0.0021	0.3451	0.0014
neutral	0.6069	0.0132	0.3368	0.0431

$+ Pi = 1$, where Pc equals the probability that correct position information is available and Pi the probability that there is no position information) and that identity information is available ($I = Ic + Ii = 1$, where Ic equals the probability that there is correct identity information and Ii that there is not). In other words, the model has as a basic assumption that localization and identification are independent processes. This assumption leads to the following four equations for the four response classes:

$$P{+}I{+} = \{Pc + (1/5)\,Pi\}\{Ic + (1/8)\,Ii\}$$
$$P{-}I{+} = \{(4/5)\,Pi\}\{Ic + (1/8)\,Ii\}$$
$$P{+}I{-} = \{Pc + (1/5)\,Pi\}\{(7/8)Ii\}$$
$$P{-}I{-} = \{(4/5)\,Pi\}\{(7/8)Ii\}$$

In these equations the fractions 1/5 and 4/5 and 1/8 and 7/8 are the probabilities of guessing correctly or incorrectly the position (there were five positions in the display) or the identity (there were eight different letters) when no location or identity information is available. Table 3.5.2 presents the same equations after multiplication, together with the observed proportions for the four classes of responses for the no foreknowledge (neutral) and foreknowledge (cued) condition separately.

Table 3.5.2 The 'independent processes' model expressing the probability of a response in each response category as a multiplicative combination of the identification probability (Ic and Ii) and the localization probability (Pc and Pi). See text for further explanation.

					neutral	cue
$P{+}I{+} =$	$Pc\,Ic$ +	$(1/5)Pi\,Ic$ +	$Pc(1/8)Ii$ +	$(1/5)Pi(1/8)Ii$	0.6069	0.6514
$P{-}I{+} =$		$(4/5)Pi\,Ic$		+ $(4/5)Pi(1/8)Ii$	0.0132	0.0021
$P{+}I{-} =$			$Pc(7/8)Ii$ +	$(1/5)Pi(7/8)Ii$	0.3368	0.3451
$P{-}I{-} =$				$(4/5)Pi(7/8)Ii$	0.0431	0.0014

Because P is independent of I it follows that

$$P{+}I{+} + P{+}I{-} = Pc + (1/5)Pi.$$

So, Pc (and Pi) can be estimated.

For the no foreknowledge (neutral) condition the values obtained are

$$Pc = 0.9297$$
$$1 - Pc = Pi = 0.0703$$

Because I is independent of P, values for Ic and Ii can be derived in a similar way. These values are

$$Ic = 0.5658$$
$$1 - Ic = Ii = 0.4342$$

Using these parameters in the equations in table 3.5.2 leads to the values of expected probabilities for the no foreknowledge condition presented in table 3.5.3.

Table 3.5.3 Expected and observed proportions and the deviations for the four response categories in the no foreknowledge condition of the identity and location task.

	Expected (model)	Observed	Deviation
$P+I+$	0.5853	0.6069	−0.0216
$P-I+$	0.0349	0.0132	+0.0217
$P+I-$	0.3585	0.3368	+0.0217
$P-I-$	0.0214	0.0431	−0.0217

As the table shows, the expected probabilities deviate markedly from the observed probabilities. In particular, if the deviations are compared with the benefits obtained in this experiment, 0.0444, it appears that the fit is simply not good enough. So, there is something wrong with our independence assumptions.

Because it is very likely that localization is independent of identification (and not unlikely that identification depends upon localization; see, e.g., Nissen, 1985 and Müller and Rabbit, 1989a, for evidence; see also section 3.4), we retained the localization parameters, Pc and Pi, and determined the conditional probabilities for identification, i.e., $Ic|Pc$ and $Ii|Pc$, and $Ic|Pi$ and $Ii|Pi$. When Ic and Ii are replaced by the appropriate conditional identification probabilities, the equations in table 3.5.2 make it possible to derive these values because Pc is given now. The obtained values are:

$$Ic|Pc = 0.5992$$
$$Ii|Pc = 0.4008$$

$$Ic|Pi = 0.1252$$
$$Ii|Pi = 0.8748$$

So it appears that the probability of identifying an item indeed heavily depends upon the item's being localized. The probability that there is identity information given that there is no location information is much lower than the probability that there is identity information given that there is location information. (Of course, with the present parameters the observed probabilities are exactly 'predicted'. We simply solved four equations with four unknowns.)

We now repeat this analysis for the foreknowledge of position condition to see what changes are brought about by position cueing. For the cue condition, the localization parameters are:

Pc $= 0.9957$
$1 - Pc = Pi = 0.0043$

The conditional identification probabilities are:

$Ic|Pc = 0.6043$
$Ii|Pc = 0.3957$

$Ic|Pi = 0.5428$
$Ii|Pi = 0.4572$

Three features of these parameters are worthy of notice. Firstly, consider the localization parameters. The striking point is – as was already apparent from the data – that localization is virtually perfect, but not perfect. So there is not always nominal position information. This is the more surprising because a clearly visible, exact, and always valid cue was used. We return to this point further on.

Now consider the identification parameters for the correct localization cases. The striking point here is that these parameters are virtually identical to those found in the no foreknowledge condition. The difference is only 0.0051. So it appears that, given that an item is correctly localized, the identification probability is essentially the same in the no foreknowledge and in the foreknowledge condition. This strongly suggests that cueing has its effect through improved position information, or, that the effect of cueing is indeed mediated by improved position information, as suggested in section 3.4.

Lastly, consider the two remaining parameters, $Ic|Pi$ and $Ii|Pi$. Two features of these parameters are of interest. Firstly, these values considerably deviate from those found for the no foreknowledge condition. This result is somewhat surprising because it is very difficult to think of any reason why, *without* effective position information, identification accuracy should be higher or lower in a cueing condition than in a no cueing condition. No position information is no position information, independent of whether the condition is a foreknowledge condition or a no foreknowledge condition. Secondly, the values obtained are very close to the values $Ic|Pc$ and $Ii|Pc$. So, while the items were incorrectly localized, the identification parameters suggest otherwise. The most parsimonious explanation for this combination of findings is that the items were effectively localized but that, in this two-response task, on a few trials the position names were simply forgotten before responding.

Taken all together, the results obtained and the analysis presented are consistent with, and support, the assumptions that in our dot cueing task

1. foreknowledge of position results in perfect effective position information,
2. identification accuracy given effective position information, i.e., $Ic|Pc$, is (virtually) the same in the foreknowledge and in the no foreknowledge condition,
3. identification benefits are mediated, or brought about, by the improved position information (without foreknowledge of position there is not always correct effective position information and without effective position information the identification accuracy is very low).

It is not difficult to work out that pivotal assumptions 1 and 2 are inter-dependent: if 1 (2) is correct then 2 (1) is also correct, and if 1 (2) is incorrect then 2 (1) is also incorrect. In the next section we first use these assumptions to specify in detail how benefits are effected in the localization-plus-identification task described in this section and in the original identification task described in sections 3.3 and 3.4. Then we show that it is reasonable to assume that assumption 1, and therefore also assumption 2, is really correct. Readers who are not interested in these details and who (a) already firmly believe that improved position information is at the basis of the cueing effect, and, (b) also believe that equation (3.4.1), i.e.,

delta $I = g(1 - P_{nc})$

(with $P_{nc} = Pc$ in the no foreknowledge condition) really captures what happens in the dot cueing identification task, can safely skip that section and turn to section 3.7.

3.6 Benefits

With the two assumptions mentioned in the previous section we are in the position to work out in detail how benefits are effected in the dot cueing tasks. First, consider the identification plus localization task.

The expected proportion of correct responses in the identification-plus-localization task is given by the row labelled $P+I+$ in table 3.5.2. Expressing the identification probabilities as conditional probabilities, $I|P$, and rearranging the terms, the expected proportion correct in the no foreknowledge condition can be written as

$$P+I+ = Pc\ \{Ic|Pc + (1/8)Ii|Pc\} + Pi\ \{(1/5)Ic|Pi + (1/40)Ii|Pi\}. \quad (3.6.1)$$

In the foreknowledge condition with $Pc = 1$ the expected proportion equals

$$P+I+ = \{Ic|Pc + (1/8)Ii|Pc\}. \quad (3.6.2)$$

So, the expected benefit, delta $P+I+$, equals (3.6.2) − (3.6.1), or,

$$(1-Pc)\ \{Ic|Pc + (1/8)Ii|Pc\} - Pi\ \{(1/5)Ic|Pi + (1/40)Ii|Pi\}$$
$$= (1-Pc)\ [\{Ic|Pc + (1/8)Ii|Pc\} - \{(1/5)Ic|Pi + (1/40)Ii|Pi\}]. \quad (3.6.3)$$

Because for a fixed Pc the last four terms can be considered as 'constants', we can summarize this function with

delta $P+I+ = a(1 - Pc)$.

In words, the amount of benefit found is a fraction, a, of the 'room for improvement', where the 'room for improvement' consists of the proportion of trials in the no foreknowledge condition on which the item was not localized, $1 - Pc$.

It is not difficult to repeat the analysis just presented for the identity-only condition, i.e., the naming task discussed in sections 3.3 and 3.4. For this condition the expected proportion of correct responses is given by the sum of the rows labelled $P+I+$ and $P-I+$ in table 3.5.2 (remember, in the identity-only experiments subjects were not asked to give position information, so we have to sum over position information available and position information not available). Summing the terms and using conditional identification probabilities, the expected proportion correct in the no foreknowledge condition can be written as

$$I+ = Pc \{Ic|Pc + (1/8)Ii|Pc\} + Pi \{Ic|Pi + (1/8)Ii|Pc\}. \tag{3.6.4}$$

In the foreknowledge condition with $Pc = 1$ the expected proportion equals

$$I+ = \{Ic|Pc + (1/8)Ii|Pc\}. \tag{3.6.5}$$

So, the expected benefit, delta $I+$, in the identity-only condition equals (3.6.5) – (3.6.4), or

$$\begin{aligned}(1 - Pc) &\{Ic|Pc + (1/8)Ii|Pc\} - Pi \{Ic|Pi + (1/8)Ii|Pi\} \\ &= (1 - Pc) [\{Ic|Pc + (1/8)Ii|Pc\} - \{Ic|Pi + (1/8)Ii|Pi\}].\end{aligned} \tag{3.6.6}$$

We can summarize this function with

delta $I+ = b(1 - Pc)$,

and, because this Pc is the Pc in the no foreknowledge condition and therefore equals P_{nc} in equation (3.4.1), this is the hypothesized relation we presented as a tentative model in section 3.4 (see also Van der Heijden et al., 1989).

In the foregoing analysis two assumptions were used: the assumption of perfect effective position information in the foreknowledge of position condition (i.e., the assumption that in this condition $Pc=1$) and the assumption that the identification probability, given that there is effective location information, $Ic|Pc$, is identical in the foreknowledge and no foreknowledge conditions (for evidence see section 3.5). Just because of the first assumption, a third assumption was not needed: the assumption that also the identification probability given no effective location information, $Ic|Pi$, is identical in the foreknowledge and no foreknowledge conditions. The first two assumptions are interdependent. The last assumption, however, is completely independent of the first two.

The first two assumptions are critical and possibly theoretically debatable.

The last assumption is less critical and is a-priori reasonable. As already stated, there is no reason to expect different identification probabilities given *no effective position information* in the no foreknowledge and in the foreknowledge condition. (One reason why the obtained parameters suggest otherwise was mentioned in section 3.5.) Fortunately, only this latter, independent, assumption is needed to show that also the other two assumptions are nearly correct.

If the first two assumptions are dropped and only the latter assumption is maintained, it is not difficult to show that the *difference* in expected benefits obtained in an identity-plus-location condition and in an identity-only condition, delta $I+P+$ – delta $I+$, equals

$$(X - Pc)(4/5) \{IcIPi + (1/8)IiIPi\}$$

where X stands for the proportion of trials with effective position information in the foreknowledge of position condition. (The assumption of perfect position information is replaced by the assumption that this quantity equals the unknown value X. All terms involving the second assumption – identical conditional identification probabilities – disappear by taking the difference between the two benefits, delta $I+P+$ – delta $I+$.) Fortunately it is possible to estimate the value of X.

Van der Heijden et al. (in prep.) presented an identity-plus-location task and an identity-only task to the same group of Ss under completely identical conditions. We discussed the identity-plus-location task extensively in the previous section. Delta $I+P+$ equalled 0.0444. The benefit obtained in the identity-only task was 0.0326. So, the observed difference, delta $I+P+$ – delta $I+$, equalled 0.0118. Therefore we can write

$$(X-Pc)(4/5) \{IcIPi + (1/8)IiIPi\} = 0.0118$$

Using for Pc and $IcIPi$ the parameters derived in section 3.5 for the no foreknowledge condition, i.e., $Pc = 0.9297$ and $IcIPi = 0.1252$, the equation can be solved. The estimated value of X is 0.9926, and is indeed very close to 1.000 as assumed earlier. So, it seems that the assumption of virtually perfect effective position information in the foreknowledge condition – and therefore also the assumption that the conditional identification probability $IcIPc$ is nearly the same in the foreknowledge and in the no foreknowledge condition – is not very far from the mark.

Taken all together, it appears that the tentative model, introduced in section 3.4

$$\text{delta } I = g(1 - P_{nc})$$

is substantiated by a detailed analysis of the data and really seems to summarize what happens in the single-item recognition task. It is the improved position information in the foreknowledge condition that is at the basis of, or mediates, the improved identification performance. (Of course, this is an attractive, simple, outcome; the experimental manipulation consisted in providing better position information. Neither in the course of information processing nor of our analysis has any additional magic shown up.)

3.7 Transient and sustained

In single-item recognition experiments with accuracy as the dependent variable, it is investigated whether performance increases in the foreknowledge condition as compared with the no foreknowledge condition. To make improvements possible, an experimental situation is created whereby, in the no foreknowledge condition, only on a proportion of the trials can the item be named correctly. To this end the target is presented in a rather degraded way: a low luminance or target–background contrast, a short exposure duration, a position at some distance from the fixation point. Such a degraded target does not really 'stand out'. The target is neither spatially nor temporally well defined.

Exactly this way of target presentation appears to be essential to produce benefits in the foreknowledge condition in single-item tasks with accuracy as the dependent variable. (In multiple-item tasks other factors might be essential. See, e.g., Egly and Homa, 1984, and Müller and Findlay, 1987.) We know from a series of experiments that not all ways of target degradation work. For instance in our work in which we controlled the baseline performance level by using an aftercoming pattern mask, no benefits were observed (see, e.g., Van Werkhoven, Wolters and Van der Heijden, 1986, and Fleur, Lapré, Van der Heijden and Wolters, 1986). Also Müller and Findlay (1987) were unable to find really reliable foreknowledge effects in a single-item condition where a backward mask was used to control the accuracy level. From the literature it is well known that, in order to get the same level of performance, the exposure duration has to be much longer in a condition with backward masks than in a condition without (see, e.g., Eriksen, 1980). Just because of this longer exposure duration under backward masking the target is spatially and temporally well defined. It is the aftercoming mask that interferes with target identification. (With forward masks, that more or less hide the target, benefits show up again. See Van der Heijden et al., in prep.)

In the foreknowledge condition in the dot-cueing task, one dot is located on, or very close to, the position of the impending target. (In the no foreknowledge condition five dots are presented simultaneously, one close to the position of the impending target.) The appearance of such a clear position cue in a visual field in which nothing else happens is an abrupt, localized, temporal and spatial incongruity, a change, or something new. Such an occurrence is spatially and temporally well defined. The experiments showed that, under the exposure conditions used, the dot-cueing procedure produced benefits. So, the problem we are faced with is: How can a spatially and temporally well-defined visual event (i.e., a dot cue) be of any help in a task requiring the handling of a spatially and temporally ill-defined visual event (i.e., a target), presented in close temporal and spatial contiguity? Of course, the general type of answer has to be: because the cue has, or brings something, the target lacks and needs. This general type of answer can be worked out in at least two (related) ways, one emphasizing the temporal aspect, the other the spatial aspect. Let us have a brief look at both types of answers.

The difference between the two types of visual events – temporally and spatially well-defined events and temporally and spatially ill-defined events – can be phrased in terms of two different types of retinal ganglion cells and corresponding retina–brain pathways: X-cells or parvo-cells and Y-cells or magno-cells. (See, e.g., Stone and Dreher, 1982, Kandel and Schwartz, 1985, chapters 28–29, Livingstone and Hubel, 1988, DeYoe and Van Essen, 1988, and Zeki and Shipp, 1988.) The Y-cells are at the basis of what is named the *transient* channel, or, the *magno* cellular pathway. Y- cells are approximately evenly distributed over the retina. They have short latencies and rapidly conducting axons. Y-cells have large receptive fields and respond transiently, especially when changes – movements, onsets, offsets – are involved. The X-cells are at the basis of what is called the *sustained* channel, or, the *parvo* cellular pathway. X-cells are mainly concentrated in the fovea. The X-cells have longer latencies and the axons of X-cells conduct more slowly. They have smaller receptive fields and respond in a sustained way. X-cells are probably involved in the transportation of detailed pattern and colour information.

Using this transient–sustained dichotomy, the help provided by the cue can be conceptualized in the following way. Assume that for a correct recognition response, activity in both the transient and sustained channel is needed. As stated, in the experiments under discussion, the targets presented are barely visible. It is possible that under such impoverished viewing conditions the transient or magno pathway is not triggered by the target on all trials. A clearly visible, abrupt, location cue, however, will trigger this pathway on all trials. A weak target in close temporal and spatial contiguity to this cue can then possibly profit from the fact that the transient pathway is appropriately triggered, albeit by an extraneous event. In this view a dot-cue serves as a substitute for an insufficiently clear and abrupt onset of a stimulus by activating the transient channel when the stimulus itself does not, or does not sufficiently, activate this channel.

There is, however, an alternative way in which the dichotomy of transient and sustained channels possibly can be used to describe the difference between the two types of visual events. At the basis of this description is the view that the X or parvo-cells and the Y or magno-cells are not only distinct retina–brain pathways, but are also at the basis of two anatomically and functionally distinct information processing systems within the cortex. Kandel and Schwartz (1985, p. 382) propose two major intra-cortical pathways, corresponding to the transient and sustained channels, that project to different extrastriate areas. It is suggested that these areas process functionally-distinct aspects of the visual stimuli (see also Ungerleider and Mishkin, 1982, and Mishkin, Ungerleider and Macko, 1983; for extensions and refinements see, e.g., DeYoe and Van Essen, 1988, pp. 224–5, Livingstone and Hubel, 1988, p. 744, and Zeki and Shipp, 1988, p. 315).

The first intra-cortical pathway is thought to be a continuation of the X-cell's or parvo-cell's path. It projects via areas V2, V3 and V4 to the inferotemporal areas. It is the pathway we briefly described in section 1.10. It is suggested that this pathway processes identity information, i.e., is concerned with the 'what'. It is often postulated that no location information is connected with the identity information in the inferotemporal areas. The proposition is that identity is represented independently of position (see, e.g., Mishkin et al., 1983).

The second intra-cortical pathway, not mentioned in section 1.10, is thought to be a continuation of the Y-cell's or magno-cell's path. It projects via V2, V3 and V5 to the posterior parietal area. The suggestion is that this pathway is concerned with the spatial relations among objects, i.e., deals with the 'where'. It is often suggested that no identity information is connected with the location information in the posterior parietal area (see, e.g., Mishkin et al., 1983). The idea ___ ty and location are independently represented by separate cortical ___ e segregation just mentioned is probably only a matter of degree. At ___ vel there is an overlap in structure and function of the channels: see, ___ nd Aine, 1984, Livingstone and Hubel, 1988, and Zeki and Shipp, ___ s are connected and operate in complex, interactive, networks.) ___ rom this two-systems view the help provided by the cue can be ___ the following way. Assume that for a correct recognition response, ___ and location information is needed. Because of the impoverished ___ ditions, on a number of trials in the no foreknowledge condition ___ rmation is available but no position information. The clearly ___ cue provides exactly this and only this location information. One ___ explanation was introduced by Butler and Currie (1986, p. 207). In their view it is possible that 'the absence of position information may prevent the subject from "seeing" an item, even though the item has been identified, because the visual system would have no information about where to fixate in order to gain more information or to confirm the initial perception'. Just because in our type of task the subjects sometimes claim not to 'see' the target, this suggestion is quite attractive.

In both descriptions, a cue can serve as a substitute for an insufficiently clear and abrupt onset of a stimulus and activate the transient channel when the stimulus does not, or not sufficiently, activate this channel. The emphasis is different, however. In the first description, the transients' function is to signal onsets, news or changes. In the second description the function of transients triggered by the cue is to provide position information, needed for a correct recognition response or for 'seeing' the target.

3.8 Change, position and attention

In the two explanations described in the previous section a basic assumption is that the transient channel provides essential information: change or position. In the single-item task the target presentation does not always present that information. The cue then functions as a substitute, providing the information needed.

In this way cueing produces the benefits observed in this type of task. The question we now have to consider is: Is it indeed position as suggested in sections 3.4, 3.5 and 3.6 or is it possibly change that is at the basis of the cueing effect?

There are three pieces of empirical evidence that seem to contradict the view that it is change as such and that further support the view that it is indeed position information that is at the basis of the cueing effect.

- Firstly, also in the neutral condition in the single-item tasks with dot cues, the appropriate transient channel is triggered by one of the five simultaneously appearing dots. However, benefits are only observed with one, single, dot. So sheer appropriate change information seems *not* to be *sufficient* to complement the information transmitted by the sustained channel.
- Secondly, facilitating effects of foreknowledge of position in single-item detection and recognition tasks with accuracy as the dependent variable are also found with visual cues that are not in close proximity to the target's position. For instance, Bashinski and Bacharach (1980) demonstrated benefits with arrow cues positioned close to the fixation point (see section 3.1). So, a 'change' reported by the appropriate transient channel seems *not* to be *necessary*. Also a channel from another position can convey the infor- mation lacking.
- Thirdly, facilitating effects of foreknowledge of position have also been demonstrated without any visual cues at all. Egly and Homa (1984), for instance, verbally instructed their subjects where to expect the target. Clear benefits were found (see section 3.1). So, no visual transients reporting change have to be involved at all.

From these observations it follows that an abrupt change in close proximity to the target position is not only insufficient as an explanation for the cueing effect; abrupt changes appear even to be unnecessary. Improved position information, however, suffices. So it must be position information that is at the basis of the foreknowledge of position effect. There is no reason to doubt the conclusion we earlier arrived at.

Within our theoretical considerations, however, this conclusion leads to a paradoxical situation. As stated in section 3.7, experts suggest that identity and location are independently represented by separate cortical systems. How then can improved position information in one or another cortical system A, result in improved recognition accuracy, while identity information must come from another cortical system B? Of course, to solve this problem, some magic is needed, and we propose that it is exactly attention's job to solve this paradoxical situation. More specifically we propose that attention functions by addressing the identity information, while starting from the position information. In section 3.9, and especially in Chapter 8, I further elaborate this proposal. In this section we briefly consider the question of how a cue can bring it about that attention 'gets' or 'arrives' at the appropriate position where it has to start its beneficial effect.

With regard to this question, two cases have to be distinguished. In the first case, there is only one abrupt visual event: a change in, or very close to, the appropriate position, just as in our dot cueing tasks. In the literature the assumption is that such an abrupt visual event recruits attention at its position by triggering the transient system. Breitmeyer and Ganz (1976), for instance, state that the transient system is 'part of an "early warning system" that orients an organism and directs its attention to locations in visual space that potentially contain novel pattern information' (Breitmeyer and Ganz, 1976, p. 31). In the past many investigators have pointed out that such sudden events, i.e., isolated abrupt changes, immediately and automatically attract or catch attention (see, e.g., Titchener, 1908, pp. 204–5 in Yantis and Jonides, 1984; Jonides and Yantis, 1988; Berlyne, 1960; 1966). Jonides (1981; 1983) pointed to the automatic and immediate attention-catching properties of such abrupt visual events, used as cues. Todd and Van Gelder (1979), Krumhansl (1982), Yantis and Jonides (1984) and Jonides and Yantis (1988) demonstrated clear (processing) advantages for a visual event with an abrupt onset as compared with events with one or another type of gradual or masked onset.

In the second case, there is not an abrupt visual event in the appropriate position. There is either an abrupt visual event in another position of the visual field, as in Bashinski and Bacharach's (1980) central arrow study, or there is no abrupt visual event at all, as was possibly the case in Egly and Homa's (1984) study with advance verbal position instructions. Then attention is either initially captured at a wrong position (the arrows) or is at the position of the fixation point or simply at an unknown position (the verbal instruction). In this case a further (voluntary? cognitive? controlled?) step is needed to get attention at the appropriate position. (In Chapter 4 we return to the problem of the 'movements' of attention.)

Taken together, it seems that, with regard to the problem of how attention arrives at the appropriate position, two different processes have to be distinguished: one related to transients and one apparently not really related to transients (possibly something like a fast, 'attention-at-position-catcher' and a slower, controlled 'attention-to-position-forcer'). This distinction was earlier emphasized and further substantiated by Jonides (1981; 1983; see also Van der Heijden, 1989). A related distinction was recently made by Weichselgartner and Sperling (1987). They distinguish two partially concurrent attentional processes: a fast, automatic, process that records the cue and its neighbouring events, and a relatively slow, controlled, process that records the stimulus to be attended to and its neighbouring events (see also Jonides, 1981, p. 196, who distinguishes two components in the processing of a cue: an automatic and a non-automatic component).

3.9 An early operation

Posner (1980, p. 6) mentions a number of studies, e.g., Grindley and Townsend (1968) and Mertens (1956), that were not successful in demonstrating attentional effects with single-item displays, i.e., with 'empty visual fields'. With his own studies as a starting point he elaborates one possible reason why

> many previous efforts were not successful in finding improvements in RT or threshold detection in similar experiments. One reason is that the overall effect seems to get smaller as the task is made more difficult .... If the effect really is smaller in complex tasks, I believe that this may be because subjects have to reorient attention from visual input to internal structures. If subjects are required to discriminate between a letter and a digit, for example, calling attention to a position in space will not be very useful in an empty field such as used in these experiments. Subjects will have to reorient attention from spatial position to the area in memory that is available for analysis of the discrimination .... These ideas fit with the usual observation that knowledge of spatial position only helps complex tasks when the field is cluttered. In tasks where there are good methods of quickly summoning attention, one might be better off not to know where the stimulus will occur rather than having to reorient from visual position to semantic code.
>
> (Posner, 1980, pp. 7–8)

Posner et al. (1980, p. 168) present exactly the same argument: 'Spatial cues will be of great help in complex cluttered fields because they tell the subjects which stimuli are to be dealt with; in an empty field they may or may not help, depending upon the difficulty of reorienting from the location to the internal lookup of item identity.'

In fact, what Posner suggests is that in this type of task, identity information suffices. In his view, there is *no need* for attention to start from a 'visual input', a 'visual position' or a 'position in space'. In his view the task is performed more adequately when attention is directly directed to the 'semantic code', 'the area in memory ... available for analysis' or the 'item identity'. It will be clear that this position is a variant of the late selection views (see Chapter 2).

Contrary to Posner's suggestions, however, the data and analyses of our single-item recognition tasks show

- that position information is close to essential for performance in the no foreknowledge condition in the identification task; (See the conditional identification probabilities in section 3.5. It is not completely essential, because identification accuracy without effective location information is above chance. To the latter finding we return further on.)
- that foreknowledge of the position where the item is going to appear significantly improves performance; and

– that benefits are (mainly) mediated by improved position information in the foreknowledge condition as compared with the no foreknowledge condition and (virtually) not by an improvement in identification accuracy given that there is effective position information. What foreknowledge of position seems to effect is firstly an improvement in localization; not an improvement in identification.

In this way the data and analyses presented in sections 3.5 and 3.6 convincingly show that it is simply not true that subjects might be better off not to know where the stimulus will occur (or occurs) rather than having to reorient from visual position (or visual input) to semantic code (or identity). So, the important problem still to be solved is *why* position information is so important in these types of tasks. Why is selection in the single-item task early selection starting from position? We elaborate two possibilities.

One possibility is that visual information is automatically registered as a visual code – something like features on a position – but that, to derive an identity code, this information has to be selected and a subsequent identification process has to be started or triggered. This is a version of the 'early selection' view but a very unattractive version. As we have seen in Chapter 2, the orthodox early selection view holds that, because there is a limited capacity for further processing, a subset of the information presented is selected. But in our type of task only one single letter is presented, not a complex letter array. Only this single letter has to be processed. Therefore neither a limited capacity processing channel nor a limit in attentional capacity itself can really be the reason for not processing the letter. So it seems that this 'first select then identify' proposal is not an adequate one. It requires a stretching of the capacity notion beyond all reasonable bounds (see also section 3.0).

A second possibility is that visual information is automatically registered as a visual code and also automatically further processed into an identity code. In this view the visual position or visual information is needed to retrieve or address the identity code. This 'first identify then select' proposal is what I formerly called, the process of 'postcategorical filtering' and 'selection' (Van der Heijden, 1981; Van der Heijden, Hagenaar and Bloem, 1984). Available identities are addressed by attention by means of the visual information that gave rise to these identities and this visual information in its turn is addressed via its position (so, the addressing sequence is: appropriate position → features on appropriate position (i.e., 'object') → corresponding identity).

Of course, the problem with this view is why such a complex addressing procedure is necessary, given that in a single-item task only one identity is available. The answer might be that it is simply not true that only one identity is available. Knowledge of the set of potential answers, residual activation from previous trials, and expectations about what is going to be presented next, etc., might entail that on each trial, besides the identity triggered by the target, a number of alternative identities is available. (The task can be regarded as a 'pseudo' multiple-item task.) These identities as such, however, provide no information about which one is the adequate one. At the level of identities there is only identity information. So, in a sense, there is an identity competition or a problem in identity selection. Position information has to solve this competition. For that job it needs 'features on position' as an intermediate. The sequence position → features on position → identity can unambiguously decide between the alternative identities.

This view is consistent with Styles and Allport's (1986) analysis of performance in a real multiple-item task. They speculate about an '"attentional spotlight" ... in *retinotopic* co-ordinates ... wherever the "spotlight" is directed, activity in corresponding, retinotopic cortical units is temporarily enhanced. The transient, enhanced activation presumably also propagates (after some delay) to coding systems "down-stream" (including the non-retinotopic identity and relative position codes)' (Styles and Allport, 1986, p. 199). In this proposal we easily recognize: appropriate position (spotlight in retinotopic coordinates) → features on appropriate position (corresponding retinotopic cortical units) → corresponding identity (non-retinotopic identity).

Moreover, this view is also consistent with our finding that there is an – albeit very small – above chance identification accuracy without effective knowledge of position ($IclPi = 0.1252$; see section 3.5). Just because of target presentation, the correct identity is often among the available identities, independent of whether it can be addressed or not. Consequently, when one of the available identities is selected at random, the target has a higher than chance probability of being the selected identity.

Taken together it seems that in the tasks discussed in this chapter one or another 'selective' operation operates upon a 'visual' or 'early' representation. It is likely that this operation starts from 'position' and uses the 'early' information to select one identity from among a number of available identities. The execution of this operation can be equated with 'paying attention'. (Exactly this addressing and selecting process might create the illusion that letter detection is capacity limited whereas luminance increment detection is not. See Shaw, 1984, and Müller and Findlay, 1987, for the relevant evidence.)

3.10 RSVP

Further important evidence for a selective mechanism, starting from position and addressing an 'early', 'visual', representation, comes from a complicated single-item recognition task with accuracy as the dependent variable; the rapid serial visual presentation (RSVP) task. In the pure form of this task, a sequence of items is presented at a rapid rate, one after another, at the same spatial position. This task can be regarded as a single-item task because at each moment in time only one single element is presented.

To the best of our knowledge, Eriksen and Collins (1969) were the first to use the RSVP task. In their task the number series 1 to 9, with one of the nine digits missing, was presented in order at digit intervals varying from 50 to 100 ms. In a 'before' condition subjects were told a digit name prior to each trial. The task was to determine whether it was presented in the series or not. On half the trials the digit was the actual omitted digit. In an 'after' condition the name of the critical digit was only given after termination of the trial. So, in this condition subjects had to look for the gap in the series. The authors comment:

> A phenomenal analysis of these search tasks suggests that the performance in the before condition depends on some type of preattentive or filtering process. If the sequence is presented at a rate of approximately 50 msec per digit, two or three scattered digits are perceived clearly with the rest going by unnoticed. If S is asked to look for a specific digit, this digit then stands out in the presentation as one of those perceived clearly. In the after condition, on the other hand, detection of a gap in the number series seems to require that each of the successive numbers be perceived in order to detect the gap. This requires a much slower rate of presentation, approximately 200 msec per digit.
> (Eriksen and Collins, 1969, pp. 489–90)

An experiment supported this phenomenal analysis.

Eriksen and Collins's task is a very special type of task, however. At the end of section 2.7 we concluded with Kahneman and Treisman (1984) that in nearly all experimental tasks two distinct functions are controlled by different aspects of the information presented: stimulus choice by one property, and response choice by another property. In Eriksen and Collins's study, however, shape, i.e., a specified digit, determines stimulus choice as well as response choice. So, it is not unlikely that here we have a situation in which two different selective mechanisms are concerned with the same stimulus property. This focussed cooperation might result in the digits standing out perceptually.

Subsequently, a number of experiments were reported in which indeed the two different functions were controlled by different stimulus aspects. Lawrence (1971, Exp. 1) asked subjects to report the word in a series of words that differed from the others by virtue of being in upper case letters. Accuracy in this task was quite high, but depended upon the speed of item presentation. There were about 83% correct responses at a speed of 10 items/second and 58% at a speed of 20 items/second. When an error was made, the intrusion of the word immediately following the target was the most frequent. Lawrence (1971, p. 87) states 'When an error of this type is made, Ss are quite confident that the reported word is the capitalized word'.

Broadbent and associates (see, e.g., Broadbent, 1977; McClean, Broadbent and Broadbent, 1982; Gathercole and Broadbent, 1984; Broadbent and Broadbent, 1987) further investigated and extended this task. In all experiments coloured items were used. Subjects had either to name the (unique) colour of a prespecified (unique) item or to name the (unique) item in a prespecified (unique) colour. For present purposes, the most interesting experiment is experiment 1 of McClean et al. (1982). Subjects had either to name the letter in a specified colour

Table 3.10.1 Frequency (per cent) with which attributes used in responding
originated from various temporal positions. Data from McClean et al.
(1982, Exp.1). See text for further explanation.

	\u2013Serial position in list					
	\u20132	\u20131	T	+1	+2	T+ +1
Condition L|C	8.2	8.2	58.8	17.0	7.8	75.8
Condition C|L	7.8	8.4	65.1	11.5	7.2	76.6

(condition L|C) or the colour of a specified letter (condition C|L). Items were
projected at a rate of approximately 15 items/second. Table 3.10.1 presents the
results.

In this table are given the frequencies (per cent) with which attributes
originated from two positions (\u20132) and one position (\u20131) before the target
position, from the target position (T) and from one (+1) and two (+2) positions
after the target position. The table shows that, as in Lawrence's (1971) study,
accuracy is rather high (see the column T). Furthermore, the table shows that also
in this task most errors come from position +1, i.e., the position immediately after
the target position. A further interesting feature of these results is that the sum of
reported attributes from the target position and the immediately following
position is about the same for the two conditions (see column T+ +1).

The unique feature of the RSVP task, of course, is that there is no uncertainty
with regard to spatial position; all items are presented on the same spatial
position. There is, however, uncertainty with regard to the moment that the
selective operation has to be started from that spatial position. It appears from
these and related experiments that a great number of, more or less strictly
specified, stimulus features are effective in triggering the selective process. It is
these features that resolve the temporal ambiguity and determine the 'when' of
the selective operation in the RSVP task.

The results are now easily explained in terms of a two-stage process, i.e., in
terms of a selective operation that starts from the fixed spatial position and
addresses 'early', 'visual', information, to select the target identity from among
other available identities. First, to initiate the selective process, the target has to
be detected (the *uppercase* word, the *red* letter, the letter *N*). Then the response
has to be selected (what word, what letter, what colour). If the target is detected
relatively early, the correct target features can be addressed and the correct
response is selected. If the target is detected relatively late, the second process
can only start selection when the target features are already replaced by features
of the subsequent item. Then the item in the next temporal position is selected.

Figure 3.10.1 serves to illustrate the principles underlying this reasoning. In
the upper panel, the 'average' case is depicted. The solid part of the upper line
represents the interval of time that the information needed for target detection and
initiating the selective process is available. The solid part of the lower line

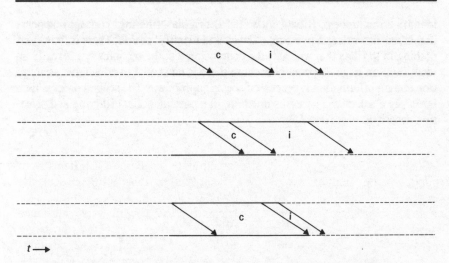

Figure 3.10.1 Tentative model accounting for addressing and selecting in the RSVP task (see text for further explanation).

represents the interval of time that the visual information needed for response selection is available. After these intervals of time the information is replaced by the subsequent visual information. The oblique arrows represent the addressing and selecting process. The upper part stands for the moment of initiation and the bottom part for the moment of becoming effective. The part of the figure labelled 'c' gives the correct selections, the part labelled 'i' the intrusions (subsequent information is erroneously addressed and selected).

In the middle panel it is shown what happens when the information needed for starting the selective process is available later than the information needed for response selection. In this situation there are fewer correct responses and more intrusions. This panel can be taken to represent what approximately happened in McClean et al.'s (1982) L|C condition (see table 3.10.1). In the lower panel the information needed for triggering the selective process is available earlier. Now there are more correct responses and fewer intrusions. This panel indicates what approximately happened in McClean et al.'s (1982) C|L condition (see table 3.10.1). It is worthwhile to note that in the present account in all three cases the sum of correct reports and intrusions from the next temporal position is indeed approximately the same (see the column labelled T+ +1 in table 3.10.1).

The results and the analysis presented strongly suggest that the addressing and selecting process starts at (the fixed) position (see also Keele, Cohen, Ivry, Liotti and Yee, 1988), and simply deals with the information available, i.e., features on position: if the target is still available, the target features; if the subsequent item has already appeared, the features of that item.

Broadbent and associates strongly suggest that this second process is an identification process. Broadbent's (1958) original 'filtering' concept reappears in this recent work as a two-stage 'detect and identify' notion. There is, however, nothing in the data that warrants the conclusion that the second stage is really an identification stage. Especially because there is no spatial overload, the assumption that all information is processed seems appropriate. The second process then is simply a selection process: something like postcategorical filtering and selection described in section 3.9.

Chapter 4

Single-item detection and recognition tasks with latency as the dependent variable

4.0 The field

In the type of task to be discussed in this chapter the stimulus situation is again extremely simple. One clear, suprathreshold, target-stimulus is presented in an otherwise empty field, i.e., on the moment of target presentation there is only one, spatially localized, event. 'Clear suprathreshold' can be taken to mean that after presentation of the stimulus no uncertainty is left with regard to identity and position of the stimulus. Subjects are instructed to react as fast as possible to this stimulus, and reaction time, RT, is the main dependent variable. The target can appear in one of several positions. (In most experiments only two target positions are used.) A cue, preceding the target, gives information about the likely position of the impending target. The questions of interest are whether this foreknowledge of position as a result of cueing has any effect on the speed of reaction to the target, and, if so, how these effects have to be described and interpreted.

In the previous chapter we saw that it is rather difficult to demonstrate beneficial effects of foreknowledge of position in threshold single-item detection and recognition tasks with accuracy as the dependent variable. Furthermore we saw that benefits, if found, were generally quite small. This was explained in terms of the available room for improvement. To assess benefits, performance in the foreknowledge of position condition has to be compared with performance in a no foreknowledge, or neutral cue, condition. With accuracy as the dependent variable this introduces a limit. Because one cannot be correcter than correct, in the foreknowledge of position condition an improvement is possible only on a proportion of trials equal to the proportion of trials that were not yet correct in the no foreknowledge of position condition (see section 3.3).

With latency, i.e. RT, as the dependent variable there is not a comparable limit. Because one can be faster than fast, in principle, an improvement in RT is possible on all foreknowledge of position trials. This leads one to expect that there is more, and more robust, evidence for beneficial effects of foreknowledge of position in tasks with RT as the dependent variable than in tasks with accuracy as the dependent variable. A first brief look at the literature clearly confirms this expectation. In recent years quite a lot of papers were published, reporting (substantial) positive effects of foreknowledge of position in single-item paradigms with RT as the dependent variable.

As with tasks with accuracy as the dependent variable, also in this field of research two types of tasks have been used: detection tasks and recognition tasks. With *detection* tasks subjects have to signal as fast as possible the appearance of one or another target, for instance the flashing of a dot or of a square of light, in one of the alternative target positions (see Posner, Nissen and Ogden, 1978, for the first attempts to demonstrate benefits with this type of task). With *recognition* tasks subjects have to indicate as fast as possible what the target, e.g., a letter appearing in one of the alternative positions, is (see Eriksen and Hoffman, 1974, for the first firm demonstration of benefits with this type of task).

As might be expected from the previous chapter (see section 3.8), and as will further appear in subsequent sections, for the tasks now under discussion a second distinction is also highly relevant. This distinction concerns the types of cues used to inform the subjects about the (likely) position of the impending target. We only consider visual cues or indicators (for verbal cues see further on). Two types of visual cues are distinguished (see also Jonides, 1981; 1983). The criterion for this distinction is mainly the position of the cue. Let us term the two types of cues location cues and symbolic cues. A location cue is a visual event, for instance a short-duration small dot, appearing at or very close to one of the alternative target positions. A symbolic cue is a visual event, for instance a bar or an arrow, appearing in a 'neutral' position, for instance in, or close to, the centre of the display. With symbolic cues, subjects are provided with a rule that specifies how the cue has to be interpreted, e.g., 'an arrow pointing to the right indicates that the target will appear at the right' (or at the left; see Shepherd, Findlay and Hockey, 1986).

In the recent years, positive effects of foreknowledge of position on RTs in single-item tasks have been demonstrated with all types of tasks that we now can distinguish: detection tasks with symbolic cues, recognition tasks with symbolic cues, detection tasks with location cues and recognition tasks with location cues (see sections 4.2 and 4.3). But for this type of experiment to really reveal something of interest about the possible involvement and operation of attention, at least two conditions have to be met.

The first condition has already been extensively discussed: exposure durations (and/or exposure conditions) have to be used that do not allow useful eye movements (see section 2.8). For the reasons for requiring this condition, the reader is referred back to section 2.8. It is attentional effects we are interested in; not acuity effects. In the context of the experiments to be discussed in this chapter, 'exposure duration' has to be interpreted as: 'Interval between the onset of the cue and the offset of the target', i.e., the duration of the whole information presentation sequence. (Sometimes, subjects are verbally informed where the target is going to appear. It will now be clear why we do not discuss these experiments. 'Exposure duration' is then not only extremely long, allowing useful eye movements in the direction of the position of the impending target, but also ill-defined.) Unfortunately, exactly in the field of research we are now concerned with, often 'exposure durations' were used that were much too long (and volumes of journals have been wasted with post hoc 'explanations' why that did not really matter). In a later section we consider a further reason for not considering experiments with large cue–target intervals: the observation that with longer delays adverse effects on RTs, i.e., 'inhibition', may be observed.

A second condition the experiments have to meet is that the position cues should convey only more adequate position information than neutral cues and not any other extra information. In some experiments reported in the literature, however, position cues also provided information about the type of response that was most likely to be made, e.g., about whether the left hand or the right hand had to be used, or whether a movement to the left or to the right had to be made. This happens when type of response and position of the target are correlated (e.g., when a target at the left requires a left hand response and a target at the right a right hand response). The reason for imposing this condition will be clear. We are not interested in this differential response or motor preparation but in the effects of central attention. (In general, to observe the latter effects, 'expectations' and 'intentions' have to be kept fixed because 'intentions' and 'expectations' can influence overall RTs in the same way as central attention does, thereby resulting in spurious central attention effects. See Chapter 2; see also Posner et al., 1978, for this issue in relation to single-item tasks.)

The two requirements specified above leave us with a rather small number of experiments that can really tell us something about the effects of attentional involvement in suprathreshold detection and recognition tasks with RT as the dependent variable. But, there is a reason to even further restrict the amount of literature to be discussed. This reason we discuss in the next section.

4.1 The neutral condition

It is generally assumed – and there is substantial evidence to support this assumption – that in the type of task under discussion two classes of preparatory processes with influences on RTs have to be distinguished: general warning or alerting processes reflecting, for instance, the development of expectations and intentions over time (see, e.g., Posner and Boies, 1971) and specific preparatory processes reflecting the 'development' of central attention over time (see, e.g., Jonides and Mack, 1984). It therefore seems that in the ideal paradigm for investigating the specific preparatory effects of foreknowledge of position on RTs with single-item tasks two experimental conditions have to be used: a foreknowledge or informative cue condition (a 100% informative cue precedes the target), and a no foreknowledge or neutral cue condition (a noninformative neutral cue precedes the target).

The paradigm is ideal if and only if (a) RTs obtained in the neutral condition reflect the effects of the general warning or alerting processes, and (b) RTs obtained in the foreknowledge condition reflect the same general warning effects plus the effects of the specific preparatory processes. The *difference* between the RTs obtained in the two conditions is then an uncontaminated indication of the effects of the specific preparatory processes, i.e., of the attentional benefits we are interested in.

Moreover, by systematically varying the interval between onset of cue and onset of target (the Stimulus Onset Asynchrony, SOA) in this ideal paradigm, and by calculating the difference between the two conditions per interval, the development of the effects of the specific preparatory processes over time can be traced. (Just because general as well as specific preparatory processes develop over time, functions relating RTs to SOAs for the foreknowledge condition only, as for instance reported by Tsal, 1983, are completely uninterpretable; then there is no baseline condition that can be used to isolate the contribution of the specific preparatory processes. See, e.g., Eriksen and Murphy, 1987, Van der Heijden, Wolters and Enkeling, 1988, and Yantis, 1988.)

In their, now classic, single-item recognition task with RT as the dependent variable, Eriksen and Hoffman (1974) indeed used this ideal paradigm. After Posner and Snyder (1975) and Posner et al. (1978), however, most investigators in the field use a slightly different paradigm (see also Bashinski and Bacharach, 1980, in Chapter 3). In this paradigm, the informative cue is not 100% informative, but gives correct position information on only a fraction, e.g., 80%, of the trials (valid trials) and incorrect or misleading information on the remaining fraction, e.g., 20%, of the trials (invalid trials). So, two types of trials are distinguished when an informative, i.e., a non-neutral, cue is presented, and the mean RTs observed with both types of trials can be compared with the mean RT observed in the neutral condition. For both types of trials the comparison provides an indication of the effect of the specific selective preparatory processes given the cue validity used. Because for valid trials the comparison generally assesses a 'benefit' in performance and for invalid trials a 'cost', this paradigm is known as the cost–benefit analysis of reaction times (see Jonides and Mack, 1984).

As stated, most investigators in the field use this paradigm for assessing the effects of selective preparatory processes. Remington and Pierce (1984) even suggest that not using this paradigm is a serious error (p. 394). Nevertheless, there is a serious problem with this paradigm. Basically the problem is, that it is far from clear how a task is performed given a cue validity of less than 100%. There are at least two possibilities. The first is that subjects 'probability match' over trials (see, e.g., Jonides, 1983, and Eriksen and Murphy, 1987, p. 305 for this point of view). With an 80% cue validity, subjects might prepare on 80% of the trials for the indicated position and on 20% for (one of) the alternative target position(s). The second possibility is that with a smaller than 100% cue validity subjects are prepared somewhat less than optimally for the indicated position and somewhat more than minimally for the nonindicated position(s). (See, e.g., Shaw, 1978, 1980, and 1984, for this type of optimal capacity allocation model; see, however, also Jonides, 1983, and Van der Heijden, 1989; see also section

6.7.) Of course, just because it is not known what happens – discrete probability matching vs continuous trade-off – the results obtained with the cost–benefit paradigm are very difficult to interpret. This is the more so because what exactly happens might depend upon the type of cue used: a location cue or a symbolic cue (see, e.g., Jonides, 1981; 1983; Van der Heijden, 1989; see also section 6.7). The results obtained under a 100% cue validity are easy to interpret, because it is reasonable to assume that subjects are then always and also optimally prepared for the indicated target position. So it seems that a 100% validity condition has to be preferred.

In an impressive paper, Jonides and Mack (1984) also criticize the cost–benefit paradigm, but on completely different grounds. In their view it is not the less than 100% valid informative cue that introduces the problems but the noninformative neutral cue. They correctly recognize that neutral and informative cues must be identical with respect to all their effects except that of triggering the specific preparatory effects. Failing to meet this condition implies that the relative magnitudes of costs and benefits estimated by subtraction of RTs would be rendered meaningless (see Jonides and Mack, 1984, pp. 31–2). They further show that lots of experiments fail to meet this condition. There are often factors that only impact on the neutral condition, or, the neutral condition often yields response times that not only reflect general warning effects, in common with the informative cue condition (see Jonides and Mack, 1984, pp. 32–40).

Jonides and Mack's (1984) remedy is quite drastic, however. In their view in most research the neutral or no foreknowledge condition can simply be deleted: valid and invalid trials suffice. To discover 'whether there are specific preparatory effects elicited by informative cues … it is sufficient to discover merely whether performance differs with valid and invalid cues and whether differences between these conditions grow with the interval between cue and target' (Jonides and Mack, 1984, p. 41). So, what they propose is to change the cost–benefit analysis into a cost-plus-benefit analysis. But, while in this way the *existence* of specific preparatory effects might be demonstrated, no information at all is obtained about the *character* of these effects. A cost-plus-benefit can result because of facilitation of performance, i.e., a benefit, on valid foreknowledge trials and normal or average performance on invalid foreknowledge trials, because of normal performance on valid foreknowledge trials and delayed performance, i.e., costs, on invalid foreknowledge trials, etc. In other words, from the difference between performance with valid and invalid cues, not very much can be learned of the underlying processes. Moreover, just because there are already serious difficulties in interpreting performance with a less than 100% cue validity (see a previous paragraph), there is not very much hope that the difference in performance observed with valid and invalid cues can be interpreted in a reasonable way.

Finding out something about underlying processes and operations is the main aim of the information processing approach. Therefore to really get some insight into the general and especially into the specific preparatory processes in the type of task we are concerned with, the inclusion of a neutral condition seems essential (see also Eriksen and Murphy, 1987; Van der Heijden et al., 1988). Indeed, Jonides and Mack (1984) recognize that it is sometimes valuable to include a neutral condition. Then, however, informative and neutral cues have to be carefully chosen: 'the cues used for neutral and informative conditions should be matched as closely as possible. This includes matching them on physical appearance, on potential to alert subjects generally, and on ease of encoding' (Jonides and Mack, 1984, p. 41). And with that requirement one can only agree.

We are now in a position to specify what experiments will be discussed in the next sections. These are experiments using either symbolic cues (section 4.2) or location cues (section 4.3) that (a) include an appropriate neutral condition, and, (b) measure central attentional effects uncontaminated by peripheral effects (eye movements) or alternative central effects (e.g., differential expectations and intentions). Because, with these restrictions, only a few experiments with a 100% cue validity remain, we also have to include experiments using a less than 100% cue validity. From these experiments we only consider the valid and neutral trials.

4.2 Symbolic cues

In single-item suprathreshold detection and recognition tasks a cue precedes the appearance of the target. Two different types of visual cues have been used in the recent past: location cues and symbolic cues. In this section the results obtained with symbolic cues are discussed. The location cue results are discussed in section 4.3.

A symbolic cue is a clearly visible visual object, e.g., an arrow or a digit, appearing in a neutral position, generally in the centre of the visual display. In principle the *position* of the cue conveys no information with regard to the position of the impending target (in fact, it often does). If symbolic cues are used, subjects are also provided in advance with a rule specifying how to interpret the cue, e.g., 1 stands for upper-left quadrant, 2 for upper-right quadrant, etc., or, arrow pointing to the right stands for target at the right and arrow pointing to the left stands for target at the left. Remington and Pierce (1984, exp. 2) reported the results of a detection task and Eriksen and Hoffman (1974) of a recognition task employing symbolic cues. In both experiments also a neutral cue condition was included. The neutral cue conveyed no information with regard to the position of the impending target but only time information, just as the symbolic cue.

Detection tasks

In Remington and Pierce's (1984) experiments the target was a small dot. Subjects were to react as quickly as possible to the onset of this dot by pressing a single key. The dots could occur either to the left or to the right of fixation at eccentricities of either 2 or 10 deg. The informative cue was an arrow that appeared above the fixation point. The cue was valid on 80% of the trials and invalid on the remaining 20% of the trials. In their second experiment also a neutral cue was used. This cue was a cross that appeared immediately above the fixation point. The cross indicated that the target was equally likely to occur at the left and at the right. In their experiment 2, six SOAs between cue and target were used: 50, 100, 150, 250, 400 and 550 ms. Table 4.2.1 presents the results obtained for the valid and neutral cue condition and their differences for the relevant range of SOAs (we estimated these data from their figure 2).

Table 4.2.1 Mean RTs (ms) for neutral and foreknowledge trials for two target distances and three cue–target SOAs in the single-item detection task reported by Remington and Pierce (1984, Exp. 2). The row labelled delta gives the estimated benefits.

Eccentricity	2 deg			10 deg		
SOA (ms)	50	100	150	50	100	150
Neutral	292	275	282	308	286	288
Valid	279	255	251	289	265	261
Delta	13	20	31	19	21	27

Three important features are readily apparent from this table.

– For the neutral (and the valid) cue condition, RTs decrease initially with increasing SOA, signifying a development or growth of the cue-induced general alerting effects over time.
– RTs with valid cues are smaller than with neutral cues, indicating positive effects of specific preparatory processes induced by the informative cue, i.e., benefits.
– The differences between RTs obtained with neutral cues and valid cues, i.e., the benefits, increase with increasing SOAs, signifying a development or growth of the specific preparatory processes over time.

Recognition tasks

In Eriksen and Hoffman's (1974) experiment the targets were the capital letters A, H, M and O. Subjects had to name the letter as fast as possible. The target could appear in one of four, equally spaced, positions on the circumference of an imaginary circle with a radius of 1 deg. The informative cue was a black bar, 0.5 deg long, with the near end 0.5 deg from the target position. It constituted an imaginary radius from the centre of the display through the indicated position. This cue was always valid. In the neutral condition a black dot, appearing over the fixation point, was used. It indicated that the four positions were equally probable. In the experiment, four SOAs (?) between cue and target were used: 0, 50, 100 and 150 ms. Table 4.2.2 presents the results for the informative and neutral cue condition and their differences for the range of SOAs used.

Table 4.2.2 Mean RTs (ms) for neutral and foreknowledge trials for four cue–target SOAs in the single-item recognition task reported by Eriksen and Hoffman (1974). The row labelled delta gives the benefits.

SOA (ms)	0	50	100	150
Neutral cue	389	377	376	376
Valid	388	365	356	348
Delta	1	12	20	28

Inspection of the table shows that the same three features as found with the detection task of Remington and Pierce (1984) show up in this recognition task.

- In the neutral (and the informative) cue condition RTs decrease with increasing cue–target SOA, indicating a growth of a cue-induced general alerting effect.
- On average, the RTs obtained in the informative cue condition are smaller than those found in the neutral cue condition, indicating a positive specific preparatory effect of informative cues, i.e., benefits.
- The differences between the RTs, i.e., the benefits, strongly suggest that this positive effect is virtually absent at an SOA of 0 ms and increases with increasing SOA over the range of SOAs investigated, so indicating a development or growth of the specific preparatory effect over time.

Taken together, it seems that with symbolic cues both detection tasks and recognition tasks show essentially the same basic phenomena over the relevant range of SOAs: growing general alerting effects and, additionally, growing specific preparatory effects or benefits.

Two further, what can be called 'strategy effects', observed with symbolic cues, have still to be mentioned. The first concerns the effect of cue validity. While the available reliable evidence is quite scarce, there is some evidence that the magnitude of the positive effect of symbolic cues depends on their validity. If the cue reliably indicates the position of the impending target a larger positive effect is observed than with a less reliable cue (see Shepherd et al., 1986; see also Hughes, 1984, for a systematic investigation of this effect but with very large SOAs). Of course, the difference between neutral cues (50% validity) and informative cues (80% validity) in Remington and Pierce's (1984) study supports this supposition (see table 4.2.1). At this point it is worthwhile to remember that in the accuracy experiment, reported by Müller and Findlay (1987) and referred to in section 3.1, a peculiar kind of 'double' symbolic cue and rather low cue validities were used. It seems that under such conditions only (very) small benefits have to be expected.

The second strategy effect shows up in a comparison of mixed and blocked presentations. Posner (1978; see Hawkins, Shafto and Richardson, 1988, p. 488) investigated the effect of two levels of target eccentricity – parafoveal and peripheral targets – in a position-cueing paradigm. There were either blocks of trials devoted to one eccentricity, or the two eccentricities were randomly mixed in a series of trials. With eccentricity blocked, identical benefits were found for the two eccentricities. With target eccentricities mixed, larger benefits for peripheral than for parafoveal targets were observed. Hawkins et al. (1988) investigated the effect of three levels of target luminance in blocked and mixed designs. With target luminances blocked, identical benefits for the different luminance levels were observed. With luminances mixed, increasing benefits with decreasing luminances were found. (Unfortunately, in the latter experiment 'exposure duration' was much too long.)

4.3 Location cues

A location cue is a visual event, e.g., a short duration dot, appearing in, or very close to, one of the alternative target positions. Possamai (1986) reported the results of a detection task and Van der Heijden et al. (1988) of a recognition task employing location cues. In both experiments also a neutral cue was used.

Detection tasks

In Possamai's (1986) experiment the target consisted of a small cross that occurred with equal probability in one of three locations: either at fixation or at 7 deg to the left or to the right of fixation. Subjects had to press a single key as fast as possible when the target appeared. The location cue consisted of a luminance increment of one out of three diodes that were located slightly below the three alternative target positions. There was no correlation between the location of the cue and that of the target, or, all cues had a validity of 33 1/3%. So, the cues were not informative. In the experiment five SOAs were used: 50, 75, 100, 250 and 500 ms.

For this experiment we define trials with a peripheral cue and the target subsequently appearing in the indicated position as valid trials, and trials with a central cue and the target subsequently appearing in one of the two alternative peripheral positions as neutral trials. Table 4.3.1 presents the results for these two types of trials and their differences for the relevant range of SOAs (we estimated these data from Possamai's figure 2).

Table 4.3.1 Mean RTs (ms) for neutral and foreknowledge trials for three cue–target SOAs in the single-item detection task reported by Possamai (1986). The row labelled delta gives the estimated benefits.

SOA (ms)	50	75	100
Neutral	340	329	320
Valid	333	318	314
Delta	7	11	6

Three important features appear in this table.

- For the neutral (and the valid) cue condition, RTs decrease with increasing SOAs, indicating a development or growth of general alerting effects over time.
- RTs with valid cues are somewhat smaller than with neutral cues, indicating a positive specific preparatory process induced by the valid location cue. (The size of the benefit is probably somewhat underestimated because neutral cues were presented foveally and valid cues peripherally, making relatively faster responding to the neutral cue possible; see section 2.8.)
- The differences between the RTs obtained in the two conditions, i.e., the benefits, appear fairly constant with increasing SOAs, suggesting that there is no development or growth of the specific preparatory processes in the interval of time considered here.

Recognition tasks

In Van der Heijden et al.'s (1988) recognition task the targets were the letters E, K, M and O. The target could appear in one of two positions: either at 3 deg to the left or to the right of a central fixation dot. As cues, a luminance increment of a dot at a distance of –2.5, –0.5, 0, +0.5 or +2.5 deg of visual angle from the fixation point was used (a minus means to the left, a plus to the right of the fixation). A luminance increment of a peripheral dot served as a location cue and the luminance increment of the central dot as a neutral cue (the dots at –0.5 and +0.5 served as symbolic cues). In experiments 1 and 2 the validity of the location cue was 100%. In experiment 3 the cue validity was 50%. The three experiments had SOAs of 33, 66, 99 and 132 ms in common.

For the present experiments we define valid trials and neutral trials in the same way as for Possamai's (1986) experiment. Table 4.3.2 presents the results, averaged over the three experiments (to this averaging we return later).

Table 4.3.2 Mean RTs (ms) for neutral and foreknowledge trials for four cue–target SOAs in the single-item recognition task reported by Van der Heijden et al. (1988). The row labelled delta gives the estimated benefits.

SOA (ms)	33	66	99	132
Neutral	467	460	456	454
Valid	461	453	448	447
Delta	6	7	8	7

The table shows that

- In the neutral (and the informative) cue condition RTs decrease with increasing SOAs, indicating a growth of general alerting effects.
- RTs in the valid cue condition are smaller than in the neutral cue condition, i.e., valid cues induce specific preparatory processes that bring benefits (again, the size of the benefits might be somewhat underestimated because of the positions of neutral and valid cues).

– The differences between the two cueing conditions are constant over the range of SOAs, suggesting that there is no growth or development of the specific preparatory process over this interval of time.

Taken all together it seems that with location cues both detection tasks and recognition tasks show essentially the same basic phenomena for the relevant range of SOAs: growing general alerting effects and constant specific preparatory effects or benefits.

Two further phenomena observed with location cues have still to be mentioned. The first phenomenon concerns the effect of cue validity. The available literature strongly suggests that location cues have a positive effect on RTs to targets in or close to their position, independent of the validity of the cue. Remember that Possamai's (1986) cues had a validity of 33 1/3%, i.e., were not informative. Posner and Cohen (1984) even demonstrated positive effects with, what can be called, a negative cue validity of 10%; the cue specified the alternative target position more reliably. Eriksen and Yeh (1985, Exp. II) found a far from significant difference of about 5 ms between a 100% and a 40% validity condition. Van der Heijden et al. (1988) found no essential differences between their first two experiments (a cue validity of 100%) and their third experiment (a validity of 50%). Just because of this finding we averaged the results of the three experiments in table 4.3.2.

The second phenomenon concerns the effect of the distance between the position of the location cue and of the target. In general, for beneficial effects to show up it is not necessary that the cue is on, or very close to, the position of the impending target. With cues in the neighbourhood of this position benefits are also obtained. There is, however, evidence, obtained with very long cue–target intervals (see, e.g., Shulman, Wilson and Sheehy, 1985; Shulman, Sheehy and Wilson, 1986) and with short cue–target intervals (Van der Heijden et al., 1988), that RTs monotonically increase with increasing cue–target distances. Figure 4.3.1 illustrates this effect. So, the rule seems to be, the closer the more effective

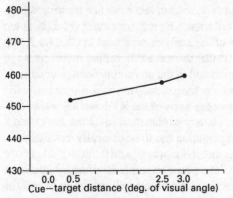

Figure 4.3.1 The 'distance' effect: RT as a function of cue–target distance. (From Van der Heijden et al., 1988.)

the location cue. (See also La Berge, 1983, and La Berge and Brown, 1986, on this issue, but notice the confounding with retinal acuity and of variables interacting with retinal acuity, such as forward masking, in these studies.)

4.4 Attention?

The standard explanation for most of the results just described, whether obtained with symbolic cues or with location cues, is, of course, in terms of attention and more specifically in terms of a 'spotlight of attention'. The explanation runs approximately as follows. There is an attentional mechanism, limited in its spatial extent, that can be likened to a spotlight. The help of this attentional mechanism is needed for rapid detection and identification and therefore for (fast) responding. This attentional mechanism can move its focus just as a spotlight can. These movements of visual attention take time. When there is no foreknowledge of the position of an impending target (i.e., with neutral cues) attention starts moving only after appearance of the target. Intermediate RTs are then to be expected. With foreknowledge of position provided by a location cue or by a symbolic cue, the attentional mechanism can already start to move in the direction of that position before the target is presented. If a target indeed appears at that position, RTs are fast and benefits are observed. When a target appears at another position, however, RTs are lengthened because attention has to turn its steps and move its focus from the expected location to the unexpected location. Costs are then observed. (See, e.g., Posner, 1980; Posner, Cohen and Rafal, 1982, p. 188; Posner, Snyder and Davidson, 1980, p. 172; Shulman, Remington and McClean, 1979; Remington and Pierce, 1984; Hughes, 1984; Tsal, 1983; for variations on this theme see, e.g., Eriksen and St. James, 1986.)

Some authors, however, suggest alternative explanations, not invoking the concept of attention. All these alternative explanations are in terms of 'response bias' or 'criterion shifts' (see, e.g., Duncan, 1980; Sperling, 1984; Shaw, 1984; and Müller and Findlay, 1987; see also section 3.2). The explanation simply states that subjects lower their criterion, i.e., require less evidence for responding, at a cued position, and/or raise their criterion, i.e., require more evidence, at the uncued positions. Of course, in terms of the analysis presented in Chapter 2, this criterion explanation basically suggests that there is a differential involvement of intention in the foreknowledge condition and in the no foreknowledge condition. Stronger intentions to react in the foreknowledge condition as compared with the no foreknowledge condition might be at the basis of the RT benefits, is the idea. So, before we can endorse and elaborate any explanation invoking the concept attention, this simple criterion shift explanation has to be critically evaluated.

Some experiments strongly suggest that it is extremely difficult to exclude one or another criterion shift explanation. The prime example is given by Posner et al. (1980). In their Experiment 4, these authors presented either a digit (4 or 7) or a letter (D or Q). Subjects were presented a single response key. They had to press the key whenever a digit was presented and to refrain from responding if a letter was presented. There were four alternative target positions. With neutral cue trials the target was equally likely to appear at any of the four positions. With cued trials, an arrow pointed to one of the four positions. This cue was valid in 79% of the trials.

> In this paradigm RTs to the expected position were very fast, but error rates were always much higher than in unexpected or neutral trials. Subjects found it very difficult to withhold responding when a nontarget occurred in the expected position. This result indicates that there is a strong tendency to react with a false alarm to a visual event occurring in an expected position. Subjectively, it felt as if one were all set to respond when an event occurred in the indicated position, and it was very frustrating to inhibit the response while waiting to determine if it was a digit (target). When an event occurred in an unexpected [?] position, it felt as though the answer was already present by the time one was ready to make the response. These subjective impressions fit very well with the idea that the attentional system is responsible for releasing the response rather than for the actual information relevant to the decision that a target was present.
>
> (Posner et al., 1980, p. 167; [?] mine)

This experiment, however, had one very peculiar feature. Subjects had to respond when a digit was presented and to refrain from responding when a letter was presented, i.e., the task used was a go–no-go task. So, the 'intention' to react was not fixed for all trials but was also experimentally manipulated. More specifically, on about 40% of the trials it was an item in the indicated position that required a response, while only on about 10% of the trials did an item in one of the three nonindicated positions require a reaction (i.e., on about 3% per position). So, there was a substantial correlation between position of the item (relative to the position indicated) and response required or not.

With regard to the 'premature and false reactions' observed in such a situation, Gibson (1941) had already remarked:

> It is significant that this happens almost exclusively when the subject has adopted a muscular attitude, which suggests that the effect is produced by strong intention rather than strong expectation ... it will frequently occur when an extraneous stimulus is substituted for the expected one, and there is evidence that the frequency of this occurrence is proportional to the similarity of the substituted to the expected stimulus.
>
> (Gibson, 1941, p. 785)

When, in a subsequent experiment, Posner et al. (1980) fixed the intention to react by requiring a response on all trials and thereby removed the correlation, the high number of anticipation errors indeed disappeared. (Moreover, there were clear benefits when the stimulus occurred in the expected position and costs when it occurred in the unexpected position in comparison with the neutral condition; to this finding we return further on.)

In the experiments described in sections 4.2 and 4.3 a response was required on each trial, so there is no reason to suppose that differential intentions were involved in the foreknowledge and in the no foreknowledge condition. There are, however, more reasons to reject a criterion shift explanation. We mention three of these reasons.

Firstly, Eriksen and Hoffman (1974), using symbolic cues, and Van der Heijden et al. (1988), using location cues, obtained reliable cueing effects in suprathreshold letter *recognition* tasks with RT as the dependent variable. As just stated, Posner et al. (1980) in their letter–digit task with 'intentions' fixed demonstrated clear benefits (and costs). If these results are due to criterion shifts that have the effect that less evidence is required for initiating a reaction in the foreknowledge of position condition, then an increase in errors has to accompany the decrease in RTs. No such effects were reported, however. Therefore these findings are incompatible with the view that a criterion shift, based on differential intentions, is responsible for the benefits.

Secondly, an explanation in terms of criterion shifts leaves a number of phenomena described in sections 4.2 and 4.3 unexplained. For instance, it is very difficult to see how such an explanation would deal with the distance effect reported by Shulman et al. (1986) and Van der Heijden et al. (1988). Because uncued locations had equal probabilities of target occurrence, the criterion shift explanation would have to assume that the amount of shift would not only depend on the probability of target occurrence (a reasonable assumption), but also on spatial distance of the target from the cued location (an ad hoc assumption). See also Hawkins et al. (1988, p. 489) for this argument. Other evidence that poses serious difficulties for the criterion shift explanation consists of the difference in development of benefits for location cues (constant with SOA) and for symbolic cues (growing with SOA). Posner et al. (1980, p. 172) and Posner (1980, p. 21) have also listed a number of further empirical findings that are not consistent with the criterion shift explanation. The reader is referred to Posner's papers for further details.

Thirdly, reliable effects of cueing are also obtained with *non-informative* location cues. (See, e.g., Possamai, 1986; Van der Heijden et al., 1988. Posner and Cohen, 1984, reported even positive effects with a negative cue validity.) But if a cue conveys no information about the location of the impending target, then there is no reason to assume that subjects lower their criterion for that position (and/or raise it for the alternative positions). Just for this reason 'one can more confidently assume that an attentional mechanism is brought into play by a non-informative cue than by an informative one' (Possamai, 1986, p. 247).

Taking all together, it seems that an alternative explanation in terms of criterion shifts has to be rejected. As far as we know, explanations in terms of differential 'expectations' have never been considered and it is indeed very difficult to see how such explanations can account for the data (see also section 3.2). So, it seems that an explanation in attentional terms has to be preferred. This is not to say that in the experiments described intentions and expectations do not play a role. These factors codetermine the RTs obtained. The important point is that in properly designed experiments these factors do not differentially affect the RTs observed in the different experimental conditions. Then any differences found between conditions can properly be ascribed to the operation of attention (or to 'expectation restricted to position', but let us call that 'attention').

In the next two sections we describe how attention operates in the type of task under discussion. Because the location cue experiments produced the simplest pattern of results we discuss these data first. Section 4.6 is concerned with attention's involvement in the symbolic cue experiments.

4.5 Location cues and 'spotlight'

With informative and non-informative location cues (see, e.g., Possamai, 1986; Van der Heijden et al., 1988) and even with very low validity location cues (see, e.g., Posner and Cohen, 1984), and with short SOAs, targets in or close to the cue's position are responded to faster than targets appearing further away. So, location cues facilitate in one way or another responding to targets occurring in their neighbourhood, the amount of facilitation decreasing with increasing cue–target distance. This effect is already apparent at very short SOAs (see, e.g., Posner and Cohen, 1984; Possamai, 1986; Van der Heijden et al., 1988) and is constant over an initial range of SOAs. The problem is how to explain these results.

Just as in the dot-cueing experiments discussed in Chapter 3, the appearance of a location cue in a visual field in which nothing else happens is an abrupt, temporally and spatially sharply localized, incongruity, a sudden change, or something new. However, contrary to the situation discussed in Chapter 3, in the suprathreshold experiments we are now dealing with, the target is also a sharply defined temporal and spatial incongruity, a sudden change, or something new. So, the situation we are now confronted with is one consisting of two abrupt events in close temporal and spatial contiguity. And the problem to be solved is: How can a first sudden event be of any help in responding to a clearly visible second sudden visual event appearing close in time and space?

In line with Cornsweet's (1970) assumption that the attention mechanism can be conceived as a high level feature detector, the feature being 'change' (Cornsweet, 1970, p. 433), it is possible to try an explanation involving only changes or onsets, and no extra attentional mechanism. For instance, it is possible to postulate that a second change at a certain spatial position is more easily detected than a first one. However, such a hypothesis is quite unintelligible and unattractive as an explanation because it does not explain *why* that should be the case. There is, for instance, nothing in the properties of the transient channels as such that leads to the prediction that the presence of a first change adds something to the detection of a second one (see section 3.7). So, it is far from clear why benefits should arise. Moreover, also a 'distance effect' is not one of the properties of the transient channels transmitting this information to higher centres (see section 3.7). So, it is also far from clear why a nearby second change should be faster detected than a second change somewhat further on.

It therefore seems that change detection as such is not sufficient to explain the relevant phenomena. As in Chapter 3, and in line with Breitmeyer and Ganz's (1976) hypothesis, we have to assume that an abrupt change does something extra: it attracts attention to its position in space. At least two pieces of experimental evidence obtained in single-item tasks with RT as the dependent variable provide positive support for this supposition.

First, Posner and Cohen (1984) and Maylor (1983, in Maylor, 1985) used, besides single-cue trials, also double-cue trials in which a location cue appeared at the left side and at the right side of fixation simultaneously. The two simultaneous cues were followed by a single target at one side of the fixation point. Both Posner and Cohen and Maylor found that benefits were approximately halved by this double cueing as compared with single cueing. This strongly suggests that it is not the prior changes as such that determine task performance; just because of double cueing there were always prior changes close to the target position. So, change is not sufficient. Something extra must be involved. The findings are at least consistent with Posner and Cohen's (1984) suggestion that additionally attention is involved and that reduced benefits are observed because 'attention cannot be split to the two sides when both are cued' (Posner and Cohen, 1984, p. 539). Given this assumption the results are easily understood. With double-cue trials attention is attracted by only one of the two cues. Because the target appears at that position in only 50% of the cases, benefits brought by attention are halved as compared with the single-cue condition.

Second, Yantis and Jonides (1984, Exp. 2) compared RTs to abrupt-onset items and gradual no-onset items in a single-item paradigm. For no-onset items, irrelevant segments of a figure that camouflaged the item faded, thereby gradually revealing the target item. For onset items an irrelevant figure faded and then a new display item was abruptly illuminated at that display position. Other work had shown that performance with onset items was superior to performance with no-onset items (Yantis and Jonides, 1984, exp. I; Todd and Van Gelder, 1979). This finding is, of course, consistent with the view that abrupt-onset items automatically attract attention to their position and gradual no-onset items do not. The important point in the present study was that subjects knew where the item to be reacted to was going to appear and that they were instructed to 'pay attention' to that spatial position. In this way, the differential attention-capturing power of onset items and no-onset items was neutralized. Both types of items could now equally profit from attention. The results indeed indicated that when attention is appropriately directed in advance, there is no advantage for abrupt onsets over gradual no-onsets. This result strongly suggests that the positive effects of abrupt onsets are not brought about by changes as such but by attracting attention to their position. Attending to the relevant position in space adequately compensates for the adverse effects of the absence of the abrupt onsets; changes as such are not necessary.

What the location-cue experiments seem to show, then, is that a second sudden visual event or change (i.e., the target) in close temporal and spatial contiguity with a first visual event (i.e., the cue) benefits from the fact that attention was caught by properties of that first event, in the sense that it can be responded to faster. The fact that, over a range of SOAs, an aftercoming stimulus benefits from location cue presentation, indicates that this cue-induced attending is not sharply localized in time (remember, the event attracting attention is). The fact that not only targets in the cued position, but, albeit to a lesser extent, also more distant targets benefit, indicates that attention is not sharply localized in space (remember, the event attracting attention is). It seems that not an object, but an approximate region in visual space is attended, with the efficiency of attention decreasing with increasing distance from the cue position. (See also La Berge, 1983; La Berge and Brown, 1986; Downing and Pinker, 1985, for demonstrations that, with attention directed to a restricted spatial position, reaction times to objects at other positions increase with their distance from the focus.) Indeed, all this strongly suggests the workings of a kind of 'spotlight' with a focus and a penumbra, and possibly with a task dependent diameter and shape (La Berge, 1983; see, e.g., Yantis, 1988, for a number of different shapes). Benefits and distance effect are produced because, in a sense, there is an attentional 'overflow' from cue to target, both in space and in time. Furthermore, the development of this overflow seems to be automatic, fast, and independent from the information conveyed by the location cue, if any.

However, as already stated, the target appearance is also a localized temporal and spatial incongruity or an abrupt change. So, the target is also capable of recruiting, and will possibly recruit, attention at its position. But then a remaining problem is: How can the cue-induced recruitment of attention to the position of the (impending) target be of any help in responding to a target that itself is perfectly capable of attracting attention to its position?

A reasonable answer can be found starting from the assumption that a visual event with an abrupt onset recruits attention to its position nearly immediately, but not immediately. This is a reasonable assumption, especially because the idea is that not a change as such, but attention captured or attracted by that change, is at the basis of the benefits, and attracting or capturing something takes at least some time. So, let us suppose that attention only 'arrives', i.e., becomes effective, at the position of a sudden event x ms after the onset of that event. Then such a stimulus event presented in isolation and of duration T is unattended during the first x ms and attended during the remaining $T - x$ ms. Now consider two of these events in sequence and close to each other in space. If the first event (the location cue) precedes the second event (the target) by an interval (SOA) larger than x ms, the position will already be attended to upon arrival of the second event. The second event will then be attended to during its whole time course, T. The extra attention received during the interval of time x explains the benefits observed. Moreover, because no more can be gained than this extra attention during the interval of x ms, benefits will be constant for SOAs larger than x ms. This interpretation of what happens is consistent with the data presented in section 4.3. Moreover the data presented there strongly suggest that the interval x, i.e., the time needed for a location cue to attract attention at its position, is smaller than (or equals) 33 ms. (With SOAs smaller than x ms either less or no benefits are predicted on the present view.)

An attentional 'overflow' in space and time, resulting from 'location cues', is clearly adaptive. This becomes apparent if we look at real life situations instead of at the artificial event–event situations used in the laboratory. Often an attention-catching property, for instance the movement of the head of an animal, is not the only property that has to be attended to. It is the whole animal that just moved its head that has to be attended and possibly responded to (and often very fast). Attending to the head only when it moves is not of very much use.

4.6 Symbolic cues and 'movement'

With symbolic cues and a rule for how to interpret the cue, targets indicated by the cue are responded to faster than non-indicated targets. So, symbolic cues facilitate responding to targets in the position they signify. At short SOAs this effect is not yet apparent (see, e.g., Eriksen and Hoffman's, 1974, data in table 4.2.2). The effect grows with increasing SOAs (see section 4.2).

Of course, the appearance of a symbolic cue in an empty visual field is also a localized temporal and spatial incongruity, an abrupt change, or something new. It is reasonable to assume that, because nothing else happens in the visual field, attention is automatically and nearly immediately recruited by, and at the position of, this abrupt change. Now, however, this change does not occur in close spatial contiguity with the second relevant visual event or change, the target. Therefore, no immediate spatial 'overflow' is to be expected. So, why benefits and why increasing benefits with increasing SOAs?

Two possibilities can easily be excluded. The first is that the cue has no effect at all and that the target, because it is also a clear temporal and spatial incongruity, simply attracts attention itself. Given this view, neither benefits (nor costs) nor SOA effects can be explained. A second possible view states that a cue has only an adverse effect with the smaller SOAs, because the capture of attention by the target is temporally prevented by a voluntary, active or 'controlled' interrogation of the cue. (Von Helmholtz in section 2.1 can be interpreted as providing this suggestion: Only 'so soon as nothing new is to be noticed [at the position of the symbolic cue], [attention] passes, in spite of our will, to something else'.) While this view can possibly explain part of the SOA effect, benefits remain completely unexplained. So, neither 'no effect of symbolic cues', nor 'adverse effects of symbolic cues' can cope with the pattern of results. One or another explanation in terms of 'positive effects of symbolic cues' is needed.

To understand the results obtained with symbolic cues, the standard explanation, presented at the beginning of section 4.4, seems to offer the best starting point. One ingredient of this 'spotlight of attention' metaphor, we already needed in the last section to explain the location cue results: There is something like a 'spotlight of attention' that is limited in size. Objects falling under that spotlight are responded to more rapidly than other objects. For the symbolic cue experiments now under discussion the second ingredient of this metaphor is of crucial importance: the assumption that by one or another, cue informed, voluntary intention the position of this spotlight can be 'moved' or 'transferred' in visual space.

Given this metaphor, the explanation runs as follows. For benefits to be observed, the message, conveyed by the symbolic cue, has to be derived and used in one or another way (the rule has to be applied). A logical analysis, given the metaphor, suggests that after cue interpretation, attention has to be disengaged from the cue position where it was 'trapped', has to 'move' to the expected position and has to engage at that position (Posner, Walker, Friedrich and Rafal, 1984). If it takes some time to interpret the cue (a reasonable assumption) and to disengage and move attention to the position of the (impending) target, no benefits are to be expected with short SOAs. The target itself, also a clear and abrupt isolated event, can then attract attention to its position before these preparatory processes are finished. If, with longer SOAs, attention can indeed move to the position of the impending target and arrive there before target appearance, or before the target itself attracts attention, benefits are to be expected just as with location cues. (It is again essential to assume that the target does not immediately, but only nearly immediately, attract attention; see, however, section 4.5 where we already introduced this assumption – the interval of duration x – to account for the benefits observed with location cues.) Due to variations in 'interpretation' times, 'disengaging' times and 'moving' times, increasing benefits for a range of intermediate SOAs are to be expected. The assumption that the 'movement' is controlled by a 'voluntary kind of intention' is an appropriate starting point for explaining the 'validity' and 'strategy' effects described in section 4.2.

At present, within this conceptualization, the most heavily debated research problem concerns the dynamics of the 'movement' of attention, i.e., the problem of how the spotlight of attention changes from one position to another. The problem investigated is whether attention moves continuously, passing through positions between cue and (expected) target position, or whether attention jumps discretely from one position to another position. Both assumptions, the assumption of a time-consuming movement (see, e.g., Posner et al., 1980; Posner, 1980) and the assumption of an instantaneous jump consisting of a 'fading' at one position together with the simultaneous arising or slow development or buildup of attention at another position – something like the time-consuming opening of a gate (see, e.g., Sperling and Reeves, 1980; Reeves and Sperling, 1980) – provide adequate starting points for the explanation of the temporal aspects of the data (see La Berge and Brown, 1986, for a description of various types of shifts and movements).

There are three, often cited, single-item studies with RT as the dependent variable that were concerned with this issue. Unfortunately the conclusions the investigators reached on the basis of their research do not agree. Shulman, Remington and McClean (1979) concluded that attention moves in an analogue, continuous manner through visual space. Also, according to Tsal (1983) the attentional focus travels continuously through visual space. In his view the velocity is independent of the distance to be traversed: approximately 1 deg per 8 ms. According to Remington and Pierce (1984), however, the shift of the focus of attention is either discrete, or, continuous with a velocity proportional to the distance to be travelled.

It is not necessary to describe this research in detail. Recent critical evaluations have made clear that all three studies suffered from serious flaws (see, e.g., Eriksen and Murphy, 1987; Yantis, 1988; Van der Heijden et al., 1988). Two important problems the three studies have in common are

– the absence of a neutral condition (Shulman et al., 1979; Tsal, 1983; Remington and Pierce, 1984, Exp. 1) or the neglect of the neutral condition in a critical comparison (Remington and Pierce, 1984, Exp. 2). As a result, a precue's general warning or alerting effect could not or was not controlled or partialled out (see section 4.1 for the importance of this factor);
– the involvement of targets at different retinal eccentricities in the critical comparisons (Shulman et al., 1979, 8 and 18 deg; Tsal, 1983, 4, 8, and 12 deg; Remington and Pierce, 1984, 2 and 8 deg). As a result, distance to be travelled and retinal eccentricity are completely confounded. (It is possible to vary distance while keeping eccentricity fixed by positioning the targets and the cue on the circumference of an imaginary circle around the fixation point.) So, the effect of absolute retinal position and the interaction effects of absolute position with other factors were not controlled or partialled out (see section 2.8 for the importance of this effect).

As stated, Eriksen and Murphy (1987) critically evaluated the 'movement' literature and pointed to several serious weaknesses. They conclude:

How attention shifts from one locus to another in the visual field is still an open question. Not only is the experimental evidence conflicting, but the experiments are based on a string of tenuous assumptions that render interpretations of the data quite problematic. This reflects not so much on the design of the experiments as on the uncertain state of our knowledge of the phenomena of attention.

(Eriksen and Murphy, 1987, p. 305)

The fact that even these authors themselves do not distinguish between results obtained with location cues (Tsal, 1983) and symbolic cues (Shulman et al., 1979; Remington and Pierce, 1984) convincingly supports their point of view. (See also Yantis, 1988, for the same problem.)

4.7 The function of attention

Some two thousand years ago a lamp or a light was seen as a useful metaphor for describing the function of the eyes:

> The light of the body is the eye: if therefore thine eye be single, thy whole body shall be full of light. But if thine eye be evil, thy whole body shall be full of darkness. If therefore the light that is in thee be darkness, how great is that darkness!

Or, in a more modern translation:

> The lamp of the body is the eye. If your eyes are sound, you will have light for your whole body; if the eyes are bad, your whole body will be in darkness. If the only light you have is darkness, the darkness is doubly dark.
>
> (The Sermon on the Mount; Matthew, 6, 22–3)

Of course, this metaphor makes at least some sense. At first sight there are some striking similarities between the function and way of operation of a light and the function and way of operation of the eyes. Just like the light of the lamp the eyes are essential for seeing. Just like the light of a lamp the eyes are limited in the size of the region of the visual world that can be effectively dealt with. And just as the light of a lamp can be directed to parts of the world of interest so can the eyes be directed to important regions in the visual world.

But we now well know that eyes are not really lights or lamps. There are no eye-emitted rays. (While Aristotle had already rejected the theory of eye-emitted rays, this idea nevertheless reigned until the nineteenth century. Bidloo (1649–1713), a Dutch professor at the University of Leyden, rejected the theory on the basis of the cat-test. 'He locked himself in a completely dark room together with a cat and after some time appeared with the news that he had not seen one single ray.' Van Hoorn, 1972, p. 105.) Light enters the eyes from the outside world. Lamps emit light, eyes absorb light.

Nowadays, within the information processing approach, exactly the same light-of-a-lamp analogy is used, now, however, not to illuminate the working of the eyes, but to characterize the operation of central attention in vision. The attentional mechanism is likened to a spotlight that can move in visual space or to the beam of a searchlight, with the option of altering the focus. (There is also the, closely related, 'zoomlens with variable power setting'; see, e.g., Eriksen and Rohrbaugh, 1970; Eriksen and Yeh, 1985; Eriksen and St. James, 1986.) I introduced this view in section 4.4 and used it in section 4.5: Location cues and 'spotlight'. The question we now have to address is: What is the function of this spotlight?

It is generally accepted that there are three important components in the attention-as-a-light analogy. First just as a light is needed for seeing, so attention is needed for the processing, i.e., the detection and identification, of information. Second, just as a spotlight or searchlight can only illuminate a limited region of the world, so also attention can deal only with a limited region of the visual world. And third, just as a spotlight or a searchlight can be pointed at important and interesting regions in the world, so can one or another mechanism – the attentional mechanism – concentrate its 'resources' at the spatial position (or internal representation of the spatial position) containing the information to be processed (see, e.g., Kahneman, 1973; Shaw, 1978; Jonides, 1980; 1983; Eriksen and Yeh, 1985; Eriksen and St. James, 1986; Murphy and Eriksen, 1987).

The shift in what the lamp-metaphor stands for strongly suggests that there is progress in science and that a definite choice has been made: The cat-tests have convincingly proved that the lamp is no longer adequate as a metaphor for the working of the eyes, and the information processing approach has convincingly shown that it is appropriate for characterizing the operation of central attention in vision. As a matter of fact, however, this choice has not been made in current information processing research. It is generally suggested that the eye and attention perform exactly the same function. The eye, but also attention, allow us to see (i.e., process, identify and recognize information, in information processing terms). Attention is like an 'internal eyeball' (Skelton and Eriksen, 1976) or, attention is the 'mind's eye' (Jonides, 1980; 1981; 1983). Both attention and the eyes are like lamps. We quote Jonides (1983) to illustrate this conviction.

> When one wishes to concentrate on a particular spot in the visual field, one should shift fixation so that the spot's image falls on the most sensitive area of the retina, the fovea. The reason for this is quite clear: non-foveal portions of the retina are not nearly as sensitive in processing visual images as is the fovea itself. Consequently, when careful analysis of a visual stimulus is warranted, foveal input is engaged. In a sense [?], one could claim that the visual resolving power of the retina is limited, and foveation is the mechanism that permits one to overcome this limitation on a local basis.
>
> Apparently, a mechanism like foveation exists at a different level of the visual system as well. A number of experiments have established that subjects can shift their internal allocation of processing resources from one location in the visual field to another without shifting gaze .... The function of movements of the mind's eye seems as clear as that for movements of the body's eye: The processing capacity of the visual system is limited, and concentrating resources on a particular spatial locus is just another way of overcoming this limit on a local basis. It is not clear, of course, why two mechanisms have developed to overcome this limitation, a central and a peripheral one.
>
> (Jonides, 1983, p. 247; [?] mine)

And indeed, that is very far from clear.

There are, of course, attempts to specify why different 'attentional' mechanisms have developed to solve the same, or closely related, problems.

> There are three kinds of "directing": One that involves the whole body – e.g., a predator selects a prey animal out of a flock by running in its direction – ; one that involves parts of the body or receptor organs (e.g., head or eye

movements, or turning the ears); and finally there is covert orienting by merely directing attention towards the selected object. I propose that these three kinds of directing are related .... They complement each other (for example, one or the other may be the most efficient, depending on the "grain size" of the selection problem) ....

(Neumann, 1987, p. 385)

But are we really to believe that we select a deer by running, a rabbit by appropriate eye movements and a fly by covert changes of attention, i.e., that it is 'grain size' that determines which mechanism is called upon?

In my view it is exactly the duplication of the same 'processing' or 'directing' or 'whatever else' function that makes nearly all current attentional theories very unattractive. And this becomes more so, the more the properties of the attentional mechanism mimic the properties of the external eye, e.g., its inhomogeneous acuity and its movements (see section 2.8).

It is very difficult to see, for instance, what attention adds to the functioning of the external eye if

the attentional field might be conceived as varying in the level of information processing or extraction that occurs. In the focus of the attentional field, stimuli are processed to a high level with considerable extraction of detail. Subtended into the visual field, this area of high-level information extraction may be no more than a degree of visual angle. Surrounding this high-level processing area there may be an area where only gross information is extracted.

(Eriksen and Hoffman, 1972b, p. 204, also quoted in Eriksen and St. James, 1986)

Eriksen and Hoffman (1972b) point to the close correspondence between James's and their own characterization of attention and the characteristics of the eye. But remember, James regarded the eye and its movements as an attentional mechanism (see section 2.2).

When, moreover, also movements of attention are postulated that resemble in nearly all respects the overt saccadic eye movements (see, e.g., Jonides, 1980; Remington and Pierce, 1984; see also section 4.6) it becomes completely dark why, after all, we still need eyes (or, alternatively, why something like central attention ever evolved).

In my view, the 'spotlight' metaphor has much to recommend it. It is, however, too much an 'external eye' metaphor, as far as its account of the *function* of attention in visual information processing is concerned, to be taken really seriously as a metaphor for visual central attention. It is the duplication of function, inherent in nearly all contemporary theories of visual attention, that strongly invites us to look for an alternative function for the spotlight of attention. Furthermore, the empirical data do not really support this interpretation of the 'spotlight' metaphor. The experiments discussed in this chapter, just as the experiments discussed in Chapter 3, provide no reason to assume that attention is involved in the processing, i.e., identification or categorization, of the information.

One observation, described earlier in this chapter, has to be emphasized in this context. That observation is that, neither with location cues nor with symbolic cues, is there any indication of stronger attentional effects in recognition tasks than in detection tasks (the reader is invited to compare the data in tables 4.2.1 and 4.2.2, and in tables 4.3.1 and 4.3.2!). For correct performance in recognition tasks, detailed information is needed. For suprathreshold detection tasks, however, no detail at all is needed. Global or very gross information, possibly even only information about the onset of the event, suffices for task performance. So, if attention has to do with the detail of information processing, as Jonides (1983), Eriksen and Hoffman (1972b) and Eriksen and St. James (1986) and many others suggest, benefits observed in recognition tasks can possibly be accounted for. The fact that benefits are also observed with the detection tasks and the fact that these benefits are of the same order of magnitude as in the recognition tasks, remain, however, completely unexplained.

So, it seems better to search for another function of the spotlight of attention, one that has nothing to do with information processing and with the detail of information processing. The question then is: What can really be said about the function of attention on the basis of the experiments presented in this chapter? The answer is simple. What the experiments showed is that responding is *faster* with attention than without. So, a real possibility is that the prime function of attending, as apparent in the type of tasks discussed in this chapter, is in the *time* domain. To get rid of the unwanted duplication of function we can, consistent with the data presented in this chapter, grant the eye and its movements the task of providing the needed grain size in space and assign the spotlight of attention and its 'movements' the job of providing the required grain size in time (faster responding then simply falls out as a byproduct of attention's main job: providing order in time).

A related conclusion was already reached by Posner (1980).

Although orientation to the periphery allows [the?] detection [response?] to occur more quickly, it does not provide an increase in the retinal grain and thus does not produce strong [?] acuity changes. Attention represents a system for routing information and for control of priorities. It does not provide a substitute for the sensory specific wiring intrinsic to the visual system.
(Posner, 1980, p. 9; see also Posner et al., 1980, p. 167; all [?] mine)

Let us have a further look at the eye and its movements and attention and its 'movements', to assess the viability of this position.

4.8 Attention and eye movements

It is often assumed that the position of eye fixation is related to the direction of attention. Not only in everyday life is what somebody is attending to, inferred from where a person is looking at. The assumption also underlies research using eye movement registration techniques to investigate cognitive processes. (See, e.g., Kahneman, 1973; Rayner, 1977.) In line with this assumption some investigators assume that attention is always locked to fixation; they regard the movements of the eye as the movements of attention (see, e.g., James, 1890/1950; Haber, 1983). We have seen, however, that there is abundant evidence that the direction of attention and the position the eye is pointing at need not necessarily coincide. Moreover, there is at least some evidence that the direction of attention can – continuously or abruptly – change during an eye fixation (see section 4.6). So, to perform its functions, the visual system seems to have at its disposal (at least) two kinds of 'directing' or two means for 'selecting' parts of the visual world. The eyes can be directed by means of overt changes in eye position (see section 2.8) and central attention can be directed by means of – still secret – covert movements of attention (see section 4.6).

It is worthwhile investigating what exactly the relation between covert attentional orienting and overt changes in eye-position by means of (saccadic) eye movements is. It is reasonable to assume that the two ways of directing complement each other in one way or another (Neumann, 1987, p. 385). The study of the relation between the two ways of spatial sampling can reveal *how* they exactly complement each other, and thereby provide important insights in the function of both kinds of directing. In this section we briefly comment upon some of the research concerned with this issue in the context of suprathreshold single-item detection tasks with RT as the dependent variable.

In the literature, discussion of this issue is generally started without any clearcut hypothesis (see, e.g., Posner, 1980; Posner and Cohen, 1984; Shepherd et al., 1986). The logical possibilities for the relationship between covert attentional orienting and overt eye movements are listed and the literature and experimental evidence is evaluated to see what logically possible relation is best in accord with the data. The reason for this state of affairs might be that it is tentatively assumed that both kinds of directing serve essentially the same function: providing spatial grain. Then they complement each other only in the sense that either overt orienting or covert orienting performs the job; 'for example, one or the other may be the most efficient, depending on the "grain size" of the selection problem' (Neumann, 1987, p. 385). The question 'which one performs the job?' is then simply an empirical question. One has to wait and see. A real relation or interaction is then not expected and no sensible hypothesis can be formulated.

For Posner (1980) the logically possible relationships run from 'complete dependence' (common system) via 'efference theory' and 'functional relation' to 'complete independence' (no relation). Shepherd et al. (1986) distinguish the same possible relationships: 'identical', 'interdependence' (i.e., a common resource) and 'completely independent'. After evaluating the evidence, Posner (1980) concludes to a functional relationship. Shepherd et al. (1986) conclude to an asymmetric reciprocal relationship. These conclusions are based on two pieces of evidence:

1. the evidence that it is possible to shift the focus of attention without moving the eyes, i.e., the benefits found in the absence of eye movements (see the research discussed in this and the previous chapter);
2. the evidence that attention seems to 'move' to the target position prior to a saccadic eye movement to that position, i.e., the evidence for a presaccadic attention shift (see, e.g., Wolff, 1987; Posner, 1980; Shepherd et al., 1986).

It is, however, not too difficult to make sense of, and even to predict, this pattern of results. The starting assumption then is not that the eye as a spotlight and attention as a spotlight complement each other in the sense that now the one, then the other, performs the job. The starting assumption is that the eye and its movements and attention and its 'movements' have different functions and that they complement each other in the sense that both overt orienting and covert orienting are involved in performing the job: that there is not redundancy or duplication but a real cooperation or collaboration. So, let us assign the eye and attention a different function with which they can adequately deal.

We know that the eye provides spatial grain or acuity (see section 2.8). There is no reason to assume that the eye or 'the retina' can determine temporal priorities. The prime function of the eye is in providing or increasing the spatial grain. Eye movements are involved in ordering and structuring information in space, by enlarging the foveal angle over time. So, let us assume that the eye is for spatial resolution over time. We saw that attention was capable of speeding up responding (see section 4.8). There is no reason to assume that attention can increase retinal grain or visual acuity. The prime function of attention is something like providing or increasing the temporal grain. Movements of attention seem to be involved in ordering and structuring information in time by assigning temporal priorities in space. So, let us assume that attention is for temporal resolution over space.

If this interpretation is indeed correct, then it entails that it is covert attention, in cooperation with higher order processes, that determines whether, and if so where, the eye has to move. In this view, a (saccadic) eye movement is just another response that can be given temporal priority by attention. If attention can perform its temporal ordering function in agreement with the quality requirements of the total information processing system, no overt eye movement is called for. If processes, responsible for the performance of one or another type of task, complain about the quality or spatial grain of the visual information they are supposed to work upon ('cannot read it') an eye movement is called for. In a way, the eye is the spotlight, in the service of attention (remember the Sermon on the Mount). Over time, attention directs its spotlight to positions needing increased spatial grain.

From this interpretation it follows that:

1. Covert attentional movements are not always followed by overt (saccadic) eye movements (it is possible to 'look out of the corner of the eyes' without

making an overt eye movement). If there is sufficient spatial grain no overt eye movement is called for.

2. Overt (saccadic) eye movements to a position in space follow always a covert attentional movement to that position in space (the 'post attentional eye shift'; see, e.g., Bryden, 1961, for a spectacular example). If there is insufficient spatial grain an overt eye movement is called for.

But these two conclusions simply rephrase the empirical evidence Posner's (1980) conclusion (functional relationship) and Shepherd et al.'s (1986) conclusion (asymmetric reciprocal relationship) are based upon. It is worthwhile noticing that these conclusions follow because of the basic assumption we used: Attention has its own, unique, function; it structures information in time. Attention has no job in the *processing* of the information.

Within this view, and consistent with the data and analysis presented in Chapter 3, the effect of attending can then be regarded as creating a 'path of least resistance' capable of connecting the position given temporal priority with input information and input information with the response mechanism in use for performing the task. The effect of foreknowledge of position described in the present chapter can then be regarded as a kind of advance internal preparation consisting of the selection of a particular position whose impending content is allowed priority in the control of the response. It is important to note that in this view it is again position and only position that is at the basis of the cueing effects. And position information is the only information a pre-cue has to offer.

Of course, the view here proposed would gain considerably in strength if it could be shown that just after a saccadic eye movement, attention is at the fovea, i.e., that during and shortly after the movement attention has stayed at the same position in an environmental (or spatiotopic) coordinate system. Unfortunately there is no unambiguous experimental evidence. However, after demonstrating that in a (very) artificial situation this need not be the case, Posner and Cohen (1984) conclude that 'under the more usual conditions of natural vision, attention moves in advance of the eyes but returns to the fovea as the eye moves' (Posner and Cohen, 1984, p. 550). At the end of the next section we briefly return to this issue.

4.9 Inhibition

In 1961, B. Babington-Smith reported 'An unexpected effect of attention in peripheral vision'.

Arrange a number of small objects such as keys, coins, etc., on a table and fixate a point among them from some convenient distance, say 3 ft. Maintaining fixation of the point selected, attend to one of the objects and try to see or describe it in detail ... the object selected for attention becomes hazy and may even disappear. The effect may persist for seconds at a time or it may be fleeting or fluctuating; but other objects in the field remain steadily visible meantime. It is well known that the whole visual field may disappear when it is 'stabilized', and some people report that this occurs with steady fixation. The blurring or disappearance of small regions selected for deliberate attention is, however, a different matter and suggests some form of central interference.

(Babington-Smith, 1961, p. 776)

Several recent studies have reported a related phenomenon, i.e., what is called, an inhibitory effect, in single-item experiments with latency as the dependent variable. Under certain conditions, RTs to targets at a cued position are larger than to targets at an uncued position (see, e.g., Posner and Cohen, 1984; Maylor, 1985; Maylor and Hockey, 1985; Posner, Cohen, Choate, Hockey and Maylor, 1984; Possamai, 1986; see also Klein, 1988, for a related study). Because the phenomenon has been brought under experimental control only very recently, much more research is required to really establish the conditions giving rise to this inhibitory effect. Here we briefly summarize and comment upon the, theoretically most important, results reported up to now.

Posner and Cohen (1984) were the first to report the phenomenon. They displayed three box outlines on a cathode ray tube, a central one and two peripheral ones. As a cue, one of the two peripheral boxes was brightened. A target appeared either in the centre box (on a proportion of 0.60 of the trials) or in one of the peripheral boxes (0.10 each; 0.20 of the trials were catch trials). The cue was noninformative with regard to the position of the target; it only gave temporal information. The SOA varied from 0 to 500 ms. As to be expected with location cues, a significant advantage for a target in the cued location, i.e., benefits, were found for the first 150 ms. For SOAs larger than 300 ms, however, this initial facilitation was replaced by a significant cost; RTs to targets at the cued side were larger than to targets at the uncued side. So the early advantage to the cued side was followed by a subsequent loss.

From subsequent experiments Posner and Cohen (1984) concluded that

- inhibition does not arise from attentional orienting but from the energy change present at the cued location (double cueing, i.e., cueing of both peripheral positions simultaneously, resulted in significant inhibition but not in significant facilitation; no inhibition was observed with central, symbolic, cues, i.e., when there was no energy change prior to the target at the cued position);
- inhibition after externally controlled overt orienting (i.e., orienting by means of an eye movement, controlled by location cues) is primarily mapped in environmental (or spatiotopic) coordinates, not in retinotopic coordinates (i.e., it is not linked to a part of the retina).

The second conclusion was subsequently extended by Maylor and Hockey (1985, exp. 3). They showed that also after externally controlled covert orienting (i.e., orienting by means of an internal movement of attention) inhibition is mapped in environmental coordinates. The first conclusion was, however, contested by Maylor (1985). She therefore tested a prediction, suggested by Posner et al. (1984), that inhibition should also be observed when there was a peripheral energy change prior to target presentation but attentional orienting to the target was prevented. No inhibition was observed, however, in a dual-task experiment that abolished attentional facilitation. (The secondary task was a saccadic eye movement in response to an unpredictable jump of a to-be-tracked, slowly moving, spot in the vicinity of the fixation point.) So, an energy change as such is not sufficient for inducing inhibition.

Maylor (1985) furthermore repeated the double cueing experiment and showed that double cueing produced not only less facilitation, as Posner and Cohen (1984) reported, but also less inhibition than a single cue. This finding is consistent with the view that each cue in the double cueing experiment will attract attention to its position on about 50% of the trials and that subsequently only the cued position that was also attended will show inhibition (see also section 4.5). Averaged over trials, facilitation and inhibition should then be about half of the effects found in a single-cue condition where the cue attracts attention on all trials. Maylor concludes 'that externally controlled orienting is a necessary condition to produce inhibition. However, not every event in the visual periphery results automatically in externally controlled covert orienting. Indeed, such orienting can be reduced or even prevented by additional information present in the visual field, or by the requirements of secondary tasks' (Maylor, 1985, p. 189).

For two reasons Maylor's (1985) 'orienting' hypothesis has to be favoured over Posner and Cohen's (1984) 'energy change' hypothesis.

– First are Maylor's experiments showing covariation of initial facilitation and subsequent inhibition; the rule seems to be: no inhibition without previous facilitation (see also Klein, 1988).
– Second is the generality of the inhibition phenomenon, showing that inhibition does not simply occur after stimulation, but only after one or another 'action' has been initiated. Inhibition is not only observed with manual reactions after overt or covert orienting. Inhibition is generally observed after a first (covert or overt) reaction if the second reaction is directed to the same position in space. A second overt manual reaction to a target is delayed (Maylor and Hockey, 1985, exp. I). A second saccadic eye movement to a target is delayed (Vaughan, 1984). A manual response after a saccadic eye movement is delayed (Posner and Cohen, 1984). A saccadic eye movement after covert orienting is delayed (Maylor, 1985, experiment 2). And, as elaborated in a previous section, it is exactly 'orienting', i.e., covert attention, that is concerned with the 'initiating' of such actions.

So, for the moment, it seems safest to assume that inhibition is a delayed consequence of attentional orienting, or, that attentional orienting to a position in space has two effects in the temporal domain: an initial facilitation for that position and inhibition later on.

Recent research revealed some further interesting properties of the inhibitory component of attentional orienting. First, it appeared that this inhibition is not only observed in the periphery, but also in the fovea (Maylor and Hockey, 1985, experiment 4; Possamai, 1986). Moreover, inhibition in the fovea is observed at substantially shorter SOAs than in the periphery (Possamai, 1986). This is congruent with the assumption that covert attention is initially at the fovea and only moves elsewhere later on as we suggested in section 4.8. Secondly, inhibition is not restricted to the originally stimulated location. Also nearby locations are affected, the effect decreasing with increasing distance from the stimulated location (Maylor and Hockey, 1985, experiment 2). So it seems that, as far as spatial properties are concerned, inhibition mirrors the 'spotlight' of facilitation (see section 4.3). This observation strongly supports the view that inhibition is really some kind of aftereffect of attentional facilitation. Thirdly, it seems that inhibition not only occurs after attention is summoned away from the cued location as Posner and Cohen (1984) suggested. Consistent with Babington-Smith's (1961) observations, it appears that, even if there is no incentive at all to move attention away, facilitation is followed by inhibition (Possamai, 1986). Moreover, also when cue and target both appear at the fovea, inhibition is observed (Maylor and Hockey, 1985; Possamai, 1986).

All results together make it unlikely 'that the inhibition builds up over the same time interval as facilitation but is simply masked by the larger facilitation resulting from covert attention' (Posner and Cohen, 1984, p. 549). It rather seems that inhibition follows facilitation after some interval of time, independent of whether attention stays or is summoned away. 'Thus the two components ... appear to combine to produce a spatial [?] mechanism that responds efficiently to novelty in the visual environment' (Maylor and Hockey, 1985, p. 786; [?] mine) and that avoids spatial positions already responded to.

If all this is correct, i.e., if inhibition *follows* facilitation in time as a kind of aftereffect, and if it is true that inhibition is mapped in environmental (spatio-topic) coordinates, than it follows that facilitation is also mapped in environmental (spatiotopic) coordinates. And that is in essence what we suggested in section 4.8. (The issue whether, and, if so, why inhibition is only observed with location cues and not with symbolic cues, needs further investigation.)

Moreover, if all this is correct, attention seems to have two opposite effects in time, just as a fixation of the eye has two opposite effects with regard to space. An eye fixation entails that a part of the visual world is projected on the high acuity region of the fovea, while the rest of the visual world is projected on a region of lesser acuity (see section 2.8). Attention entails that a part of the visual world is given the highest temporal priority initially, while that region is assigned a lower, or even negative, priority later on (see also section 4.8).

4.10 The Stroop effect

Also some versions of the Stroop (1935) test are really single-item recognition tasks with RT as the dependent variable. (We already introduced this task in section 2.7.; see Dyer, 1973a, for an extensive review of the early research with this task.) The usual procedure with this task as a test is to present Ss with cards containing (a) a series, e.g., 10 rows of 10 colour patches, (b) a series of (100) colour words, and (c) a series of (100) colour words written in non-corresponding colours. The first card is used for colour-naming, the second card for word-reading and the third card can be used for colour-naming and for word-reading. For each card and task the total time for naming all colours or reading all words is measured. The important finding is that if the colours on the third card have to be named, performance is far inferior to performance on the first card; a great delay in colour-naming is found and often also a large number of errors is observed. The delayed colour naming with the combination card is generally called the Stroop phenomenon or Stroop effect. Interestingly, if the words on this card have to be read, virtually no differences with word-reading on the second card are found, i.e., it is very difficult to demonstrate a 'reversed' Stroop effect.

In the context of this chapter, one modification of this task is of particular importance. This modification was introduced by Dalrymple-Alford and Budayr (1966). Instead of using the lists of items, they measured single response latencies for tachistoscopically presented single Stroop stimuli and single colour patches. The same effects as with cards one and three of the original task were observed: a large delay in colour naming with the incongruent combinations. Sichel and Chandler (1969) and Hintzman et al. (1972) used the same procedure, but besides the incongruent combinations (the word naming a different colour) and neutral stimuli (a colour patch), also congruent combinations (word and colour name the same) were used. Hintzman et al. found that the latencies for the congruent combinations were somewhat smaller than for the neutral stimuli. (Unfortunately, RTs with congruent combinations are difficult to interpret. If subjects erroneously report the word, instead of the colour, the error goes unnoticed.) This first modification was of importance because a very complex, multiple response, task was reduced to a much more tractable, simple single-trial task. (See section 2.10.)

Most explanations for the Stroop phenomenon presented in the past started from the basic assumption that all dimensions of a single item, i.e., its colour, size, shape, etc., are processed in parallel. So, more responses become available, resulting in severe 'response competition' (see, e.g., Treisman, 1969; Kahneman, 1973; Morton, 1969; see, however, Broadbent, 1971, p. 176, for an alternative view). Dyer (1973a) summarizes these views by stating:

> Perhaps the best present explanation for response competition includes both Treisman's (1969) claim of an inability to focus on either the color or word analyzers and Morton's (1969) assumption of a single response channel.
>
> (Dyer, 1973a, p. 118)

The explanation was completed by adding an assumption about the relative speed or relative strength of the internal responses to the colour and to the word. In his review, Dyer (1973a) states:

> Most of these explanations have considered the phenomenon in terms of response competition with a stronger reading response to the irrelevant word aspect of the stimulus dominating and delaying the color-naming response.
>
> (Dyer, 1973a, p.114)

and

> Almost every investigator of the color-word phenomenon since Stroop (1935) has viewed the further increase in color-naming time when the patches are words as a direct result of this faster assignment of spoken words to written stimuli than to colors and the resulting conflict between this faster response to the irrelevant word aspect of the stimulus and the response to the relevant color aspect of it.
>
> (Dyer, 1973a, p.116)

Following Stroop (1935), Klein (1964), Morton (1969) and Dyer (1973a), most authors preferred an explanation of Stroop interference with colour naming and the absence of interference with word reading in terms of the relative speed of processing the word (fast) and the colour (slow), i.e., in terms of a horse race model (see, e.g., Cohen and Martin, 1975; Palef and Olson, 1975; Posner and Snyder, 1975; Seymour, 1977; Proctor 1978; Regan, 1978; see also the end of section 1.7). This relative speed explanation is not correct, however. Several studies in which the colours were preexposed, thus giving a speed advantage to the colour horse, failed to show any sign of a reversed Stroop effect with colour naming, comparable to the regular Stroop effect (see, e.g., Neumann, 1980; Van der Heijden, 1981; Glaser and Glaser, 1982).

Because substantial interference has been reported from position words (top, bottom) on position naming but not from positions on position word reading (see, e.g., Fox, Shor and Steinman, 1971; White, 1969; Shor, 1970) and from numerals on the naming of numerosity but not from numerosity on the reading of numerals (see, e.g., Flowers, Warner and Polansky, 1979), the conclusion has to be that something like 'stimulus–response compatibility' is the factor of importance. Responses to the less compatible aspect, i.e., the aspect that has to be named, are strongly hampered by responses to the compatible aspect, i.e., the aspect that can be read. Responses to the compatible aspect are not interfered with by the responses to the less compatible aspect.

Moreover, the orthodox explanation is also incomplete as an account of what happens in Stroop tasks and variants of the task because it only specifies where the interference stems from. The explanations are mainly concerned with the processing of information; not with the selection of information. But a basic observation with these tasks is that subjects, while facing serious difficulties, can nevertheless perform the task quite accurately. In other words, the subjects are successful in selecting the correct response. This selection aspect of the Stroop task has nearly completely been neglected in the literature. In one way or another the interference appeared much more interesting. (In Chapter 6 we return to this bias.)

With regard to the selection aspect, Van der Heijden (1978; 1981) argued that one or another form of late selection cannot be the mechanism involved. Both responses, the one derived from the colour and the other originating from the word, are equally task relevant and important. So, at the level of responses it cannot be determined which one is the correct one (see also section 3.9). In one way or another, early information has to be used to address and select the correct response. Van der Heijden (1978; 1981) suggested that, with colour naming, position and colour features, and with word reading, position and word features, are used in this response-addressing process. 'Postcategorical filtering' and 'selection' were the terms coined for this process (see also section 3.9). Indeed, it was the Stroop task showing 'response competition', suggesting parallel processing of both form and colour, as well as effective selection, that prompted this conceptualization.

Unlike most other authors, Kahneman and Henik (1981) explicitly addressed the question how in Stroop and Stroop-like tasks the correct response is ultimately selected. (Remember, subjects nearly always come up with the correct answer.) In their model, and in nearly all models concerned with performance in Stroop tasks, this question is really problematic just because of the assumption that all attributes of the stimulus are processed in parallel and that therefore all the responses associated with the object's properties are facilitated and available as responses. How then to arrive at the correct, for instance the colour-derived, response, and how to avoid, for instance, the word-derived response? According to Kahneman and Henik (1981) 'A final stage of processing is concerned with a task-directed choice among the responses that have been evoked'. They adequately add that in their experimental task 'color-information is used at two different stages, to find the relevant stimulus and to control the color-naming response'. So, also in their view, position and colour-information are used in one or another way to arrive at or address the correct response. In Chapter 8 we return to this selection issue and formulate it anew.

Recently the Stroop task has become quite popular, not for finding out how interference exactly originates or how the relevant dimension is exactly selected, but for getting some insight into what happens with the representation corresponding to the irrelevant varying dimension, e.g., with the word when the task is colour naming. In some theories it is argued that that information is lost by passive decay (see, e.g., Van der Heijden, 1981) but in other theories it has been argued that that information is actively inhibited (see, e.g., Neill, 1977; 1979; see also Tipper, 1985). The issue is investigated by presenting a series of Stroop stimuli in which the irrelevant colour word that had to be ignored on trial n

becomes the ink colour name on trial $n + 1$. Several studies have shown that such a 'suppress(!)–say' sequence incurs a 'say' reaction time cost (see, e.g., Dalrymple-Alford and Budayr, 1966; Neill, 1977; Neill and Westberry, 1987; Beech and Claridge, 1987). The same effect can be demonstrated with pictures and letters (Allport, Tipper and Chmiel, 1985; Tipper, 1985; Tipper and Cranston, 1985). The relation between this inhibition effect (resulting from ignoring) and the inhibition effect discussed in section 4.9 (resulting from attending) still remains to be worked out.

Chapter 5

Multiple-item detection and recognition tasks with accuracy as the dependent variable

5.0 The partial-report task

The topic of this chapter is the operation of central attention with multiple-item arrays and with accuracy as the dependent variable. As stated in Chapter 1, attention can be operationally defined as the benefits observed in detection and/or recognition performance as a result of appropriate selection, emphasis, or priority instructions, as compared with conditions without such instructions. This definition, however, creates some problems with the type of task discussed in this and in the next chapter. What is, with multiple item arrays, a valid and comparable neutral condition, i.e., a condition without selection, emphasis, or priority instructions with which performance in the 'attend' condition can be compared? For 'complex' tasks an appropriate neutral condition is much more difficult to find than for 'simple' tasks.

One solution to this problem was introduced by Sperling (1960) at the start of the information processing approach. He compared performance in an 'attend' condition, after a suitable transformation, with performance in a 'free-report' condition. In his partial-report task Sperling (1960) presented displays with rows of letters or digits, e.g., displays consisting of three rows, each containing four letters. The subjects were instructed to keep their eyes fixated on a central fixation point. Then the display was exposed for 50 ms. The subjects were asked to make a partial report, i.e., to report only the items from one row in the display. A symbolic cue was used: the instruction as to which row was relevant on a trial was coded as a tone, occurring just before, during, or at various intervals after exposure of the display. A high, medium or low tone specified report of the upper, middle or lower row, respectively. It was impossible for the subjects to predict before the tone occurred, which of the rows would be specified.

Sperling's primary interest was in the duration and capacity of a visual memory (see section 5.2). He wanted to tax this memory and, therefore, mainly used post-cues instead of pre-cues. With the tone immediately after offset of the display the subjects averaged about 3 items out of a maximum of 4. With increasing tone delays the number of items correct decreased, until, at a cue delay of about 300 ms, an asymptotic level of about 1.5 items correct was reached.

Sperling (1960) also measured performance in a whole-report task, i.e., in a task in which a display of letters and/or digits is presented briefly and the subject is asked in advance to report as many items as he can. In this task the subject's performance appears remarkably constant. With exposure durations ranging between 15 and 500 ms and with displays containing from 6 to 18 items, the subjects average about 4.5 items correct. So, with displays with three rows of four letters in this task, the subjects average about 4.5/3 = 1.5 letters correct per row. That is the asymptotic level of performance in the partial-report task.

With the shorter tone-delays in the partial-report task more items per row are named than in a whole-report task. This positive difference in favour of the partial-report task found with the shorter display–cue intervals is called the 'partial-report superiority'. For Sperling this partial-report superiority measured capacity and duration of the visual memory, but also the efficiency of selection (see Averbach and Sperling, 1961, p. 211). And given a number of assumptions this partial-report superiority can indeed be regarded as the benefit. But let us have a look at the most important assumption.

Sperling used the whole-report task as a neutral condition. To assess efficiency of selection he compared performance in the partial-report condition with performance in the whole-report condition. This might be an adequate procedure for assessing capacity and duration of a visual memory, but such a comparison has serious drawbacks for estimating benefits. The main problem is that it is far from clear whether, in such a comparison, the relevant difference is only 'appropriate instructions' versus 'without such instructions' (see for this requirement Jonides and Mack, 1984, in section 4.1). It is very likely that in the comparison between partial-report and whole-report performance, also strategy differences, time differences and differences in memory-load are involved (see, e.g., Dick, 1969; 1974, and Merikle, 1980, p. 288, for a discussion of these problems). Then, however, the partial-report superiority is not a valid estimate of benefits. While, initially, most researchers used Sperling's method, exactly for this reason later on a slightly different paradigm and another comparison was generally preferred. To that paradigm we return in section 5.1.

Nevertheless, one topic in this field of research is of special relevance. It is the topic concerned with the question of which types of stimulus attributes – besides location – are capable of producing the high initial level of performance, i.e., the question of which attributes afford efficient selection. From subsequent symbolic cue plus rule research, it appeared that not only when the cue directly specified the position of the relevant items, but also when it indirectly specified the location via colour of the items, e.g., high tone: red letters, low tone: blue letters (see, e.g., Clark, 1969; Von Wright, 1968; 1972; Dick, 1969; see also Bundesen, Pedersen and Larsen, 1984; Bundesen, Shibuya and Larsen, 1985), via brightness (see, e.g., Von Wright, 1968; see also Bundesen et al., 1984), via shape (Von Wright, 1968; Turvey and Kravetz, 1970; see also Bundesen et al., 1984), or via size (Von Wright, 1970) the same result was found: position might be most efficient (see., e.g., Nissen, 1985), other visual attributes afford efficient selection too. Other studies, however, showed that this is not the case, and that no, or only very small, positive effects are found, when the cue specified a subtle visual property such as upright letters vs letters rotated through 180 degrees (Von Wright, 1970). Moreover, the initial research strongly suggested that no partial-report superiority at all was found when the cue specified a derived property such as letters vs digits (Sperling, 1960; Von Wright, 1968; 1970; but see below), vowel vs consonant (Von Wright, 1970) or letters ending with the vowel /E/ vs letters ending with the vowel /I/ (Coltheart, Lea and Thompson, 1974).

The letter–digit, i.e., category cueing, research deserves some further discussion. As stated, with category cueing either no (Sperling, 1960; Von Wright, 1968; 1970), or only very minor (see, e.g., Dick, 1969; 1971; Von Wright, 1972; Merikle, 1980) effects were observed. Contrary to these results and contrary to his expectations, Merikle (1980, Exp. 3) found quite successful selection by category membership! This result was subsequently corroborated by Duncan (1983). Moreover, by means of a sophisticated and rigorous mathematical analysis, Bundesen and associates (Bundesen et al., 1984; Bundesen et al., 1985; Bundesen, 1987; Shibuya and Bundesen, 1988) were able to demonstrate rather efficient selection by category membership. Bundesen et al. (1984) even showed that selection by a 'physical' feature, such as angular vs curved letters, is less efficient than selection by category membership (see, however, also Bundesen, 1987, table 2).

Merikle (1980, p. 288) tried to answer the question why in some studies efficient selection by category membership is found and in others not. In his view, category cueing may only show up when the partial-report cue is presented considerably before display onset (see also Duncan, 1983, p. 534, for the same suggestion). In my view, this suggestion is nearly correct but not completely correct. Indeed, a major difference between the successful and unsuccessful studies was in the moment of presentation of the partial-report instruction. In fact, in the unsuccessful studies this instruction was varied from trial to trial; before each trial 'letter' or 'digit' was specified. In the successful studies, however, the instruction remained the same for a series of trials; before a block of trials the 'letter naming' or 'digit naming' instruction was given. In other words the major difference was not so much in the time of presentation of the instruction; the major difference was in 'cueing varied' vs 'cueing blocked'.

The important difference between 'cueing varied' and 'cueing blocked' is not so much in the operation of attention but in the role played by higher order expectation (and/or intention). With instructions varied, this expectation has to change from trial to trial. Moreover, what was relevant on trial n might become irrelevant on trial $n+1$ and what was irrelevant on trial n might become relevant on trial $n+1$. With instructions blocked, a consistent expectation can be maintained for a whole series of trials. What was relevant on trial n is also relevant on trial $n+1$, and what was irrelevant on trial n remains so on trial $n+1$. In other words, with instructions blocked, the operation of attention and of expectation are completely conflated. Attention and expectation closely cooperate in the performance of the task. This cooperation with blocked presentations and the absence of this cooperation with varied presentation might have a number of important consequences for the interpretation of the results obtained with letter–digit partial-report tasks.

First, because with partial-report instructions blocked a complete confounding and cooperation of attention and expectation is likely, it is not surprising that efficient selection by category membership – even more efficient than selection by a 'physical' feature like 'angular vs curved' where such a confounding does not exist – is easily found (see the research of Bundesen and associates).

Second, because with partial-report instructions blocked an optimal preparation is possible but with whole-report instructions it is not (report 'only letters' allows for a more appropriate preparation than report 'letters and digits'), a comparison between performance in the two conditions is biased in favour of the partial-report condition. It is likely that this biased comparison leads to the erroneous conclusion of efficient 'attentional' selection on the basis of category membership (see Merikle, 1980; Duncan, 1983).

Third, because with partial-report instructions varied, just as with the whole-report instructions, no optimal preparation is possible, a comparison between performance in these two conditions is not necessarily incorrect. It is exactly this comparison that in the past led to the conclusion that no, or only very small, effects of attentional selectivity can be demonstrated with category cueing (see Sperling, 1960; Von Wright, 1968; 1970), while substantial effects are easily demonstrated with a large number of 'simple' physical features.

5.1 The partial-report bar-probe task

At about the same time that Sperling introduced the partial-report task, Averbach and Coriell (1961) introduced a different form of (post) stimulus sampling, called the partial-report bar-probe task. Their stimulus displays contained two linear letter arrays. A visual indicator, a barmarker, was used to indicate the position of one of the letters. The barmarker was very close to the relevant letter and functioned therefore as a location cue. The exposure duration of the letters was 50 ms, and the barmarker appeared either before, simultaneously with, or at various moments after display presentation at a randomly chosen position. The subject was to report which letter (had) occupied the position indicated. So, in this task, the report of only one letter was required.

Figure 5.1.1 gives an impression of Averbach and Coriell's results. With the barmarker before appearance of the display, the proportion correct is rather high (about 75% correct). With increasing display–marker intervals a fast decrease in proportion correct is observed, until, at an interval of about 250 ms, performance becomes asymptotic (about 35% correct). So, as far as effects of moment of presenting the report instruction are concerned, there are no obvious differences between Sperling's (1960) results and Averbach and Coriell's (1961) results.

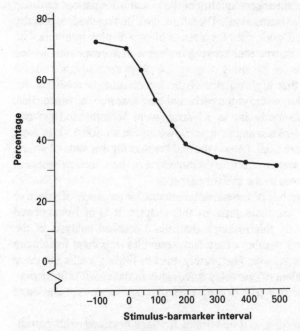

Figure 5.1.1 Percentages correct as a function of stimulus-barmarker interval in a partial-report bar-probe task.

Both the partial-report task and the partial-report bar-probe task seem to measure the same processes as a function of probe delay (see the joint publication of Averbach and Sperling, 1961).

In Averbach and Coriell's study and in the later studies using the partial-report bar-probe task no neutral condition was used. (Also Averbach and Coriell were primarily interested in the duration and capacity of a visual memory; see section 5.2.) To assess the effectiveness of the cue-induced selective processes another comparison is, albeit implicitly, generally used. In this comparison the moment of presentation of the cue relative to the stimulus display is of crucial importance. The underlying logic can best be made clear by first considering the two extreme conditions. First, consider a cue far ahead of the stimulus display. Subjects then have sufficient time to localize the cue and react (covertly) to it. So, this condition can be considered as a condition with appropriate advance selection instructions or appropriate foreknowledge of position. Now consider the situation with the cue far behind the display. Then, at the moment of presentation of the cue, most visual information will have disappeared (see, e.g., Sperling, 1960; Coltheart, 1980a). So, this condition can be regarded as a condition without appropriate selection instructions. With cue presentation moments in between the first and second extreme position, the appropriateness of the instruction will gradually decline.

Unfortunately, in this comparison 'quality of the visual information' covaries with 'appropriateness of the instruction'. Therefore, with this method, especially the effects obtained with advance cues for a range of cue–display intervals, i.e., with appropriate selection instructions varying in degree of appropriateness, are of fundamental importance for the study of attention. With such advance cues it is reasonable to assume that high quality visual information is available for selection. Unfortunately, however, in the early and later research, advance cues, and especially cues substantially far in advance, were seldom used (to one exception, the research of Eriksen and associates, we turn in section 5.9). In most research only post-cues were used. (Again the main reason for this state of affairs was that most researchers were not primarily interested in the selection aspect in the task under discussion, but in the memory aspect.)

Nevertheless, this research is of fundamental interest for the study of selective attention and is therefore the main topic of this chapter. It is of fundamental interest because it is exactly this research that, via a detailed analysis of the errors, and after removing a number of artefacts, provides important insights in the early versus late selection issue. Fortunately, the key finding leading to these insights is largely independent of cue delay and quality of the visual information. We conclude this section with a brief description and one possible explanation of exactly this finding.

One of the most spectacular and consistent findings obtained with partial-report bar-probe tasks using linear arrays is the sharply W-shaped serial position curve for correct responses. Accuracy of report is highest in the middle position and in the two end positions of a linear array and is appreciably lower in between (see, e.g., Averbach and Coriell, 1961; Townsend, 1973; Campbell and Mewhort, 1980; Mewhort, Campbell, Marchetti and Campbell, 1981; see also figure 5.7.1).

Averbach and Coriell (1961, p. 309) already provided the beginning of an explanation:

> Why, then, doesn't performance reach 100 per cent? The reason is *not* that some letters are outside the fovea, since individual letters exposed in any of the ... positions of the array are clearly legible. The explanation seems to lie, rather, in the fact that letters in some positions, although perfectly legible by themselves, are not legible in the context of the array .... All subjects show the same distribution, in which performance is better at the centre and ends, and poorer in between.

Later on, this 'context' explanation was further elaborated. According to Estes (1978) there are two factors that in combination produce this W-shaped function. The first is the central–peripheral gradient of acuity. The second factor is lateral masking, i.e., the adverse effect on identification of a letter caused by a (mask) letter presented in close temporal and spatial proximity. The first factor is well documented (see section 2.8). The second factor – unique for multi-element displays – has been brought only recently under rigorous experimental control.

Nevertheless, research has provided substantial evidence for the importance of this factor and has also revealed several of its properties (see section 7.7).

In Estes's (1978, p. 188) view these two factors – retinal acuity and lateral masking – can account for the W function for correct reports in the following way. Lateral masking would be greatest in the interior of the array where each letter has two neighbours, and least at the ends where the letters have only a single, foveal, neighbour, and a blank space at the peripheral side. This explains the high level of performance with the end items. Visual acuity is highest in the fovea and decreases towards the periphery. This explains the high level of performance with the centre items. The two explanations in combination explain the complete W-shaped serial position curve.

Van der Heijden (1987) presented a numerical example showing that with these two simple assumptions indeed a broad range of W-shaped functions can be generated (see figure 5.1.2). The combination rule used for this numerical example was the lateral-inhibition equation for the eye of the Limulus, presented by Cornsweet (1970, pp. 293–300),

$$Oi = Ii - \sum KjiOj.$$

Applied to letters in a linear array this equation can be read as: The ultimate level of activation for a letter on position i in the array, Oi, equals its initial or input

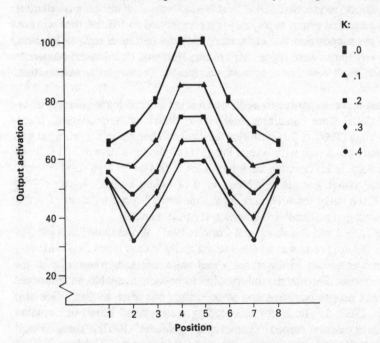

Figure 5.1.2 Numerical example demonstrating how lateral masking transforms an input (.0) in W-shaped serial position curves (.1, .2, .3 and .4).

level of activation Ii (determined by retinal acuity) minus the sum of the inhibitory influences received from other letters in the array, $\sum KjiOj$ (with Kji reflecting the severity of lateral masking). The figure shows that Estes's (1978) explanation cannot easily be dismissed (see also Chapter 7, and Hagenzieker and Van der Heijden, 1990). But subsequent research showed that more is involved. To that research we return further on.

5.2 Early selection?

The experimental results mentioned in the foregoing sections led to a coherent and nearly generally accepted view of the first stages of visual information processing. The major emphasis in this view was on an initial, large capacity information store, a memory with fast decaying information. The availability of information *after* stimulus presentation was regarded as the important and exciting finding. (It is interesting to note the titles of some of the first papers, like 'Short-term memory in vision', and 'Short-term storage of information in vision'.)

The nature, or degree of encoding, of the information retained in this store was mainly inferred from the results of the investigations concerned with the problem of which stimulus attributes were effective in producing a partial-report superiority effect (see section 5.0). The rule used was: If an attribute is effective in producing a partial-report superiority it is represented and, if not, then it is not. This led to the supposition that elementary physical attributes such as location, colour and brightness were represented in this store and that derived properties such as letter, digit, vowel or consonant, i.e., identity or categorical information, were not.

So, partial-report experiments addressed a stage of precategorical representation, or, a visual store containing solely raw, literal, or 'unprocessed' information. Sperling (1960, p. 26) identified this 'information storage' (i.e., what was experimentally observed) with 'visual image' (i.e., the subjective image induced by the stimulus). In his opinion, the information in this initial high capacity store was not only visual, but also visible; a kind of fading image. Neisser (1967) summarized the early research and coined the term 'iconic memory' for this briefly persisting visual and visible analogue of the stimulus.

Sperling (1960) and Averbach and Coriell (1961) also assumed that identity information did not become available automatically in their type of task. Identity information was neither in the initial visual store, nor somewhere else in the processing system. For identity information to become available an additional operation was necessary: items had to be 'read', one after another. (See also Mackworth, 1962; 1963a, b, for this reading assumption.) Later, this reading process was variously named 'synthesizing' (Neisser, 1967), 'categorizing' (Broadbent, 1971) and 'transfer to a more endurable memory' (Coltheart, 1975).

A basic underlying assumption was that only one item could be read at a time (see, e.g., Neisser, 1967, p. 103; Broadbent, 1971, p. 173). This limited capacity reading process, that combines the processes of selection and of identification, together with the short availability of the material to be read, was generally held responsible for the limited number of correct reports in whole-report experiments and for the fast decrease of partial-report performance with increasing cue delays (see Coltheart, 1980a, pp. 186–7, for a detailed presentation of these assumptions).

While the main emphasis was on iconic memory and its properties and on the identification aspect of the reading process, something like 'central selective attention' – the topic we are interested in – was not completely forgotten. Sperling stated

the finding that only 4 or 5 letters can be reported after a brief exposure dates back to the last century. My contribution has been, I think, to show that these few letters can be arbitrarily selected from a considerably larger number of letters which are available momentarily and shortly after the exposure ....
(Averbach and Sperling, 1961, p. 211; see also Sperling, 1960, pp. 24–5)

As we have seen, however, this finding also dates back to the last century. Von Helmholtz carefully documented this ability (see section 2.1). Nevertheless, the clear demonstration and objective measurement of the possibility of arbitrary selection without the involvement of eye movements, and the flexibility of this process in a properly controlled situation, was the major contribution of Sperling's (1960), Averbach and Coriell's (1961) and later iconic memory research.

Coltheart (1975) summarized all the results in a model, that he called 'the conventional view of iconic memory':

brief displays are held in a form of storage which is of high capacity, is subject to rapid decay and is visual in nature .... Because of the rapid decay ... items which are to be retained long enough to be reported must be transferred ... the S can at least choose which of the items will be transferred .... The untransferred residue being rapidly lost through decay ....
(Coltheart, 1975, p. 43)

Of course, the choice of items is based on the vis   information available in the precategorical, literal, store. (See also Coltheart 1980a, p. 225.) This view is the orthodox early selection position with, as basic assumptions,

(a) a limited capacity for processing (i.e., for identifying or categorizing) information;
(b) a selection process intervening in a stage containing literal (not yet identified) information;
(c) selection is selection for processing (i.e., for identification or categorization).

It will be clear that these are essentially the visual equivalents of the early selection assumptions of Broadbent's (1958) filter model (see section 2.4). It will also be clear that – except for the (limited capacity) processing assumptions – this view is consistent with the conclusions we reached in the two previous chapters. Attention deals with, or addresses, early information (see Chapter 3). 'Choice' and 'arbitrary selection' are mainly means for creating structure in time (see Chapter 4). Let us now see what assumptions have to be rejected and what assumptions can be maintained.

5.3 Error analysis

A second, important, line of relevant evidence came into being when theorists appreciated that with a detailed analysis of the error data, appreciably more information could be extracted from the results of partial-report and especially from partial-report bar-probe tasks than generally was assumed. Initially, in partial-report bar-probe tasks, with only a few exceptions (see, e.g., Eriksen and Rohrbaugh, 1970; Townsend, 1973; Dick, 1974), only proportions correct were used as data. These proportions correct were taken as unbiased measures of the subject's ability to identify the cued items. When subjects made an error, it was simply taken for granted that this error was a 'reading' error, and such a reading error was interpreted as a failure of perceptual analysis, or as a failure of identification. A further analysis of errors was not seen as relevant. Estes's (1978) explanation of the W-shaped serial position curve forms a clear example of this way of thinking (see section 5.1). In this explanation only retinal acuity and lateral masking determine performance per position. But, as stated, more is involved.

In the 'reading' notion, identification and selection are combined. So, for correct 'reading' in a partial-report bar-probe task, more is required than identification alone. Subjects must also locate the relevant item relative to the barmarker and select the so located item. Therefore, errors may reflect failures of identification, but also failures of localization. So, an analysis of errors is of crucial importance. Such an analysis of errors with linear arrays was presented by Townsend (1973) and Dick (1974), but especially Mewhort and associates have collected a complete set of relevant data.

Mewhort and associates used 8-letter linear arrays and a barmarker as a probe. The letters were randomly selected without replacement from the whole alphabet of 26 letters. They distinguish two types of errors: Intrusion (or item) errors and location errors. A response is scored as an intrusion error when the subject reports a letter not present in the stimulus array and as a location error when the subject reports a letter that was in the array but on another position than the one indicated. Since, from the 26 letters of the alphabet, there are 8 letters in the array – the target and 7 nontargets – and 18 letters not in the array, failures of identification should on the average result in numbers of intrusions and location errors in the proportion of 18 to 7. In other words, if errors are really failures of identification, as the orthodox iconic memory view suggests, appreciably more item errors (18 opportunities) than location errors (7 opportunities) are to be expected. That is, however, not what is found. The, for our purposes, most important results are:

- Appreciably more location errors than intrusion errors are found (see, e.g., Townsend, 1973; Mewhort and Campbell, 1978; Butler, 1980; Campbell and Mewhort, 1980; Mewhort et al., 1981; Mewhort, Marchetti, Gurnsey and Campbell, 1984; see also figure 5.7.1).
- Most location errors consist of responses naming an item adjacent to the item indicated by the probe, i.e., are, what are called 'near' location errors (see, e.g., Dick, 1974, table I; Mewhort and Campbell, 1978; Campbell and Mewhort, 1980; Mewhort et al., 1984).
- Location errors have an M-shaped serial position curve. They approximately mirror correct responses that have the complementary W-shaped serial position curve (see section 5.1). So, the relative accuracy across the array is high when the number of location errors is low and vice versa. For intrusions, this interrelated pattern of accuracy and errors is not that apparent (see, e.g., Mewhort and Campbell, 1978; Campbell and Mewhort, 1980; Mewhort et al., 1981).
- The decrease in accuracy which is observed as the cue is delayed (see figure 5.1.1), is largely matched by an increase in location errors and only to a small extent by an increase in intrusions (see, e.g., Townsend, 1973; Mewhort et al., 1981; Mewhort et al., 1984).

It will be clear that, in particular, the large number of location errors and the spatial distribution of these errors is not what is expected on the basis of the traditional early selection view. Moreover, also, the dissociation between the effect of probe delay on location errors (a large increase) and on intrusions (a minor increase) is not consistent with the orthodox iconic memory view. According to that view the decrease in performance with increasing probe delays reflects decay of information in iconic memory (Neisser, 1967): a loss of information similar to a fading image. But if errors indeed result from attempts to identify a progressively degrading sensory representation, a large increase in failures of perceptual analysis and therefore in number of intrusions is expected and only a relatively small increase of location errors. So the results seem opposite to that predicted by the fading image analogy.

Taken all together, the error data seem to provide no evidence at all supporting the traditional interpretation of performance in partial-report bar-probe tasks. What the error data strongly suggest is that it is not so much problems of *identification* but problems of *localization* that impose the major limitations to performance in partial-report bar-probe tasks. From 'selection' and 'identification', combined and confounded in the term 'reading', it seem to be factors related to selection (i.e., to localization) and not to identification that mainly determine task performance. This result makes it necessary to come up with an alternative interpretation of performance in partial-report bar-probe tasks. Mewhort and associates developed such an alternative.

5.4 Late selection?

To account for the results obtained in partial-report bar-probe tasks, especially for the large number of location errors, and also for the results obtained in a number of related tasks, Mewhort and associates proposed a 'dual-buffer' model. This model is the front end to a larger word-identification model (see, e.g., Mewhort and Campbell, 1981, and Mewhort, 1987, for a detailed description). Five components of the overall model are involved in the bar-probe task: a feature buffer, an identifier, a character buffer, an attentional mechanism and a short-term memory.

According to the model a representation of the stimulus first enters the feature buffer, a precategorical store containing representations of physical attributes of the stimulus. The identifier, operating in parallel on all the information in this buffer, identifies the items and stores its results along with location information in the second store, the character buffer. The attentional mechanism operates on the identity and location information in this character buffer. It selects a code, suitable for output, from the character buffer and passes it to short-term memory. So, in this model, attentional selection comes after identification. The ambiguous 'reading' concept is decomposed into two independent subprocesses: identification and attentional selection. In my view, this decomposition is a major theoretical accomplishment.

This 'dual buffer' model, together with the assumptions that there are differences in saliency of spatial information at the different positions in the character buffer (to 'explain' the W-shaped serial position curve for correct reports), and the assumption that there is a faster loss of location information as compared with identity information in the character buffer (to 'explain' the dissociation between the effects of probe delay on intrusions and location errors), is capable of explaining most of the results. It is not clear, however, how it is explained that most location errors are near location errors. (See, however, Mewhort, 1987, p. 347, for an exhaustive listing of additional assumptions. These assumptions are certainly sufficient to explain everything. See also section 5.7.)

Because an essential and theoretically important assumption of the dual-buffer model is that selective attention (i.e., the attentional mechanism) operates in, what is called, the character buffer and not in, what is called, the feature buffer, it is of importance to consider how the two buffers are defined. This is the more so because a recent theoretical discussion between Chow (1986) and Mewhort, Butler, Feldman-Stewart and Tramer (1988) has at least shown that an extremely close reading of the dual-buffer doctrine is required.

Campbell and Mewhort (1980, p. 140) introduce the feature buffer as 'a memory which stores the feature information. The visual persistence described by Eriksen and Collins (1968) and by Di Lollo (1977) likely reflects the operation of the feature buffer'. Mewhort et al. (1981, p. 51; see also Mewhort and Campbell, 1981, p. 61, and Mewhort et al., 1988, p. 730) add 'The feature representation is precategorical, and the buffer's capacity is unlimited; that is, the buffer preserves spatial and other physical attributes of the display. Thus, the feature buffer holds raw data concerning the shape of each letter; for example, different features would be involved in upper- and lowercase letters'.

Campbell and Mewhort (1980, p. 141; see also Mewhort et al., 1981, p. 51, and Mewhort et al., 1988, p. 730) describe the character buffer as 'a visual–spatial buffer. The buffer preserves the spatial arrangement, but as the buffer is postidentification, it involves a more abstract representation than the idea of an image (or icon) would suggest'. Mewhort and Campbell (1981, pp. 62–3) work out what they mean by abstract: 'By abstract we mean that the character buffer holds identified characters, items with labels, not basic features. Further, the characters, themselves, are abstractions not images'. Mewhort et al. (1981, p. 51 and p. 62) identify the character buffer with the nonimage postidentification store studied by Rayner, McConkie and Zola (1980). The latter describe the information in this store as 'independent of specific visual (case) characteristics' (Rayner et al., 1980, p. 224).

Taking all together, the important point is that the feature buffer equals what was called 'Iconic memory' in the 'conventional view of iconic memory' (see also Butler, 1982, p. 119), but that, contrary to the conventional view, in the 'dual buffer' model, this is not the store addressed or used by attention in the partial-report bar-probe task (see Mewhort and Butler, 1983, p. 33, and Mewhort et al., 1988, p. 730). For that task the character buffer is the relevant store. The identification mechanism assigns each character and the probe a position in the character buffer (a process not unlike the subscription of an item in a matrix; see Mewhort et al., 1988, p. 730). The attentional mechanism retrieves an item on the basis of this position information from the character buffer.

So, in a sense, in the dual-buffer account, attentional selection in the partial-report bar-probe task is not really selection in vision (see, e.g., Van der Heijden, 1986; 1987). The feature buffer plays the role of visible 'fading image' but is simply neglected by attention (in fact, it plays no role whatsoever in the dual-buffer account except in storing to-be-identified information). And, while the character buffer is granted a role in visual perception, especially in the integration of information across eye movements and in the continuity of perception (see, e.g., Mewhort et al., 1981, p. 62; Mewhort and Campbell, 1981, p. 63; Mewhort and Butler, 1983, p. 33) it can neither be equated with visible persistence nor with what is visible in vision; details are lost (Mewhort et al., 1981, p. 51; Mewhort and Campbell, 1981, p.63), the information is independent of specific visual characteristics (i.e., A = a at this level; Rayner et al., 1980, p. 224), or, is abstract. Furthermore, according to the model, there is virtually no loss of identity information in this store, but visible persistence is only of a very limited duration (see, e.g., Coltheart, 1980a).

Coltheart (1984; see also Coltheart, 1980a) strongly supported this view of what happens in partial-report bar-probe tasks by presenting a closely related model. He distinguishes three memory components: a precategorical visual feature buffer, a postcategorical character buffer and a response buffer. The high-capacity feature buffer contains rapidly decaying features, the postcategorical character buffer contains identity information and episodic information (tags with information about particular physical properties), the response buffer contains the item to be reported. A 'sensory registrar' takes care of loading the feature buffer. A 'character-identifier' operates in parallel upon the information in the feature buffer and creates tagged identity representations in the character buffer. In partial-report tasks, the cue controls the transfer of one character from the character buffer to the response buffer. (This transfer process is regarded as a limited capacity, and possibly even serial, operation.)

The two views described in the preceding paragraphs are examples of late selection models. Selection takes place at a postcategorical level where identity information is available. The selective process uses the episodic information represented at this level (tags or relative spatial position) for distinguishing relevant and irrelevant information. While an initial high capacity feature buffer containing rapidly decaying visual information (iconic memory or a fading image) is still recognized, it plays no role in the selection of information in these models (see, e.g., Coltheart, 1984, p. 282). This late selection position has as basic assumptions:

(a) an unlimited capacity for processing (i.e., identifying) information;
(b) a selection process operating in a stage containing identified information;
(c) selection is selection for further operations, e.g., for storage in a response buffer or for overt report.

Formulated in this way, it will be clear that these late selection models are visual variants of Deutsch and Deutsch's (1963) late selection model. There is, however, an important difference. The mechanism responsible for selection is changed. Deutsch and Deutsch's 'weightings of importance' (i.e., one or another kind of higher order expectation) is replaced by something like Broadbent's attentional selection (i.e., one or another kind of selective operation dealing with position). In these models Von Helmholtz's attention intervenes at the level of James's expectation. However, theoretical caprioles come with a price. In this case 'early' information, i.e., information that is peripherally available, has to be duplicated 'late', i.e., at a more central level (Mewhort's character buffer preserves spatial arrangement and Coltheart's character buffer contains episodic information in the form of tags). The interesting question is therefore: Are these aberrant late selection models really correct? Do we really have to reject the conclusion we arrived at in Chapter 3: Attentional selection in vision is early selection?

5.5 M and W functions: localization

In our view the data upon which Mewhort et al.'s (and also Coltheart's) information processing model is based do not really force one to believe that selection in partial-report bar-probe tasks is not early selection in vision, but late selection in one or another 'buffer' containing abstract identity and position information. Certainly, the data strongly suggest that it is very worthwhile distinguishing between identification and localization in 'reading'. Mewhort and associates correctly emphasized this important point and the related point that localization is an important factor in partial-report performance. However, especially with pre-cues, simultaneous cues and post-cues at the smaller ISIs, there is nothing in the data that really suggests that the visual and visible representation, whose duration is measured in visible persistence studies, plays no role in bar-probe tasks and that information at the postcategorical level, for instance tags, labels, or relative spatial position in a character buffer, is used for distinguishing and addressing the relevant information. In short, in our view, there is no need for the counterintuitive late selection position for the range of target–probe delays that are of interest for the study of attention in vision. Let us look at some aspects of the data again.

As stated in section 5.1, one of the most spectacular and consistent findings obtained with partial-report bar-probe tasks using linear arrays is the sharply W-shaped serial position curve for correct responses (see, e.g., Averbach and Coriell, 1961; Townsend, 1973; Campbell and Mewhort, 1980; Mewhort et al., 1981). Originally, in the dual buffer account, this phenomenon was 'explained' in terms of saliency of positional information in the character buffer (see, e.g., Mewhort et al., 1981, p. 56 and p. 62). Other explanations are possible, however. In this section we discuss target localization problems. In the next section we look again at Estes's (1978) explanation in terms of retinal acuity and lateral masking. In section 5.7 we present a combination of these two explanations.

With regard to localization, Mewhort (1987) distinguishes three kinds of difficulties that can result in faulty selection by the attentional mechanism: 'Probe alignment errors reflecting spatial drift during the target–probe interval, data inversion within the buffer itself, and mislocalization by the attentional mechanism' (Mewhort, 1987, p. 347; see, however, also Mewhort et al., 1981, p. 62). In Mewhort et al. (1988) the latter, somewhat mysterious, difficulty has disappeared and only 'probe misalignment' and 'inversions within the character buffer' are maintained (Mewhort et al., 1988, p. 730). So, in the following analysis we also restrict our discussion to the latter two error sources.

The important point now is, of course, that 'probe misalignment' – an error in the process of relating the probe's position to the target's position – is not a unique kind of error to be found with late selection only. There is no reason to assume that this type of error indicates a problem at a postcategorical level. Also, with early selection, probe alignment problems can be an important source of errors. So, this type of error cannot be claimed in favour of the late selection view because it simply does not discriminate between the early and late selection views. Data inversion – kermess in character buffer; see Mewhort et al. (1988, p. 732) – possibly does. Therefore, the first important question to be answered is: Is it – for the range of SOAs of interest for selection in vision – 'probe misalignments' or 'inversions' that are largely responsible for the errors, and consequently for the W-shaped serial position curve for correct responses (and for the complementary M-shaped serial position curve for location errors)?

At least two pieces of evidence strongly suggest that, for SOAs relevant to the study of attention in vision, mainly probe misalignments and not data inversions in a character buffer are at the basis of erroneous responses. The first comes from a simulation study of Mewhort et al. (1988; see also section 5.7). These authors simulated performance in a bar-probe task as a function of probe delay. Of importance are the two parameters they used for simulating localization performance: PA, indexing the probability of correct probe alignment, and IL, indexing the probability that an item will retain its correct position within the character buffer. For the shortest probe delay the probabilities used were 0.85 and 0.95 for PA and IL, respectively. This choice of parameters strongly indicates that, with selection in vision, the simulation only produced acceptable results when it was assumed that the probability of probe misalignment is rather high and considerably higher than the probability of data inversion in the character buffer. (Mewhort et al., 1981, p. 62, preferred an explanation in terms of 'inversions' or 'spatial clarity in the buffer' rather than in terms of 'alignment'!)

The second piece of evidence comes from an experiment that compared performance with preexposure and postexposure of the barmarker (Hagenaar, in prep.). The first surprising finding was a strong *increase* in number of location errors with increasing preexposure of the barmarker. These location errors cannot result from inversions in the character buffer (kermess has not been started yet) and must therefore be due to probe misalignments. Of even more importance is the fact that the development of the number of location errors was virtually symmetrical around an SOA of 0 ms. Location errors increase in the same way with increasing preexposure as with increasing postexposure of the barmarker. This result is not in accordance with the assumption that precise spatial information about items in the buffer is lost as the target–probe interval increases. Then, with post-cues 'inversions' are an additional source of errors, and more location errors are to be expected with increasing postexposure of the barmarker (both misalignments and a growing number of inversions contribute) than with increasing preexposure (only misalignments contribute). The results strongly suggest that only the operation of relating the barmarker to the letter array is the process of critical importance (and that the absolute SOA is a critical variable in this operation).

Further evidence that these misalignment errors are, at least in large part, responsible for the W-shaped serial position curve for correct responses (and possibly mainly for the M-shaped curve for location errors) comes from a slightly modified bar-probe task. From the literature it appears that, if subjects are asked to indicate only the *position* of the probe, the serial position curve of correct position responses can also take on a W-shape (see, e.g., Mewhort and Campbell, 1978; Tramer, 1981; Hagenaar, 1990; but see Townsend, 1973, for a counter example).

Hagenzieker, Van der Heijden and Hagenaar (1990) further investigated localization performance with this position-naming task. In their bar-probe task the arrays consisted of the digits 1 through 7, always in sequence and in the same position. So, the name of the digit and the name of the position were always identical. Subjects had to name the (position of the) digit indicated by a barmarker. Any digit in the string could serve as the target digit. Two target luminances were used: bright and dim. In the, for our purposes, relevant condition, the barmarker preceded the stimulus by 100 ms (SOA = −100 ms). Figure 5.5.1 shows the proportions correct responses per target position for the bright and dim luminance condition separately. (It is very worthwhile to note that there is no effect of luminance condition in this localization task.)

The figure shows that also with a substantial preexposure of the barmarker the position curve for correct responses is strongly W-shaped. (Virtually all errors were near location errors, suggesting a 'distance effect' as observed with location cues in single-item studies; see section 4.3.) But, according to the dual-buffer doctrine, with preexposure of the barmarker, the attentional mechanism can address a virtually intact representation in the character buffer; precise spatial information is initially available and is only subsequently 'lost as the interval separating target and probe increases' (Mewhort et al., 1988, p. 730). In the experiment, however, there was a *negative* target–probe interval. So, the pattern

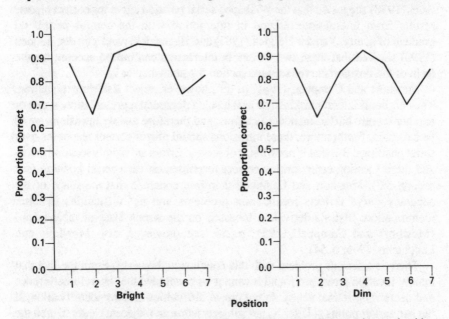

Figure 5.5.1 Proportions correct per position (1–7) in the digit naming task with preexposure of the barmarker. Panel at the left: Bright luminance condition. Panel at the right: Dim luminance condition. (Data from Hagenzieker et al., 1990.)

of results depicted in figure 5.5.1 cannot be due to 'inversions' in the character buffer. Consequently, it must be due to 'misalignments'.

Of course, in the traditional letter bar-probe task, the barmarker has to be used to locate the target in exactly the same way as in this digit bar-probe task. So, in the letter task exactly the same alignment problems are encountered. Therefore it can also be concluded that at least a large part of the W-shaped serial position curve for correct reports in the traditional bar-probe task (and of the M-shaped serial position curve for location errors) has to be attributed to the subject's limited ability to locate the probe relative to the target. And, as stated, that finding cannot be claimed in favour of late selection models.

Nevertheless the localization literature indicates that the W-shape function obtained in the localization task is generally much higher and also somewhat flatter than the one observed in the orthodox bar-probe task (see, e.g., Mewhort and Campbell, 1978; compare also figures 5.5.1 and 5.6.1). Therefore the subject's limited ability to locate the probe relative to the target can only account for part of the W function. There must be another factor involved. Is this factor data inversion within the character buffer or are other factors involved?

5.6 M and W functions: lateral masking

Estes (1978) suggested that the W-shaped serial position curve for correct reports results from lateral interference in interaction with the central–peripheral gradient of acuity. Van der Heijden (1987) and Hagenzieker and Van der Heijden (1990) showed that these two factors in interaction can indeed account for the form of the position curve (see also section 5.1 and Chapter 7).

Mewhort and Campbell (1981, p. 56), however, reject Estes's explanation. They argue: If lateral masking has as a result a degraded representation in one or another feature buffer, misidentifications, and therefore mainly intrusions are to be expected. Furthermore, these intrusions should mirror correct responses over serial positions. But that is not what is observed. Errors are mainly location errors and these location errors mirror correct responses on each serial position (see section 5.3). Mewhort and Campbell therefore conclude that the shape of the accuracy curve reflects localization problems and not difficulties in letter identification.. 'Estes's derivation focussed on the wrong class of mechanism' (Mewhort and Campbell, 1981, p. 56; see, however, also Mewhort and Leppmann, 1985, p. 54).

There is a serious problem with this conclusion, however. From the fact that mainly location errors are found it cannot be concluded that lateral interference and decreasing retinal acuity do not create difficulties in letter identification. If the barmarker points at letter X, but subjects name an (adjacent) letter Y then the conclusion that there were no problems with the identification of Y is warranted, but not, however, the conclusion that there were no problems with the identification of X. Exactly the fact that a location error was made prevents the correct assessment of identification performance on the probed position. So, even while errors are mainly location errors, an underlying W-shaped identification curve as specified by Estes's (1978) explanation cannot be ruled out.

The problems we are now faced with are, (a) how to determine whether the accuracy curve also reflects letter identification difficulties, and (b) if so, how to assess the size of these effects per target position. Fortunately, Hagenzieker et al.'s (1990) study provides the information we need. The study included, besides the position naming task described in section 5.5, also an orthodox letter naming bar-probe task. The letter naming task was identical to the digit naming task in all respects, except that the digits 1 through 7 were replaced by strings of seven randomly chosen letters. Figure 5.6.1 shows the proportions of correct reports per target position in the condition where the barmarker preceded the array by 100 ms, i.e., in the condition where only 'misalignment' errors and no 'inversions' are to be expected (see section 5.5). As in figure 5.5.1 the data are presented for the bright and dim luminance condition separately.

As stated in section 5.5, the variable luminance condition had virtually no effect on performance in the digit naming task (see figure 5.5.1). Figure 5.6.1, however, shows a huge effect of luminance condition in the letter naming task. In general, if a variable affects performance in one task but not in another the presence of a unique component in the first task and not in the latter is strongly supported. It is exactly that component that is sensitive to, and reflects the different levels of, that variable. Let us apply this principle to the data obtained in the position naming task and in the letter naming task.

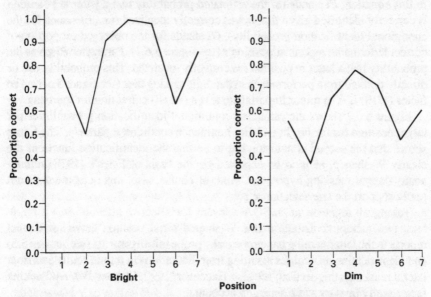

Figure 5.6.1 Proportions correct per position (1–7) in the letter naming task with preexposure of the barmarker. Panel at the left: Bright luminance condition. Panel at the right: Dim luminance condition. (Data from Hagenzieker et al., 1990.)

The digit naming task measures probe alignment and probe alignment only. Because of preexposure of the barmarker, inversions could not influence the results. Because always the digits 1 through 7 in series and on the same position were used as stimuli there were no identification difficulties (the absence of any effect of luminance condition supports this conclusion). Because of preexposure of the barmarker, also in the letter naming task inversions could not influence the results. In this task exactly the same probe alignment factor must have been involved as in the position naming task. However, the digit naming task shows that that factor is not affected by luminance condition. So, the letter naming task must involve a second, unique, factor, that has nothing to do with localization, and that is strongly affected by luminance condition. It is obvious that it is an identification component – that plays no role in the digit naming task but is essential in the letter naming task – that is strongly affected by luminance condition. So, the first conclusion has to be that the letter naming accuracy curve also reflects identification difficulties.

For extracting the identification component, hidden in the correct reports obtained in the letter naming task, a simple mathematical model suffices. Hagenzieker et al. (1990) used the following equation:

$$Ei = \frac{Oi - (1/19)Ii}{Pi}$$

In this equation, Ei stands for the estimated probability that a letter at position i is correctly identified given that it was correctly localized (i.e., Ei stands for the conditional identification probability). Oi stands for the observed proportion of correct letter name reports at position i (see figure 5.6.1). Parameter Pi gives the probability that a letter in position i is correctly localized. This probability can be directly derived from performance in the digit naming task (see figure 5.5.1). The factor $(1/19)$ Ii is of minor importance; it is a (small) correction for guessing.

Figure 5.6.2 shows the estimated conditional identification probabilities per target position for the bright and dim luminance condition separately. The figure shows that the second conclusion has to be that the identification functions are clearly W-shaped, as is to be expected on the basis of Estes's (1978) retinal-acuity–lateral-masking hypothesis. And, of course, also, this outcome does not really support the late selection view.

Taking all together, at an SOA relevant for selective attention in vision, at least two factors contribute to the W-shaped serial position curve for correct reports in the letter naming bar-probe task: probe misalignments (see section 5.5) and identification difficulties resulting from limitations in retinal acuity and from lateral masking (this section; see also Hagenaar, 1990, Chapter IV). And neither factor really favours a late selection account.

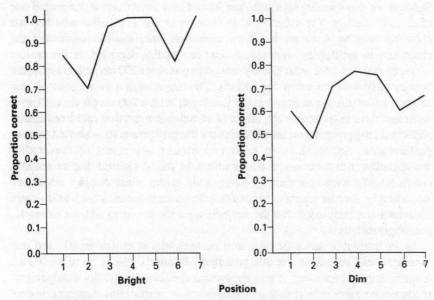

Figure 5.6.2 Estimated proportions correct identifications per position (1–7) with preexposure of the barmarker. Panel at the left: Bright luminance condition. Panel at the right: Dim luminance condition. (Data from Hagenzieker et al., 1990.) See text for explanation.

5.7 An alternative

In the last two sections we presented a detailed analysis of performance in an atypical bar-probe task: the indicator preceded the display. We analysed performance in exactly this condition because our main interest is in attention in vision. In this context the factors that contribute to the sharply W-shaped serial position curve for correct reports are of most importance. We showed that at least two factors determine this serial position curve: probe alignment (see section 5.5) and lateral masking in combination with retinal acuity (see section 5.6). Both factors are most parsimoniously regarded as influencing the stream of information processing relatively early, and therefore seem to support the early selection view.

Recently, strong support that it is indeed early selection under these conditions was provided by an unsuspected source. Mewhort, Johns and Coble (in press) concluded on the basis of a series of experiments that, under these conditions, subjects do not select from a postcategorical representation, but use the probe to select a part of the precategorical representation for perceptual analysis! The experimental paradigm that led them to this important conclusion was the paradigm introduced by Pashler (1984). Although in that paradigm RT is the main dependent variable, we had better consider the results of that research here.

Pashler modified the bar-probe task so that it provided a latency measure. Subjects were shown displays with four As and four Es. An arrow designated one of these characters. The subject had to indicate as fast as possible whether that character was an A or an E. There were two letter-quality conditions: the characters in the display were either clear or visually degraded. In the critical exposure condition the letter display was preexposed for 200 ms before appearing concurrently with the arrow for 150 ms. The late selection views contend that subjects address items at a postcategorical level. With a 200 ms preview, there is sufficient time to overcome the effect of stimulus degradation on identification and to load the postcategorical store with the identity information needed for task performance. So, there is no reason to expect any effect of the quality manipulation. But there was a strong effect. In the 'decreased display quality' condition RTs were considerably longer than in the 'clear display' condition. Accordingly, Pashler rejected the idea that the postcategorical store was the store addressed and concluded that the subjects used the arrow to address the early, precategorical, data.

In an intriguing series of experiments, Mewhort et al. (in press) used this paradigm and variations on this paradigm. Pashler's results were replicated (experiment 1). Moreover, it was shown that the stimulus quality manipulation produced the same effects with preexposure of the arrow indicator (experiments 3 and 4). Consistent with our analysis Mewhort and associates conclude that in these conditions subjects use the probe to focus on a narrow part of the precategorical internal representation, i.e., use early information. In vision, selection is really selection in vision.

In a typical bar-probe task, however, an arrow *following* the display indicates the item to be reported. In the recent past most investigators used this typical bar-probe task because they were more interested in memory than in the operation of central attention in vision (see section 5.2). Mewhort and associates also used the quality manipulation paradigm to see what happens with this exposure sequence. Also, under these conditions there were small, albeit non-significant, quality effects (experiments 2 and 3). However, as a result of the large numbers of errors, the very large RTs and the real possibility of a speed–accuracy confound in this condition, the data cannot be very well interpreted. So, the issue of where, i.e., at what level, the selective mechanism intervenes in a typical, post-barmarker, bar-probe task is still open. The rest of this section is devoted to this issue.

In research using the partial-report bar-probe task for studying memories in vision, instead of the operation of central attention in vision, the factors that contribute to the reduction in accuracy of report with increasing probe delays are regarded as of most importance. So, let us also have a brief look at what factors determine this decrease in accuracy with increasing probe delays.

In the last, and in my view rather desperate, defence of their late selection position, Mewhort et al. (1988) argue that three factors are involved:

- a decreasing probability that an item will remain in the character buffer after a specified time, i.e., a decreasing item retention;
- a decreasing probability that the probe will be assigned to the character buffer position which matches its position in the display, i.e., a decreasing probe alignment;
- a decreasing probability that an item will retain its correct position within the character buffer after a specified time, i.e., a decreasing location retention (see Mewhort et al., 1988, p. 731).

By means of a Monte-Carlo simulation study, Mewhort et al. (1988) show that an implementation of these assumptions is capable of producing all relevant probe-delay data, i.e., the probe-delay data for correct reports, for location errors and for item errors. They conclude: 'the simulation based on the dual-buffer model, an implementation of the late selection position, provides a very good fit to the data ...' (Mewhort et al., 1988, p. 733).

Two remarks about this conclusion have to be made, however. Firstly, the factors implemented by Mewhort et al. do not really discriminate between the early and late selection position. While the last factor is possibly unique to the late selection position (is it really?), the first two are certainly not. The view that part of the decreasing accuracy is due to probe alignment problems is completely compatible with the early selection view (see section 5.5), and something like item availability or item retention has always been a basic ingredient of the early selection explanation (see section 5.6). So, the latter two factors cannot be claimed in favour of the late selection view (see, e.g., Van der Heijden, 1987). Secondly, what Mewhort et al. (1988) basically do is to solve a set of equations with two unknowns by using three, time-dependent, parameters. (At each probe delay the sum of the proportions of correct reports, location errors and item errors equals 1.00. So, if two are known, the third is given.) Such a set of equations can also be solved with two time-dependent parameters. An approximate solution with three parameters is not a major scientific accomplishment.

As just stated the early and late selection views have two causal factors in common: probe alignment and something like item availability or item retention. Of course, the late selection argument loses all its force if it can be shown that exactly these two factors can account for all the interesting findings obtained with partial-report bar-probe tasks at any arbitrary small probe delay or combination of small probe delays: the spatial distribution of correct reports, the spatial distribution of location errors, the spatial distribution of item errors, etc., etc. In this section we show that the combined 'probe alignment/lateral masking and retinal acuity' explanation has indeed sufficient power to account for all interesting observations obtained with the bar-probe task. To this end, we use a numerical example (we are only interested in the qualitative pattern, not in the exact quantitative results that vary from experiment to experiment).

Table 5.7.1 presents, in terms of probabilities, the essence of the two explanations that in combination have to account for performance in the bar-probe task.

The row labelled $I+$ makes explicit the retinal-acuity–lateral-masking explanation at some, arbitrary probe delay or combination of probe delays. It gives the probability of correct item identity information per array position for positions 1 to 8 (note that the distribution is W-shaped, as postulated by this explanation; see section 5.6). The row labelled $I-$ gives the complements, i.e., the probabilities that correct identity information is not available.

Table 5.7.1 Probability values used in a numerical example implementing the retinal-acuity–lateral-masking explanation (rows $I+$ and $I-$) and the probe-alignment explanation (rows Cue Position 1, 2, ..., 8). (See text for further explanation.)

Item Position		1	2	3	4	5	6	7	8
$I+$		.80	.40	.60	.90	.90	.60	.40	.80
$I-$		.20	.60	.40	.10	.10	.40	.60	.20
Cue Position	1	.70	.30						
	2	.40	.40	.20					
	3		.10	.60	.30				
	4			.05	.90	.05			
	5				.05	.90	.05		
	6					.30	.60	.10	
	7						.20	.40	.40
	8							.30	.70

In the rest of the table the alignment-difficulty-of-probe explanation is specified in terms of probabilities per probe position. (In fact, in these rows something like the distance effect observed with location cues, described in Chapter 4, is implemented.) For instance, the table specifies that a probe at item position 3 is correctly aligned on 0.60 of the trials, is misaligned to the left on 0.10 of the trials and misaligned to the right on 0.30 of the trials (see: Cue Position 3).

The combination of explanations can result in four different, covert, outcomes: both position correct and identity correct ($P+I+$), position correct and identity incorrect ($P+I-$), position incorrect but the identity (on that incorrect position) correct ($P-I+$), and position incorrect and identity (on that incorrect position) also incorrect ($P-I-$). Per position, the expected values for these four different outcomes can simply be obtained by multiplying (and summing) the appropriate item and position probabilities. Table 5.7.2 presents the resulting values.

Table 5.7.2 Covert outcomes of combination of explanations per target or cue position. *P+I+*: Position and identity correct; *P+I–*: Position correct and identity incorrect; *P–I+*: Position incorrect and identity on that position correct; *P–I–*: Both position and identity on that position incorrect (see text for further explanation).

		P+I+	*P+I–*	*P–I+*	*P–I–*
Cue Position	1	.560	.140	.120	.180
	2	.160	.240	.440	.160
	3	.360	.240	.310	.090
	4	.810	.090	.075	.025
	5	.810	.090	.075	.025
	6	.360	.240	.310	.090
	7	.160	.240	.440	.160
	8	.560	.140	.120	.180

From table 5.7.2, the expected probabilities per position for correct reports, location errors and intrusions are easily derived. The formulas that have to be used are

$$P(\text{correct}) = P+I+ + (1/25)\ P–I– \tag{5.7.1}$$

$$P(\text{Loc.error}) = P–I+ + (7/25)\ P+I– + (6/25)\ P–I– \tag{5.7.2}$$

$$P(\text{Intrusion}) = (18/25)\ P+I– + (18/25)\ P–I– \tag{5.7.3}$$

Formula (5.7.1) states that the probability of a correct response equals the probability that both position and identity are correct plus a fraction of the probability that position was incorrect and the identity on that incorrect position was also incorrect. The latter factor estimates the probability of a correct guess, given incorrect position information. There are 26 (letters of the alphabet) minus 1 (the item is incorrectly recognized, so its name is excluded) equals 25 possible recognition responses. One of these 25 possible responses consists of the name of the target (formulas (5.7.2) and (5.7.3) have to be interpreted in a similar way).

Table 5.7.3 presents the expected probabilities per position and averaged over positions (X), and the left panel in figure 5.7.1 presents the results in graphical form. The reader is invited to compare this figure with figure 3, panel 1, in Mewhort et al. (1981, p. 56), reproduced in the right panel of figure 5.7.1. The latter figure shows the average performance for a group of subjects over probe delays of 0, 40, 80, 120 and 160 ms.

Table 5.7.3 Expected proportions correct reports, location errors and intrusions, per target or cue position (see text for further explanation).

		Correct	Location E	Intrusion
Cue Position	1	.5672	.2024	.2304
	2	.1664	.5456	.2880
	3	.3636	.3988	.2376
	4	.8110	.1062	.0828
	5	.8110	.1062	.0828
	6	.3636	.3988	.2376
	7	.1664	.5456	.2880
	8	.5672	.2024	.2304
	X	.4771	.3133	.2097

What this excercise shows is that, with the combined 'retinal-acuity–lateral-masking' and 'probe alignment' explanations, it is easy to construct a complete pattern of results that shows all important characteristics for any arbitrary (combination of) relatively small probe delay(s):

– the 'correct' distribution is sharply W-shaped;
– the 'location error' distribution is sharply M-shaped and mainly complements the 'correct' distribution;
– there are more location errors than intrusions;
– the 'intrusion' distribution is U-shaped or mildly M-shaped.

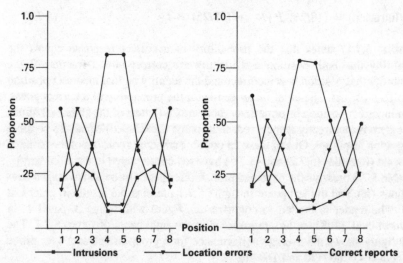

Figure 5.7.1 Proportions responses per position for three different response categories as obtained in a numerical example (panel at the left) and as reported by Mewhort et al., 1981 (panel at the right). See text for further explanation.

It will be clear that the combination of explanations used yields mainly near location errors and only few far location errors (see table 5.7.1 and equation (5.7.2)). From tables 5.7.1 and 5.7.3 it is also readily apparent that the correct localization distribution is higher and somewhat flatter than the correct identification distribution. In short, the combination explanation is capable of accounting for all relevant results obtained in partial-report bar-probe tasks.

The main conclusion from this section and the previous sections is, that neither the data obtained with pre-cues and simultaneous cues, nor the data obtained with post-cues at relevant SOAs force us to assume that visible persistence, i.e., the precategorical feature buffer, or, stated bluntly, vision, plays no role in partial-report and partial-report bar-probe tasks. There is no need for the counterintuitive late selection view. It appears that the early selection assumption of the orthodox iconic memory view can adequately account for (most of) the results. So, we conclude, as in Chapter 3: Attentional selection in vision is early selection.

This conclusion remains valid, even when one wishes to maintain Mewhort and associates' important theoretical contribution: the decomposition of the ambiguous 'reading' concept into the two independent subprocesses of identification and attentional selection. In this context it is important to notice that the combination of explanations presented in this section is completely consistent with, and even implements, that point of view: the processing parameters and the selection parameters in table 5.7.1 are mathematically independent and simply multiplied for obtaining the probability estimates. However, with this point of view, early selection has not to be interpreted as selective processing. Early selection then stands for selective addressing of available responses by means of early, visual, information: something like 'postcategorical filtering' and 'selection' (see Van der Heijden, 1981; see also sections 3.9 and 4.10). We now turn to some further positive evidence in favour of the early selection view.

5.8 Early selection: circular arrays

The previous sections showed that, with linear arrays, peculiar and unique phenomena are observed that easily obscure and even distract from important information about the working and properties of selective attention. Probe alignment errors, differential retinal acuity and differential lateral masking introduce so many complications that the issues of real interest are nearly completely obscured. Of course, positioning the items on the circumference of an imaginary circle removes all problems that go with the use of linear arrays; retinal acuity, lateral masking and effectiveness of the barmarker are the same for the different positions in a circular array. Moreover, within the range of acceptable array sizes, appreciably fewer probe alignment errors are to be expected with circular than with linear arrays, and, as a result, the phenomena of interest are more readily apparent. The reason for this is very simple. Items on the circumference of an

Table 5.8.1 Length of linear arrays and radius of circular arrays with equivalent inter-item spacings. The formula used is $L = 2 \pi R$ (L and R in degrees of visual angle). Xs indicate often-used array sizes.

Length of linear array (L)	Radius of circular array (R)
1	0.16
2x	0.32
3x	0.48
4	0.64
5	0.80
6	0.96x
7	1.11x
8	1.27

imaginary circle are generally much wider spaced than items in a row. Table 5.8.1 illustrates this effect. For each linear array length the radius of a circle with equivalent inter-item spacing is given.

So, we leave the linear array studies and turn to the simpler circular array studies. In this section we pursue the early–late selection issue one step further. The important point we want to make is that within the circular array tradition, as opposed to the linear array tradition just described, the early selection assumption has never been really doubted (see, e.g., Eriksen and Steffy, 1964; Eriksen and Collins, 1969; Eriksen and Rohrbaugh, 1970; Keele and Chase, 1967; Lupker and Massaro, 1979; Van der Heijden, 1984; 1986; Van der Heijden, Schreuder, De Loor and Hagenzieker, 1987). There was not only no reason to doubt the early selection position. Results obtained with circular arrays in tasks concerned with the early–late selection issue strongly indicated that selection in this type of task is early selection. We discuss two lines of evidence: Keele and Chase's (1967) study and the research of Van der Heijden and associates.

Keele and Chase (1967) used circular, ten-item, arrays. The interesting feature of their study is the error analysis used to assess the visual similarity between response letter and target letter when an error was made. For this analysis they collected all error data in three stimulus–response matrices: one for short probe delays (0 to 100 ms), one for intermediate delays (250 to 500 ms) and one for very long delays (1000 to 5000 ms). After some further operations, these matrices were correlated with a matrix giving the percentage overlap for each pair of letters (i.e., the visual confusability for each pair of letters). The correlations found were 0.37, 0.17, and 0.17 for short, intermediate and long delays, respectively. All correlations were significant, indicating that at least part of the error responses were visually similar to the target. More important, however, is the observation that the correlation was greater at short delays than at longer delays, indicating that, especially with the (important for the study of attention) short delays, error responses resemble the target item. Of course, this pattern of results is clearly consistent with, and supports, the view that early information plays an important role in partial-report bar-probe tasks.

In our research concerned with the problem of the locus of central selection in bar-probe tasks, we further investigated this role of early information. To this end, we tested a prediction that directly follows from the early selection views. The prediction is that the function relating one type of errors – real misidentifications of the target – to probe delays has to exhibit an inverted U-shape. This early selection prediction was independently derived by Van der Heijden (1984, p. 452) and Mewhort et al. (1984, p. 295).

Our reasoning was as follows. The early selection views maintain that the bar-probe is applied to the contents of a precategorical visual store, containing rapidly decaying, literal stimulus information (i.e., to a rapidly fading visual image). With short probe delays, the bar-probe is applied to a visual store containing high quality visual information. Depending upon the stimuli and exposure conditions used, a certain proportion of misidentifications is to be expected. With very long probe delays, the probe is applied to the contents of a store containing virtually no visual information. Responding will be mainly based on guessing and there is no reason to expect an abundance of misidentifications. With *intermediate* probe delays, however, the probe is applied to a store with contents that are somewhat, but not fully, decayed. Especially then, misidentifications are to be expected. So, misidentifications should start at a certain level at the shorter probe delays, should increase with increasing intermediate probe delays, and should decrease again at the larger probe delays, i.e., the function relating misidentifications to probe delays should exhibit an inverted U-shape.

Mewhort et al. (1984) also argued that early selection views predict an inverted-U function for misidentifications. Their reasoning is essentially the same, except that they assume that with the larger probe delays responses are selected from a pool of stored categorized items that have been read-in non-selectively before the probe arrived ('nonselective transfer'). Also then, there is no reason to expect an abundance of misidentifications with the larger probe delays.

So, early selection views predict that the function relating misidentifications to probe delays should exhibit an inverted U-shape. It is very difficult to see how late selection views, maintaining that the bar-probe is applied to the contents of a categorical store in which identity information is retained as abstract codes, can predict an inverted-U function for misidentifications.

The experimental problem is, of course, how to isolate the genuine misidentifications. The classification of errors used in the analysis of performance in partial-report bar-probe tasks is only a descriptive classification and fails to give the wanted information. As the equations in section 5.7 show, an item error or intrusion, for instance, can result from an error of identification, but also from a failure of localization combined with a failure of identification (see equation 5.7.3); a location error can result from a failure of identification, from a failure of localization and also from a failure of localization combined with a failure of identification (see equation 5.7.2). So, both error categories contain misidentifications and contain more than misidentifications only, or, none of the error types distinguished in the analysis of partial-report bar-probe tasks measures all and only misidentifications. To test the prediction a paradigm is needed that permits the isolation of the misidentifications.

In our paradigm, four pairs of items were used. The pairs were chosen in such a way that *genuine misidentification of an item mainly resulted in the naming of the other member of the pair and virtually never in the naming of a member of another pair*. With a proper stimulus composition this property of the stimuli allowed us to estimate the number of genuine misidentifications (see Van der Heijden, 1986, for an extensive description of the paradigm and the analysis). We collected two sets of items that sufficed these conditions: four pairs of colours (see Van der Heijden, 1984) and four pairs of letters (see Van der Heijden et al., 1987). The set of colour items was obtained by trial and error in pilot experiments. To choose the set of letters, the confusion matrix reported by Van der Heijden, Malhas and Van den Roovaart (1984) was used. (See Heisser, 1988, for the details of this selection procedure.)

We ran five experiments that allowed us to assess the function relating real misidentifications to probe delays. In experiments I and II the colour patches were used and in experiments III, IV and V the letters. Table 5.8.2 presents the proportions of misidentifications as a function of probe delays. The table shows that in all five experiments the proportions of misidentifications first increase and then, with larger probe delays, decrease.

Table 5.8.2 Proportions of genuine misidentifications as a function of probe delay for two experiments with colours as items (Van der Heijden, 1984) and three experiments with letters as items (Van der Heijden et al., 1987). The maximum proportion of misidentifications is in brackets.

Experiment		Probe delay (ms)				
		0	100	200	300	400
Colour	(I)	.141	.172	(.180)	.159	
Colour	(II)	.135	.156	(.187)	.167	
Letter	(III)	.068	.079	(.115)	.111	
Letter	(IV)	.174	.193	(.204)	.201	
Letter	(V)	.154	(.200)	.199	.185	.176

In evaluating the size of the effects at least three points have to be taken into account. First, we are inspecting here a small subset (the genuine misidentifications) of a subset (the item errors) of a subset (the error responses) of the total number of responses. Of course, only small effects are to be expected with such a small part of the data. Second, the data in table 5.8.2 are the raw proportions of misidentifications, uncorrected for guessing. An appropriate correction for guessing sharpens the inverted U-shape. Third, our item selection procedures only maximized within-pair errors. Only with perfect stimulus material, channeling all and only identification errors to the category misidentifications, is the maximum effect to be expected.

If these considerations are taken into account, the conclusion is allowed, that the total pattern of results strongly suggests that misidentifications really first increase and then decrease with increasing probe delays. In other words, the data strongly suggest that the function relating misidentifications to probe delays has indeed an inverted U-shape. This strongly suggests early selection in the present type of task, especially for the, for the study of selective attention, relevant range of probe delays.

Taken all together, the linear array data do not force one to accept the late selection hypothesis. Pashler (1984) and Mewhort et al. (in press) provided the important evidence in favour of early selection for bar-probe tasks with pre-cues and simultaneous cues (see section 5.7). The probe-alignment findings (see section 5.5) plus the retinal-acuity–lateral-masking phenomena (see section 5.6) can adequately account for the results obtained with postexposure of the bar-marker (see section 5.7: a simplistic one-factor early select-and-process, i.e., the 'read', explanation has to be replaced by a more realistic two-factor explanation). The circular array data that allow a better view at what is really going on also provide supporting evidence for the early selection view. So, as in Chapter 3, the conclusion has to be: early selection. Finally, we are in a position to have a brief look at some of the properties of this early selection mechanism.

5.9 Eriksen's early research

C.W. Eriksen was the first to see the real importance of the bar-probe paradigm as a tool for investigating attentional processes. In his view, not the memory aspect, emphasized by most investigators (see section 5.2), but the selection aspect is what makes this paradigm very worthwhile.

> This perseverating image, or as Neisser (1967) termed it, icon, has generated considerable interest, but an equally if not more interesting characteristic of this experimental technique is the means by which attention can be selectively directed in a matter of milliseconds to the relevant stimulus item.
>
> (Eriksen and Collins, 1969, p. 254)

While nearly all visual information processing psychologists tried to assess properties of the newly discovered visual memory, Eriksen and associates started a line of research that tried 'to account for the selective capacity of humans and lower animals as well to respond to certain stimuli and effectively ignore others that appear equally potent on physical and time dimensions' (Eriksen and Lappin, 1967, p. 368).

Because for Eriksen selective attention is in essence 'the process by which one of a number of equally potent stimuli is selected and processed and the others ignored ...' (Eriksen and Rohrbaugh, 1970, p. 331), he positioned the items on the circumference of an imaginary circle around the fixation point, i.e., made the items 'equally potent'. Furthermore, in the initial research the experimental technique was to present the displays at an energy level that led to above-chance accuracy but appreciably less than 100% correct performance. In most experiments also, conditions with leading indicators were included. So, different levels of appropriateness of foreknowledge of position with constant quality of visual information (see section 5.1) could be investigated.

From Eriksen's early research with circular arrays and accuracy as the dependent variable two sets of results are of special importance. The first set contains indications of the *temporal* properties of the selective process and the second set indications of the *spatial* properties. The two sets of results are of importance because together they lead to a complete characterization of attentional selectivity with multi-item displays in vision.

In Eriksen and Collins's (1969) study temporal properties were investigated. The duration of the selective process was the topic of main concern. The authors used different kinds of indicators, but here we only briefly discuss the results obtained with the 'arrow head' indicator: a symbolic cue consisting of a black arrowhead located at the centre of the circular display and rotated in its directional orientation to designate one of the letters. To obtain estimates of the time required to process this symbolic cue, or to apprehend its meaning, the indicator was presented at various lead times before the occurrence of the display. (R was 0.9 deg of visual angle and the number of items presented simultaneously, N, was 6. A control condition showed that there were virtually no probe alignment errors.) It was found that performance improved until the indicator led the display by approximately 200 ms. The correct conclusion from this result was that 'This asymptotic value would indicate the *maximum* time required for precise selection to take place' (Eriksen and Colegate, 1971, p. 321; italics mine).

Unfortunately, this important result has not entered the literature subsequently in a proper way. Eriksen and Colegate (1971, p. 321) also state 'Research indicates that the selective process requires between 200 and 300 msec (Eriksen & Collins, 1969; Averbach & Coriell, 1961)'. Since then a 'cue-decoding time' for symbolic cues of 200–300 ms seems generally accepted (see, e.g., Eriksen and Hoffman, 1973, pp. 158–9; Coltheart, 1980a, p. 210; 1980b, p. 64). But, as I have set out elsewhere, Averbach and Coriell were *not* interested in the duration of the selective process; in line with the 'memories-in-vision' bias of that time they were only interested in estimating 'effective storage time', i.e., the temporal extent of the newly discovered visual memory (see Van der Heijden, 1987, p. 434). And as just described, Eriksen and Collins (1969) only found a *maximum* cue decoding time of 200 ms. Because the asymptotic performance is determined by the slowest cue decoding time of the slowest subject, the average cue decoding time must be considerably smaller. In fact, figures 2 and 3 in Eriksen and Collins (1969) show that for the arrowhead most to nearly all of the increase in performance is between a simultaneous cue and a pre-cue leading by 100 ms. So, what Eriksen and Collins's data show is that with *symbolic* cues there is indeed a substantial cue-decoding time (see also section 4.6). The modal cue-decoding time, however, is appreciably smaller than 200 ms, and not between 200 and 300 ms (see also Lupker and Massaro, 1979, p. 67).

In Eriksen and Rohrbaugh's (1970) study spatial properties of the selective process were investigated. The effect of physical spacing between adjacent items was, besides the effect of number of items presented simultaneously, the topic of main concern. A symbolic cue – a line pointing in the direction of the target – was used. In their first experiment spacing was varied by either grouping the items close together on adjacent positions on the circumference of the imaginary circle or by distributing the same number of items over all positions ($R = 1.1$ deg of visual angle; $N = 4$, 8 or 12). It appeared that performance was significantly poorer in the 'grouped' condition, i.e., with the closer spacing, than in the 'distributed' condition, i.e., with the larger spacing. Near location errors were also somewhat more numerous in the 'grouped' condition than in the 'distributed' condition. Of course, this finding is not surprising. Also with circular arrays with items closely spaced, probe alignment errors are to be expected. It was furthermore found that accuracy decreased with increasing number of elements presented, this independent of the spacing of the items. Moreover, accuracy monotonically decreased from pre-cue (100 ms before stimulus presentation), via simultaneous cue, to post-cue (50 ms after display presentation).

A subsequent experiment appeared to rule out the possibility that part of the spacing effect was caused by contour interaction effects or lateral masking (see section 5.1). However, the function for 'letters' in their figure 3 is not completely clear with regard to this issue. In our view the presence of lateral masking cannot really be excluded. Nevertheless, the authors conclude that the spacing effect was attributable to a greater tendency for subjects to confuse the target letter with an immediately adjacent one (Eriksen and Rohrbaugh, 1970, p. 342).

Eriksen and Rohrbaugh (1970) brought the temporal and spatial properties together in a model for selective attention accounting for performance in bar-probe tasks: the variable-power lens analogy. The cue-delay effect (Eriksen and Collins, 1969) and the spacing effect (Eriksen and Rohrbaugh, 1970) are the crucial observations upon which the model is based.

> One way in which spatial proximity could affect an attention process would be if selectivity required time for spatial precision. Prior research has shown (...) that selective attention can require 200–300 msec. Further, Eriksen and Collins (...) have found that during this time the icon is decreasing in clarity or legibility. Let us assume that attention is somewhat analogous to a variable-power lens. At low power settings, a large field of view is obtained, but with little detail or information about the individual elements in the field. As the power of the lens is increased, the field narrows, but with a large increase in

the detail that can be resolved about the elements still remaining in the field. If the analogy is carried further and selective attention is compared to a focusing of the lens, and if it is assumed that this focusing process requires time, then the effect of spatial proximity between letters in the display could be interpreted in the following manner.

Attentional focus is at a low power setting with a wide field of view until the probe is presented. When the probe occurs, the attentional system begins to focus on the probed location, but during the time the focusing is occurring, the icon of the display is decaying. If there is insufficient time – before the display decays beyond intelligibility – for attentional focus to reduce the field to encompass only the probed element, two or more letters may still be in the attentional field. This could lead to confusion as to which of these letters was the probed element. Accuracy in identifying these several alternatives could also be expected to be less, since the power of the attentional field has not had time to increase to a maximum resolution. This lack of sufficient time for complete attentional focusing would thus result in errors from two sources: confusion as to which of several elements was the probed one, and less resolution or identification accuracy for the elements remaining in the attentional field.

The data ... are commensurate with such a model. These data indicate that confusions did occur with immediately adjacent letters, but more important, they also show that the tendency for these confusions increased with decreasing time for attentional focusing. If the indicator preceded and terminated 100 msec. before the display, not only was performance in identifying the target letter better, but there was virtually no tendency to confuse an immediately adjacent letter with the target. When there was less time for attentional focusing, as when the probe was simultaneous with the display or was delayed 50 msec. after it, adjacent-letter confusions became more frequent and identification accuracy of the target letter decreased. This result is consistent with our expectations (outlined above) for the event that the attentional field did not have time to focus to the maximum before the display icon decayed.

(Eriksen and Rohrbaugh, 1970, pp. 338–9)

At this point it is worthwhile to notice three features of this variable-power lens model.

- Firstly, two spatial aspects have to be distinguished: the size of the field of view of the lens (wide or narrow) and the position the lens is pointing at (left, right, etc.).
- Secondly, corresponding with these two spatial aspects, two 'movements' of the lens have to be distinguished. Explicit is the increase in power or the focusing of the lens over time. But this focusing is focusing on one spatial position, so also some kind of directing or pointing of the lens over time is involved.

- Thirdly, the size of the field of view of the lens, i.e., its power setting, determines the *degree* or level of processing of the information within its range (in this way the model accounts for the identification aspect of task performance). The position the lens is pointing at – but also its size of field of view – determines what information, i.e., from what position, is processed (in this way the model accounts for the selection aspect of task performance).

It will be clear that, as in the 'reading' notion (see section 5.2), in this 'zoom lens' metaphor of selective attention the processes of selection and of identification are inextricably interwoven. They can be distinguished, but not separated. Attention is in the business of identifying the items it selects or in the business of selecting items it has to identify. Moreover, in this model, global or approximate selection goes together with shallow processing, and precise selection with thorough processing. In the next chapter we return to this and to related proposals.

5.10 Attention and processing

To assess where we have arrived now, it is worthwhile distinguishing three different theoretical issues, that are in principle independent but in fact often (implicitly or explicitly) sold in combination: issues related to the function of central attention, the early vs late selection issue, and the limited vs unlimited capacity issue.

Let us first have a look at the function of attention. In section 4.7 we saw that, for one or another reason, it is not generally agreed within information processing psychology that information processing, i.e., the identification or categorization of visual information, is most parsimoniously accounted for in terms of 'hardware'. Whereas it is difficult to see what else is needed besides the visual information processing system together with an appropriate eye movement system, most investigators agree that in addition 'something else' is needed. The main idea here is not that 'something else' is needed for directing the eye to the regions of interest and that the visual system then takes further care of the processing of information. The main idea is that 'something else' is also needed for the processing of information within a fixation. More specifically, a great number of authors have as a basic assumption that (selective) attention is not only involved in the selection of information, but also in, and even needed for, the processing of visual information. Most of these authors conceive selective attention as a spotlight (see section 4.4) or as a zoom lens (see section 5.9). It is assumed that the information that is in focus or within the beam is processed in detail, whereas information falling outside the beam is not processed or receives only very gross (preattentive) processing (see, e.g., Eriksen and Rohrbaugh, 1970; Eriksen and Hoffman, 1973; Eriksen and Murphy, 1987; Kahneman and Henik, 1981; Broadbent, 1982; La Berge, 1983; Kahneman and Treisman, 1984). The 'reading' notion, with selection and processing combined, clearly reflects these ideas.

In order to avoid the duplication of function in eye and attention we tried to assign attention a proper and unique role. We suggested as a real and attractive possibility that the prime function of attention is in the time domain, not in the space domain (see section 4.7). More specifically we assumed that attention is for temporal resolution over space and for assigning temporal priorities (see section 4.8).

The important point now is, that nothing in the data presented in this chapter really contradicts this view. In fact, in section 5.7 we showed that the orthodox 'reading' notion, combining selection and identification, is not really needed to account for the performance observed with bar-probe tasks. (Notice that the zoom lens model is simply a variant of the 'reading notion'.) Just as Mewhort and associates, we decomposed the reading notion into two independent subprocesses. One subprocess deals with the identification of the information. Retinal acuity and lateral masking determine the quality of its results. The second process is an early selection process. It is in principle independent of the identification process. Position of the probe in space and time, and spacing of the items determine the outcome and the quality of this operation. In the model this selective process is not involved in the identification of the information. It selects one from among a number of simultaneous alternatives. To account for performance in the bar-probe task it is sufficient to assume that it selects a position in space and assigns temporal priority to the item related to that position and not to items related to other positions. Nevertheless this view is not the received view. In the next chapter we will meet various versions of the reading notion again (and again).

After what has been said in this chapter, not very much more has to be said about the early vs late selection issue. It appeared that there is no need for the late selection assumption. Early selection, or selection in vision, can adequately account for the results (see sections 5.7 and 5.8). Of course, in line with the analysis presented in sections 3.9 and 4.10, and also in line with the decomposition just briefly discussed (see also section 5.7), this early selection is most parsimoniously interpreted as 'selective addressing', not as 'selective processing'.

Much more has to be said about the limited capacity vs unlimited capacity issue. The reason is that in the past the early vs late selection issue and the limited capacity vs unlimited capacity issue were not regarded as independent issues, but sold as combinations (see section 2.7). A stand with regard to the selection (processing) issue implied a stand with regard to the processing (selection) issue, was the idea. Exactly this, in my view erroneous, conviction is at the basis of the rather generally accepted point of view that the data presented in this chapter contain one important piece of evidence that can be taken as supporting the limited capacity notion: the evidence in favour of the early selection view. This evidence has been abused in two different, but related, ways in the recent past. Both ways quite forcefully suggest that by accepting the early selection view one also accepts the limited capacity view.

In the first way of reasoning, the general evidence in favour of early selection was regarded as the end of a general line of argumentation. The conclusion was: The information processing system has indeed a limited central capacity for processing information. The grounds for this erroneous conclusion had already ripened in an early stage of theorizing. In Broadbent's (1958) influential filter model and in all subsequent variations of this model, limited central capacity and the protecting mechanism of early selection were inextricably connected. Just because the system was supposed to have a limited central capacity, it required or needed early selection: one or another kind of filter (Broadbent, 1958; 1971) or attenuator (Treisman, 1960), that had to protect the system from going under. But from 'limited capacity therefore early selection' it does not follow 'early selection therefore limited capacity'. (This is the fallacy of affirming the consequence; Popper, 1959.) Early selection is what is observed; limited central capacity is only an a-priori theoretical notion.

In the second way of reasoning, the detailed evidence in favour of early selection was regarded as specifying the capacity limits in detail. From the observation that it appears easy to select on the basis of elementary physical attributes (e.g., position or colour) but not on the basis of identity or categorical information (letter, digit) it was concluded that physical attributes were represented in the system but derived properties were not (see sections 5.0 and 5.2). This was taken as proof of the point of view that the system has indeed a limited capacity for categorizing, identifying or processing information. But from 'is not represented and can therefore not serve as the basis for selection' it does not follow 'cannot serve as the basis for selection and is therefore not represented'. (Indeed, again the fallacy of affirming the consequence.) Effectiveness of selection is what is observed; that some information is not represented is simply postulated by the a-priori limited capacity notion. (It is perfectly possible that identity information is represented in the system but that it is only difficult to select or even inaccessible for central selection. For this argument see, e.g., Coltheart, 1984; Duncan, 1981; Pashler, 1984; see especially section 3.9 where this possibility is worked out in detail.) Thus, also from the detailed evidence in favour of early selection, nothing really follows about the processing capacity of the human information processing system.

So, from early selection as a given, nothing about the processing capacity of the system really follows. In Alan Allport's words:

> behavioral evidence about the relative efficiency of "selection" – i.e., the relative efficiency of *selective cueing* – is simply irrelevant to questions about the level of processing accorded to the "unselected information". To put it another way, the controversy regarding "early" versus "late" selection has systematically confused "selection" as selective *cueing* and "selection" as selective *processing*. Once the distinction is made clear, there may even be no controversy.

> (Allport, 1987, p. 409)

Taking all together, the results presented in this chapter provide some insight into where, i.e., at what stage of information processing, selection occurs. The data strongly suggest that attentional selection is early selection, or, that, in vision, attentional selection is really selection in *vision*, not in one or another higher order memory containing abstract information. To the problems of whether there are really processing limitations and whether attention is really in the business of identifying or categorizing visual information we return in the next chapter.

Chapter 6

Multiple-item detection and recognition tasks with latency as the dependent variable

6.0 The start

This chapter is concerned with the research on characteristics of selective attention as observed with multiple-element displays and latency (RT) as the dependent variable. It was exactly this research that brought surprising discoveries. The results were surprising because they were not anticipated on the basis of theories formulated to explain the data obtained with earlier research using accuracy (or a crude overall latency measure) as the dependent variable. Also the research itself is quite surprising. It is no longer benefits, but costs due to response competition (see section 4.10), that are regarded as the basic data. In this section we first briefly sketch the theoretical background that made the results surprising. In the next two sections, we describe the basic findings that forced the change from benefits to costs. The rest of the chapter can be regarded as a desperate search for the characteristics of selective attention in vision.

In the early 1970s Eriksen and associates changed their variant of the circular bar-probe task with accuracy as the dependent variable (see section 5.9) into a bar-probe task with RT as the dependent variable. In their first publication they are very explicit about their theory-derived convictions:

> An essential characteristic of a concept of selective attention is the ability to respond in a predetermined or preset way to only one or a small subset from a number of equally potent stimuli. The operation of selective attention in visual perception can be demonstrated in the following experimental arrangement: If a large number of letters or digits are simultaneously exposed for a brief duration, the human O is typically able to report only a small number, approximately four. Under the same conditions, if the O is told to report only the stimulus designated by a black bar or similar indicator, he can by some process, select this particular stimulus and report it with perfect accuracy. A necessary condition for this demonstration is the overload of information provided the O. The existence of a limited channel capacity is implied by the concept itself. Without such a limit, there would be no necessity for selective attention, as all stimuli would then be processed with equal accuracy at all times.
>
> (Eriksen and Hoffman, 1972a, p. 169)

So, the concept of selective attention is primarily characterized in terms of an ability to select, i.e., an ability to respond in a predetermined way to only one from a number of equally potent stimuli. The operation of selective attention can be demonstrated by a subject's ability to select information with perfect accuracy. In short, selective attention selects and is very good at that.

The concept of selective attention is, however, immediately brought into relation with concepts regarding the capacity of the information processing system (see also section 2.7). The operation of selective attention is necessary because a subject has only a limited capacity to process, i.e., to identify or categorize, the information, and perfect selection is necessary, otherwise capacity is wasted. If there were unlimited capacity for processing information there would be no necessity for selective attention. All stimuli would then be processed.

An assumption, not explicit in the quotation, but nevertheless strongly present in the background, is that it is actually attention that is responsible for the processing, and that it is actually attention that is limited in capacity (remember Eriksen and Rohrbaugh's, 1970, zoom lens model of selective attention, discussed in section 5.9). So, lurking in the background is the 'reading' assumption, combining, within the concept 'attention', the concepts 'selection' and 'processing'. In fact, this assumption was the dominant assumption of those days (see also section 5.2).

This 'reading' assumption, together with the available data, led to two basic convictions with regard to the 'attentional processing' of visual information.

The first basic conviction was that items (i.e., letters, digits, etc.) are processed serially, i.e., 'read' one after another (see also section 5.2). Eriksen and Hoffman are convinced that the processing, i.e., the identification, of the separate stimuli is serial in nature (see, however, section 5.9). In this context Eriksen and Hoffman (1972a, p. 169) refer to a study by Eriksen and Colegate (1971). Also Neisser (1967, p. 103) had proposed this serial processing hypothesis. Broadbent (1971, p. 173) pointed to Mackworth's (1963a) research in support of the serial processing of information. And the same idea was expressed by Treisman (1969, p. 293) where she states 'There is quite strong evidence that true division of attention is difficult or impossible and serial processing necessary both with two or more inputs and with tests for two or more targets.'

A second basic conviction at that time was that all dimensions of a single item, i.e., its colour, size, shape, etc., are processed in parallel. The experimental task that mainly provided the evidence underlying this idea of parallel processing of all dimensions of a single item was the test devised by Stroop (1935; see section 4.10). According to Treisman (1969) the different dimensions of an item are processed by different 'analysers'. A review of the Stroop literature forced her to conclude 'These findings suggest that focussing on particular perceptual analysers while excluding others may be difficult or impossible' (Treisman, 1969, p. 295). According to Kahneman the same data show that 'There is little evidence that an intention to attend to a particular dimension of experience can prevent the perceptual interpretation of other dimensions' (Kahneman, 1973, pp. 110–11).

So, at the start of the 1970s the theoretical assumptions with regard to selective attention were:

- selective attention selects and does so with nearly perfect accuracy,
- selective attention is also essential for or involved in the processing of the information.

In combination these two assumptions form the 'reading' assumption.

With regard to the processing of visual information the convictions were:

- the system, i.e., attention, has a limited capacity for processing information,
- with multiple-item digit or letter arrays the elements are processed one after another,
- all attributes of a selected item are processed in parallel.

Let us now have a look at the empirical evidence that challenged most of these assumptions and convictions.

6.1 The Stroop effect I: non-equivalent items

We just saw that in the early 1970s the basic convictions were that the items in a multiple-item array are processed in series, but that all dimensions of a selected single item, i.e., its colour, brightness, size, shape, position, etc., are processed in parallel. As stated, the experimental task that mainly provided the evidence underlying the idea of parallel processing of all dimensions of a single item was the test devised by Stroop (1935; see Dyer, 1973a, for an extensive review of the early research with this task).

We already introduced this task in section 4.10, so at this place a short summary suffices. The usual procedure with the Stroop test is to present Ss with cards with colour patches (card 1), colour words (card 2), and colour words written in non-corresponding colours (card 3). The important finding is that if the colours on the third card have to be named, performance is far inferior to performance on the first card: a great delay in colour-naming is found and often also a large number of errors is observed (the Stroop phenomenon or Stroop effect). If the words on this card have to be read, virtually no differences with word-reading on the second card are found, i.e., it is very difficult to demonstrate a 'reversed' Stroop effect. The Stroop effect is generally explained in terms of response competition. The idea is that in this task word reading cannot be prevented (i.e., word and colour are processed in parallel) and that the word reading response interferes with the colour naming response (see section 4.10).

Two modifications of the task are important. The first modification reduced this complex, multiple-response task to a much more tractable, simple single-trial task (see, e.g., Dalrymple-Alford and Budayr 1966; Sichel and Chandler, 1969; Hintzman et al., 1972; see also section 4.10). The second, and in the context of this chapter really important, modification was introduced by Dyer (1973b). He correctly noted that for the Stroop effect to obtain it was not essential that the word itself was in colour, i.e., that integral combinations of words and colours were used. Kamlet and Egeth (1969) used white words on small rectangles of colour and Dyer and Severance (1973) presented black words followed by a colour patch that consisted of a series of Xs. In both studies a delay of colour naming was found when the words were incongruent colour names. So, at least some spatial and temporal separation of the word and colour was allowed.

Dyer (1973b) extended these findings by really separating colours and words. In his colour naming task, black colour words and non-word colour patches were presented simultaneously, one 2 deg to the right and the other 2 deg to the left of a central fixation point. The sides where word and colour appeared were randomly varied from trial to trial. The exposure duration was 100 ms, so no useful eye movements could be made. Incongruent, neutral and congruent combinations were used. The important result was that also with this bilateral presentation procedure, incongruent names delayed colour naming and congruent colour names produced some facilitation, this relative to the neutral condition in which, instead of words, a series of Xs were presented together with the colour. Dyer concluded 'The results clearly indicate that this bilateral presentation of the color and word produces a large portion of the color-naming interference that occurs with individual presentations of conventional Stroop stimuli where the word and color are integrally combined', and 'Parallel processing of the separated word and color is clearly demonstrated by the facilitation and interference for color naming' (Dyer, 1973b, p. 316).

Subsequently, a great number of authors have replicated Dyer's finding (see, e.g., Van der Heijden, 1978; 1981; Gatti and Egeth, 1978; Merikle and Gorewich, 1979; Kahneman and Henik, 1981; Kahneman and Chajczyk, 1983; Van der Heijden, Hagenaar and Bloem, 1984; Hagenaar and Van der Heijden, 1986). So, not only with integral combinations but also with spatially separate presentation of colour and word, colour-naming interference is obtained. Spatial separation of (relevant) colour and (irrelevant) word in no way obliterates the Stroop effect. However, studies using integral combinations as well as separate presentations strongly indicate that the effect of the colour words is appreciably smaller with separate presentation of colour and word (see, e.g., Kahneman and Henik, 1981; Van der Heijden et al., 1984; see also Kahneman and Chajczyk, 1983, p. 500). To the possible theoretical implications of this difference we return in Chapter 8.

With the orthodox Stroop task, not only colour-naming interference is obtained. An equally important, although quite boring, finding is the negligible interference from colours on word-reading. Van der Heijden (1978; 1981, exp. I) investigated whether this result can also be reliably replicated with the procedure of separate bilateral presentation of the word and colour aspect. Virtually no interference was found. So, it is not spatial separation as such that introduces peculiar, Stroop-like, effects. The word-reading outcome, together with the colour-naming results mentioned above, lends strong support to the point of view that the integral combination of words and colours is not a necessary condition for producing the theoretically interesting Stroop phenomena. With spatially separate presentations similar phenomena are easily demonstrated.

Dyer's (1973b) results led to a large number of further variations and generalizations (see, e.g., Neumann, 1980; Van der Heijden, 1981), but, in the present context, these latter results are not really of importance. What is of importance is that the change from a single-item task (integral combination) into a multiple-item task (separate presentation) did not result in a dramatic change of results. This strongly suggests that there is not only parallel processing of the different attributes of a *single* item (Treisman, 1969; Kahneman, 1973). Also (different attributes from?) *different* items are apparently processed in parallel.

Of course, this outcome is damaging for the basic conviction that the items in a multiple-item array are processed in series. Moreover, just because of the parallel processing, the results also strongly suggest that, if selective attention indeed selects and processes, its selective performance is far from perfect. So, either the 'attention processes' assumption or the 'perfect selection' assumption is seriously challenged. To the problem whether only different attributes of different items (e.g., the colour of the patch and the shape of the word) can be processed in parallel, we turn in the next section.

6.2 The Stroop effect II: equivalent items

Given the evidence for parallel processing (of different attributes?) of different items obtained with spatially separate Stroop stimuli, i.e., with displays with 'non-equivalent' or 'non-equipotent' multiple items, the correctness of either the attention-processes hypothesis or the nearly-perfect-selection hypothesis has to be seriously doubted. It can be argued, however, that with such 'non-equivalent' inputs a unique and peculiar stimulus situation is created and that therefore the violation of one of these assumptions is simply an exception that can only be observed with colour item/word item displays. Then, of course, the important question is, whether the results obtained with 'equivalent' multiple-item arrays are in accord with the conviction that items are processed in series. In this context especially the research of Eriksen and associates with multiple-letter arrays is of importance.

The results of the first bar-probe study using RT as the dependent variable reported by Eriksen and associates seemed to support all prevailing convictions (see Eriksen and Hoffman, 1972a). Problems, however, already arose in a second study (Eriksen and Hoffman, 1972b). In that study RTs to voice a target letter were studied as a function of the spatial and temporal proximity of noise elements. The target was indicated by a barmarker. Two types of noise elements were used: letters and black discs. In this section we mainly look at the results obtained with letters as noise. In section 6.6 we look at the effects of the black discs.

It is of importance to know that in Eriksen and Hoffman's study the capital letters A, H, U, and M served as alternative target letters and simultaneously as noise letters. For present purposes the important result was that, especially with simultaneous appearance of target and noise, appreciably larger RTs were observed with the letters as noise than with the discs. To explain this unexpected pattern of results Eriksen and Hoffman (1972b, p. 204) surmised that 'A noise element can achieve recognition on some trials more rapidly than the target element itself and thus either engage the encoding process so that the target is somewhat delayed from encoding or, in the case of a parallel encoding process, result in response competition between the two letters that have been identified'. So, the possibility of some parallel processing of letters cannot be excluded.

In subsequent research Eriksen and associates, clearly aware of the theoretical importance of their observations, further investigated this unexpected effect (see, e.g., Eriksen and Hoffman, 1973; Eriksen and Eriksen, 1974; 1979; Eriksen and Schultz, 1979; Eriksen, Coles, Morris and O'Hara, 1985; see also Hoffman, 1975; Keren, 1976). Eriksen and Hoffman (1973) and Eriksen and Eriksen (1974) were particularly interested in the effect of the nature of the noise letters. In their experiments the Ss had to move a lever in one direction if the target was a member of a set of two (for instance, an H or an M), and in the other direction if it was a member of another set of two letters (for instance an A or a U). In Eriksen and Hoffman's (1973) experiment either (1) a single target was presented, or the target together with (2) letters from the same set (response compatible noise), (3) letters from the other set (response incompatible noise), or, (4) a mixture of letters from both sets. In Eriksen and Eriksen's (1974) experiment either (1) a single target was presented, or, the target together with a series of letters composed of (2) the same letter (identical noise), (3) the other letter from the same set (response compatible noise), (4) one of the letters from the other set (response incompatible noise), or, (5) other letters (neutral noise). Eriksen and Hoffman used circular arrays and a barmarker, appearing simultaneously with or at various intervals before the exposure of the array, to indicate the target. Eriksen and Eriksen used linear arrays, having the target always in the centre.

The most important results of these experiments were:

- Even with very large intervals between cue and display (350 ms) and also if the target is always in the same position, so that there is no spatial uncertainty at all, effects of the noise letters are observed.
- These effects of noise letters strongly depend upon their response relationship with the target letter. Noise letters from the same set as the target, whether physically the same or not, cause little delay in responding. Noise letters from the other set give a large delay in reaction to the target. Noise letters belonging to neither set give intermediate delays.
- The size of the effects appeared to depend upon the target–noise distance. (To this finding we return in sections 6.4 and 6.5.)

From their results Eriksen and Eriksen (1974, p. 147) conclude:

Since the effect of noise is strongly determined by its response compatibility with the target letter, support is given not only to the conclusion that the effects of noise are the result of response competition or interference, but further that this results from at least some of the noise stimuli being processed along with the target to the point where they are identified enough to tend to elicit appropriate responses.

So, again, parallel processing of equivalent items.

Eriksen, Coles, Morris and O'Hara (1985) further substantiated this conclusion. In their experiment subjects responded with a thumbpress of one hand to one letter and with the thumb of the other hand to a second letter. As in previous experiments, reactions were delayed when the letter to be responded to was presented together with the alternative target. But, more importantly, they also report that the occurrence of a correct response was frequently accompanied by an EMG in the arm appropriate to the response-incompatible noise letter. In line with their earlier conclusions they interpret this observation as indicating that the noise letters were processed to the point of incipient response activation simultaneously with the target letter.

Eriksen and associates' letter paradigm is not the only paradigm yielding Stroop-like interference effects with equivalent or equipotent stimuli. Van der Heijden (1981) and Glaser and Glaser (1982) reported similar findings with word–word combinations (see, however, also La Heij, 1988). Moreover, the effects are not restricted to multiple-item arrays with highly compatible items, i.e., items that can be read. The same phenomena have been repeatedly demonstrated with colour–colour combinations, i.e., items that have to be named (see, e.g., Van der Heijden, 1981; Glaser and Glaser, 1982; Hagenaar and Van der Heijden, 1986).

All these results strongly suggest that there is not only parallel processing of different attributes of different items (section 6.1). Also the same (form or colour) attributes of different items are apparently processed in parallel. The non-equivalent colour-word situation is apparently not a unique or peculiar stimulus situation, and the Stroop phenomenon is not merely a curiosity. Exactly the same effects are easily demonstrated with equivalent items.

Again, the outcome of the experiments is damaging for the conviction that the items in multiple-item arrays are processed in series. Appreciably more parallel processing is going on than was initially anticipated. Moreover, because of the apparent parallel processing, the findings also suggest that, if selective attention selects and processes, its selective performance is not very impressive. So, again, either the 'attention processes' assumption, or the 'perfect selection' assumption, has to be seriously doubted.

6.3 Objects

Response competition originating from an irrelevant item – the phenomenon described in the last two sections — became of paramount importance in research and theorizing in visual selective attention. It was nearly generally agreed that response competition could be used as a kind of a measuring stick for spatial (and temporal) properties of selective attention in vision. Response competition provided an unambiguous indication of where, to what region in visual space, selective attention had been directed.

The underlying idea is rather simple. The basic assumption is, what we called, the 'reading' assumption: attentional selection and the processing (i.e., identification) of information are the two sides of a coin. Attention selects and attention is needed for and involved in the processing of information; what is selected is (subsequently) processed and what is processed was (first) selected. So, if it is known what was processed, it is also known what was selected, and therefore, to where selective attention was directed. Of course, response competition originating from an irrelevant element is a clear sign that that element was identified. If response competition is observed, it follows that that element was selected and processed. So, response competition provides an indication of where selective attention had been directed.

In this section and the next two sections we describe to what results research using this reponse competition logic led. The main question we are concerned with is: Is attention directed at objects (this section) or at larger (section 6.4) or still larger (section 6.5) regions of visual space? What does the response competition logic reveal about the spatial (and temporal) properties of attention in vision?

The assumption that attention in vision addresses (internal representations of) single objects, or the (internal representation of the) exact spatial position a single object occupies, in short, the 'perfect selection' assumption, is very attractive and has often been defended (see, e.g., Neumann, 1980; 1987; Duncan, 1984; Van der Heijden et al., 1984; Allport, 1987). There are indeed a number of experiments supporting this assumption (see Neumann, 1987, pp. 385–6 for a brief overview). Among these is an important series of experiments by Kahneman and Henik (1981; see also Kahneman and Chajczyk, 1983; Kahneman and Treisman, 1984). Moreover, Kahneman and associates foster an attention-selects-and-processes, i.e., a reading, theory. In their view, attention is a limited resource (see also Kahneman, 1973) that is involved in and needed for the processing of information. Therefore Kahneman and Henik can investigate the point of view that attention is directed at objects by using a response competition paradigm and the response competition logic. Because 'attention addresses objects' is a parsimonious assumption, worthy of being defended, it is worthwhile to have a closer look at this and subsequent research to see whether this view is really tenable when response competition is used as a measuring stick.

According to Kahneman and Henik, the objects of attention are segregated or organized as 'perceptual units' by a preattentive process: an early stage of information processing that tentatively parses the visual 'field' (see also Neisser, 1967). After segregation attention can select one of the objects, or attention can be directed to or called by one of the objects. This focussing of attention on one object has two results:

- Attention facilitates all the responses associated with properties or elements of the selected object (an irrelevant attribute or element of an attended object will attract, and waste, its share of attention).
- The focussing of attention on an object prevents the processing beyond the preattentive stage of other, nonselected, objects; so unattended objects lose most or all of their ability to evoke instrumental responses (Kahneman and Henik, 1981; see also Kahneman and Chajczyk, 1983).

Kahneman and Henik find support for their view in the outcome of a series of experiments in which a variant of the Stroop task was used. Especially in their experiment 3 an elegant paradigm was used without confounding covarying variables. In the relevant part of that experiment, subjects were exposed to a pair of words, one on either side of the fixation point. One of the words was coloured, and the other was always black. Subjects had to name as fast as possible the colour of the coloured word. Three conditions were used with, as stimuli,

1. a coloured neutral word and a black neutral word,
2. a coloured incompatible colour word and a neutral black word,
3. a coloured neutral word and a black incompatible colour word.

Note that in condition 2 the relevant colour and the irrelevant incompatible colour word are united in one object, while in condition 3 colour and colour word are distributed over two spatially separated objects (in condition 1 there is no incompatible colour word).

The mean RTs in the three conditions were 858, 1017 and 858 ms, respectively. So, no effect at all of an 'external' incompatible colour word was found (RT condition 3 – RT condition 1 = 858 – 858 = 0). Only a severe interfering effect of an 'internal' incompatible colour word was observed (RT condition 2 – RT condition 1 = 1017 – 858 = 159). Subsequently, Van der Heijden et al. (1984) essentially replicated this result in two experiments in which Kahneman and Henik's paradigm was slightly modified and extended. Of course, given the response competition logic described at the beginning of this section, this pattern of results is completely consistent with Kahneman and Henik's view: attention can be directed to one perceptual object and exclude all others.

Nevertheless, because this result was opposite to the results first reported by Dyer (1973b) and subsequently by many others using spatially separated Stroop stimuli (see section 6.1), Van der Heijden et al. (1984) doubted the conclusion that the 'external' black words were not processed. They considered the possibility that these words were indeed processed, but that, in the paradigm as used, their effects did not show up in the RTs measured. Their reasoning was as follows.

In Kahneman and Henik's paradigm, the stimuli from the, apparently very difficult, 'coloured incompatible colour word and neutral black word' condition (i.e., condition 2) are randomly mixed with stimuli from the other two, apparently much easier, conditions. (It is likely that this condition 2 is so difficult because an 'internal', genuine, Stroop conflict has to be solved; see sections 4.10 and 6.1 for evidence.) But in such a mixture of subtasks it is often the most difficult condition that determines task performance in all subtasks (see, e.g., Eriksen and Eriksen, 1974, p. 145; Eriksen and Eriksen, 1979). In a sense, with a composite of subtasks, often a processing strategy is used that is optimal (i.e., adequate and efficient) for dealing with the most difficult subtask, but non-optimal, inefficient or too time-consuming, for the easier subtasks.

Van der Heijden et al. tested this idea by removing the internal colour-word conflict in this paradigm, thereby eliminating the difficult condition that, according to their reasoning, prevented an effect of external words from showing up. This was achieved by replacing the internal, incompatible, colour words by, in all relevant respects equivalent, neutral noncolour words. To see whether there was an effect of external words, three conditions were used. All conditions had a coloured neutral word whose colour had to be named. This word was either accompanied by

1. a black compatible colour word (C)
2. a black neutral word (N), or
3. a black incompatible colour word (I).

The first column of Table 6.3.1 presents the results obtained.

Table 6.3.1 Mean naming times (ms) of the colour of a neutral word. Column at the left: Pure paradigm with only coloured neutral words. Column at the right: Mixed paradigm. C, N, and I: Congruent, neutral and incongruent black external colour word. See text for further explanation. (From Van der Heijden et al., 1984, exp. II and III.)

C	554	695
N	565	681
I	602	690
Mean	574	689

Just as in Dyer's (1973b) study and many other studies a highly significant effect of the external incompatible colour word was found (condition I – condition N = 602 – 565 = 37). Moreover, also some facilitation from the external congruent colour word is indicated (condition N – condition C = 565 – 554 = 11).

The second column of table 6.3.1 gives the results obtained with essentially the same stimuli, but now presented together and mixed with the very difficult internal colour-word conflict stimuli in a random sequence. Two features are readily apparent:

1. the mean RTs are much higher now, showing that in a mixture of subtasks the most difficult condition indeed strongly influences performance in the easier subtasks,
2. no differential effect of the black words is observed in this situation where the most difficult condition influences performance in the easier subtasks.

What the data in table 6.3.1 seem to show is, that one cannot conclude from 'no differential effect of black colour words' (column two) that 'black colour words are not processed' (see column one). It is likely that in all experiments using this paradigm the (black) external words were processed, but that in the experiments involving very difficult subtasks effects of their presence were simply masked by other factors and therefore could not be noticed.

Kahneman and Henik were aware of this problematic aspect of their theory. A number of other experiments in their study showed that statements like 'Because selective attention to objects is effective ... the involuntary reading of a distant color word can be prevented by focussing attention on the relevant visual object ...' (Kahneman and Chajczyk, 1983) are much too strong. In nearly all experiments some differential effect of the external words was observed. So, the irrelevant object is processed sufficiently to cause measurable interference.

Two directions are possible now. Either one maintains the assumption that (selective) attention addresses objects (i.e., the 'perfect selection' assumption) and rejects the response competition logic (based on the 'attention processes' assumption). Or one maintains the response competition logic but then one has to reject the assumption that attention is capable of selecting objects. Kahneman and associates – and as we will see in the next two sections nearly all authors – select the latter possibility. They maintain the response competition logic.

Kahneman and Henik explain the discrepancy between their theoretical views and the observations by rejecting the hypothesis 'that the selectivity of attention is perfect' (see also Kahneman and Treisman, 1984, p. 46, for the point of view that the occurrence of Stroop interference in a stimulus situation like this represents 'at least a partial failure of selective attention to objects'). In their view the results show that '[T]he allocation of attention to a perceptual object facilitates all the responses that are associated to its properties, but facilitation also spills over to neighboring locations'. In fact, the unfortunate conclusion they ultimately arrive at is that '[T]here appears to be a spread of attention, with the selected object as its focus'.

For three reasons this conclusion is unfortunate. Firstly, the change from 'attention is directed to an object' to 'a spread of attention, with the selected object as its focus' is not a minor reformulation, but an essential change in the conceptualization of the spatial properties of selective attention. In fact the change from 'objects' to 'region in space' alters the theory into a 'spotlight' view of attention that we already introduced in section 4.4 and that we will meet again in the next section. Secondly, nearly all formulations of the spotlight view and related views face serious difficulties in explaining how the relevant object is ultimately selected. If selective attention fails either partly or completely, what is then doing the ultimate selection? Thirdly, after all, there is abundant evidence for efficient and virtually perfect object selection given adequate exposure conditions (the crowded linear arrays used in partial-report bar-probe tasks are responsible for the errors made in that task!); subjects need not make mistakes, not even in the most difficult versions of the Stroop task.

6.4 Spotlight with shifting focus

If the response competition logic is correct, than it follows that central attention is not capable of accurately addressing objects in visual space. Staying within the logic, the conclusion has to be that attention addresses a larger region in visual space than the region occupied by the object. This easily leads to the notion of attention as a kind of spotlight or searchlight, illuminating a circumscribed and limited region of visual space (see also sections 4.5 and 4.7), and that can move or shift its focus independent of the direction in which the eye is pointing (see also section 4.6). Many authors have proposed one or another variant of this attention-as-a-lamp idea in the recent past (see Chapter 4 for references; see Eriksen and Murphy, 1987, and Yantis, 1988, for critical evaluations of aspects of this metaphor, especially of the movement aspect). So, it must be a very attractive and powerful metaphor.

Among the research that can be taken as supporting this view is an important series of studies by Eriksen and associates (see, e.g., Eriksen and Hoffman, 1972b; 1973; Eriksen and Eriksen, 1974; Eriksen and Schultz, 1979). Eriksen and associates defend an attention-selects-and-processes theory (see sections 5.9 and 6.0; see, however, also section 6.5). Therefore Eriksen and associates can investigate the view that attention addresses a limited region in visual space by using a response competition paradigm and the response competition logic. Let us have a closer look at this and some subsequent research.

The spotlight view of selective attention was (apparently) introduced within visual information processing psychology by Eriksen and Hoffman (1972b). These authors suggest that it may be that visual attention has a locus in the visual field that actually can be measured in terms of the degrees of visual angle it subtends.

> The attentional field might be conceived as varying in the level of information processing or extraction that occurs. In the focus of the attentional field, stimuli are processed to a high level with considerable extraction of detail. Subtended into the visual field, this area of high-level information extraction may be no more than a degree of visual angle. Surrounding this high-level processing area may be an area where only gross information is extracted.
>
> (Eriksen and Hoffman, 1972b, p. 204)

Of course, to serve any useful function the attentional field must have the possibility to move, or, shift focus. Therefore, the authors assume that '[T]his central processing mechanism ... does not necessarily have to be locked to the eye in terms of its operation. That is, the attentional focus can be centred on a part of the visual field that does not correspond to the fovea' (Eriksen and Hoffman, 1972b, p. 204).

Within the response competition logic a 'spacing' effect – a decrease of the severity of response competition stemming from a to-be-ignored noise object with increasing target–noise separation – constitutes the critical evidence for the spotlight view. The underlying reasoning is quite simple. If the target is in the focus of attention, the to-be-ignored noise objects receive less attention, and therefore less processing, the greater their distance from the target. With a sufficiently large target–noise distance, the noise is not processed at all. The less an item is processed, the less response competition it can cause. And if an item is not processed at all, no response competition is to be expected.

Eriksen and associates have used the response-competition paradigm described in section 6.2 and the response competition logic as described above to elucidate properties of selective attention as a spotlight of limited size. In all these experiments a very small set of targets was used. These targets were divided into two sets, one set requiring one response, the other set another response. The target item either appeared alone, or, together with other stimulus elements. These latter elements were associated either with the response on the target (compatible noise), with the other response (incompatible noise), or not associated with any response (neutral noise).

Eriksen and Hoffman (1973) used 12-letter circular arrays around a central fixation point. A line indicator preceded exposure at variable intervals. The subject responded to the target with a right or left lever press, dependent upon the set which the target belonged to. RTs were larger when the target lay in close proximity to incompatible letters rather than to compatible letters, and, more importantly, there was an inverse relationship between the interference of incompatible letters and their distance from the target letter. So there was a clear spacing effect. Eriksen and Hoffman (1973) indeed interpret this decreasing interference with increasing distance in terms of selective attention directed at a small region in the visual field. 'The focus [of attention] would appear to be approximately 1 deg of visual angle, with the margin extending slightly more ... and the rest of the field constituting the fringe' (Eriksen and Hoffman, 1973, pp. 159–60).

An alternative explanation not in terms of a spotlight of attention is possible, however. The exposure duration was 1000 ms and the indicator preceded the display. Therefore, the subjects had more than sufficient time to make a saccadic eye movement to the target position. But when the target is fixated, letters adjacent to the target fall on positions of higher retinal acuity than letters two or three positions removed. Accordingly, the decreasing interference with increasing distance, i.e., the spacing effect, can simply be interpreted in terms of parallel processing and retinal acuity after a saccadic eye movement (see section 2.8).

In later research Eriksen and Eriksen (1974) used linear arrays in a similar type of task. (See, e.g., Eriksen and Eriksen, 1979, Eriksen and Schultz, 1979, and Eriksen et al., 1985, for similar studies.) The target always appeared in the centre of the array, so subjects had sufficient time before stimulus exposure to move the hypothetical spotlight to the target position. Again, decreasing interference from incompatible letters with increasing target–noise separation, i.e., a spacing effect, was found.

While Eriksen and Eriksen are very careful in interpreting this outcome, they nevertheless maintain the imperfect-attentional-field interpretation: 'S cannot prevent processing of noise letters occurring within about 1 deg of the target due to the nature of processing channel capacity and must inhibit his response until he is able to discriminate exactly which letter is in the target position' (Eriksen and Eriksen, 1974, p. 143). Broadbent agrees and proposes as a good rule that [selective attention operates in such a way that?] events more than 1 degree from the target are unlikely to interfere (Broadbent, 1982, p. 271). And also Eriksen and St. James (1986, p. 233) interpret this effect in terms of 'a graded dropoff in processing resources corresponding to William James's conception of a focus, a margin, and a fringe'.

But again these linear array data neither warrant such an interpretation nor support such a rule. With linear arrays having the target in the centre, an increase in target–noise separation results in the noise letters being projected on retinal positions with reduced retinal acuity. So, also for this experiment, the spacing effect can simply be interpreted in terms of parallel processing and retinal acuity; no spotlight of attention is needed. (Eriksen and Schultz, 1979, pointed out two alternative ways, besides attention, in which target–noise separation could have affected performance: contour interactions, affecting acuity, and, indeed, slower processing of stimuli impinging on retinal areas further removed from the fovea centre; see also Eriksen and Eriksen, 1979.)

However, the fact that it is *possible* to reinterpret the spacing effect in these studies in terms of retinal acuity does not rule out the possibility that an attentional spotlight of limited size is involved in the processing of visual information. It is possible that there are also genuine spacing effects resulting from the spatial characteristics of selective attention. The confounding with retinal acuity then only entails that the contribution of the hypothetical spotlight cannot be properly assessed. So, is there further evidence supporting the view of attention as a spotlight of limited size?

To investigate whether there is indeed an attentional spotlight of limited size, displays with large target–noise distances should be used. This was done in a number of colour-naming experiments in which a variant of the Stroop colour-word task was employed (see, e.g., Whitehouse, Somers and Egeth, cited in Egeth, 1977, p. 289; Gatti and Egeth, cited in Egeth, 1977, p. 291; Gatti and Egeth, 1978; Merikle and Gorewich, 1979; Kahneman and Chajczyk, 1983). On each trial the subjects saw a centrally located colour patch, with noise words above and below. Gatti and Egeth (1978) used target noise separations of 1, 3 and

5 deg. To ensure readability of the words very large letters were used. They found that interference of incompatible, and facilitation of compatible, colour words decreased with increasing distance, but, more importantly, interference of incompatible colour words was still clearly present at the largest distance. Merikle and Gorewich (1979) extended the task by varying also the letter size in order to compensate for reduced retinal acuity at wider distances. They essentially replicated the results of Gatti and Egeth (1978) for their largest letters. Kahneman and Chajczyk (1983) reported essentially the same results. So, the conclusion has to be: If there is indeed a spotlight, then it is certainly not of a limited size. (Gatti and Egeth (1978) and Merikle and Gorewich (1979) favour an explanation of their results and those of Eriksen and associates in terms of limitations in visual acuity for the noise letters; not in terms of a spotlight of attention.)

Gatti and Egeth's (1978) and Merikle and Gorewich's (1979) paradigms are appropriate for studying the size of the hypothetical spotlight, but are not suitable for investigating the exact spacing effects produced by the spotlight of attention. Possible attentional effects due to spacing are again completely confounded with effects due to retinal acuity. To decide whether there is indeed a spacing effect, resulting from the spatial characteristics of an attentional mechanism, spacing and acuity have to be unconfounded. Hagenaar and Van der Heijden (1986) unconfounded spacing and retinal acuity by positioning the items on the circumference of an imaginary circle. So all stimulus elements were projected on positions of equal retinal acuity. In two experiments response competition in a colour-naming task was investigated as a function of colour–noise separation. No effect of target–noise distance was observed in these experiments, a result at variance with the predictions of the spotlight view.

Eriksen and St. James (1986), on the other hand, obtained a clear and unambiguous spacing effect in a response competition paradigm, in which acuity and spacing were also correctly unconfounded (see also Murphy and Eriksen, 1987, for similar results). These authors, however, correctly observe that much too much response competition is observed to really support the view that there is an attentional spotlight of limited size. They therefore enlarge the field served by attention and interpret their results in the context of another model for spatial selective attention, the zoom lens model. To that model we turn in the next section.

Taken all together, the research using response competition as a measuring stick has not produced much convincing evidence that selective attention can be modelled as a spotlight of limited size, engaged in the processing of information. The hypothesis that the spotlight has a limited size is not easily substantiated. Most spacing effects that at first sight supported such a view are more parsimoniously explained in terms of the 'outer' eye and connected neural apparatus and parallel processing of information.

Two conclusions are possible now. Either one maintains the assumption that (selective) attention addresses limited regions in visual space (the 'perfect selection' assumption) and rejects the response competition logic (based on the attention-processes assumption). Or, one maintains the response competition logic but then one has to modify the spotlight view of attention stating that attention is capable of addressing limited regions in visual space. Albeit not explicitly, most authors opt for the latter possibility. They maintain the response competition logic. The modifications and adaptations they suggest, however, are an undisciplined crew.

Most authors favour an explanation of the results in terms of failures of central selective attention, or, in terms of an attentional mechanism with imperfect precision (see, e.g., Neumann, 1980; 1984; Broadbent, 1982; Kahneman and Treisman, 1984). The title of Gatti and Egeth's paper is 'Failure of spatial selectivity in vision'! This type of conclusion is unfortunate, however, because in these types of tasks subjects make only very few errors. So, how is selection accounted for?

Other authors try to cope with the results by assuming that attention was not really involved in the processing of the (very) distant noise information. If I understand Broadbent (1982) correctly, then such identity specific interference is an example of the 'breakthrough of the unattended' (Broadbent, 1982, p. 257). Kahneman and Chajczyk state that reading isolated words requires 'some attention, though not much of it' (Kahneman and Chajczyk, 1983, p. 508). Such conclusions are, however, very unfortunate. One cannot have and use the response competition logic as a measuring stick for the spatial properties of central attention and at the same time deny its most essential assumption (see section 6.3).

6.5 Zoom lens

If the response competition logic is correct it follows that central attention does not always address a limited region of visual space. On occasions, a much larger region is 'effectively' dealt with. Few authors correctly saw this consequence of the response competition logic and were willing to draw and defend the appropriate conclusion. Among the noticeable exceptions are Eriksen and associates (see, e.g., Eriksen and Yeh, 1985; Eriksen and St. James, 1986; Murphy and Eriksen, 1987), and, while not working with the response competition logic, Jonides (1980; 1981; 1983). Both Eriksen and associates and Jonides defend the view of visual attention as a processing resource that can be distributed and concentrated in the visual field, independent of foveal fixation. Eriksen and associates use a response competition paradigm and the response competition logic to study properties of visual spatial attention. In this section we discuss their research. In section 6.7 we have a closer look at Jonides's theory and data.

Just because a much greater degree of spatially parallel processing is apparently going on than an object view and a spotlight view of attention can encompass, another analogy is needed if one wants to maintain the assumption that attention is involved in the processing of visual information. Eriksen and

Rohrbaugh (1970) already proposed such an analogy: the variable-power, or, zoom lens analogy (see section 5.9). The basic and ideal properties of the zoom lens analogy for visual spatial attention have recently been described by Eriksen and Yeh (1985) and Eriksen and St. James (1986). The three most important properties are listed below.

1. Just as a zoom lens can vary in its field of view, so can the spatial distribution of attention vary continuously from the entire visual field to an area subtending as little as a fraction of a degree of angle.
2. Just as a zoom lens has a reciprocal relation between the size of the field of view and its magnification or resolving power for detail, so is the concentration of attentional resources, i.e., the processing capacity per unit area, inversely related to the size of the area attended ('the number of units of information being processed per unit of time is essentially constant', Eriksen and Yeh, 1985, p. 595).
3. Just as it takes for a zoom lens a measurable interval of time to change from one state (i.e., field-of-view-size and amount-of-detail combination) to another, so it also takes a finite amount of time for visual attention to change from one state (i.e., size-of-attentional-field and resource-concentration combination) to another state. In other words, there are gradual transitions between states.

Eriksen and Hoffman (1972a) were the first to test the zoom lens model in a multi-element task with RT as the dependent variable. They regard their results as a complete confirmation of the Eriksen and Rohrbaugh (1970) model. But unfortunately, the exposure times were much too long, so the results of this experiment have to be seriously doubted. Eriksen and Hoffman (1972b) reported a second test. They failed to find evidence pointing to a gradual focussing of processing and therefore rejected the model. But again, the exposure time was much too long (2 seconds!), and it is therefore not clear whether this rejection was correct. Until 1985, the zoom lens analogy disappeared from the scene. Then, after having given a completely satisfactory account of their data in terms of Jonides's two-state attentional model (see section 6.7), Eriksen and Yeh (1985, p. 595) reintroduced the zoom lens model as a 'more apt analogy'.

Eriksen and St. James (1986) start to investigate (aspects of) the zoom lens model using a response competition paradigm and the response competition logic. They present their subjects 8-letter circular arrays centred on the fixation point. Letter exposure duration was 50 ms. On each trial, one, two or three adjacent positions were cued by means of one, two or three location cues (short black bars just below the position(s) of the letter(s)). Either the target letter S (requiring a lever movement in one direction) or C (requiring a movement in the opposite direction) appeared in the cued region. There were seven distractor conditions: neutral noise; a repetition of the target letter one, two or three positions outside the cued area (compatible noise at distance 1, 2 and 3); the opposite letter one, two or three positions outside the cued position (incompatible noise at distance 1, 2 and 3). All other positions were randomly filled with the response-neutral letters A, N and H. The cues – duration 50 ms – were presented 200, 100 or 50 ms before or upon offset of the letters, i.e., at SOAs of 200, 100, 50 and –50. (Because trial presentation was blocked by SOA, the 200 ms SOA is too long.) We evaluate the results of this experiment against the background of the three basic zoom lens properties mentioned at the beginning of this section.

1. The results are consistent with the view that there can be a very large attentional field; significant interference from incompatible noise at all three distances was obtained. This, however, we already knew from the data discussed in section 6.4. Of more importance is the fact that the results are not consistent with the view that attention can be highly focalized, subtending as little as a fraction of a degree of angle (Eriksen and Yeh, 1985, p. 595; Eriksen and St. James, 1986, p. 227). Even at the 200 ms SOA, so, after what must have been a sufficient interval of time for the zoom lens to contract before the letters are presented, a significant and differential effect of the noise letters is still observed. Eriksen and St. James (1986, p. 233) conclude that this result suggests that there are limits to how finely the attentional focus can be drawn. Of course, this conclusion is completely consistent with the results mentioned in sections 6.3 and 6.4. If attention selects and processes, then it selects and processes much too much.

2. At first sight, the data seem in accord with the assumption that there is a reciprocal relation between size of the attentional field and amount of processing resources. Fastest RTs are observed with one position cued, intermediate RTs with two positions cued, and largest RTs with three positions cued. Eriksen and St. James (1986), however, favour another explanation for this result. (In their view, this increase in RT is attributable to a change in the discriminative difficulty of the task with increasing cued area size.) They virtually eliminate the reciprocal relation assumption as a testable hypothesis by proposing an 'optimal allocation of attentional resources' principle.

It is very worthwhile to have a closer look at this principle because 'If this principle is valid, it will be extremely difficult to demonstrate experimentally that processing efficiency decreases with increased size of the focus due to a thinning out of resources in the focus field' (Eriksen and St. James, 1986, p. 235). The principle says 'in nearly all experimental situations, the subject should be conceived of as having a reservoir of attentional resources he/she can draw upon to apply to tasks as they become more attention demanding (i.e., are perceived by the subject to be able to benefit from more attentional resources)' (Eriksen and St. James, 1986, p. 228). Eriksen and St. James find indeed evidence that suggests to them that the subjects were able to draw upon additional attentional resources to compensate for an increase in focus size (see Eriksen and St. James, 1986, pp. 227–8). So, this second property of the zoom lens analogy is not of very much help to decide between alternative views. A zoom lens external mechanism renders this property unobservable.

3. With the 'optimal allocation' principle added, it is far from clear what the critical experimental evidence has to be for supporting the point of view that the precision of focus improves gradually over time. Of course, the cue–target SOA and the distance of the incompatible noise letters from the cued area are the critical variables. But, if 'the subject should be conceived of as having a reservoir of attentional resources he/she can draw upon to apply to tasks as they become more attention demanding (i.e., are perceived by the subject to be able to benefit from more attentional resources)' then we should expect that subjects apply more resources in the difficult short SOA conditions than in the easy long SOA conditions (remember, SOAs were blocked). Then, increasing resources can possibly compensate for decreasing SOAs and no differential predictions can be generated. So, by introducing the 'optimal allocation of attentional resources' principle, Eriksen and St. James also eliminate the gradual transition assumption as a testable hypothesis!

Nevertheless, let us have a brief look at the data and the interpretation of the data. For Eriksen and St. James, the distance of the incompatible noise letters from the cued area and the cue–target SOA are the critical variables. Eriksen and St. James's data show a clear main effect of spacing, i.e., of target–noise distance! (See also Murphy and Eriksen, 1987, for the same result.) Interference from incompatible noise letters decreases with increasing distance from the cued region. It is important to realize, however, that a spacing effect as such is not the critical evidence in favour of the zoom lens analogy. A spacing effect is also compatible with the spotlight view of attention (but the spotlight view is not compatible with the very large attentional fields). We briefly return to this spacing effect at the end of this section and in Chapter 8.

The critical evidence for the zoom lens analogy has to come, in one way or another, from the RT–SOA functions. Unfortunately, the RT–SOA functions for incompatible noise letters at different distances reported by Eriksen and St. James do not reveal very much. For their first experiment a significant interaction is reported, but that analysis included the neutral noise condition (see section 4.1 on general and specific preparatory effects) and the too-long SOA of 200 ms (see section 2.8 on retinal acuity and eye movements). It is very doubtful whether, with an analysis restricted to the proper subset of data, the interaction is still significant. In a second experiment the interaction was not significant.

Taking all the evidence together, it is clear that the evidence in favour of a zoom lens model for spatial attention is not really overwhelming. Moreover, the zoom lens analogy is not very attractive as a model for visual information processing and visual spatial attention (see also Murphy and Eriksen, 1987, pp. 584–5 for a number of reservations and a complete reinterpretation of the results). Especially with the 'optimal allocation' principle added, the analogy seems compatible with any conceptualization of the processing of visual information. The assumption of a wide field of view together with 'very much resources' gives essentially unlimited capacity parallel processing; the assumption of a narrow field of view and only 'a little bit of resources' is compatible with limited capacity serial processing. As a result, the analogy used in combination with the response competition logic has virtually no predictive or discriminative power. For example, it will be clear that the zoom lens analogy has no problems at all in accounting for the identity-specific interference effects observed with (very) large target–noise separation (Gatti and Egeth, 1978; Merikle and Gorewich, 1979; see the previous section). The simple assumption of a large attentional field size, including both target and noise, suffices. Unfortunately the analogy is also consistent with a complete absence of identity specific interference in these tasks, if that should have been the result obtained. The simple assumption of a small attentional field concentrated on the target position and excluding the noise suffices.

So, in its present formulation, the zoom lens analogy is so broadly construed that no real, differential, predictions can be derived. The analogy, however, encounters a second, serious difficulty, just as for the spotlight view. Essential is, of course, again the finding that the attentional field cannot be finely tuned, but has a, for selection, too-large irreducible size of about 1.5 to 3 deg around the cued area (Murphy and Eriksen, 1987, p. 584). Subjects, however, often perform with nearly perfect accuracy in the type of task under discussion. So the real problem is: How can selective attention correctly select if it is far from capable of adequately addressing the to-be-selected information or the corresponding region in visual space? How to account for correct selections?

Again two directions are possible now. Either one maintains the assumption that attention can be finely tuned (the 'perfect selection' assumption) and rejects the response competition logic (based on the 'attention processes' assumption). Or one maintains the response competition logic, but then one has to modify the zoom lens view of attention. Modifications of the object view (see section 6.3) and the spotlight view (see section 6.4) appeared quite easy. It seemed that the assumption of a somewhat larger attended field – from object to limited region and from limited region to the whole visual field – simply sufficed. With the zoom lens analogy this simple solution is not possible anymore. The possibility of paying attention to the whole visual field is already one of its assumptions. Moreover, it will now be clear that such a solution is a solution in the wrong direction. It now becomes apparent that it is the correct, finely spatially tuned, selections that are problematic and that have to be accounted for. Indeed, it seems that, if one wants to maintain the response competition logic the price to be paid consists of the loss of the selectivity of selective attention. There is no reason to praise the information processing approach for such a scientific accomplishment. Instead of solving problems by giving temporal priority to wanted information (see Chapter 4), attention now creates the problems by processing unwanted information. That price is much too high.

One issue remains to be discussed in this section: the spacing effect. As stated, contrary to Hagenaar and Van der Heijden (1986; see section 6.4), Eriksen and St. James (1986) and Murphy and Eriksen (1987) obtained a genuine and unambiguous spacing effect. At the present it is not completely clear what factor is responsible for this difference in results. The two experiments differed in a great number of ways: number of elements presented, type of elements presented, size of the spacings investigated, etc. One difference, however, might have been essential: Eriksen and St. James (1986) and Murphy and Eriksen (1987) used location cues and Hagenaar and Van der Heijden (1986) either no cues (Experiment I) or advance symbolic cues (Experiment II; 150 ms SOA). A spacing effect might be unique to location cues. As described in Chapter 4, in single-item studies using location cues, a related distance effect has been reported (see section 4.3). Another phenomenon that is possibly related consists of the near location errors observed in partial-report bar-probe tasks using location cues (see section 5.3). To these observations, that deserve much more investigation, we briefly return in Chapter 8.

6.6 Filtering costs: the Eriksen effect

In the last three sections we saw how the response competition logic forced investigators to ever larger attended fields; from (the location of) objects (section 6.3) to larger but still limited regions of visual space (section 6.4) to the entire visual field (section 6.5). Still larger is impossible. Crudely stated, 'parallel processing' is the outcome of this response competition research. And, because attention is thought to be responsible for this parallel processing, the selective function of attention has (nearly) completely gone. However, it is exactly this selective function of selective attention that is the topic of our concern. We therefore, for the moment, leave the response competition logic. In the next three sections, we first turn to research that elucidates other important aspects of visual central attention that can possibly shed some light on what is going on in multiple-item tasks. In section 6.9 we briefly return to some research using the response competition logic, and in section 6.10 I present a critical evaluation of the response competition logic.

As stated, in the early 1970s Eriksen and associates changed their variant of the circular bar-probe task with accuracy as the dependent variable (see section 5.9) into a bar-probe task with latency as the dependent variable because

> if the O is told to report only the stimulus designated by a black bar or similar indicator, he can by some process, select this particular stimulus and report it with perfect accuracy.
>
> (Eriksen and Hoffman, 1972a, p. 169)

With 'perfect accuracy', accuracy measures cannot reveal anything anymore. But possibly a latency measure can reveal further properties of selective attention. And indeed it did.

A newly detected phenomenon of importance goes under the names 'cognitive masking' (Eriksen and Schultz, 1978) and 'filtering costs' (Kahneman, Treisman and Burkell, 1983; Treisman, Kahneman and Burkell, 1983; see also Kahneman and Treisman, 1984). Because these terms imply 'explanations', I prefer the neutral term 'Eriksen effect' (see further on). It is the general effect that speeded choice responses, even to a highly discriminable relevant stimulus, are delayed by the simultaneous occurrence of whatever other types of visual events, this in the absence of lateral masking (see section 5.1) and of response competition (see sections 6.1 and 6.2).

Apparently, the phenomenon was first reported by Eriksen and Hoffman (1972b; see, however, James, 1890/1950, pp. 430–1) in a letter reading experiment (see also section 6.2). In that experiment two classes of noise elements were employed: other letters or black discs. The target could appear in one out of twelve positions on the circumference of an imaginary circle and was indicated by a simultaneous barmarker. Three target–noise distances were used (0.5, 1, and 1.4 deg). While the noise letters impaired performance much more than the discs, also clear delaying effects on RTs with the discs were observed at all target–disc distances. The effect was largest with simultaneous presentation of target and discs and decreased with increasing advance presentation of the target.

Eriksen correctly noticed the potential importance of the phenomenon and further investigated it. Eriksen and Schultz (1978) demonstrated the same effect, now with target position fixed. Either an A or an H appeared directly above the fixation point. Subjects had to move a lever in one direction for the A and in the other for the H. The target was either presented alone or together with patches of colours, solid geometric forms (triangles, diamonds, etc.), or random patterns of line segments forming 'pseudo' letters. In all conditions the presence of such extraneous stimuli in the visual field slowed reaction time to the target. The mean RTs were 292, 330, 327 and 319 ms for letter alone, together with geometric forms, colours and random lines, respectively. Essentially the same results were reported by Kahneman and Chajczyk (1983, exp. 2 and 4) for a colour naming task. In that experiment, a coloured bar always appeared at fixation, so also in these experiments, there was no uncertainty of target position. In some conditions irrelevant neutral words appeared above and/or below fixation. These irrelevant neutral words substantially delayed colour naming relative to the bar-alone condition. (Table 8.6.1 presents some of the data.)

Kahneman et al. (1983) systematically investigated the effect in a series of five experiments. In their first experiment they found a highly significant delay in reading a single word when an irrelevant, but highly discriminable, object – a patch of random dots – was added to the display. In the second experiment they showed that not only reading responses but also naming responses to shapes and colours are significantly delayed if a highly discriminable irrelevant object is presented simultaneously. The, in the present context, most important results come from Kahneman et al.'s experiments 3 and 4. (We discuss the results of their experiment 5 in section 6.8.) These experiments revealed three new findings.

– Firstly, it appeared that the delay in reading a word increased as more irrelevant objects (clusters of three red shapes) are added. Each additional object seemed to produce an additional increase in RT. To Kahneman et al. this finding suggests 'that each irrelevant object contributes separately to the interference and perhaps requires active exclusion from attention' (p. 515).

- Secondly, the Eriksen effect virtually completely disappeared when the task was changed from a (n-alternatives) reading task into a (one-alternative) detection task ('press a key if a word is present and refrain from responding if not'). According to Kahneman et al. 'Knowledge of presence suffices for a positive response to a target in search, but a time-consuming focussing of attention to its location could still be required to read a word or to make other specific discriminations of its properties' (p. 515). A related 'effect' shows up with target repetition. Eriksen and Eriksen (1974; see also Murphy and Eriksen, 1987) found delayed responding to a target letter in a speeded choice reaction task when the display contained letters identical to the target. In search tasks with redundant targets, in which only a target-present response is required, the opposite effect, facilitation, is found (see, e.g., Van der Heijden, 1975; 1981; Van der Heijden, La Heij and Boer, 1983; Van der Heijden, Schreuder, Maris and Neerincx, 1984).

- Thirdly, and as we shall see later on, most importantly, the Eriksen effect is completely eliminated if the position of the target is cued in advance. (Remember, increasing advance presentation of the target also reduces the delaying effect of irrelevant noise; Eriksen and Hoffman, 1972b.) Kahneman et al. (1983, exp. 4) marked the position at which the word to be read would appear by a row of dots just beneath the location of each letter (i.e., a location cue was used). The dots appeared 88 ms before the word. This precue substantially reduced the reading latency even when no irrelevant objects were present in the display and, nevertheless, completely eliminated the interference produced by the irrelevant objects.

For three reasons, I regard this latter observation, i.e., the observation that the Eriksen effect can be completely eliminated by advance cueing, to be of fundamental importance. First, because it provides a kind of signature of this type of interference that makes it possible to distinguish it from other sources of interference (for instance, interference as result of lateral masking). Second, because 'The fact that it disappears with precueing links the delay to attention rather than to peripheral interference' (Treisman et al., 1983, p. 527). To this point we return further on. And third, because, just because a position, not an object, is cued, it follows that attention is capable of addressing positions, independent of what is subsequently going to appear in that position.

Kahneman and associates tentatively conclude 'that the filtering cost represents a delay in the appropriate deployment of attention, whether this involves focussing on the target or excluding the distractors' (Kahneman et al., 1983, p. 517). Of course, this tentative conclusion is completely consistent with the assumption that it is both, i.e., that on a (small?) proportion of the trials attention is first attracted or captured by a distractor (that has to be 'excluded') and only then turns to the target (that has to be 'focussed').

In an intriguing study, Treisman et al. (1983) substantiated the point of view that the Eriksen effect is indeed an attentional effect observed when more 'objects' are presented simultaneously. They demonstrated that the effect is strongly affected by the spatial organization of the display. On each trial they either presented a word alone or a word plus a coloured frame (a rectangle, hexagon or ellipse outlined in black and filled in pink, green or yellow). When a coloured frame was presented, the word was either in the frame, or outside the frame at the opposite side of the fixation point. Subjects had to read the word as fast as possible. The results clearly showed that the irrelevant frame causes less delay when it surrounds and covers the word than when it is shown on the opposite side of fixation and is an independent perceptual unit. The results are interpreted as indicating that a delay is incurred when two distinct perceptual objects compete for attention. This interpretation was further substantiated by the finding that a small gap in the frame in *exactly the same spatial position* is detected more efficiently in a secondary task if the word to be read is in the frame than when word and frame are spatially separate (see also Hoffman and Nelson, 1981, and Hoffman, Nelson and Houck, 1983, for essentially the same results).

6.7 Jonides: probability matching

Jonides's (1980; 1981; 1983) studies are certainly among those that contain important indications about what is going on in visual selective attention tasks using multiple-item displays. Basically, Jonides was interested in developing a 'resource model' capable of accounting for the results obtained in one type of task: a visual search task with advance visual cues of less than 100% validity (see also section 4.1 on costs and benefits).

In Jonides's search tasks the subjects had to 'search' – directed eye movements were not possible – through circular eight-letter arrays, to determine whether either the target letter 'L' or 'R' was present (i.e., the task was the two-choice detection task introduced by Estes and Taylor, 1964). RT was the dependent variable. Just before array presentation a cue appeared that signalled the target location with some probability. The typical result obtained with this task is, that RTs are faster when the cue correctly indicates the position of the target, i.e., there are benefits on valid trials, than when it indicates another position, i.e., there are costs on invalid trials (Jonides, 1980; 1981; 1983). With uninformative, i.e., neutral, cues, intermediate RTs are obtained (Jonides, 1980, exp. 2).

Jonides (1983; see also Jonides, 1980, p. 111) ultimately arrived at what he called a 'two-process model'. Basically the model states that attentional resources can be allocated in one of two ways: the resources can either be evenly distributed throughout the display area so that all stimuli are processed in parallel, or the resources are concentrated on an area containing a single item and processing is serial. (This model can be regarded as a variant of the zoom lens model investigated by Eriksen and associates, discussed in section 6.5, except that Jonides does not postulate the gradual decrease of the attentional field size over time.) For the visual search task with advance cues this means that 'The extent of resource allocation to the cued location is always fixed, by hypothesis. Consequently, an item may either receive the benefit of having all the available processing resources applied to it if it is cued and attended, or share in the resources equally'. With different kinds of advance cues 'a difference in the effectiveness of the cue, according to the two-process model, causes a change only in the proportion of trials on which the cued location receives preferential treatment' (Jonides, 1983, p. 248).

To account for the effects of different levels of cue validity, as reported by Jonides (1980, exp. 2), a more precise assumption about 'effectiveness of the cue' or 'proportion of trials' is needed. Jonides (1980) suggested that, with location cues, subjects go through a probability matching procedure, somehow matching the probability of applying all resources to the cued position first with the probability that the cue indicates the target correctly, i.e., with the probability of cue validity (Jonides, 1980, p. 111). Then, if the cued item is processed first and is a target searched for, fast RTs have to be expected. If the cued item is processed first but is not a target, the remaining display items will then be examined simultaneously until a target is identified. In this case, long RTs have to be expected. On trials on which the cue did not attract attention all items are supposed to be processed simultaneously. On these trials an intermediate mean RT has to be expected. In a more elaborate analysis of Jonides's (1980; 1983) results Van der Heijden (1989) found clear support for these assumptions (see also Eriksen and Yeh, 1985, for supportive evidence).

By using the two-process model and the probability matching hypothesis it is possible to demonstrate to what important outcomes Jonides's selective attention research led. In the context of this study the differential effects of two different types of cues – location cues and symbolic cues (see also Chapter 4) – are of special interest. The analysis presented in the subsequent paragraphs is taken from Van der Heijden (1989).

Jonides (1983) varied the efficiency of the cue in drawing attention to the indicated location by using two different kinds of advance cues. On (efficient) location-cue trials an arrowhead appeared close to the letter position. On (less efficient) symbolic-cue trials an arrow also preceded the letter displays, but it was positioned in the centre of the imaginary circle containing the letters. With both types of trials cue validity was 50%.

The next four equations combine the assumptions of the two-process model and the mean RTs reported by Jonides (1983) for location valid (1), location invalid (2), symbolic valid (3), and symbolic invalid (4) trials, respectively:

$$Pl\,RT+ \; + \; (1-Pl)\,RTn \; = \; 529 \tag{1}$$
$$Pl\,RT- \; + \; (1-Pl)\,RTn \; = \; 683 \tag{2}$$
$$Ps\,RT+ \; + \; (1-Ps)\,RTn \; = \; 569 \tag{3}$$
$$Ps\,RT- \; + \; (1-Ps)\,RTn \; = \; 644 \tag{4}$$

In these equations $RT+$ stands for mean RT on valid trials with attention at the cued location, $RT-$ for mean RT on invalid trials with attention at the cued location, and RTn for mean RT on trials with distributed attention. Pl and Ps stand for the probabilities that a location cue and a symbolic cue attract attention at or direct attention to the indicated position, respectively:

These are four equations in five unknowns ($RT+$, $RT-$, RTn, Pl, and Ps) and therefore no unique solution is possible. Nevertheless, it is possible to calculate the relative efficiency of the two types of cues. Subtracting (1) from (2) and (3) from (4) gives, respectively:

$$Pl \;\; (RT- \; -RT+) \; = \; 154 \tag{(2)-(1)}$$
$$Ps \;\; (RT- \; -RT+) \; = \; 75 \tag{(4)-(3)}$$

Division shows that $Pl : Ps = 154 : 75 = 2.05$, or, that, given that the two-process model is correct, a location cue is about twice as effective in attracting or directing attention than a symbolic cue ($Pl = 2.05\ Ps$). Of course, this result entails that, if there is probability matching, then there is either probability matching on location cue trials or on symbolic cue trials, but certainly not on both. Because it is likely that subjects probability match with location cues (see, e.g., Jonides, 1980, exp. 2; Eriksen and Yeh, 1985; Van der Heijden, 1989) we have to conclude that they do not with symbolic cues. And, of more importance, the analysis indicates that subjects do not very often effectively use the symbolic cues.

The same analysis can be used to demonstrate an essential difference between location cues and symbolic cues. It appears that with location cues no 'controlled' or 'willed' strategy is followed. The effect of a location cue seems to be produced automatically without any voluntary control. This can be illustrated by the results reported by Jonides (1981, exp. II). In that experiment again symbolic cues and location cues were used. One group of subjects – the attend group – was instructed to attend to the cue and a second group of subjects – the ignore group – was instructed to ignore the cues. Cue validity was only 12.5%; in fact, the cue was not informative. The next four equations give the assumptions of the two-process model and the results obtained with the location cues for valid attend (5), invalid attend (6), valid ignore (7), and invalid ignore (8) trials. Pa and Pi stand for the probabilities that the location cue attracts attention under the attend and the ignore instruction, respectively.

$$Pa\,RT+ + \; (1-Pa)RTn \; = \; 666 \tag{5}$$
$$Pa\,RT- + \; (1-Pa)RTn \; = \; 761 \tag{6}$$
$$Pi\,RT+ \; + \; (1-Pi)\,RTn \; = \; 714 \tag{7}$$
$$Pi\,RT- \; + \; (1-Pi)\,RTn \; = \; 812 \tag{8}$$

Subtracting (5) from (6) and (7) from (8) gives

Pa $(RT- -RT+) = 95$ $((6) - (5))$
Pi $(RT- -RT+) = 98$ $((8) - (7))$

Division shows that $Pa : Pi = 95 : 98 = 0.97$, or, in words, location cues are as effective whether subjects are instructed, and try, to attend to the cue or try to ignore the cue. In a sense, subjects cannot but attend to the location cue's position.

In contrast, the use of a symbolic cue appears to be under some 'strategic' or 'voluntary' control. The next four equations present model and results obtained with the symbolic cues for valid attend (9), invalid attend (10), valid ignore (11), and invalid ignore (12) trials. Pa and Pi stand for the probabilities that the symbolic cue is used for attending to the indicated position under the attend and the ignore instruction, respectively.

$Pa\,RT+ + (1-Pa)RTn = 679$ (9)
$Pa\,RT- + (1-Pa)RTn = 740$ (10)
$Pi\,RT+ + (1-Pi)\,RTn = 763$ (11)
$Pi\,RT- + (1-Pi)\,RTn = 761$ (12)

Subtracting (9) from (10) and (11) from (12) gives

Pa $(RT- -RT+) = 61$ $((10) - (9))$
Pi $(RT- -RT+) = -2$ $((12) - (11))$

This result shows that symbolic cues are effective under the 'attend' instruction, but appear not to be used at all under the 'ignore' instruction. (A comparison of equations $((10) - (9))$ and $((6) - (5))$ again shows the far greater efficiency of location cues than of symbolic cues in attracting or directing attention.)

The outcome of our analysis – automatic effects with location cues but not with symbolic cues – is completely consistent with the outcome of Jonides's (1981) study, devoted to an investigation of differences between symbolic cues and location cues. He examined differences between these cues on three different criteria for distinguishing between voluntary and automatic processes and concluded: 'According to all criteria, one of the cues [the location cue] was shown to induce shifts of attention more automatically than the other [the symbolic cue]. This indicates two separable modes of control over the allocation of attention' (Jonides, 1981, p. 187 [inserts mine]). All this also strongly supports our point of view that (single-item) research with location cues and with symbolic cues should be clearly separated and not simply mixed together and forced under one explanation (see Chapter 4).

The observation that with location cues probability matching fairly accurately accounts for the results but that this probability matching cannot be modified or modulated by explicit, ignore, instructions seems paradoxical. After all, probability matching seems not to be really an automatic process, but to result from one or another cognitive or high level strategy. In relation to this issue,

Jonides (1981, p. 196) remarks 'a reasonable explanation might be that the operation of the peripheral cue is not completely automated. Perhaps there are two components to its processing: an automatic and a nonautomatic one. The automatic component is revealed by the identical differences between invalid and valid trials for the attend versus the ignore conditions. The nonautomatic component is revealed by the change in invalid minus valid response times with cue validity.' (See also Weichselgartner and Sperling (1987) for two partially concurrent attentional processes: a fast, automatic, process and a relatively slow, controlled, process.)

Of course, it is not completely clear how this suggestion has to be worked out so that the paradoxical phenomenon of 'automatic probability matching' can be understood. A possibility, however, is that a location cue in Jonides's experiments always calls attention to its position (the automatic component) but that an additional step is involved in which it is determined whether attention has to stay at that position or has to 'move elsewhere' (the nonautomatic component). If the outcome of this latter component is determined by validity only (and not by instruction, etc.) the paradox is solved. One way in which validity can induce the level of matching observed is by means of the invalid trials. Just because continued attending on invalid trials brings a huge cost (see Jonides, 1980, exp. 2) this attending is 'punished' and therefore 'extinguished' on each invalid trial.

If this analysis is correct, then there is a peculiar, but essential, difference between the ways in which validity effects are produced with location cues and with symbolic cues. With location cues validity effects originate because of withdrawal of attention from the indicated position on a proportion of trials. With symbolic cues the validity effects are produced by directing attention to the indicated position on a proportion of trials. (It will be clear that, if this analysis is correct, the 'attend' and 'ignore' instructions are, in a sense, opposite instructions with location cues and with symbolic cues; they require 'stay' and 'move' with location cues and 'move' and 'stay' with symbolic cues.)

Two further remarks have to be made in relation to Jonides's work. First, it will be clear that the results discussed shed a somewhat strange light on the cost–benefit technique of analysing RTs in selective attention tasks. (We introduced and criticized this technique in section 4.1.) As stated there, Jonides and Mack (1984) suggest that the difference 'RT invalid – RT valid' (i.e., costs plus benefits) offers most of the time the information wanted. The results presented in this section show, however, that two qualifications are needed. First, with location cues only a fraction, q, of the underlying costs plus benefits is estimated, where q approximately equals the validity level used. Second, with symbolic cues, only a fraction, say p, of this fraction is estimated. This strongly suggests that the cost–benefit analysis, especially when used in combination with symbolic cues, is not a very sensitive technique for assessing attentional effects. (See for further comments on the cost–benefit technique section 4.1.)

Second, Jonides's work is not only relevant because it teaches us something about cues. It has much broader implications. At the end of his study, Jonides very adequately generalizes his results where he concludes that it is not so much the location cues, but 'certain stimulus characteristics' that may be sufficient to engage automatic shifts of attention (Jonides, 1981, p. 201). This generalization brings the attention-capturing properties of location cues quite close to the attention-capturing properties of distractors that are thought to be at the basis of the Eriksen effect (see section 6.6). Moreover, the work also suggests at least a beginning of an explanation of how the Eriksen effect is solved. We suggested in section 6.6 that the Eriksen effect arises because on a (small?) proportion of the trials attention is first attracted or captured by a distractor (that has to be 'excluded') and only then turns to the target (that has to be focussed). This 'turns to the target' can be equated with 'the withdrawal of attention' that is presumably at the basis of the validity effect observed with location cues. But, of course, all these issues deserve much more investigation.

6.8 Events

It is quite likely that abrupt onsets have a special status in (visual) information processing and that abrupt onsets are at the basis of the Eriksen effect (see section 6.6) by triggering automatic shifts of attention (see section 6.7; see also Chapter 3). An abrupt onset is a temporal (and spatial) discontinuity just as a movement, a change or a disappearance. The perceptual salience of such events, for instance of a moving object, is obvious.

> The generality of this observation is readily apparent to anyone viewing a complex scene with a moving object in it: Until the movement begins, the object can seem completely invisible: At movement onset the object's location is immediately and compellingly manifest, almost without effort on the part of the observer.
>
> (Yantis and Jonides, 1984, p. 601)

There is indeed substantial evidence for the special status of onsets with regard to the attracting or capturing of attention. We already mentioned that Eriksen and Hoffman (1972b) observed that the delaying effects of irrelevant black discs decreased with increasing advance presentation of the target. So, when there are no simultaneous onsets, the Eriksen effect seems to disappear. Kahneman et al. (1983, experiment 5) investigated a related issue. In their experiment a word had to be read. The word was accompanied by a number of unreadable irrelevant distractors. All items had abrupt onsets and offsets, but the distractor elements were presented at various asynchronies with respect to the target. When abrupt onsets or offsets of irrelevant elements occurred simultaneously with abrupt target onset, severe interference was observed, i.e., RTs were significantly longer than in a word-alone condition (the Eriksen effect). When, however, the irrelevant elements were preexposed (800 ms in advance of the target) and either continuously present until target offset, or removed well in advance of target onset (300 ms after distractor onset and 500 ms before target onset), no delay in responding was observed. So it seems that advance presentation of the distractors has the same effect as precueing the target position and as advance presentation of the target.

Kahneman et al. (1983, p. 519) conclude that 'the cost of filtering [i.e., the Eriksen effect] should be attributed, at least in part, to competition between events rather than between objects. It is the simultaneous *appearance* rather than the concurrent *presence* of target and distractors that causes difficulties in the processing of the relevant object' ([insert mine]). The fact that also a severe delay was observed when offsets of the irrelevant elements coincided with the onset of the target strongly supports their conclusion: Events, abrupt onsets (and abrupt offsets) have a special status in (visual) information processing.

The fact that no delays are observed in the condition in which the distractors are presented well in advance and maintained in the field when the word is added, can be explained in two ways that differ in emphasis. First, it can be assumed that under these exposure conditions the irrelevant elements lose all their power to attract and maintain attention at their position. This explanation emphasizes the absence of erroneous attentional reactions (see also section 4.9 on 'inhibition'). Alternatively, it can be assumed that under these conditions the target always automatically captures attention because it is the only abrupt onset or event present. This explanation emphasizes the occurrence of obligatory attentional selections.

For Kahneman et al. (1983) the first alternative is the most attractive. In their view

> Filtering costs can be reduced or eliminated by preventing potential distractors from diverting attention away from the target. Advance presentation of distractors or advance knowledge of their positions can reduce their effect, even when the location of the target remains uncertain. Indeed the familiar benefits of precueing a target position could arise mainly or entirely from the information that the cue provides about the locations to be excluded from processing ... the image of an attention spotlight directed at the target could be misleading. The operation of attention may be more accurately modeled as the casting of a shadow or a mask on potential sources of distraction that should be ignored.
>
> (Kahneman et al., 1983, p. 520)

Yantis and Jonides (1984) emphasize the other point of view. In their theoretical position they combine a neurophysiological and an information processing view. They agree with Breitmeyer and Ganz (1976; see also Chapter 3) that the transient system, responding to abrupt changes such as onset, offset and movement, is involved. They combine this view with the assumptions of the prevailing theories of attention: 'Although processing resources are scarce, the assignment of attention by an efficient allocation schedule (e.g., on the basis of a preparatory cue or salient stimulus feature) can overcome these limitations, resulting in quite efficient performance' (Yantis and Jonides, 1984, p. 605). Their hypothesis is that, because abrupt onset is a property to which the visual system is very sensitive, attention is rapidly and involuntarily captured by a stimulus having this abrupt onset property, when no other abrupt onset stimuli are present. In other words, 'the activation of a so-called transient channel causes a rapid shift of resources to the task of monitoring events on the activated channel' (Yantis and Jonides, 1984, p. 605).

Yantis and Jonides test their hypothesis in a visual search task. In the search task subjects have to indicate as fast as possible whether, among a number of distractors, a specified target is present (positive trials) or not (negative trials). It has often been demonstrated that, with alphanumeric characters as targets and distractors, the search time linearly increases with increasing number of distractors (see, e.g., Atkinson, Holmgren and Juola, 1969; Van der Heijden, 1975). This 'display size effect' is substantial and is, given an appropriate choice of targets and distractors, quite resistant to practice effects (see, e.g., Shiffrin and Schneider, 1977; Schneider and Shiffrin, 1977). When, however, the position of the target is precued by a marker, a strong reduction of the latencies is observed and the display size effect nearly completely vanishes (Holmgren, 1974).

Yantis and Jonides used display sizes of two and four items. In each display, one item had an abrupt onset. The other, no-onset, items were introduced by gradually removing line segments that initially camouflaged them. On target-present trials the target was either the abrupt onset item or (one of) the gradual no-onset item(s). The data of interest are the slopes of the display size functions for these two types of positive trials. If an abrupt onset indeed captures attention no, or virtually no, effect of display size is to be expected if the target is the only item with an abrupt onset. If the target is a no-onset item the usual display size effect is to be expected.

In a first experiment (Yantis and Jonides, 1984, exp. 1) a spectacular difference in slopes was found. The slope of the display size function for onset targets (7.9 ms/item) was appreciably smaller than for no-onset targets (24.5 ms/item). In two replications (Yantis and Jonides, 1984, exp. 3), one with abrupt camouflage removal, and one with gradual camouflage removal, a somewhat smaller effect was observed. Nevertheless, the experiments clearly showed that an abrupt onset seems to function in a way similar to Holmgren's (1974) advance barmarker (see Jonides and Yantis, 1988, for essentially the same results).

Nevertheless, one feature of the data, present in all three replications, was at variance with the predictions. The capture view predicts a flat display size function for abrupt onset targets. The experiments showed consistently (small) positive slopes. As a possible explanation, Yantis and Jonides suggest that attention is captured on *almost* all of the trials, but that on a small proportion of the trials – their quantitative estimate is 0.10 – capture is not effective. In their view 'this mixture assumption appears to give a reasonable post hoc account of the otherwise unpredicted nonzero abrupt onset slopes' (Yantis and Jonides, 1984, p. 617). However, this post hoc account is not really necessary. The 'abrupt-onset-location-cue' was not 100% valid. In fact, it was uninformative with regard to the position of the target (a 50% validity and a 25% validity with display size 2 and 4, respectively). Given Jonides's work on probability matching (see section 6.7), that suggests that subjects sometimes withdraw attention in order to avoid 'punishment', a positive slope is certainly not surprising.

Recently, Jonides and Yantis (1988) investigated whether an abrupt onset is simply one example out of a large number of stimulus characteristics, all capable of capturing attention. In other words, they investigated whether onsets really have a unique status with regard to visual spatial attention. They compared the attention-capturing capabilities of one onset item among no-onset items with those of one item with a unique hue or brightness among items with another hue or brightness. The abrupt onset was the only stimulus characteristic that appeared capable of capturing attention. So, abrupt onsets really have a unique status in visual information processing; 'onset can produce attentional capture, whereas two other salient visual features that have frequently produced powerful effects in other visual tasks – colour and intensity – cannot' (Jonides and Yantis, 1988, p. 354).

6.9 Capture in Stroop tasks: the Kahneman effect

The information processing approach is primarily interested in voluntary attention and voluntary shifts of attention. Subjects are instructed to perform one or another task and in the interpretation of the data the researcher assumes that they indeed behave according to the instruction. However, certain stimulus characteristics may be sufficient to engage automatic shifts of attention. Jonides's work concerned with the properties of location cues certainly supports this view (see section 6.7). Also the Eriksen effect clearly shows that there is more involved in task performance than voluntary shifts of attention (see section 6.6). It appears that events, abrupt onsets (and offsets), can severely influence task performance by automatically attracting attention (see section 6.8; see also Lambert, Spencer and Mohindra, 1987, and Müller and Rabbit, 1989b).

Almost all experiments involving the presentation of multiple-item stimuli and the measurement of RTs reported in the last 25 years, and all experiments concerned with the Stroop phenomenon discussed in this chapter, use basically the same stimulus presentation conditions. Subjects look at a fixation point in an otherwise blank field. Then, suddenly, sometimes after presentation of a cue, all items appear simultaneously. Of course, all items are clearly above threshold, otherwise the measurement of latencies would not make very much sense. Moreover, all items have abrupt onsets. So, automatic shifts of attention are certainly involved. The important question that has to be discussed now is whether the abrupt onsets have automatically influenced the direction of selective attention in these experiments in such a way that that has led to erroneous conclusions with regard to the operation of voluntary attention.

The view that automatic capture has led to erroneous conclusions with regard to the operation of voluntary selective attention cannot easily be dismissed. Given automatic selections of irrelevant items, it is even possible to maintain – completely in line with the serial 'reading' assumption – that response competition originating from an irrelevant element is observed in multiple-item tasks because on a (small) proportion of trials an irrelevant object initially attracts or captures all attention and is therefore processed before the correct element is selected and processed. In other words, it is possible to maintain the point of view that it is the Eriksen effect that is at the basis of the Stroop effect observed with multiple-item displays. In this section we investigate the viability of this position.

At first sight, this 'capture' explanation seems very farfetched. Remember for instance Dyer's (1973b) stimuli: a colour patch at one side and a, in nearly all respects different, black word at the opposite side of the fixation point. Subjects always have to name the colour of the colour patch. Or remember Eriksen and Eriksen's (1974) stimuli with the target position fixed at fixation. It seems that with such stimuli there is not much reason to expect wrong initial selections. Nevertheless, the possibility that even with such stimuli wrong selections (sometimes) occur is very real (see section 6.6: the Eriksen effect).

Kahneman and Chajczyk (1983) believe that '[B]ecause selective attention to objects is effective ... the involuntary reading of a distant color word can be prevented by focussing attention on the relevant visual object' (p. 498). They nevertheless address the question whether the involuntary reading of a word presented *outside the main focus of attention* will be effected by the simultaneous presentation of a second irrelevant word. The reason for this endeavour is that Stroop results reported in the literature need not necessarily lead to a 'spotlight' or 'zoom lens' view of attention. As an alternative to such a shared or distributed attention view that allows (some) parallel processing of multiple items, they suggest an anomalous object selection model, the 'attentional capture' model. This model is indeed based on erroneous selections.

In the attentional capture model as formulated by Kahneman and Chajczyk it is assumed that in a colour-naming task with a colour patch as the target and external words as distractors, one irrelevant external word captures attention. The processing of this word is normal but the processing of a second irrelevant external word is then prohibited or at least severely disturbed. It is worthwhile to note that Kahneman and Chajczyk assume that there is only an effect of attentional capture on the processing of the irrelevant words; not on the processing of the relevant colour. They simply maintain that attention always immediately correctly addresses the relevant colour on each trial (see also Kahneman's object selection position in section 6.3). Capture does not prevent perfect object selection (!). Capture is a game only played in the suburbs.

Kahneman and Chajczyk investigate the sharing, or distributed attention, versus capture (outside the focus of attention) issue in a series of four experiments. The experiments have a similar design. On each trial a horizontal coloured bar is briefly shown at the fixation point. The subject's task is to name the colour of this bar. Simultaneous with the target either a neutral word, a congruent colour word, or an incongruent colour word appears, either above or below the bar. So far, the task is a straight-forward modified Stroop task with spatially separate presentation of colours and words as described in section 6.1. The important innovative feature of Kahneman and Chajczyk's research is that on half of the trials a second, neutral, word is presented on the other side of the bar. The question of interest is, how this additional neutral word affects the latencies in the different conditions of this Stroop task, i.e., how it affects interference (on incongruent trials) and facilitation (on congruent trials).

The results of the experiments are really surprising. The addition of a neutral word considerably reduces Stroop interference and facilitation. Table 6.9.1 presents the results of Kahneman and Chajczyk's first experiment (the results of the other three experiments are essentially the same).

Table 6.9.1 The effect of an additional neutral word on mean RTs (ms) in a modified Stroop task. See text for further explanation (Kahneman and Chajczyk, 1983, exp. 1).

	Modified Stroop	Modified Stroop + Neutral Word	Reduction
Incongruent	682	650	32
Neutral	610	614	
Congruent	561	585	24

The table shows that the neutral word approximately halves the interference (the difference between Incongruent and Neutral decreases from 72 to 36 ms) and the facilitation (the difference between Neutral and Congruent decreases from 49 to 29 ms).

According to Kahneman and Chajczyk (1983, p. 498) '[T]he reduction (dilution) of Stroop effects by another visual object indicates that the reading of color words has been disrupted'. What they want to find out is how this disruption is brought about. They correctly reject sensory interaction or lateral masking as an explanation because their second experiment showed that the reduction of interference also reliably occurred with a word–word distance of about 7 deg of visual angle. They also show that the reduction has nothing to do with the fact that the additional item is a (neutral) word that can evoke a response. Essentially the same effect is observed if a row of 'x's, instead of a word, is used as the irrelevant stimulus (experiment 3). What remains is one or another central, attentional, explanation. Can the reduction be explained by attentional capture?

The attentional capture model tested by Kahneman and Chajczyk simply assumes that on one-word trials the word is always processed together with the target. On each two-word trial besides the target, just one of the two words is processed, as if the other were not present. The word processed is 'selected' at random. The critical prediction from this model is that performance on incongruent (congruent) two-word trials is a 0.50 – 0.50 probability mixture of performance observed in the one-word neutral condition and the one-word incongruent (congruent) condition. This prediction can be tested for the means as well as for the variances.

For the means this prediction entails that the addition of a neutral word should reduce interference (and facilitation) by 50%. The reductions in interference observed were 50% (exp. 1), 64% and 53% (exp. 2), 31% and 18% (exp. 3), and 62% (exp. 4). With regard to the viability of their capture model in relation to the means, Kahneman and Chajczyk conclude:

> Although this model was violated in several of our experiments (including Experiment 3 and the studies in which some neutral words cause little dilution), a pattern of approximately 50% dilution has appeared in more than half of the studies of dilution conducted in our laboratory. The recurrence of this observation suggests that the simple capture model is valid, at least under some conditions. Within a sharing model, the observation of 50% dilution would be entirely coincidental .... The observed amount of dilution is compatible with a process of "early capture". Color words and neutral words appear to attract attention equally, in spite of the fact that the color words are both frequently repeated and relevant to the task.
>
> (Kahneman and Chajczyk, 1983, p. 506)

For the variances the prediction from the simple capture model entails that the variance in a dual condition consists of a 'within' component plus a 'between' component. The within component is associated with the variability of the RTs in the two one-word conditions comprising the dual word condition. The between component is associated with the difference between the means of these two conditions. Kahneman and Chajczyk derived predicted variances for the two-word conditions from the one-word conditions for each subject separately. The observed values were generally lower than the predicted values. Kahneman and Chajczyk conclude 'dual displays produce fewer very fast or very slow RTs than were predicted by a simple capture model. A more complex version of capture or some model of attention sharing will be required to explain the variability in the data' (Kahneman and Chajczyk, 1983, p. 507).

Taking all together, it seems that Kahneman and Chajczyk's theoretical tools are not sufficient to explain the results obtained. Nevertheless, Kahneman and Chajczyk's (1983) experiments are certainly among the most important experiments that the visual information processing approach has produced. In these experiments a new and rather unexpected phenomenon is demonstrated (the Kahneman effect). Kahneman and Chajczyk correctly recognized that this phenomenon must have its basis in the involuntary capturing of attention by irrelevant noise elements. It was possibly the assumption that object selection is always perfect, and that capture of attention by irrelevant simultaneous objects does not interfere with this perfect object selection, that prevented the bringing into correspondence of data and simple capture theory. In Chapter 8 we return to this aspect of the Kahneman effect.

At this point, the really important question to be answered is: Is it possible to maintain the point of view that it is the Eriksen effect – the involuntary capture of attention by irrelevant items – that is at the basis of the Stroop effect observed with multiple-item displays? This question needs a two-fold answer.

First, Kahneman and Chajczyk's (1983) results clearly show that it cannot be excluded that at least a (large?) part of this Stroop effect is due to attentional capture by a distractor. For how large a part is at the present far from clear. We know of no published replications of the Kahneman effect. In our attempts to replicate Kahneman and Chajczyk's findings, Van der Heijden, Van Gelder, Vermeulen and Winkel (in prep.) found that the effect only reliably showed up when no fixation point was used!

Second, other evidence shows that it can be excluded that the complete Stroop effect observed with multiple-item displays can be accounted for in terms of the Eriksen effect. The essential observations are the following. In section 6.6 we already pointed to one important feature of the Eriksen effect: the effect completely disappears with appropriate precueing of the target position or pre-exposure of the target (see also section 6.8). We already stated there that we regarded that phenomenon as a kind of signature of the Eriksen effect. So, with correct selection, no Eriksen effect is observed. The Stroop effect, with equivalent or nonequivalent items, however, does not disappear with the same appropriate precueing of the target position or preexposure of the target (see, e.g., Eriksen and Hoffman, 1972b; Eriksen and Hoffman, 1973; Eriksen and Eriksen, 1974; Eriksen and St. James, 1986; Murphy and Eriksen, 1987; Neumann, 1980; Van der Heijden, 1981; Van der Heijden et al., 1984; Hagenaar and Van der Heijden, 1986; Glaser and Glaser, 1982). So, also with correct selections, still a Stroop effect is observed.

This persisting identity specific interference, found with correct object selection, can be regarded as a kind of signature of the Stroop effect as observed with multiple-item displays. And exactly this feature of the Stroop phenomenon seems of fundamental theoretical importance. Just because it shows up with *correct object selection*, it strongly indicates that also nonselected information can cause interference. It therefore strongly suggests that the nonselected information is really processed, or that the processing of information occurs in parallel. If this is correct, then attending is selection of information, not processing of information. Or, there is 'sharing' as far as processing is concerned and sometimes 'capture' with regard to selection. In short, it seems that Mewhort's decomposition of the 'reading' notion into 'processing' and 'selection' is supported by these data (see Chapter 5). But selection is not always voluntary selection.

6.10 The response competition logic

To assess where we have arrived now, it is worthwhile distinguishing again three different, and in my view independent, theoretical issues: issues regarding the function of attention, the limited vs unlimited capacity issue and the early vs late selection issue (see also section 5.10). Let us first look at the function of attention.

To avoid an unwanted duplication in eye and attention I suggested in section 4.7 that it is much more profitable to assign attention a function in the time domain, granting the eye an important job in the spatial domain. In Chapter 5 we saw that the results obtained with multiple-item tasks with accuracy as the dependent variable did not contradict this view. That this view is not the generally received view will by now be clear. In the present chapter we saw how wide-spread the opinion is that selective attention is not only involved in the selection of information, i.e., in making information explicit in time, but also in, and even needed for, the processing of information, i.e., in making explicit parts in space (see especially sections 6.3, 6.4, 6.5 and 6.9).

The question whether the data presented in this chapter really provide supporting evidence for the received conventional select-and-identify, i.e., 'read' view, and against our alternative view is a quite embarrassing question. The reason is, that in this chapter we did not meet the 'attention processes' component of the 'reading' assumption as a decent scientific hypothesis to be critically evaluated. We were confronted with it as an established scientific fact forming the basis of the response competition logic: response competition as a measuring stick!

At the beginning of section 6.3, we introduced this response competition logic: attention selects and processes (the 'reading' assumption); for response competition originating from an irrelevant item to be observed, that irrelevant item must have been processed; so response competition can be used as a kind of measuring stick for assessing where in the visual field attention had been directed. Let us face the question: Is the response competition logic really tenable?

There are at least three reasons that strongly indicate that the response competition logic must simply be rejected. The first reason was already presented in section 6.5. The logic leads to at least one unacceptable consequence. We saw that the attractive assumption that (selective) attention addresses objects, or the exact spatial location objects occupy, had to be rejected (see section 6.3; see also section 6.9 for Kahneman's remarkable solution). Also the much less attractive assumption that (selective) attention is capable of addressing a too-large but still limited or circumscribed region of visual space appeared not to be tenable (see section 6.4). At least on occasions an even much larger region of space seemed to be dealt with (see section 6.5 on the zoom lens analogy). With such an ever widening field attention is dealing with, response competition is possibly adequately accounted for. The problem however is, that the larger the field, the worse selection, i.e., the ordering in time, is accounted for. By maintaining the response competition logic the spotlight views and zoom lens views lose the selectivity of selective attention.

Of course, losing the selective function of selective attention is not really a scientific accomplishment of thirty years' visual information processing research. In fact, it is a major theoretical disaster. ('Because of a *failure* in appropriately directing *scarce resources*, the efficient selection of visual information is *not* adequately accounted for', is not a theoretical summary of a major research effort to be very proud of!) This outcome on its own is sufficient reason for rejecting the response competition logic and the underlying assumption that attention (capacity, resources) is involved in the processing of information (see also section 6.5).

The second reason is that the response competition logic as used in the recent past is not empirically sound. Here we only point at the 'Kahneman effect', that strongly indicates that at least a (large) part of the Stroop effect observed with multiple-item arrays can be accounted for in terms of attentional capture (and the rest in terms of parallel processing, see section 6.9). So, the spotlights and zoom lenses of the past accounted for much too much interference. Moreover, the phenomenon of attentional capture itself strongly suggests that, after all and albeit involuntarily, attention is often directed at localized events or circumscribed regions of visual space (see sections 6.6, 6.7 and 6.8).

The third reason is, of course, that the response competition logic is also not logically tenable. What we meet here again is the fallacy of affirming the consquence (see also section 5.10). A correct statement is: 'If response competition then the information is processed' (and also: 'If the information is not processed then no response competition'). But from 'if response competition then the irrelevant information is processed' it does not follow 'if the irrelevant information is processed then response competition'. Being processed is a necessary condition for response competition to show up but it needs not be a sufficient condition (see Driver and Tipper, 1989, for an example). It is possible that information is processed but does not show up in response competition. In short, the logical link between being processed and response competition is rather weak. In Chapter 8 we return to this issue.

It is of importance to note that the latter logical argument is completely independent from the question whether something like 'attention', 'effort', or 'capacity' is involved in the processing of information or not. Even if the processing of information is a sufficient condition for identity specific interference to show up, nothing about the involvement of attention in this processing really follows. In fact, what we meet here, is a second fallacy of affirming the consequence, mixed up with the first one. Assume that processing is a sufficient condition for creating response competition. Then a correct theoretical statement is 'If attention processes the information, then response competition will show up'. But from this theoretical statement it does, of course, not follow that 'If response competition shows up then attention processed the information'. From this argument it might become clear that also the logical link between response competition and the involvement of attention in the processing of information is extremely weak.

In short from response competition, logically nothing follows about the involvement of attention in the processing of information. The response competition logic is critically dependent upon the 'attention processes' assumption and not the other way around. As used in practice as a methodological principle, however, it seems as if the response competition logic strongly supports the 'attention processes' assumption. But that is simply not true. So, the response competition data presented in this chapter do not force one to abandon the theoretical position that attention is not involved in the processing of information and has an important, too often neglected, function in the time domain (see also Chapter 4).

It will be clear from the foregoing paragraphs, that the data presented in this chapter do not really provide any insight into the information processing capacity of the human information processor. If attentional selection and the processing of information, combined in the 'reading' notion, are conceptually disentangled, it becomes clear that selective performance gives no real indications about processing performance (see also section 5.10). And, while it might have seemed otherwise, the present chapter was concerned with selection and not with processing. To get some insight into the information processing capacity of the system, other data are needed. In the next chapter we turn to some of the relevant data.

It will also be clear that nothing in the present chapter contradicts the view that attentional selection is early selection or selection in vision. In line with the data and analyses presented in Chapters 3, 4 and 5, this selection is most parsimoniously interpreted as selective addressing. This addressing has as a result that, despite response competition and despite attentional capture by irrelevant objects, the appropriate and task relevant response is given temporal priority. In Chapter 8 we return to attentional selection.

Chapter 7

Information processing

7.0 Introduction

As elaborated in Chapter 1, the main aim of the information processing approach is to explain observed behaviour in terms of the internal structure and functioning of the behaving organism. This functioning internal structure can be regarded as a complex causal control structure that generates the observed behaviour. A description of how this system functions in producing the behaviour constitutes the explanation of the behaviour.

In the present state of development, the information processing approach is not concerned with absolute properties of the control system (see section 1.7). In my view, its aim is to explain the differences in behaviour observed in different experimental conditions. In correspondence with this 'explicandum', its 'explicans' – the hypothetical information processor that functions as the causal control system – is basically conceived as a difference generator, capable of accounting for the differences observed. So, in explaining the data, the aim of the information processing approach is to arrive at an adequate characterization of this difference generator.

In Chapter 2 I isolated an unambiguous concept of attention: Von Helmholtz's type of attention concerned with position, location, or 'the where'. In Chapters 3 to 6 I presented the relevant data. I described and discussed the subject's behaviour observed in a diversity of selective attention tasks in which that type of attention presumably operated. The *differences* in behaviour observed in different conditions in these attention tasks are the data to be explained.

This chapter, on information processing, and the next chapter, on the function and way of operation of attention, are concerned with the explanation of behaviour as intended by the information processing approach. In this chapter the main emphasis is on, what can be called, the 'fixed' aspects of structure and function of the hypothetical information processor, i.e., on those aspects that are invariant under different attentional instructions and/or attentional operations. Chapter 8 is concerned with some of the 'variable' aspects of the human information processor, and especially with selective attention.

The main aim of this chapter is to define and design the hypothetical control system in such a way that, when the concept of attention is added, adequate explanations can result. Obviously, in this enterprise a choice is involved. One has to decide what to account for in terms of fixed aspects of structure and function of the hypothetical information processor and what in terms of the, in time and in space variable, involvement of attention. Our choice with regard to this issue is based on a simple consideration. In the recent past the term 'attention' has often been used to indicate a magical force, capable of solving quite unsolvable problems in a non-specified way (e.g., global attention 'processes' detailed information). To prevent the need of introducing an empty, magical, concept of attention our strategy will be to account for as much as possible in terms of the fixed structure and functioning of the information processor. If we are successful in this, there will be left to attention a decent job that it can handle.

With regard to the fixed aspects of structure and functioning of the hypothetical information processor two different questions have to be answered. The first is, how to conceive and model the visual information processing system so that the behaviour observed in selective attention tasks can be economically and adequately accounted for. This problem of the necessary and sufficient, i.e., minimal, model structure needed will be discussed in section 7.1. (In Chapter 8 this minimal model structure will be further elaborated.) The second question is how to conceive and model the effects of visual stimulation – light, or better, structured light – on this visual information processing system. This important problem is the main content of the remainder of this chapter. I briefly introduce the main issues here.

In very general terms, structured visual stimulation results in structured activation in the visual information processing system. The study of this stimulation-caused activation is essential for visual information processing psychology. All 'further processes', including selective attention, are based upon, make use of, or interact with stimulation-caused activation. Visual information processing as a whole can be regarded as the interaction between, or integration of, stimulation-caused activation and, what can be called, internally generated activation. The task of visual information processing research is exactly to unravel this intricate interaction. By means of realists' experiments it is attempted to specify what activation 'stimulation' from outside contributes and what activation 'the system' generates and contributes in producing the behaviour observed.

Within this general topic of stimulation-caused activation three issues are of prime importance because in these issues it is specified what the 'fixed' properties of the system are, and, consequently, where attention has to come in, what attention's job is and what the consequences of attention are.

The first issue concerns the time course of stimulation-caused activation as a function of intensity and duration of stimulation, i.e., the temporal properties of stimulation-caused activation. This topic was recently discussed by Hagenzieker (1987) and Hagenzieker and Van der Heijden (1990). In sections 7.2 to 7.5 we closely follow their exposition. Just because, in our view, attention's main task is in the *time* domain (see, e.g., sections 4.7 and 4.8), the *temporal* properties of stimulation-caused activation deserve especially detailed examination.

The second issue concerns the spatial interactions between channels activated by stimulation from outside, i.e., some spatial properties of stimulation-caused activation. Also this topic was discussed by Hagenzieker and Van der Heijden and in section 7.6 we closely follow their discussion. Of prime importance is the fact that the *temporal* properties of stimulation-caused activation, relevant to the study of attention, might be the result of *spatial* inhibitory interactions (see, e.g., Cornsweet, 1970).

The last issue concerns the processing level automatically reached by stimulation-caused activation. This issue is much better known as the LC vs UC processing issue (see also sections 2.7 and 2.9). In sections 7.9 and 7.10 we further investigate this issue by critically evaluating the prevailing assumptions about the processing of visual information. The main questions are of course: Is it really necessary to assume that the information processing system has a limited central capacity for processing information and, if so, has the limitation to be conceived *in such a way* that attention has to solve this problem?

7.1 Two levels

As stated in section 1.10, neurophysiologists and neuroanatomists nowadays distinguish a very large number of specialized information processing regions, or modules, in the vertebrate and therefore also in the human brain in general and in the parts concerned with visual information processing in particular. And, as stated in section 3.7, two major pathways are distinguished: the X- or parvo-cellular pathway, presumably concerned with 'the what', and the Y- or magno-cellular pathway, presumably concerned with 'the where' (see, e.g., DeYoe and Van Essen, 1988; Livingstone and Hubel, 1988; and Zeki and Shipp, 1988, for recent overviews). In the context of this 'information processing' chapter the most relevant pathway is the X- or parvocellular pathway. So, our first problem is: How to summarize this pathway in terms of a simple information processing model?

To find a minimal model structure compatible with the evidence, one first has to look for a broad distinction in functionally and behaviourally relevant levels of visual information processing. Fortunately, the neurophysiological and psychological literature is quite helpful in making such a distinction. It is often suggested that within the X- or parvocellular pathway, two broad groups of specialist modules can be distinguished (see, e.g., Styles and Allport, 1986, and Allport, 1987, for evidence).

Members of the first group are indicated by codes like V1, V2, V3, etc. The idea is that these regions of the visual cortex are concerned with physical properties of objects and scenes, such as colour, form or movement. In these regions the information is spatially ordered or spatially laid out. Therefore the term 'maps' seems appropriate for this group. In the inferotemporal cortex and in regions beyond the inferotemporal cortex such as the lateral hypothalamus and the substantia innominata members of a second group are found. The general opinion is that these regions are concerned with more abstract information such as identity, meaning and learned significance of visual stimuli. These specialists lack spatial order. 'Domains' seems an appropriate label for this group. Of course, it is a very intriguing thought that maps have to do with 'to see' (see, e.g., Treisman, 1977, and Crick, 1984, for this assumption), and that domains subserve 'to know'.

Information processing psychologists are only concerned with a very small part of this complex information processing pathway. As we saw in previous chapters, they mainly use verbal (letter and word) stimuli and require either a verbal or manual reaction. Nevertheless the broad distinction into two (groups of) separately localized and functionally different processing modules is also clearly noticeable in models in contemporary visual information processing psychology. Most theorists agree in postulating (at least) two representations, or separate levels of representation: a precategorical one containing unidentified information, or, a level of representation containing literal or analogue information about the sensory attributes of stimuli, and a postcategorical one containing identified information, or, a representation level containing categorized information. It is quite generally assumed that information is spatially ordered in the first representation but not in the second. (Often in models still a third representation, directly related to or concerned with 'responding' is recognized: something like a short-term memory or an output buffer.)

In the present study we have already met the map–domain distinction a number of times. In section 3.9 we saw how Posner (1980) used the distinction between 'visual input', 'position in space', and 'visual position' on the one hand and 'internal structures', 'area in memory ... for ... discrimination' and 'semantic code' on the other hand, to answer the question where attention intervenes. The same or a closely related distinction between two representations was also encountered in our discussion of partial-report and partial-report bar-probe tasks in Chapter 5. Researchers there distinguished two stores, holding different kinds of information after stimulus presentation. The first store was variously named Visual Information Store (Sperling, 1960), iconic memory (Neisser, 1967), short-term visual storage (Haber, 1969), sensory register (Shiffrin and Atkinson, 1969), and feature buffer (Mewhort et al., 1981). For the second store terms like immediate memory, more enduring memory, and short-term memory were used.

Even in models postulating more than two stages a partition into these two stages is easily recognized. For instance, in Eriksen and Schultz's (1979) continuous flow conception it is assumed that 'input channels ... feed a continuous output to feature detectors which, in turn, continuously feed to form units. The output from the form units is a priming or activation flow to the response system' (Eriksen and Schultz, 1979, p. 252). In this conception the map–domain transition can be localized quite naturally between the 'form units' and the 'response system'. In Sanders's (1983) linear stage model four stages are distinguished: stimulus preprocessing, feature extraction, response choice and motor adjustment. Here the map–domain transition is easily localized between 'feature extraction' and 'response choice'. So, also in multi-stage models, a division into two global information processing levels, one with information spatially ordered and the other not, is not difficult to find.

Again, it is a very intriguing thought that the first level representation has to do with 'to see', and the second level with 'to know'. In fact, within the information processing approach, this thought was explicitly expressed by, e.g., Turvey (1977) and Coltheart (1980a, b). Turvey (1977) distinguished between two components in iconic memory: *visible* persistence, characterized by being visible, brief, susceptible to masking, of very large capacity and in retinotopic coordinates, and, *schematic* persistence, with the properties nonvisible, of longer duration, of limited capacity and without retinotopic coordinates. Coltheart (1980a, b) makes essentially the same distinction: visible persistence, the phenomenological correlate of neural persistence at various stages of the visual system such as photoreceptors and ganglion cells, and informational persistence or iconic memory, a property of some relatively late stage in the visual information processing system (Coltheart, 1980b, p. 57).

Taken all together, it seems that there is converging support for two, functionally relevant, levels of processing in the X- or parvocellular pathway. These two levels also show up in the models of information processing as two levels of representation with different properties. The dichotomy visible–nonvisible, spatial–nonspatial, 'to see'–'to know', can possibly be used to characterize these levels. (Of course, for a complete account of task performance still a third level, close to or concerned with responding, has to be distinguished.)

Exactly these two levels and their characterization form a simple, attractive and appropriate starting point for the design of a hypothetical information processor that has to account for the phenomena observed in the selective attention tasks described in Chapters 3 to 6. Throughout the empirical part of our study, but especially in Chapters 3 and 5, we argued that attention in visual information processing tasks is really attention in vision. The recognition of two qualitatively different processing levels makes it possible to award selective attention an appropriate level of operation: the level characterized by 'to see'.

Moreover, for the topic of this chapter, a control system consisting of two levels also provides a sufficient minimal model structure. The reason why is not very difficult to see. Ideally, in the experiments we were concerned with, only factors that differentially influenced one type of internally generated activation varied: factors affecting the operation of attention. Factors addressing or influencing other sources of internally generated activation, e.g., intentions and expectations (see Chapter 2), were fixed. Nevertheless, there are more sources of internally generated activation involved. With two levels, however, we can simply assume that the effects of the nonattentional factors are collapsed into one fixed effect of a second type of internally generated activation at the second level. So, for present purposes, two levels suffice.

Taken together, in this chapter we distinguish two levels of information processing: maps and domains. Certainly, in a more complete account of performance at least a three-level control system is needed. In Chapter 8 we present such a more complete model (see figures 8.7.1 and 8.9.1; see also Van der Heijden, 1981, fig. 6.3 and Phaf et al., 1990, for outlines of three-level systems).

7.2 Time course of stimulation-caused activation

While current visual information processing theories disagree about all kinds of major and minor issues, they share, besides the assumption of two basic levels, one conviction. That conviction is, that the categorical information in the second level representation is, in one way or another, derived from or triggered by the precategorical information in the first level representation. (See, e.g., Chapter 5 for a number of examples and remember the 'reading' notion.) Figure 7.2.1 serves to illustrate this point in terms of the connectionist language introduced in section 1.10. Visual stimulation activates nodes – hypothetical neural units – in the maps and these nodes pass this stimulation-caused activation via hardware links to nodes in the domains. (To the issue whether it is necessary to assume that attention is involved in this process, we return in section 7.10.) The nodes in the maps represent the visual information on its position: features, combinations of features, and/or segregated visual objects at certain positions in the visual field. The nodes in the domains represent identity information independent of position. These nodes can be regarded as 'dictionary units' (Treisman, 1960; 1964), 'logogens' (Morton, 1969), or 'recognition units' (Kahneman, 1973). See McClelland and Rumelhart (1981), Phaf et al. (1990) and Chapter 8 for more elaborate versions of this general scheme.

A conceptualization of visual information processing as presented in the figure easily leads to the conviction that only one function is needed to characterize the time course of stimulation-caused activation for both levels of the visual information processing system. Just because the activation in the domains (D) is simply received or derived from the activation in the maps (M), the function for the maps (plus a monotonic transformation of that function for

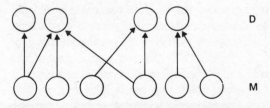

Figure 7.2.1 Nodes in maps (M) pass activation to nodes in domains (D).

the domains) seems to suffice. Of course, this assumption need not be correct. It is possible to invent very simple theoretical reasons that cast doubt on this assumption. The general idea behind these reasons is sketched in figure 7.2.2.

In the left panel of the figure, stimulation-caused activation in M is passed on to D. Nothing special happens in D. In this case, after some delay due to the time needed to transmit activation from M to D, D starts reflecting the time course of activation in M. In the middle panel a completely different situation is depicted. Here D first follows M, but inhibits itself after an additional time delay. So, after first reflecting the stimulation-caused activation in M, the time course of activation of D starts deviating from that in M: it is lower and/or shorter. A similar pattern is shown in the right panel of the figure. Now, however, D activates or sustains itself. After some time, the time course of activation in D starts deviating from that in M: it is higher and lasts longer.

Of course, these simple diagrams are not intended to represent any particular reality. They only serve to illustrate the point that, theoretically, there is no reason at all to suppose that the time course of stimulation-caused activation in the two levels we distinguished are identical or even similar. A subsequent level can always impose its own characteristics on the time course of activation it receives and so produce its own, unique, time course of activation. Only on the basis of empirical data can anything of relevance be said about the time courses of activation in the two relevant levels.

Nevertheless, in the recent literature concerned with time courses of stimulation-caused activation, it is frequently assumed that there are similarities between the time courses in M and D. In fact, as we shall see in sections 7.3 and 7.4, knowledge of time courses in M is often used as a basis for the formulation of hypotheses about the less accessible time courses in D. And, while there are simple theoretical reasons to doubt this assumption, this indeed seems an adequate and sound research strategy. The assumption of similarity of time courses, based on the assumption that stimulation-caused activation is simply passed on from M to D, is the most parsimonious starting assumption. Moreover,

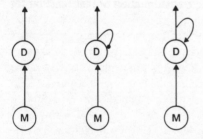

Figure 7.2.2 Three ways of how activation in maps (M) can be passed on to domains (D).

this assumption has the advantage that it makes also the data from classical visual perception research of importance for our knowledge of stimulation-caused activation in both M and D. With this assumption accepted, it is no longer necessary to restrict the discussion of the difficult information processing issues to the data produced by the information processing approach in the last few decades only.

Therefore in the first part of this chapter we follow the received opinion and use the assumption of similarity of time courses in M and D as a starting point and look where it leads us. In sections 7.7 and 7.8 we return to this assumption. There we briefly discuss whether this parsimonious assumption can be maintained or has to be rejected.

7.3 Time courses in visual perception

In this section we briefly review some relevant data with regard to time courses of stimulation-caused activation in visual perception, or, in vision, i.e., in what we called the 'maps'. For two reasons, this is an appropriate starting point for a review of literature on time courses of stimulation-caused activation in visual information processing.

First, from classical perception research, much more is known about these time courses than about time courses further up-stream in the visual information processing system. For vision, any introductory textbook provides relevant information (see, e.g., Cornsweet, 1970; Haber and Hershenson, 1974). This cannot be said for time courses of activation in, what we called, the 'domains' as investigated by the information processing approach. In fact, as we shall show in subsequent sections, at the present only speculations and educated guesses about the latter time courses exist.

Second, as we already stated, most investigators interested in time courses of activation in the domains assume that there are similarities between the time courses in maps and in domains. This allows them to borrow their hypotheses for the time courses of activation in the domains from well-known phenomena in vision, especially from well-known phenomena in brightness perception. So it is appropriate to introduce first the field they get their hypotheses from.

In studying temporal and spatial effects in visual perception, one is struck by two, apparently opposite, phenomena, resulting from different 'processing strategies' (see, e.g., Haber and Hershenson, 1974). The first group of phenomena results from a strategy that maximizes responses to light. These phenomena are encountered under conditions of relatively low light intensities. The underlying process can be characterized by the terms 'summation' or 'integration'. The second group of phenomena results from a strategy that reduces responses to steady states. These phenomena are observed under conditions of intermediate and high light intensities. The underlying processes can be characterized by the terms 'subtraction' or 'differentiation'. We discuss the two groups of phenomena, and their (hypothesized) underlying processes, in turn.

An important empirical regularity or law underlying a wide variety of temporal perceptual phenomena observed under conditions of low and intermediate light intensity is Bloch's (1885) law:

$$I.t = C \;, t < t_c.$$

In this law I is the threshold intensity of a test stimulus, t is the duration of the test stimulus, and C is a constant. The law states that in a threshold light *detection* task, the same result will be obtained as long as the product of intensity and duration of the test stimulus is maintained constant, given that the duration of the test stimulus, t, is less than a critical maximum duration, t_c. With dark adapted subjects a critical duration, t_c, of about 100 ms has been obtained in a large number of experimental determinations. In brightness *judgement* tasks it is observed that the value of t_c decreases as the energies, I, used increase (see, e.g., Ganz, 1975; Haber and Hershenson, 1974). The critical duration is also affected by the luminance of the background: light pulses presented against bright backgrounds yield much shorter critical durations than light pulses presented against dark backgrounds (see, e.g., Graham and Kemp, 1938; Barlow, 1958; Roufs, 1972; Haber and Hershenson, 1974).

An important variable that strongly affects the critical duration is the nature of the visual task. The critical duration seems to increase markedly when the task is changed from a light detection or brightness judgement task to a form discrimination or acuity task. Kahneman (1964; 1966) and Kahneman and Norman (1964) used, instead of flashes of light, Landolt-C acuity test targets. Subjects had to detect the orientation of a small gap. Critical durations of 350 and 1000 ms were found! It is, however, far from clear, how reliable these results are. Even Kahneman himself had serious doubts about these results. He called the values, obtained at the highest energy level used in the experiment, 'unexpectedly high', 'puzzling', and 'paradoxical', and concluded that his 'set of experiments does not answer the question of the determinants of temporal summation in acuity' (Kahneman, 1964, p. 561).

The results of the light-detection, brightness judgement and gap-detection tasks are generally taken to indicate that the visual system integrates or summates energy over time. For brightness detection the maximum integration interval is about 100 ms and for form perception integration intervals up to 1000 ms cannot be ruled out. So, quite extensive integration might take place under low light intensity conditions. Of course, under some circumstances integration is a desirable property. If there is very little light, collecting and retaining light over an interval of time is very useful, because

> when light intensity is very low, any strategy which allows intensity to be integrated over longer periods of time will improve the chances of detecting the presence of that energy. But the price paid for this is loss of temporal

specificity. The visual system does not record whether the pulse is long and dim, or brief and intense ...

(Haber and Hershenson, 1974, p. 122)

Under conditions of higher light energies another set of quite spectacular phenomena is easily observed. Among these phenomena are Mach-bands, simultaneous contrast and, possibly, stabilized images. Figure 7.3.1 shows a Mach band pattern, named after Ernst Mach, who first described it in 1865. The actual intensity distribution is plotted by the dashed line and the perceived brightness distribution by the solid line. The solid line exhibits a darker stripe in the region marked D and a brighter one at B. It is obvious that the brightness at these regions, called Mach bands, does not simply depend upon the intensities there. Simultaneous contrast is a related phenomenon. When a gray square is presented against a white background it looks darker than when it is seen against a black background. In general, the perceived brightness of an object depends upon the intensity of the background.

Stabilized images possibly belong to the same class of phenomena. Even during steady fixation, small eye movements still occur: involuntary saccades, drifts and tremors. Involuntary saccades occur at irregular intervals. Between these saccades, the eye drifts slowly. Superimposed upon this drift is a high frequency tremor. Around 1950 it was discovered that these movements are essential for vision. If these small eye movements are artificially eliminated, i.e., if the pattern on the retina is stabilized, the perception disappears very rapidly (Ditchburn and Ginsburg, 1952; Ratliff, 1952). If the pattern is then moved over the retina or if the brightness is changed, perception will reappear, but soon

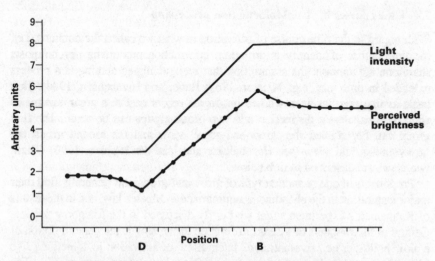

Figure 7.3.1 Mach-bands: Illusory dark and bright bands, resulting from lateral inhibition, are perceived at positions B (bright) and D (dark).

disappears again if stimulation remains unchanged (see, e.g., Gerrits and Vendrik, 1970; Cornsweet, 1970).

The latter phenomena are usually explained in terms of subtraction or differentiation; one or another kind of inhibitory interaction that occurs, at a certain time after stimulus onset, in the visual system. Cornsweet (1970), for instance, convincingly demonstrated how the disappearing perception with stabilized images, the Mach bands and the phenomenon of simultaneous contrast are easily understood by assuming lateral inhibition in the human visual system. Cornsweet is also explicit about the general lesson to be learned from these phenomena.

> To any system that learns and remembers, information about steady states is redundant. Any given condition always began (or the organism first came into its presence) as a transient event, by definition. Once it has begun, if the organism has memory, it need not be continuously reminded of the condition. If the condition stops, that, too, is a transient that will be transmitted. Thus *inhibition*, which suppresses signals from stimuli that are unchanging, would seem to perform an adaptive function.
>
> (Cornsweet, 1970, p.438)

Taking all together, two groups of phenomena in visual perception can be distinguished. Phenomena summarized in and related to Bloch's law, showing summation or integration of activation over time, and phenomena like Mach bands, suggesting subtraction or differentiation (in space) over time. In the past exactly these two groups of phenomena have been used as a source of ideas for hypothesized time courses of activation in, what we called, the domains. In the next section we turn to these hypotheses.

7.4 Time courses in visual information processing

With regard to the time course of activation in what we called the domains, i.e., the time course of identity information, information processing psychologists share one assumption: the assumption that recognizing something is a process extended in time (see, e.g., Neisser, 1967; Haber and Hershenson, 1974). This basic assumption has been worked out in the recent past in a great number of ways. Nevertheless a distinction into two broad groups can be made. The first group can be labelled the 'grow-and-grow' view and the second group the 'grow-and-shrink' view (see Hagenzieker and Van der Heijden, 1990). These two views are described in turn below.

Proponents of one or another type of grow-and-grow view generally find their major inspiration in the phenomena summarized in Bloch's law, and in the results of Kahneman's experiments that we briefly discussed in the foregoing section. Central in their models of visual information processing is the general notion of a slow build-up, i.e., summation or integration, of activation in something like 'dictionary units', 'logogens' or 'recognition units' (see section 7.2). The hypothesized integration or summation time is considerable as compared with the average duration of an eye fixation. It takes a very long time for the activation level in the recognition units to reach a maximum. The basic idea of the grow-and-grow view is depicted in figure 7.4.1. Time is represented on the abscissa, activation level on the ordinate. Let us have a closer look at some examples of this general notion to see the main characteristics of this line of thought.

Eriksen and Schultz's (1978; 1979; see also Eriksen, O'Hara and Eriksen, 1982) continuous flow or continuous growth conception is the prime example. In their view the 'maximum response in the visual system does not occur with the onset of the stimulus; it develops over an appreciable length of time' (Eriksen and Schultz, 1978, p. 4), from 100 ms for simple flashes of light to on the order of 350 to 400 ms for form stimuli. In their model, Eriksen and Schultz conceive of several processes or levels comprising the events from stimulation to response activation: input channels, feature detectors, form units and response system. 'The output from each process becomes increasingly more detailed or exact over time as energy is integrated in the visual sense organ' (Eriksen and Schultz, 1979, p. 252). Haber (1983) completely agrees with Eriksen and Schultz's view and summarizes the temporal properties embodied in that view by stating: 'Eriksen and Schultz describe from numerous experiments that stimulus clarity is not achieved instantly with stimulus onset; rather, it develops slowly, and probably continuously, over the first several 100 milliseconds following stimulus onset' (Haber, 1983, p. 6).

Grice, Boroughs and Canham (1984a), Grice, Canham and Gwynne (1984b), and Grice and Gwynne (1985) formulate essentially the same basic view using a different terminology: 'excitatory strength produced by a stimulus grows as an

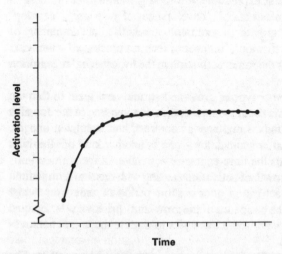

Figure 7.4.1 Activation level as a function of time according to the grow-and-grow view.

orderly function of time following onset until criterion strength is reached' (Grice et al., 1984b, p. 566). Their data and figures show that this hypothesized growth of excitatory strength extends to at least 700 ms.

Also McClelland (1979) proposed a sophisticated information processing model that shows a great similarity with Eriksen and Schultz's view. In his 'cascade' model, McClelland assumes that the – visual – system is composed of several subprocesses or processing levels. Each process is continuously active and the output of each process is always available for processing at the next level. The final output of the 'response activation process' determines which one of the possible responses will be executed. An equation is derived 'describing how activations will vary as a function of time since the onset of a stimulus' (McClelland, 1979, p. 293). This 'cascade equation' shows that, starting with stimulus onset, activation increases over time, resulting in an asymptotic activation after about 1.5 to 2.0 seconds.

A related line of thought is at the basis of Massaro's (1975) model describing the temporal course of 'visual perception'. He argues that 'the visual system appears to integrate the energy from a stimulus over time' (Massaro, 1975, p. 359), and that 'the central assumption of the model is that recognition is a temporally extended process, not an instantaneous occurrence' (Massaro, 1975, p. 366). The recognition process is characterized by a negatively accelerating function of processing time (Lupker and Massaro, 1979) that reaches asymptote at approximately 250 ms. The function therefore closely resembles the curve depicted in figure 7.4.1.

Many more examples of proposals suggesting a slow, continuous, build-up of activation over an appreciable length of time can be found in the literature. The examples given, however, suffice to indicate the essence of this theoretical position. While many different expressions are used – 'summation of energy', 'accumulation of stimulus information', 'development of response', 'development of stimulus clarity', 'growth of excitatory strength', 'accumulation of information in the form of activation', 'number of features processed' – the basic underlying idea in all cases is the same: activation in the hypothetical recognition units 'grows and grows'.

Proponents of one or another type of grow-and-shrink view seem to find the inspiration for their hypothesis about the time course of activation in the domains in phenomena like Mach-bands, simultaneous contrast, and stabilized images, i.e., phenomena in which – after some delay – one or another kind of inhibition is involved. In their proposals the time-course of activation in recognition units is characterized by a rapid growth of activation starting with onset of stimulation, followed by a decrease in activation after a short period of time even while stimulation is still present. The basic idea of the grow-and-shrink view is depicted in figure 7.4.2. What follows are some examples to outline the main characteristics of this line of thought.

Shiffrin and Schneider (1977) appear to be the first suggesting something like the grow-and-shrink view. They proposed an information processing model with

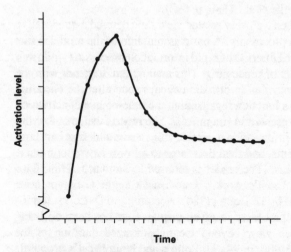

Figure 7.4.2 Activation level as a function of time according to the grow-and-shrink view.

Short-Term-Store (STS) and Long-Term-Store (LTS) as the central concepts. They state that 'the activation in STS could be extremely brief (in msec, say) and unless attention is directed to the process when it occurs or unless the sequence includes an automatic attention-calling response, then the information may be immediately lost from STS' (Shiffrin and Schneider, 1977, p. 156), and 'The various features that are activated are all placed thereby in STS where they reside for a short period before being lost (i.e., before returning to an inactive state in LTS)' (Shiffrin and Schneider, 1977, p. 163). In other words, in Shiffrin and Schneider's model the activity that is automatically produced by a stimulus is very short-lived unless it is supported by internal sources of excitation (Kahneman and Treisman, 1984).

Van der Heijden (1978; 1981) also suggested such a time-course of activation. In his model, the activation of the recognition units, termed 'counts of logogens', shows a fast increase first, soon followed by a decrease in activation according to an exponential decay function. In a later paper, the same hypothesis is formulated. 'The hypothetical effect of external activation is strong initially and decreases over time' (Van der Heijden et al. 1984, p. 466). Van der Heijden (1981, p. 192) explicitly assumes that the decrease of activation already takes place during stimulation. This latter speculation was mainly based on studies on iconic persistence (see, e.g., Dick, 1974 and Di Lollo, 1980) that appeared to show that the icon is initiated when the stimulus is presented, but runs its course independently of objective exposure duration. Exactly the same time-course of activation as suggested by Van der Heijden has been proposed by Larochelle, McClelland and Rodriguez (1980). In their view: 'Activations of logogens reach a peak shortly after stimulus presentation and then decay back to the base level as time goes on ...' (Larochelle et al., 1980, p. 692).

Krumhansl (1982) proposed a closely related view. She derived a quantitative model of visual information processing. A basic assumption of the model is that a stimulus onset initiates a brief period of rapid information processing, followed by a period with reduced rate of processing. This assumption, together with the additional assumption that encoded information decays soon after the encoding of that information, leads to a function representing the time-course of activation rather similar to the one represented in figure 7.4.2. She reports that, due to rapid information processing, the information available from a stimulus first increases to a maximum value at 110 ms, and then decreases to a lower asymptotic value until the offset of the stimulus. (The reader is referred to Stelmach, 1984, for a critical evaluation of Krumhansl's work.) Krumhansl's suggestions are quite similar to an earlier proposal by Di Lollo (1980). According to Di Lollo 'It must be ... concluded that, once processed, a given display does not keep on being reprocessed if it remains on view beyond the hypothesized duration of the recruiting phase' (Di Lollo, 1980, p. 94). Di Lollo's and Krumhansl's proposals only differ in that Di Lollo proposes that processing stops, while Krumhansl assumes that encoding does not terminate, but continues at a reduced rate.

Remarks stressing the importance of the onset of a stimulus, combined with the notion that after a very short period of time information processing declines or even terminates, are easily found in the literature. We mention a few examples. Massaro (1983) states that 'the onset of visual stimulation is more important for the visual system and we might expect that a fixed visual input at the beginning of an eye fixation will have a larger consequence than the same input later in the fixation period' (Massaro, 1983, p. 31). Rayner, Inhoff, Morrison, Slowiaczek and Bertera (1981) state that 'most of the visual information necessary for reading can be acquired during the first 50 msec that information is available during an eye fixation' (Rayner et al., 1981, p. 176). And Coltheart (1983), referring to Rayner et al. (1981), argues that 'if letter identification is so rapid ... we should not *need* to go on sampling the stimulus throughout the fixation period .... Once the text has been fixated for 50 msec or so its presence during the remainder of the fixation is irrelevant and makes no contribution to reading' (Coltheart, 1983, pp. 17–18).

In the literature more examples of proposals assuming that activation in recognition units increases fast initially and then (rapidly) decreases, are easily found. (In contemporary connectionist models, the assumption is often hardware implemented: see, e.g., the models of McClelland and Rumelhart, 1981, and Phaf et al., 1990.) The examples given, however, suffice to illustrate the essence of this line of theorizing. While many different expressions are used – 'extremely brief activation', 'a decrease in activation', 'a decrease of counts', 'a reduced rate of processing', and 'rapid identification' – the basic idea in all cases is approximately the same: activation in the hypothetical recognition units 'grows and shrinks'.

7.5 A synthesis: the Broca–Sulzer effect and a model

With regard to the time course of activation within the domains, visual information processing psychologists propose two completely different kinds of models. One group fosters models of the grow-and-grow type, another group supports models of the grow-and-shrink type. This state of affairs is the more astonishing because both proposals pretend to reflect this time course of activation under all exposure conditions. None of these investigators has ever suggested that his or her favoured time course might only appear under a restricted set of exposure conditions, e.g., under relatively low intensity conditions or under relatively high intensity conditions. Yet, light intensity might be exactly the factor that determines what type of time course – grow-and-grow or grow-and-shrink – is obtained. In this context it is worthwhile to remember that the two sets of perceptual phenomena – Bloch's law and related phenomena and Mach-bands and related phenomena described in section 7.3 – from which the two information processing hypotheses are mainly derived, are observed in relatively low and in intermediate and relatively high intensity conditions, respectively. So, it is possible that the choice of visual phenomena, used to derive and sharpen intuitions about time courses in the domains, was already biased to begin with.

If, based on the assumption that stimulation-caused activation is simply passed on from maps to domains, phenomena in visual perception are used for generating hypotheses about time courses of activation in the domains, then one has to take a visual phenomenon that applies under all relevant conditions, i.e., in the present case, encompasses the complete range of light intensities. Fortunately, there is a perceptual phenomenon that has light intensity and duration of stimulation as the important parameters. That phenomenon is the Broca–Sulzer effect, named after A. Broca and D. Sulzer, who first reported the phenomenon in 1902. Subsequently, this phenomenon has been reproduced by many authors. Possibly this phenomenon in visual perception can serve to generate a synthesizing hypothesis for the time courses of activation in the domains. So let us have a closer look at it.

Broca and Sulzer's (1902) subjects matched the brightness of a fixed-duration reference stimulus with that of a test flash having a constant luminance but a variable duration. In figure 7.5.1 the graphs of their data are plotted. The intensity of the matching reference stimulus is plotted on the ordinate and the test flash duration on the abscissa. The different functions represent various luminances of the test flash, i.e., test flash intensity is the parameter. The figure shows that under conditions of high intensity the brightness functions initially rise, reach a maximum and then decrease again for longer durations. Figure 7.5.1 also suggests that under conditions of low intensities the functions slowly rise over time and ultimately reach an asymptotic value.

Of course, of importance is that the Broca–Sulzer effect combines both sets of phenomena that have been used as a basis for generating hypotheses about the time course of activation in the domains. The upper functions resemble the one

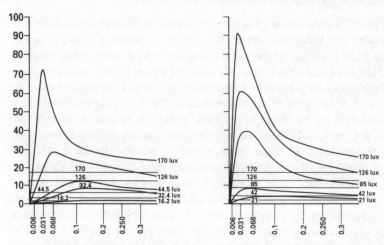

Figure 7.5.1 The Broca–Sulzer effect. Intensity of the reference stimulus is plotted on the vertical axis, test flash duration on the horizontal axis. (After Broca and Sulzer, 1902.)

depicted in figure 7.4.2, representing the hypothesized time course of the grow-and-shrink view, and the lower curves show a strong resemblance to the one depicted in figure 7.4.1, representing the time course of what we called the grow-and-grow view.

Just because the Broca–Sulzer effect combines both sets of perceptual phenomena described in section 7.3, it is worthwhile to take exactly this perceptual phenomenon as a starting point for generating hypotheses about the time courses of activation in the domains. To this end we need more insight into what happens; we need a model that makes a start in specifying the major factors involved in the Broca–Sulzer effect. Hagenzieker and Van der Heijden (1990) proposed a simple model that approximately captures what seem to be these major factors. In the next part of this section and in section 7.6 we describe this model.

According to Cornsweet 'inhibition' is the mechanism to achieve steady state suppression. This inhibition can be modelled in a number of ways (see, e.g., Cornsweet, 1970, p. 296). Consider the simple circuit depicted in figure 7.5.2. This circuit can be regarded as a 'unit' in the visual system, i.e., in the maps. (This particular circuit was taken because its properties are mathematically easily tractable.) If we consider this circuit as a unit, the figure presents the case for, what can be called, forward 'self' inhibition. Within this unit, activation, A, in X is passed on to Y via the arrow line. Y is inhibited, after some delay, by activation passing via the curled line (the curl stands for the delay).

A mathematical characterization of this circuit can be derived as follows. Assume that the activation level, A, in X, develops over time, t, and finally reaches asymptote according to an exponential growth function:

Figure 7.5.2 A 'unit' with forward 'self' inhibition.

$$A_X = b/a(1 - e^{-at}).$$ (7.5.1)

Assume further that this activation is simply passed on to Y so that after an interval of time, delta t, the activation level in Y is given by

$$A_Y = b/a(1 - e^{-at}).$$ (7.5.2)

The activation is reduced by some inhibition:

$$A_Y = b/a(1 - e^{-at}) - \text{inhibition}.$$ (7.5.3)

Assume that this inhibition is not complete, but is some fraction, W:

$$A_Y = b/a(1 - e^{-at}) - W \text{ (inhibition)}.$$ (7.5.4)

Because we assumed 'self' inhibition, the amount of inhibition is some fraction of the activation, A, itself, arriving after some time delay, c:

$$A_Y = b/a(1 - e^{-at}) - W [b/a\{1 - e^{-a(t - c)}\}].$$ (7.5.5)

Finally, assume that inhibition only takes place when the activation level exceeds a threshold, T:

$$A_Y = b/a(1 - e^{-at}) - W ([b/a\{1 - e^{-a(t - c)}\}] - T).$$ (7.5.6)

This mathematical characterization of the circuit depicted in figure 7.5.2 can serve as a simple model of what underlies the Broca–Sulzer effect. In the equation the fraction b/a determines the asymptotic value to be reached when no inhibition is present. In the model this fraction reflects the effect of light intensity.

In figure 7.5.3 time courses of activation are plotted, using the model described above. Time, t, is represented on the abscissa and activation level, A, on the ordinate. In this particular example the values of the parameters a, W, c, and T were 0.05, 0.80, 50, and 0.30 respectively. To vary the level of light energy, seven different values of b were used: 0.100, 0.080, 0.060, 0.040, 0.020, 0.010, and 0.002 respectively.

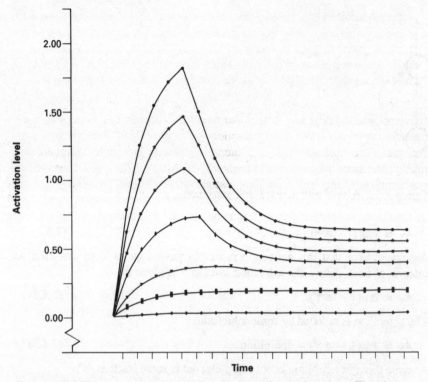

Figure 7.5.3 Time courses of activation (see text for explanation). Time is represented on the horizontal axis, activation on the vertical axis.

The reader is invited to compare figure 7.5.1, in which the Broca–Sulzer effect is plotted, and figure 7.5.3, in which the time courses of activation according to the model are plotted. The comparison shows that this simple model indeed seems to capture the main factors contributing to the Broca–Sulzer effect.

7.6 Lateral inhibition in vision

In the model described in section 7.5, inhibition was forward 'self' inhibition. There is abundant evidence, however, strongly suggesting that in vision, i.e., in the eye and in the brain, inhibition is not necessarily or not only forward 'self' inhibition, but mainly (forward) lateral inhibition (see, e.g., Cornsweet, 1970; Cowey, 1981). Cowey finds in lateral inhibition even the main reason why the visual system contains, what we called, maps:

> If lateral inhibition also occurs at the cortex and is involved in highlighting not just sharp edges but also orientation, colour, disparity, spatial frequency, size, and movement, all this is most economically achieved by having a retinotopic

representation so that the necessary interneurons for receptive field tuning lie close together. If there were no map and the cells concerned with a particular part of space were scattered throughout a visual area, the average length of their interconnecting processes would have to be much longer, and the problem of specifying them during development would be enormous.

(Cowey, 1981, p. 404; see also Cowey, 1979, p. 10)

It is important to note now that for our model to generate the time courses as depicted in figure 7.5.3, the assumption of forward 'self' inhibition is not essential. This, because (forward) lateral inhibition is capable of producing exactly the same time courses. Moreover, this lateral inhibition is completely consistent with the 'self' inhibition discussed in section 7.5. Except for the smallest units (i.e., individual neurons), 'self' inhibition can always be regarded as lateral inhibition between subgroups of units representing parts, or parts of parts, of regions, items or objects (see, e.g., Cornsweet, 1970, figs. 14-18).

In fact, it is easy to show that exactly the same functions as obtained with forward 'self' inhibition (see figure 7.5.3) are obtained with forward lateral inhibition. Consider figures 7.6.1a and 7.6.1b. In figure 7.6.1a forward 'self' inhibition is depicted, in figure 7.6.1b forward lateral inhibition. In figure 7.6.1a a unit is inhibited with a fraction, 1/2, of its input value after a certain time delay c, whereas in figure 7.6.1b a unit is inhibited with 2 x 1/4 of the input values of its *neighbours*, also after delay c. It will be clear that, if all units are assumed to have the same input values, the outcome is exactly the same in both cases.

We now show exactly the same point by using equation 7.5.6. This equation can be summarized with

$$A = X - WY. \tag{7.6.1}$$

Given forward 'self' inhibition we can specify for, say, seven adjacent positions the following series of equations:

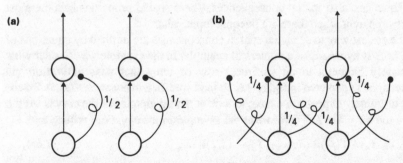

(a)   (b)

Figure 7.6.1 Schematic representation of forward 'self' inhibition (a) and forward lateral inhibition (b).

$$A1 = X1 - WY1$$
$$A2 = X2 - WY2$$
$$A3 = X3 - WY3$$
$$A4 = X4 - WY4 \qquad\qquad (7.6.2)$$
$$A5 = X5 - WY5$$
$$A6 = X6 - WY6$$
$$A7 = X7 - WY7$$

If we change over from forward 'self' inhibition to forward lateral inhibition as depicted in figure 7.6.1b, the units sending activation to the adjacent neighbours send the inhibitory inputs. Reducing the weights from W to $(1/2)W$ to keep the total amount of inhibition approximately constant, leads to the next series of equations:

$$A1 = X1 - (1/2)WY2$$
$$A2 = X2 - (1/2)WY3 - (1/2)WY1$$
$$A3 = X3 - (1/2)WY4 - (1/2)WY2$$
$$A4 = X4 - (1/2)WY5 - (1/2)WY3 \qquad\qquad (7.6.3)$$
$$A5 = X5 - (1/2)WY6 - (1/2)WY4$$
$$A6 = X6 - (1/2)WY7 - (1/2)WY5$$
$$A7 = X7 - (1/2)WY6$$

These functions are of exactly the same general format as equation 7.5.6 (or 7.6.1), and therefore result in time course curves that look the same as the functions depicted in figure 7.5.3 (with equal input values, units 2 to 6 in equations 7.6.2 and 7.6.3 have exactly the same outputs).

While the change of functions of type 7.6.2 into functions of type 7.6.3 has no consequences as far as temporal properties are concerned, it has important consequences when spatial properties are considered. Of course, equations of type 7.6.2 imply no spatial consequences at all, simply because no spatial interactions are specified. Equations of type 7.6.3, on the other hand, explicitly specify spatial interactions and therefore imply, besides the appropriate temporal consequences, also spatial consequences. These spatial properties become most clearly apparent when there are unequal input values.

The easiest way to see what spatial consequences are implied by equations of type 7.6.3 is by means of a numerical example. In the example we consider what ultimately happens in an (infinite) row of units that pass activation via connections as depicted in figure 7.6.1b (and specified in equations 7.6.3). To see what ultimately happens, we have to look at the asymptotes of the curves. At the asymptotes $Y = X - T$. Therefore at the asymptotes the equations reduce to:

$$A_n = X_n - (1/2)W(X_{n+1} - T) - (1/2)W(X_{n-1} - T) \qquad\qquad (7.6.4)$$

with n specifying the nth position in the row.

In the top row of figure 7.6.2a the input activation for a row of nine adjacent units is given. The solid line in figure 7.6.2b also presents these values. The next

	n	n+1	n+2	n+3	n+4	n+5	n+6	n+7	n+8
a) Input X	70	70	70	80	90	100	110	110	110
b) $X - T$	20	20	20	30	40	50	60	60	60
c) Inhibition I		10	12.5	15	20	25	27.5	30	
d) Output A		60	57.5	65	70	75	82.5	80	

Figure 7.6.2a The transformation as specified by equation 7.6.4, applied to the Mach-band phenomenon. Input values (X) and output values (A) for nine adjacent units. (Threshold value $T = 50$, inhibitory coefficient = 1/4.)

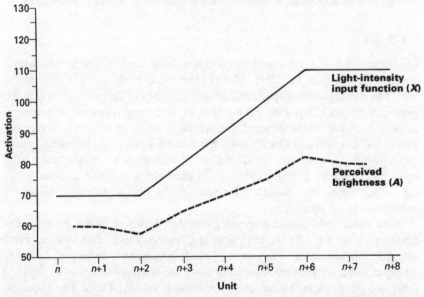

Figure 7.6.2b The input and output values (input X and output A in Fig. 7.6.2a).

two rows in figure 7.6.2a present some steps involved in applying the transformation embodied in equation 7.6.4. The last row in figure 7.6.2a gives the output values A_n, i.e., the outcome of equation 7.6.4 for each unit. This result is plotted as a dashed line in figure 7.6.2b. A comparison of this figure and figure 7.3.1 makes clear that equation 7.6.4 quite naturally generates the Mach band phenomenon (see Lindsay and Norman, 1977, for the same demonstration). So equations of type 7.6.3, summarized in equation 7.6.4, not only produce important temporal phenomena in vision like the Broca–Sulzer effect. They can also account for important spatial phenomena in vision like Mach bands.

Cornsweet (1970) already pointed out that in neural networks temporal and spatial properties are inextricably interwoven:

> we presented an extensive discussion of the lateral inhibitory interactions that occur in visual systems. These interactions have great explanatory power with respect to certain classes of perceptual phenomena that depend upon *spatial* intensity distributions. A further examination of the necessary *temporal* consequences of exactly the same machinery reveals that ... inhibition may also account for many of the temporal perceptual phenomena described ...
>
> (Cornsweet, 1970, p. 410)

(Possibly this time–space and/or space–time interrelation made Mach bands and related phenomena so attractive as a background of theorizing for the proponents of, what we called, the grow-and-shrink view.) We are now informed well enough to turn back from activation in the maps to activation in the domains.

7.7 Space

Equations 7.5.6 and 7.6.4 pretend to characterize some temporal and spatial phenomena in vision, i.e., light-induced phenomena in the maps subserving 'to see'. The two equations capture different dimensions of the same activity in the system or network. Equation 7.5.6 makes explicit some *temporal* properties of activity; it characterizes temporal phenomena in vision as observed in, e.g., the Broca–Sulzer effect and Bloch's law. Equation 7.6.4 makes explicit some *spatial* consequences. It gives the spatial pattern of activation at the asymptote. The equation is intended to characterize spatial phenomena in vision as observed in, e.g., Mach bands and simultaneous contrast. In both equations intensity of stimulation is the parameter.

Most visual information processing research, however, is not directly concerned with 'to see'. As we have seen in Chapters 3 to 6, also most selective attention experiments in vision are not directly concerned with 'to see'. In nearly all experiments subjects are required to name one or another element or object (a letter, a digit, a colour, a word, etc.). So, subjects are asked what they know, or, the experiments are concerned with information (or activation) in the domains subserving 'to know'.

In section 7.2 we tentatively assumed that stimulation-caused activation is simply passed on from the maps to the domains. We now have to face the question whether this simple and attractive assumption is really tenable or has to be rejected. Unfortunately, just as with nearly all other assumptions maintained within the information processing approach, there is sufficient evidence to maintain but not enough to really defend the assumption. The way in which the assumption has to be defended is clear, however. If there are indeed no further essential transformations between maps and domains, i.e., if the time course of activation in the domains faithfully reflects the time course of activation in the maps, then equations 7.5.6 and 7.6.4 also characterize temporal and spatial phenomena as observed in visual information processing tasks. In other words, what we have to look for are equivalents of the Broca–Sulzer effect and of the Mach band patterns in experiments in which words like 'a', '3', 'red', etc., are used as the only responses.

In this section we turn to some aspects of the information processing equivalent of the Mach band patterns, i.e., to some aspects of spatial interactions as observed in visual information processing tasks. In the next section we discuss some aspects of the information processing equivalent of the Broca–Sulzer effect, i.e., some aspects of time courses of activation in the domains.

Mach band patterns strongly suggest one or another kind of spatial interaction, e.g., lateral inhibition, in vision, i.e., in the maps subserving to see (see section 7.6; see also, e.g., Cornsweet, 1970). If activation in the maps is faithfully reflected in activation in the domains, effects of these spatial interactions must also show up in visual information processing tasks. With regard to the information processing equivalent of the Mach band patterns two groups of experimental results have to be distinguished: incidental or more or less casual observations and systematic, theory guided, investigations.

The research providing incidental observations is not really concerned with the issue of whether activation in the maps is simply passed on to the domains. The research is nevertheless of importance because it shows that, under a broad range of exposure conditions, spatial interactions also show up in visual information processing tasks. The phenomenon of relevance was already briefly described in section 5.2 (see also section 5.6). It is generally indicated with the term 'lateral masking'. In the experiments concerned with the phenomenon it shows up as an adverse effect on identification of a letter caused by a (mask) letter presented in close temporal and spatial proximity.

Research has clearly shown the importance of this phenomenon and has also revealed several of its properties. Lateral masking is not only observed with short exposure durations but also with extended exposure durations (see, e.g., Townsend, Taylor and Brown, 1971; Taylor and Brown, 1972; Estes, Allmeyer and Reder, 1976). Because with extended exposures the visual information is available during report, lateral masking appears to be a genuine visual factor and not a memory factor. Lateral masking is more detrimental in the periphery than in the fovea (Bouma, 1970; Matthews, 1973; Wolford and Hollingsworth, 1974) and with close target–mask spacing than with wide spacing (Bouma, 1970; Strangert and Bränström, 1975; Wolford and Chambers, 1983). The effect is asymmetric; masks placed on the peripheral side of the target are more effective than masks on the foveal side (Bouma, 1970; 1973; Banks, Larson and Prinzmetal, 1979; Chastain, 1982a, b; Chastain and Lawson, 1979; Chambers and Wolford, 1983). Furthermore, lateral masking is probably to some extent feature-specific, i.e., the accuracy-reducing interaction effects are larger for identical or similar letters than for dissimilar letters (La Heij and Van der Heijden, 1983; Shapiro and Krueger, 1983).

To the best of our knowledge the only systematic, theory guided, investigation of how spatial interactions in the maps show up in a visual information processing task, was performed by Hagenzieker et al. (1990). As a starting point they used equation 7.5.6. This equation was interpreted as a synthesizing information processing model with regard to time courses of activation in the domains, specifying that the grow-and-grow view is appropriate under conditions of low light intensities and the grow-and-shrink view under conditions of intermediate and higher intensities. This interpretation of equation 7.5.6 was tested by looking at the spatial consequences as given by the set of equations (7.6.3), summarized in equation 7.6.4. These equations were used in a numerical example to see what is to be expected in a partial-report bar-probe task when different luminance levels are used. In this numerical example Hagenzieker et al. 'simulated' the results expected for an intermediate luminance level and for a very low luminance level. The numerical example was concerned with linear

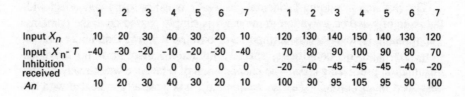

	1	2	3	4	5	6	7	1	2	3	4	5	6	7
Input X_n	10	20	30	40	30	20	10	120	130	140	150	140	130	120
Input $X_n - T$	-40	-30	-20	-10	-20	-30	-40	70	80	90	100	90	80	70
Inhibition received	0	0	0	0	0	0	0	-20	-40	-45	-45	-45	-40	-20
A_n	10	20	30	40	30	20	10	100	90	95	105	95	90	100

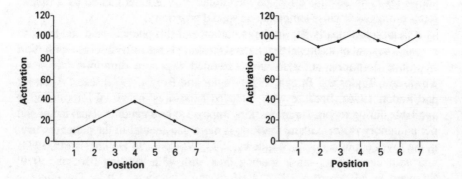

(threshold, $T = 50$; inhibitory coefficient, $(1/2) W = 1/4$; activation, A)

Figure 7.7.1 Numerical example showing the spatial effects produced by equation 7.6.4. Right panel: Above-threshold input values; left panel: Below-threshold input values.

7-element arrays, with input values reflecting a retinal acuity function. A threshold of $T = 50$ and an inhibitory coefficient of 1/4 were used. Figure 7.7.1 shows numerically and graphically what happens.

The right panel of the figure shows the spatial consequences when the input values are clearly above threshold, i.e., when inhibition is present. The left panel shows the case when input values are clearly below the threshold, T, and no inhibition is present. This numerical example shows that under conditions of 'high' intensities, the position curve is clearly W-shaped (see panel at the right). Under conditions of low intensity, i.e., with below-threshold values, the resulting position curve reflects a retinal acuity function (see panel at the left). Of course, the exact form of the functions is not of importance, because a great number of arbitrary assumptions are used (e.g., assumptions with regard to the exact type of lateral inhibition, the input values as a function of retinal acuity, the value of the threshold, T, etc.). Of importance is only the global form of the functions. The synthesizing hypothesis embodied in equation 7.5.6, applied to position in a row, predicts a retinal acuity function for low intensity conditions and a W-shaped function for intermediate intensity conditions.

To test the prediction Hagenzieker et al. (1990) used a partial-report bar-probe task. Two levels of luminance were used: a relatively high luminance condition, in which it was expected to find the traditional W-shaped curve, and a – for letter recognition – very low luminance condition, in which it was expected to find some kind of retinal acuity function. The information was sampled in a pre-cue condition and in a post-cue condition.

In both luminance conditions a sharply W-shaped serial position curve was found (see section 5.6 for the results and the analysis of the data). So, interpreted in terms of the spatial consequence equation, i.e., equation 7.6.4, both luminance conditions appeared to be conditions with above-threshold input values; under both conditions inhibition was clearly present. Because with still lower luminances letter reading became impossible in this partial-report bar-probe task, we have to conclude that the threshold, T, is very low indeed.

Interpreted in terms of equation 7.5.6 this means that under the low luminance condition no shred of evidence was found supporting the grow-and-grow view. All the data pointed at an underlying time course of activation as suggested by the grow-and-shrink view. Consistent with this view (a) the W-shaped curve was more pronounced in the bright than in the dim exposure condition (see figures 5.6.1 and 5.6.2) and (b) the W-shaped curve became more pronounced over time. In the next section we return to this important result.

7.8 Time

It is possible to take the point of view that with regard to the information processing equivalent of the Broca–Sulzer effect, i.e., with regard to the time courses of activation in the domains, most has been said already. In section 7.4 we extensively described the relevant research, i.e., what is known about the time courses of activation in the domains. In section 7.5 we argued that the time courses proposed by information processing psychologists reflect, or are consistent with, the time course of activation as apparent in the Broca–Sulzer effect. Equation 7.5.6 describes the temporal aspect of the Broca–Sulzer effect. So, if there are no further essential transformations between maps and domains, i.e., if the time course of activation in the domains faithfully reflects the time course of activation in the maps, equation 7.5.6 also describes the temporal aspects of activation in the domains.

At first sight, it seems then that we have arrived at an important theoretical result. Equation 7.5.6 (see also figure 7.5.3), interpreted as an information processing model, seems to form a simple, synthesizing, model compatible with the grow-and-grow view as well as the grow-and-shrink view. Light intensity seems to determine which view is the appropriate one. The grow-and-grow view seems to capture what happens under conditions of (very) low light intensities, and the grow-and-shrink view seems to apply under conditions of intermediate and higher light intensities.

Unfortunately, things are not that simple, and that for at least two reasons. First, the synthesizing model, embodied in equation 7.5.6, does not really represent the view defended by proponents of the grow-and-grow view. (In our view, it adequately reflects the ideas expressed by proponents of the grow-and-shrink view.) It is well known that only 'In low illumination after sufficient adaptation ... retinal receptive field properties do change-away from acting as differentiators and towards acting as photon collectors' (Marr, 1980, p. 218). Proponents of the grow-and-grow view will certainly disagree with the conclusion to which the synthesizing model seems to force us: that their view only applies under conditions of (very) low light intensities; conditions under which, for instance, letter reading is impossible. Their view was intended to account for the temporal aspects of visual information processing under all, and certainly not only under very low, intensity conditions (see section 7.5).

Secondly, this interpretation of equation 7.5.6 is also not consistent with available empirical data. As described in section 7.7, Hagenzieker et al. (1990) indeed interpreted equation 7.5.6 as a synthesizing information processing model, specifying that the grow-and-grow view is appropriate under conditions of low light intensities and the grow-and-shrink view under conditions of intermediate and higher light intensities. The spatial consequences of this interpretation were tested in a partial-report bar-probe task. A relatively high and a very low luminance condition were used. Under the low luminance condition no evidence at all supporting the grow-and-grow view was found (remember, with still lower luminances, letter reading became impossible in this task). It will be clear that the outcome of this investigation, concerned with the spatial consequences embodied in equation 7.5.6, is completely at variance with the point of view that this equation can serve as a synthesizing information processing model. The correct interpretation of equation 7.5.6 is not that the grow-and-grow view is correct under conditions of low light intensities and the grow-and-shrink view under conditions of intermediate and higher light intensities. The time courses of activation, relevant for information processing tasks, seem to be of the grow-and-shrink type only.

Fortunately, there is another way to reconcile the grow-and-grow views and the grow-and-shrink views. This reconciliation has as important features that (a) it takes equation 7.5.6 as really reflecting the underlying time courses of activation in visual information processing, and, (b) it recognizes that only the grow-and-shrink curves, obtained at intermediate and higher light intensity levels, are of relevance for visual information processing. At the basis of this reconciliation is the assumption that central (selective) attention is capable of transforming a time course of activation function of the grow-and-shrink type into one of the grow-and-grow type by adding extra activation.

In sections 4.7 and 4.8 we assigned (selective) attention a function in the time domain. Providing order in time was suggested as being attention's main job. In section 7.0 we argued that visual information processing as a whole can be regarded as the interaction between, or integration of, stimulation-caused activation and, what can be called, internally generated activation. Of course, central (selective) attention can also be regarded as internally generated activation, interacting and integrating with stimulation-caused activation. So, it is possible that exactly this integration of activations transforms an underlying grow-and-shrink time course into an 'observed' grow-and-grow time course.

This synthesizing view is quite close to the views expressed by proponents of the grow-and-grow views and of the grow-and-shrink views. As we have seen several times before, in these two groups of theories, the processing assumptions are inextricably interwoven with assumptions about how the system contributes in generating the behaviour observed, i.e., with assumptions about what function attention serves in visual information processing. From the literature it appears that in the two groups of theories the hypothesized role of attention is conceived differently.

In most grow-and-grow views attention is involved in the processing of information (see, e.g., Lupker and Massaro, 1979; Massaro, 1975; Eriksen and associates). This can be taken to mean that in these views the time courses of activation are not the result of stimulation alone. In these views attention is an essential component in visual information processing that determines the rate of growth. The activation level possibly 'grows' automatically, but 'grows', and 'grows' the more, the more attention (i.e., resources or capacity) is present. But then the proposed grow-and-grow time courses are the result of integration of stimulation-caused activation and internally generated, attentional, activation.

In most grow-and-shrink theories, on the other hand, attention performs another role. In these views, the time courses of activation are indeed only the automatic result of stimulation. Attention has nothing to do with the processing of information. Only after information is identified (processed) does attention come in. (The presence of attention then causes the *selection* of identified information; see, e.g., Shiffrin and Schneider, 1977; Van der Heijden, 1981.) So in these views the grow-and-shrink time courses are the underlying time courses, that are addressed and changed by attention to provide the desired order in time. One way for attention to provide order in time is by changing one (of several) grow-and-shrink time courses into a grow-and-grow time course, so that it becomes the dominant activation at a certain moment in time.

The analysis presented in the previous paragraphs entails that it will be extremely difficult to obtain information about the underlying, stimulation-caused, time courses of activation from selective attention experiments. What is observed will generally be the result of the interaction and integration of stimulation-caused activation and internally generated, attentional, activation. Exactly this interaction and integration will generally result in evidence favouring the grow-and-grow views, even if the underlying time course is of the grow-and-shrink type.

There is, however, one method that presumably provides a better look at the underlying time courses of activation, uncontaminated by attentional influences. This method looks at the effects over time of irrelevant, not to be selected, information. In this context it is worthwhile to remember Kahneman et al.'s (1983) Eriksen effect studies with advance presentation of the distractors (see section 6.8). The finding that under these conditions the Eriksen effect tended to disappear led these authors to the conclusion that

> the image of an attention spotlight directed at the target could be misleading. The operation of attention may be more accurately modeled as the casting of a shadow or a mask on potential sources of distraction that should be ignored.
> (Kahneman et al., 1983, p. 520)

Exactly this 'casting of a shadow' is what is to be expected from steady-state suppression (Cornsweet, 1970), and equals the shrink part of the grow-and-shrink curves. So, there is no need to invent another exotic function for attention to account for this important observation. The assumption of underlying grow-and-shrink time courses of activation for the intensity levels relevant for visual information processing, simply suffices (and the assumption that the time courses of activation in the domains faithfully reflect the time courses of activation in the maps need not to be rejected).

7.9 UC and LC again

The information processing view presented in the preceding sections is consistent with the UC processing assumption as introduced in information processing psychology by Deutsch and Deutsch (1963, pp. 27–8): 'One of the salient features of the system as proposed is that it assumes that all sensory messages which impinge upon the organism are perceptually analyzed at the highest level'. It is also quite close to, e.g., Marcel's (1983) UC processing view:

All sensory data impinging however briefly upon receptors sensitive to them is analyzed, transformed, and redescribed, automatically and quite independently of consciousness, from its source form into every other representational form that the organism is capable of representing, whether by nature or by acquisition. This process of redescription will proceed to the highest and most abstract levels within the organism. Further, within every domain of redescription, wherever more than one parsing is possible of the data presented to it, all possible parsings will be carried out and represented. The structure of systems which automatically process sensory input is distributed as well as hierarchical. Some systems depend on the outputs of others, e.g., lexical analysis of alphabetic print depends on a representation in terms of strokes and letters. However, systems such as form and color operate independently. Good evidence for such distributed processing comes from neuropsychological dissociations ...

(Marcel, 1983, p. 244)

The analysis is also consistent with current knowledge in neurophysiology about the processing capacity of the brain:

The massively parallel, apparently modular organization of processing in the nervous system does not suggest any compelling limitation on the concurrent analysis of multiple visual objects, up to and including their categorization in terms of known forms and of learned actions they afford .... Of course there may be such limitations; we simply observe that the available neurophysiology does not appear to require them.

(Allport et al., 1985)

The particular variant of the UC processing view developed in this chapter is exactly the same as the one I proposed earlier (Van der Heijden, 1978; 1981). The reason for persisting on this position is not only that this view is consistent with what others say (e.g., Deutsch and Deutsch, 1963; Marcel, 1983) or with neurophysiological evidence (e.g., Cornsweet, 1970; Allport et al., 1985). The reason is that neither in experiments concerned with the capacity issue (see, e.g., Van der Heijden, 1975; Van der Heijden, La Heij and Boer, 1983; Van der Heijden, Schreuder, Maris and Neerincx, 1984 and also the important work by Egeth and associates, e.g., Egeth, Jonides and Wall, 1972; Egeth, Folk and Mullin, 1989; Mullin and Egeth, 1989), nor in experimental work concerned with the functioning of attention (see, e.g., Van der Heijden et al., 1984; Hagenaar and Van der Heijden, 1986), nor in theoretical work concerned with these issues (see, e.g., Van der Heijden et al., 1984; Van der Heijden, 1987; 1990), can I find reasons to conclude otherwise.

Nevertheless, most theorists in information processing psychology propose a completely different view. In their theories the human information processing system has only a limited central capacity for processing, i.e., for the categorization or identification, of visual information. It is worthwhile to distinguish two different positions within this group of LC views, because the limitations are construed in two different ways.

One group of theorists suggests that the human information processing system has, what can be called, 'structural' central limitations. Broadbent (1958; 1971) postulated a central information processing channel with a limited capacity, that has to be protected by a filter (see Chapter 2). Moray (1967) thought that this central limitation was due to a limited central computation capacity such as in the central processing unit of a computer. According to Norman and Bobrow (1975), however, it is better to conceive these limitations in terms of insufficient transmission channels and stores.

It is highly likely that for visual information processing these views capture something of importance and it is not too difficult to find a number of ways to reconcile these views with the view proposed in this chapter. First, in a sense, the eye can be regarded as a 'filter' that protects the central information processing system from an overload. In section 2.8 we described this filtering function of the eye. Remember that we noted there that the eye has a built-in limited capacity. Second, in a sense, the two million (2×10^6) retinal gangion cells that transport the information from eyes to cortex can be regarded as a 'transmission channel' of severe limited capacity. Of course, their capacity exactly meets the information processing capacity of the eyes and exactly fits the central computation capacity of the brain. Nevertheless their number is very small as compared with the number of cells in the brain concerned with processing visual information (about 5×10^{10}). Third, (self) inhibition, resulting in steady state suppression, and lateral inhibition, causing interference between representations, can also be interpreted in terms of 'insufficient storage capacity' and 'insufficient transmission channels'.

In my view, especially after Cornsweet's (1970) impressive lessons, visual information processing research has neglected far too much the profound effects of (lateral) inhibition. Elsewhere I have defended the position that it is inhibition that makes human beings appear as limited capacity information processors.

> Just as a watchmaker can remove a balance thereby making the watch run much faster, so can the great omnipotent designer remove inhibition, making much more information processing possible. But then neither the watch nor the human being performs its proper functions anymore. It seems that it is (lateral) inhibition that transforms an, in principle, unlimited capacity information processing system into a, for practical purposes, severely limited capacity system, that can perform its proper functions in the world.
>
> (Van der Heijden, 1990, pp. 222–3)

Taken all together, the information processing view described in the previous sections incorporates a great number of features of the visual information processing system, that can be called, if one wishes, peripheral and central 'structural limitations'. With these features given, there is no further need to invent and introduce additional, not further specified, 'structural limitations' to account for the data observed in selective attention experiments.

7.10 Resources

A second group of theorists proposed a completely different type of limitations. They completely disagree with Deutsch and Deutsch's view that 'a message will reach the same perceptual and discriminating mechanisms whether attention is paid to it or not' (Deutsch and Deutsch, 1963, p. 28). In their view, besides the information processing system, something else is additionally required for the processing of information. For Neisser (1967), for example, the processing limitation was in 'focal attention'; an 'act of focal attention' cannot handle more than one 'unit' at a time. In Kahneman's (1973) view, there is a limited amount of general mental energy or effort that has to be distributed over the central processing components. In this view 'selective attention to inputs is the allocation of capacity to the processing of certain perceptual units in preference to others' (Kahneman, 1973, p. 135). In a recent formulation this view is expressed as follows.

> Attention can be conceived of as a limited supply of processing capacity, or resources, that can be allocated in varying amounts to different tasks ... or to different locations in the visual field ... parallel search of visual displays is the result of an even allocation of attentional processing capacity to all display positions. If the discrimination is simply enough that these distributed resources can handle the processing, evidence for parallel search is obtained. If, however, the discrimination requires greater resources, then resources are concentrated and display locations are searched serially.
>
> (Eriksen and St. James, 1986, pp. 225–6)

At first sight, it seems much more difficult to reconcile these views with the information processing view proposed in this chapter. One way out, however, is to admit that something like 'resources', 'focal attention', 'effort' or 'capacity' is indeed needed in the visual information processing tasks this study is concerned with, but not for the processing of information as defined in the present chapter, i.e., for the transition from maps to domains. So, let us try to find a possible answer to the question of what it is 'attention', 'capacity', or 'resources' are then needed for.

To find an answer to this question it is worthwhile to start with the question: Why was it ever proposed that, in visual information processing, 'resources', 'capacity' or 'attention' is needed for the processing of information? A first answer to this question is quite simple. It was the starting assumption. The assumption was implicitly part of the 'reading' hypothesis. Reading clearly seems an 'activity', requiring 'capacity', 'effort', or 'resources'. And there is nothing wrong with the idea that reading requires effort.

Originally, in the 'reading' notion (perfect) selection and identification were combined (see sections 5.2 and 6.0). So, the feeling was that this combined 'selection and identification' required effort, capacity, or resources. Subsequently, however, empirical evidence forced theorists to reject at least some aspects of the 'reading' hypothesis. Different options were chosen then.

One important option we met in Chapter 5. Mewhort and associates made 'the system' responsible for the processing of the information. Attention was left with the function of selection. In this dissociation both the processing and the selection of information are adequately accounted for (see Shiffrin and Schneider, 1977, and Van der Heijden, 1978; 1981, for related proposals).

A completely different, very influential, option we met in Chapter 6. In the spotlight views and zoom lens views attention maintained a function in the processing of information. Unfortunately, the evidence suggested that the 'scarce resources' could not be finely tuned or directed. There were 'failures in selective attention' (see, e.g., Gatti and Egeth, 1978; Neumann, 1984); the 'spot' was too large (see section 6.4), and 'zooming in' was not sufficient (see section 6.5); so, much too much information was selected and processed (see section 6.10). Within this option, processing is accounted for but selective attention lost its selective function. It only approximately selects. A further non-attentional selection is necessary to account for the subject's ability to produce correct responses (remember, subjects hardly ever make mistakes). See, e.g., Eriksen and Eriksen (1974; see section 6.4) and Kahneman and Henik (1981; see section 4.10) for such additional, non-attentional, selection proposals.

The important question now is: Why was it that some (most?) theorists favoured the second option over the first option? And why was it that, in this option, 'capacity', 'effort', or 'attention' was associated with the processing of information and not with the selection of information, when the empirical evidence forced these theorists to distinguish these two aspects in reading? If – in 'reading' – 'processing' and 'selection' are distinguished, then the 'effort' can be assigned to the processing of the information but also to the selection of the processed information. Why then attentional processing and non-attentional selection (option 2), and why not non-attentional processing and attentional selection (compatible with option 1)?

This question makes it necessary to have a closer look at the experiments that led to the second option. The relevant experiments are those using the 'response competition logic' (see sections 6.1 to 6.5). They are multiple-item experiments with latency as the dependent variable. For the latency measure to be of any use, an experimental situation has to be created in which subjects can perform the task correctly. Not simply latency, but *latency on correct trials* is the dependent variable. So correctness of response is experimentally fixed. Factors are varied and their effects on correct latencies are measured.

In general, experimenters regard what is fixed as not existing and what varies as the real thing (see sections 2.3 and 2.6). In the relevant experiments response competition varied and therefore was regarded as the real thing in need of an explanation. Correctness of selection was fixed and therefore not in need of explanation. Consequently 'capacity', 'effort', or 'attention' was assigned to the real thing: the processing of information that was held to be responsible for response competition.

It will by now be clear, that it is possible to reconcile the 'resource', 'capacity', or 'effort' view with the UC processing view described in this chapter. In this reconciliation the assumption that resources are needed for processing information, i.e., option 2, has to be rejected, and the assumption that effort is required in the selection of information, a view compatible with option 1, has to be accepted. Indeed, what is generally summarized with the term 'voluntary attention' can be regarded as the effort needed to provide order in time (see sections 4.7 and 4.8). One way to attain this goal was already pointed out in section 7.8. An attractive assumption in line with the analysis presented in this chapter is that attention, as internally generated activation, can interact with stimulation-caused activation and change a grow-and-shrink type curve into a grow-and-grow type curve. To some further details about how attention exactly performs this job we turn in the next chapter.

Chapter 8

Attention, expectation and intention

8.0 Unlimited capacity and no selection

In the recent past most prominent theorists in information processing research took limited central capacity simply as a given; as a basic fact of nature. The idea was that exactly this limited capacity made selection necessary. Broadbent (1958) introduced this view (see section 2.4) and consistently advocated it.

> Large though the brain is, any conceivable mechanism which could cope simultaneously with all possible states of the eye, the ear and other receptors, would probably be even larger. The workings of the nervous system then are likely to incorporate a good many devices aimed at economizing on the mechanism necessary .... Broadbent (1958) ... held that the limited capacity portion of the nervous system was preceded and protected by a selective device or filter, which would pass only some of the incoming information.
>
> (Broadbent, 1971, p. 9)

Others were even more convinced than Broadbent (1958; 1971; 1982).

> The human organism exists in an environment containing many different sources of information. It is patently impossible for the organism to process all these sources, since it has a limited information capacity, and the amount of information available for processing is always much greater than the limited capacity. Therefore the organism must process information selectively.
>
> (Garner, 1974, pp. 23–4)

It will by now be clear that the limited central capacity notion of this 'limited capacity therefore selection' view is debatable on many grounds (see, e.g., sections 2.9 and 7.9; see also Neisser, 1976; Allport, 1980a, b; 1987; Neumann, 1984; 1987; Van der Heijden, 1990). Nevertheless, the 'limited capacity therefore selection' view was at least a logically coherent view. If the system indeed has a limited central capacity for processing information, then, in order to survive, it had better select very carefully. (Of course, here Deutsch and Deutsch's problem immediately shows up: How to select 'very carefully' if there is only a limited capacity for processing, i.e., for really evaluating, incoming information? see section 2.5.)

Some proponents of the 'limited capacity therefore selection' view, however, went much further in the defence of their position. These authors also suggest that, if there were no central capacity limitations for the processing of information, no selection would be needed anymore. Broadbent (1971), for instance, states

If there were really sufficient machinery available in the brain to perform such an analysis for every stimulus, and then to use the results to decide which should be selected, it is difficult to see why any selection at all should occur. The obvious utility of a selection system is to produce an economy in mechanism. If a complete analysis were performed even of the neglected message, there seems no reason for selection at all.

(Broadbent, 1971, p. 147)

Basically the same idea is found in Eriksen and Hoffman (1972a):

If a large number of letters or digits are simultaneously exposed for a brief duration, the human O is typically able to report only a small number, approximately four. Under the same conditions, if the O is told to report only the stimulus designated by a black bar or similar indicator, he can by some process, select this particular stimulus and report it with perfect accuracy. A necessary condition for this demonstration is the overload of information provided the O. The existence of a limited channel capacity is implied by the concept itself. Without such a limit, there would be no necessity for selective attention, as all stimuli would then be processed with equal accuracy at all times.

(Eriksen and Hoffman, 1972a, p. 169)

It will by now also be clear where this 'unlimited capacity therefore no selection' view comes from: it simply follows from the assumption that selection is selection for processing, i.e., from the reading assumption with selection and identification combined. Of course, if all information is processed then there is no need for *selection for processing*. In short the extremely strong hold of the reading assumption apparently prevented the conception of reasonable arguments for the need for *selection for other purposes* than the processing of information.

Later on, however, some limited capacity theorists recognized a second function of selection:

There are two main interpretations of the adaptive function of selective attention, corresponding to two problems that an organism must solve. One view emphasizes the richness and complexity of the information that is presented to the senses at any one time and the consequent risk of confusion and overload (Broadbent, 1958). The other view emphasizes the diverse and incompatible response tendencies that may be instigated at any one time and the consequent risks of paralysis and incoherence (Posner, 1978; Shallice, 1972) .... It is of course quite possible – indeed likely – that organisms are threatened by perceptual overload and by response incoherence, and that different selective processes must be employed to control the two threats.

(Kahneman and Treisman, 1984, p. 29)

And, in our view, exactly this second function of attention is of fundamental importance.

Our information processing view, set out in Chapter 7, does not recognize a central processing problem as a result of the richness and complexity of available information, or, a threat introduced by perceptual overload. In our view, there is no limited central capacity providing the reason for selection. So, what we are left with is the second problem: 'response incoherence'. Even if more selective processes are employed and have to be distinguished – as Kahneman and Treisman suggest – we have to find the reason for their existence in 'the diverse and incompatible response tendencies that may be instigated at any one time'. Phrased more generally, we have to derive the need for all forms of selection from properties and requirements of actions (see also Allport, 1987; Neumann, 1987; Van der Heijden, 1990). So, let us have a brief look at actions and selections.

8.1 Actions and selections

Recently a number of theoreticians pointed out that not 'limited capacity', but exactly something like 'unlimited capacity' or 'too large capacity' is what makes selection necessary:

Although the senses are capable of registering many different objects together, effector systems are typically limited to carrying out just one action of a given kind at a time. Hence the biological necessity and theoretical importance of selection-for-action.

(Allport, 1987, pp. 396–7)

Exactly the many-to-many possible mappings between domains of sensory input and of motor output introduce

The problem ... how to avoid the behavioral chaos that would result from an attempt to simultaneously perform all possible actions for which sufficient causes exist ...

(Neumann, 1987, p. 374)

These views are not only an attractive starting point because of the 'unlimited capacity' aspect. Of uttermost importance is also the fact that the terms 'at a time' and 'simultaneously' in these two quotations (and the expression 'at any one time' in Kahneman and Treisman's quotation) strongly indicate that the basic problem the system faces is a temporal priority problem: a problem of ordering actions in time. And this exactly fits in with and complements the view on attention we introduced in section 4.7. The function of attention is in the time domain. Attentional selection has to impose order or structure in time.

Just as Kahneman and Treisman (1984), both Allport (1987) and Neumann (1987) recognize two essential forms of selection. The first form of selection is needed because there is one real 'capacity' limitation: human beings have only a limited number of effectors. So, there is a difference in capacity between the central information processing system (no capacity limitations; see Chapter 7) and the action systems or effectors (a very limited capacity; generally only one action at a time can be performed). This form of selection has therefore to solve the problem, which action, or more precisely, which category or mode of action, from the total repertoire of possible actions, has to be given temporal priority (Allport, 1987, p. 395). It determines which skill is allowed to recruit what effectors at a certain moment in time (Neumann, 1987, p. 376).

The second form of selection is needed because a selected action can generally be directed to only one among a number of simultaneously available objects at a time. In most natural situations, and also in most laboratory settings, there are, however, more potential targets to which a selected action can be directed. This form of selection has therefore to solve the problem of which object to act upon at a certain moment in time, i.e., the problem of where the action is now to be directed (Allport, 1987, p. 395). It determines from what region in space the set of parameters is taken that is allowed to specify the action in detail at a certain moment in time (Neumann, 1987, p. 376).

The first form of selection – the selection of the action – is artificially induced in the simple information processing experiments reported in this study. The experimenter 'simply' instructs the subject which category or mode of action has to be given temporal priority. In one way or another this instruction – plus a couple of practice trials – not only prevents 'the behavioral chaos that would result from an attempt to simultaneously perform all possible actions for which sufficient causes exist ...' (Neumann, 1987, p. 374); the instruction also has the quite remarkable result that subjects generally start to produce the unique, and only the unique, behaviour requested.

This wonder has not received very much attention in the information processing literature. As we saw in Chapter 2, however, early experimental psychology was explicitly concerned with this issue (see section 2.3). Members of the Würzburg school thoroughly investigated the effect of instructions with simple experimental tasks in the laboratory. Watt discovered that a thought-process would run off 'automatically' at the presentation of a stimulus-word when the task to be performed had been adequately accepted by the subject in the 'preparatory period'. Ach observed that, in this respect, there is no difference between thought and overt action (see Boring, 1957, p. 404). They came up with the theory that an 'Aufgabe' (i.e., the instruction) induced an 'Einstellung' (i.e., a set or task attitude) that involved a 'determinierende Tendenz' (a more specific selective agent) that determined when and how one or another task was going to be performed. Subsequently Gibson (1941; see also section 2.3) convincingly argued that at least two, functionally separable, factors have to be distinguished in this concept 'Einstellung' or 'set': expectations (of stimulus objects, qualities, or relations) and intentions (to react or not so to react, or to perform a mental operation). So, in information processing tasks, the instruction (plus a few practice trials) prepares the subject by inducing expectations and intentions with regard to the task to be performed (see Allport, 1980a, for an attempt to bring some of these concepts back in a modern terminology: the terminology of 'production rules').

The second form of selection – the one that solves the problem of which object to act upon by determining from what region in space the set of parameters is taken that is allowed to specify the action in detail at a given moment in time – is the form of selection with which the empirical part of our study, Chapters 3 to 6, was mainly concerned. It is the form of selection that, according to our definitions, is brought about by (selective) attention (see Chapter 2). And, of course, it is also the form of selection that we now have 'to account for' or 'to set in an explanatory framework'. The basic question we are faced with in this chapter is, how this form of selection is performed.

From what was said earlier in this section, however, it will by now be obvious that selective attention is not operating in isolation or in a vacuum. First is the instruction, preparing the subject by inducing expectations and intentions. Confronted with a stimulus, the so prepared subject performs the information processing task. And within this task performance, selective attention plays its role. It operates within the constraints set by the instruction-induced task and in cooperation with expectations and intentions.

Von Helmholtz was already well aware that there are strong dependencies between the task on the one hand and the operation of selective attention on the other. He observed that attention will only be maintained when we 'constantly seek to find out something new' or 'set ourselves new questions' about the target of our attention (see section 2.1). Unfortunately in Gibson's study the relation between expectations and intentions on the one hand and attention on the other is only recognized; a possible interaction remains opaque (see Chapter 1 for the likely reason). This is readily apparent in the following quotations.

> The attention could be directed predominantly either to the perception of the stimulus or to the execution of the response ... the important point is that the preparatory set contains aspects of both *expectation* and *intention*.
>
> (Gibson, 1941, p. 784)

> In no other field of psychology has the role of the determining tendency been so frequently investigated as in perception. As a determinant of perceptual processes, set is related to attention .... Külpe demonstrated in 1904 that what

is perceived in a tachistoscopic presentation of colored letters may be strikingly different from the colored letters presented .... The attentive set functioned as a selective agent.

(Gibson, 1941, p. 793)

It will be clear, however, that for our topic, the operation of selective attention in vision, this relation is also of fundamental importance. For an adequate theory of selective attention it is essential to know what stimulation contributes (see Chapter 7), what preparation (i.e., intentions and expectations) contributes, and what further contribution is left for the information processing system that deserves the name selective attention. Therefore the present chapter is also concerned with this issue. First, however, we isolate a 'minimal' concept of selective attention that can adequately account for something like object or region selection. In subsequent sections aspects of the relation between attention, expectation and intention and some consequences of their interaction are discussed and elaborated.

8.2 A model for the perception of visual objects

Figure 8.2.1 presents Anne Treisman's model for the perception of visual objects (Treisman, 1988; see also Treisman and Souther, 1985, and Treisman and Gormican, 1988). Because of its strengths (and also because of its weaknesses) it is worthwhile to take this model as a starting point for further theorizing about visual spatial attention. Moreover, the model was developed to account for a completely different set of experimental data than we were concerned with: data pertaining to the integration of visual information into unified wholes (see, e.g., Treisman and Gelade, 1980; Treisman and Schmidt, 1982; Treisman and Paterson, 1984). And, of course, to achieve some integration in theoretical accounts it is worthwhile to take exactly this model as a starting point and try to arrive at an integrated view.

One of the major strengths of Treisman's model is in the recognition and use of the recent anatomical and physiological discoveries of a great number of separate visual areas that are specialized in coding different stimulus properties (see, e.g., Livingstone and Hubel, 1988; Zeki and Shipp, 1988; DeYoe and Van Essen, 1988; see also sections 1.10 and 7.1). For clarity of exposition, in the figure only three modules are depicted: a colour module coding colour in colour maps, an orientation module coding orientations in orientation maps, and a location module coding positions in a map of locations.

A second major strength of the model is in the recognition of the fundamental importance and required properties of the location module in relation to the function of selective attention. In the recent past many authors emphasized the importance of spatial location in visual information processing tasks (see, e.g., Butler and Currie, 1986; see also Chapter 3). Allport, for instance, states

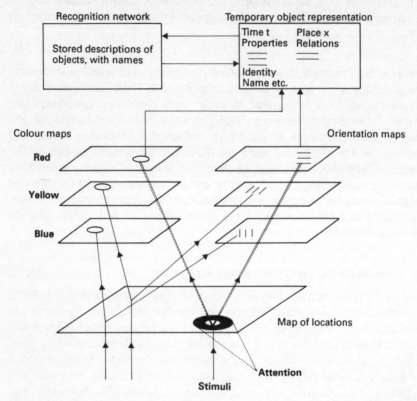

Figure 8.2.1 A model for the perception of visual objects. (After Treisman, 1988, p. 202.)

Sensory-motor communication proceeds in many parallel, specialized channels ... sensory dimensions that have been found to provide efficient selection cues for selective response (besides the explicit specification of spatial location) are also dimensions that appear to have intrinsic, *spatiotopic* representation in the brain .... I suggest that so-called "early" selective cueing (or "stimulus set") is in all cases directly or indirectly, cueing by spatial location.

(Allport, 1987, p. 410)

A basic assumption of the model is that the different sensory features of objects – their colours, sizes, orientations, (direction of) movement, etc. – are coded automatically and spatially in parallel. They simply 'trigger activation' on the appropriate position in the appropriate maps (see the dashed lines from 'stimuli' to 'maps' in the figure). This automatic coding, however, is not regarded as sufficient for object perception and object recognition. Then combinations of features, called conjunctions, are required. And here, according to Treisman, visual spatial attention comes in. When features must be located and combined or conjoined to specify objects, attention is required. Attention provides the 'glue' (Treisman and Gelade, 1980, p. 98) which integrates the separated features *in a particular location* so that the conjunction, i.e., the object, is perceived as a unified whole (see the solid lines in figure 8.2.1).

In Treisman's model 'Attention selects within a "master map of locations" that shows *where* all feature boundaries are located, but not *which* features are located *where*. Thus it distinguishes "filled" from "empty" locations, where "filled" implies the presence of any discontinuity at the feature level' (Treisman, 1988, p. 203). In other words 'The medium in which attention operates, ..., is a master map of locations that specifies *where* in the display things are, but not *what* they are. It indicates the number of elements, or filled locations, but not which features occupy which locations' (Treisman and Gormican, 1988, p. 17).

A number of investigators have provided interesting suggestions about how attention in this conceptualization might be implemented. Crick (1984) suggested that this spatial attention might consist of bursts of firing and phases of inhibition in groups of thalamic neurons. The idea is that this activity induces temporary synapses among the neurons in the maps and so codes transient conjunctions of properties. A similar speculation was offered by Styles and Allport (1986). In their proposal an 'attentional spotlight', perhaps thalamically driven and operating in *retinotopic* coordinates, binds or conjoins the features into objects:

> ... wherever the "spotlight" is directed, activity in corresponding retinotopic cortical units is temporarily enhanced. The transient, enhanced activation presumably also propagates (after some delay) to coding systems "downstream" .... Wherever the attentional spotlight stops, the activation of *all* codes driven by that region of the retina will be selectively enhanced. As a result, at any one time the *most* strongly activated code in each of many different coding domains should be *in register*, i.e., they should refer to the *same* retinal location.
>
> (Styles and Allport, 1986, p. 199)

In a related context, Allport (1987) remarks that virtually all neurophysiological evidence he is aware of indeed indicates that in the brain this type of selective function is revealed by selective enhancement of neuronal activity; not by selective inhibition or attenuation (Allport, 1987, pp. 404–5).

This selective enhancement can be equated with 'object selection'. So, with Treisman's model together with these neurophysiological speculations we have the beginning of a solution and a possible implementation in terms of 'selective attention as enhancement of activity' for the problem of object selection. But there is more. According to Allport (1987)

> [T]he really important point to recognize, ..., is that selection, in the sense of selective *cueing*, in no sense logically entails rejection or exclusion of the noncued information from further *processing*. It has certainly not been

empirically demonstrated that selective cueing *in fact* has this consequence. This being so, behavioral evidence about the relative efficiency of "selection" – i.e., the relative efficiency of *selective cueing* – is simply irrelevant to questions about the level of processing accorded to the "unselected information." To put it another way, the controversy regarding "early" versus "late" selection has systematically confused "selection" as selective *cueing* and "selection" as selective *processing*.

(Allport, 1987, p. 409)

So, also of importance is that 'In a massively parallel, activation-coded system, selective enhancement provides a possible mechanism of selective cueing that need not entail the exclusion from further processing of the noncued information, beyond the level at which selective enhancement first occurs ...' (Allport, 1987, p. 410). Therefore this object selection is also completely consistent with the 'unlimited capacity parallel processing' hypothesis and the role of attention as elaborated in Chapter 7.

Taken together, Treisman's model is an important model because it accounts for a large set of experimental data (see, e.g., Treisman, 1988, for an overview). It starts from the relevant anatomical and physiological evidence. Moreover, further elaborations of the model are at least consistent with further physiological evidence. The model correctly emphasizes the importance of spatial location. And, in the context of the present study not the least important, the (elaborated) model is also compatible with most of the theoretical conclusions we already reached in Chapter 7: 'Unlimited capacity' processing and 'selective enhancement' by selective attention.

Nevertheless, as presently formulated, the model faces (at least) two serious difficulties. One of these difficulties is related to the 'output' side of the model (see the upper two boxes in figure 8.2.1). The second difficulty is related to the 'input side' of the model (see the 'attention' input at the bottom in figure 8.2.1). We briefly indicate both problems in turn.

Let us first have a brief look at the 'output' side problem. Treisman's main interest is in 'perception' as such. Her main ambition is in finding out what perceptual operations tax the system most and which appear to take place automatically (Treisman, 1988, p. 201). It is, however, very easy to defend the general point of view that the perceptual systems are not just for 'perceiving' and the particular point of view that the visual system is not just for 'seeing'. The most important function of the visual system lies in the transformation of information in light into actions (reading, naming, walking, grasping, etc.). Vision, and all other 'perceptual systems have evolved in all species of animals solely as a means of guiding and controlling action ...' (Allport, 1987, p. 395). Exactly this point of view brings theorists like Allport and Neumann to questions like 'what action?', 'how is the action directed?', etc. (see section 8.1). This important 'action' aspect is, however, completely neglected in Treisman's model. In section 8.7 we return to this problem.

With regard to the 'input' side of the model, a number of interrelated problems can be distinguished. In Treisman's model 'attention' dangles as a kind of appendix at the bottom of the model. It simply originates nowhere. However, if attention is not considered as an extraneous 'spiritual force' (James, 1890/1950), this way of modelling immediately raises questions like 'what does attention consist of?', 'where does attention come from?', 'how does attention know what a filled position is?', 'how does attention know what filled position it has to aim at?', 'what is the mechanism of directing attention?', etc. It is exactly this type of question with which the next four sections are concerned.

8.3 Attention

Treisman conceives of visual attention as a kind of 'spotlight' that can 'fixate' positions in a 'map of locations' (see, e.g., Treisman, 1988, pp. 203 and 206). In Chapter 4 we already critically evaluated some aspects of the spotlight metaphor (see section 4.7). In the present context it is worthwhile to emphasize one of these problematic aspects: the 'attention-as-a-spotlight' metaphor is nearly always mixed up with an 'attention-as-an-inner-eye' metaphor (attention 'moves' and 'fixates'). Of course, there is an obvious reason for this problematic state of affairs: A spotlight implicitly presupposes an 'operator' and 'user' equipped with eyes and a visual system, 'looking' at the regions he deals with by using the spotlight. This homunculus is simply smuggled in, hidden in the package containing the spotlight, and seems to provide the answers to nasty questions like 'who operates the spotlight?', 'where does the operator get its instructions from?', and 'how does the operator perform its job?'. But even if one answers the question 'where does the spotlight come from?' with, for instance, 'from the thalamus!' (Crick, 1984; Styles and Allport, 1986), these questions remain unanswered.

The homunculus sold in combination with the spotlight, however, provides an important hint about the direction in which preliminary answers to our questions have to be found. This becomes clear if we realize that

– in models like those depicted in figure 8.2.1 we are trying to outline the design of a visual system capable of performing selective attention tasks (visual system 1), and
– to adequately perform his function – operating the spotlight – the homunculus also needs a visual system (visual system 2).

But, *entia non sunt multiplicanda*: two *identical* visual systems is one too many. Fortunately, however, there is still a *different* visual system left. In Chapter 3 we distinguished between the X- or parvo-cellular cortical pathway and the Y- or magno-cellular cortical pathway. In Chapter 7 we were exclusively concerned with the X- or parvo-cellular pathway. Also Treisman's model, depicted in figure 8.2.1, only represents this channel. So, up to now, only a part of the total visual system was considered (i.e., visual system 1). The Y- or magno-cellular channel is still available as a second visual system (visual system 2). The homunculus needs a visual system? Well then, let the homunculus with its spotlight have, or, even better *be* the second visual system! Of course, this move entails that we can then conceive of selective attention as an operation internal to the total visual system. A dangling appendix, called attention, is then no longer needed.

How to conceive of selective attention as a visual-system internal operation? In Chapter 2 we expressed our conviction that simple tasks have to provide the fundamental insights into human information processing. And indeed, Chapters 3 and 4 contain the basic data that indicate how this feat might be accomplished. In fact, it is the data for which an effect of selective attention is least expected: the data obtained in the *neutral* condition of the single-item tasks with accuracy (Chapter 3) and latency (Chapter 4) as the dependent variable.

Let us first have a look at the accuracy data obtained in the neutral condition of the identification-and-localization dot cueing task, discussed in section 3.5. Because of their fundamental importance we summarize these data in the left panel of table 8.3.1 (Experiment I). The right panel of the table gives a comparable set of data obtained in an experiment with slightly different exposure conditions (Experiment II).

Table 8.3.1 Results obtained in the neutral condition of two single-item recognition and localization tasks with accuracy as the dependent variable. $P+$: Position correct; $P-$: Position incorrect; $I+$: Identity correct; $I-$: Identity incorrect. The table entries are the proportions in each $P \times I$ combination.

	$I+$	$I-$		$I+$	$I-$
$P+$	0.61	0.34	$P+$	0.70	0.22
$P-$	0.01	0.04	$P-$	0.01	0.07

Experiment I	Experiment II

Our first attempt to interpret these data used a model assuming independent identity and location processing (see section 3.5). Figure 8.3.1 gives the basic structure of such a model. Information enters the information processing system in an 'input module' (V1 and/or V2?). In line with the available neurophysiological evidence the information is sent on in independent identity (X, or parvo) and position (Y, or magno) channels (see section 3.7). The identity information ultimately triggers representations in an 'identity module' (the inferior temporal cortex?). The position information addresses locations in a 'location module' (the posterior parietal cortex?) that codes information as the 'master map of locations' in Treisman's model.

An analysis of these data (see Chapter 3), but also casual inspection of the table, readily shows, however, that a model, assuming independence of position processing and identity processing as depicted in figure 8.3.1, is not capable of accounting for the data. There is a dependency; the probability that there is

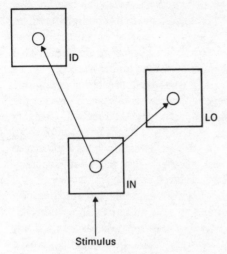

Figure 8.3.1 Independent identity and location processing model. Information enters the input module (IN) and is sent on to an identity module (ID) and a location module (LO).

identity information given that there is no location information is very low as compared with the probability that there is identity information given that there is location information (see also section 3.5). Position information seems (close to) essential for identification performance in this neutral condition. Our problem is therefore: How to conceive the relation between identity information and position information so that the data in table 8.3.1 are adequately accounted for?

The theoretically important point is now that only a minor modification is needed to bring the scheme presented in figure 8.3.1 into accordance with the data. A scheme that is in all respects consistent with the data is depicted in figure 8.3.2. First, notice that the independence model depicted in figure 8.3.1 is incorporated in this scheme. So the basic underlying assumption still is that identity processing and position processing are independent. Added is only a 'feedback' loop from the location module back to the input module. The interpretation of the scheme is as follows. If position information is fed back and identity information is available then $P+I+$ results. If position information is fed back and no identity information is available then $P+I-$ results. If position information is not fed back then $P-I-$ has to result even if there is identity information. Correct identity guessing, however, entails that also then a few $P-I+$ responses are obtained (see section 3.9 for the details of this identity guessing). In short, for a correct identification response, identity information has to be addressed by location information. The feedback loop implements this addressing in a simple way and so accounts for the basic finding that in the neutral condition position information is (very close to) a necessary, but not a sufficient, condition for a correct identification response (see Chapter 3).

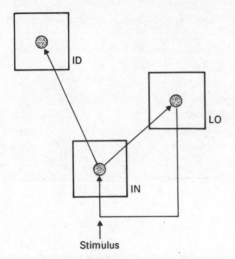

Figure 8.3.2 Independent processing model with attention-feedback loop from location module to input module.

Let us now turn to the neutral, i.e., no-cue, condition of the single-item experiments with latency as the dependent variable, discussed in Chapter 4. The important point is that the scheme depicted in figure 8.3.2 is consistent with, and can be regarded as the implementation of, a basic assumption we introduced in relation to these data. That assumption is that a visual event with an abrupt onset recruits attention to its position nearly immediately, but not immediately. More exactly, we hypothesized that such a visual event presented in isolation and of duration T is unattended during the first x ms and attended during the remaining $T - x$ ms (see section 4.5). It will be clear now that the scheme is consistent with, and implements, this assumption. The visual event of duration T is the event in the input module, the feedback can be regarded as the 'attention', and the time needed to traverse the feedback loop can be equated with the initial x ms that an uncued, neutral, item is not attended.

The operation of the feedback loop can be regarded as a visual-perception internal kind of selective attention triggered by position information or the onset of position information. So, in this view, it is not attention, coming from nowhere, that is directed at a position in a map of locations. The map of locations is the *source* of the attention. Location information – if fed back to the input module – *is* the attention. Not attention directed at position, but position directed as attention.

The operation of the feedback loop is involved in correct identification performance (see the data in table 8.3.1). The assumption, however, is that this loop is triggered by position information and contains no identity information. It is therefore difficult to see how the operation of this loop can be of any help in the identification of the input. In line with our proposals in Chapter 3 and in the subsequent chapters we therefore propose that the operation of the feedback loop has no function in the identification of the information but only in the selection of identified information. It provides the activation needed for the selection of the information as described in sections 7.8 and 8.2.

Taken all together, the scheme depicted in figure 8.3.2 can be regarded as a kind of basic circuitry combining identity processing, location processing and a built-in or hard-wired form of 'selective attention'. It implements something like 'postcategorical filtering' and 'selection'; the addressing sequence is: position $\rightarrow$ features on position (all features; not only relevant features) $\rightarrow$ identity (Van der Heijden, 1981; see also section 3.9). In subsequent sections it will become clear that it can be regarded as the kernel of the 'difference generator' (see section 1.7) which attention research in visual information processing psychology seeks.

8.4 Attention: location cues

Of course, the basic circuitry described in the last section is not worth its salt if it cannot be shown that it indeed forms a fruitful starting point for further theorizing about selective attention in vision. Fortunately it is easy to show that it is. Without many further assumptions, at least three important groups of real 'selective attention' results, all three obtained with location cues, are now easily understood.

In Chapter 3 we showed that in single-item recognition tasks with accuracy as the dependent variable the accuracy *benefits* brought by cueing, are a fraction of the room for improvement in terms of *position* information:

delta $I \; = \; g(1 - P_{nc})$.

In this equation P_{nc} is the proportion of trials for which position information is available in the no-cue condition. In the cue condition the cue was clearly visible and always valid. So, the cue provided perfect position information, i.e., $P_c = 1$. The term $(1 - P_{nc})$ therefore equals not only the *room* for improvement but also the *actual* improvement in position information as a result of cueing. In terms of the circuit depicted in figure 8.3.2, $(1 - P_{nc})$ equals the additional proportion of times that position information is fed back from the location module to the input module in the cue condition as compared with the no-cue condition. As stated in the foregoing section, if identity information is available but position information is not fed back, $P-I-$ results (we neglect the effect of guessing). If, however, in this situation position information is fed back, $P+I+$ results. In this way the additional proportion of times that position information is fed back literally produces the identification benefits observed and that is what the equation essentially expresses. The feedback loop is simply the hardware implementation of our proposition that attention causes that improved position information results in improved recognition performance and that 'attention functions by addressing the identity information, while starting from the position information' (section 3.8).

In Chapter 4 we reported that in single-item (detection and) recognition tasks with latency as the dependent variable location cues produce (rather small) latency *benefits*. This effect is already apparent at short SOAs and is constant over an initial range of SOAs. There is virtually no cue validity effect in this type of experiment. There is, however, a distance effect (see section 4.3). The explanation of these findings in terms of the circuit presented in figure 8.3.2 is very simple. In this type of experiment the clearly visible target itself is always capable of activating the feedback loop. So, shortly – i.e., our hypothetical x ms – after target presentation, activity traversing the input-module–location-module–input-module loop will arrive back at the input module. Then the single target is attended. In this situation a location precue can only produce a latency benefit by activating that feedback loop before the target does. The target is then attended earlier. This will already be the case with very small cue–target SOAs. Because no more can be gained than the extra attention during the interval of x ms, i.e., the time needed to traverse the total loop, a constant and maximum effect is to be expected for SOAs larger than x ms. And that is the result observed. In short, the complete explanation of the latency benefit is based on a simple hardware implementation – the feedback loop – of our proposition that 'a visual event with an abrupt onset recruits attention to its position nearly immediately, but not immediately' (section 4.5). The finding that there is virtually no cue validity effect in this type of experiment (see section 4.3) also follows from the assumption that the targets trigger the feedback loop automatically and nearly immediately (see also Jonides's, 1981, research in section 6.7).

The distance effect, observed in single-item studies using location cues (see section 4.3), is better considered in the context of the partial-report bar-probe tasks discussed in Chapter 5. The most important phenomena observed with these bar-probe task are: often a correct response is produced but location errors are also very frequent; the distributions of correct responses and location errors over item positions are W and M shaped, respectively (see section 5.3). Figure 8.4.1 gives an extended version of our basic circuitry, adapted for this multiple-item task. All simultaneously presented items activate their identity representations in the identity module and their position representations in the location module and all position representations feed back to their input representations (solid lines). Just because all position representations feed back, this way of stimulus presentation results in an ambiguous situation, possibly a situation without a winner (see, however, section 8.6 for a further discussion of this situation). A (pre- or post-) location cue, however, resolves this ambiguous situation. By activating a representation in the input module the cue provides extra activation for one of the representations in the location module and that additional activation also comes back via the feedback loop (dashed line). This extra activation breaks the tie in the input module, and one of the items is selected.

In terms of the model, location errors due to probe misalignments (see section 5.5) are to be expected in bar-probe tasks when cue-derived position feedback is imprecise and therefore does not exactly relate to a target position in the input

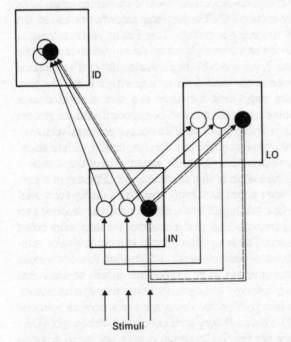

Stimuli

Figure 8.4.1 Extended independent processing model adapted for partial-report bar-probe tasks with location cue.

module. There is indeed ample neurophysiological evidence that strongly suggests that the spatial resolving power of the position channel is rather limited and that its precision decreases with increasing retinal eccentricity (see, e.g., section 3.7). Exactly these features of the position channel suffice to account for the probe misalignment part of the W-shaped serial position curve for correct reports and the (complementary) M-shaped serial position curve for location errors. The highest spatial accuracy is to be expected at the middle position (highest spatial resolving power) and at the end positions (lowest spatial resolving power but no outer neighbours). Correspondingly, on these positions the lowest number of location errors is to be expected (see also table 5.7.1 in section 5.7). It will be clear that the rather low spatial resolving power of the position channel can also be held directly responsible for the distance effect observed in single-item studies with latency as the dependent variable (see Shulman et al., 1985; 1986, and Van der Heijden et al., 1988, in section 4.3) and in multiple-item studies with latency as the dependent variable (see Eriksen and St. James, 1986, and Murphy and Eriksen, 1987, in section 6.5).

Taken all together, the scheme introduced in section 8.3 accounts in a simple and attractive way for all basic phenomena observed in selective attention experiments using location cues. Moreover, and of great theoretical importance, the feedback loop depicted in figures 8.3.2 and 8.4.1 is an implementation of early attentional selection (see section 2.7). The loop starts at, what we called, the input module and feeds back to the input module. This feature of the scheme is consistent with results discussed at various places in the empirical part of our study (see, e.g., sections 3.9, 5.2, 5.7 and 5.8). In particular, the results obtained in the bar-probe tasks discussed in section 5.8 are of importance in this context. Real misidentifications of the target first increased and then decreased as a function of probe delay. That is exactly the result to be expected with the present scheme, given that information in the input module decays progressively over time (a reasonable assumption) and that probe position functioning as 'attention' addresses this decaying early information (the basic assumption of the scheme).

The foregoing exposition makes clear that in the circuit depicted in figure 8.3.2 (and 8.4.1), we have at least a fruitful starting point for a theory for spatial selective attention in vision. One small problem with the circuit as described up to now has to be mentioned, however. That problem is that the loop, after being activated, will remain activated. The activation simply entertains and/or rein-forces itself (input–position–input–position–etc.). To prevent this continuous activation one or another provision has to be introduced. It will be clear that studies of the inhibitory effect, observed in single-item experiments with latency as the dependent variable, might provide the important clues (see our specula-tions at the end of section 4.9). This inhibitory effect observed with longer SOAs strongly suggests that it is not position information as such but 'new' position information that triggers the feedback loop that serves as attention. In other words, something like the 'onset' might be the relevant component of the position information (see also sections 3.7 and 3.8).

8.5 Attention and expectation: verbal and symbolic cues

In 'orthodox' explanations of the results obtained in location cueing experiments, there is always a perfect correlation between availability of position information and the beneficial effects of spatial selective attention. Consider the following two examples.

– 'Position cueing in single-item studies with accuracy as the dependent variable produces benefits because
  (a) on trials where the target lacks position information the cue provides exact position information, and
  (b) also on these trials attention can therefore move to the appropriate spatial position' (see Chapter 3).
– 'Position cueing in single-item experiments with latency as the dependent variable produces latency benefits because
  (a) the relevant position information is available earlier, and
  (b) attention can therefore arrive at the relevant position earlier' (see Chapter 4).

This perfect correlation between (properties with regard to) position information and (properties with regard to) spatial selective attention makes one of the two superfluous. And because position information is the more basic one, it is parsimonious to maintain position information and to delete attention. In our type of explanation presented in the two foregoing sections we did this by feeding back position information and using it as the attentional input. As a result of this operation attention became a visual-system internal activity. It appeared that the assumption that position information is fed back and functions as an attentional input sufficed to account for most of the location cue data. Only position information serving as attention and 'nothing else' and certainly no 'magic' was needed.

In a great number of experiments described in Chapters 3 to 6, however, not location cues but other types of cues or instructions were used to specify the relevant position in space. To account for selection for these experiments, besides the basic circuitry depicted in figures 8.3.2 and 8.4.1, also something else, some kind of additional 'magic', is needed. In this section we consider these experiments. We try to specify what 'magic' is needed to complement our basic circuitry so that selective performance in these tasks can also be accounted for in a parsimonious way.

Within this group of selective attention tasks, three subgroups can be distinguished: experiments in which the relevant spatial position is directly verbally specified in advance, experiments in which the relevant spatial position is indirectly verbally specified in advance by means of a 'criterion attribute', and experiments in which the relevant spatial position is specified by means of a symbolic cue. We discuss these three groups of experiments in turn.

Experiments in which the relevant spatial position was specified verbally in advance were mainly described in Chapter 6 (see, e.g., the experiments of Eriksen and Eriksen, 1974, in section 6.2, and of Gatti and Egeth, 1978, in sections 6.1 and 6.4). As in the partial-report bar-probe experiments, in these multiple-item experiments one of the items has to be selected for responding. Now, however, there is no visual pre- or post-location cue. There is only the advance verbal instruction with regard to position. The basic result obtained with this type of task is: correct selection (to the response competition phenomena we return to in later sections). How to account for this selection? In our view, the most parsimonious way to account for the selective performance in these types of tasks starts from the assumption that an advance verbal instruction with regard to position ultimately has an effect comparable to that of a location cue. This assumption entails that, in one or another way, 'higher centres' are capable of transforming the verbal message into extra activation on the relevant position in the location module (see figure 8.5.1). In other words the additional magic needed consists of 'higher centres' capable of transforming the verbal instruction into an *effective* advance *expectation* with regard to position in the location module. A system prepared in this way will then be capable of displaying the wanted behaviour: selecting the relevant item (see, e.g., Yantis and Jonides, 1984, in section 4.5 for corroborative evidence).

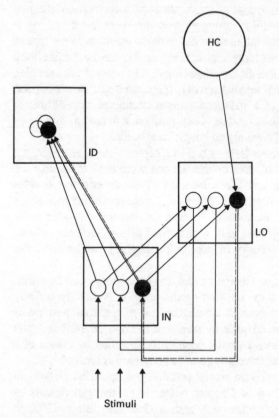

Figure 8.5.1 Extended independent processing model adapted for selection tasks with advance verbal spatial instruction. HC stands for 'higher centres'.

Experiments in which the relevant spatial position was indirectly verbally specified in advance by means of a 'criterion attribute' were mainly described in Chapter 5 (see, e.g., the partial report research concerned with the question of which types of attributes – besides location – afford efficient selection in section 5.0; see also section 3.10: RSVP tasks). Also in these multiple-item experiments one (or a few) of the items has to be selected for responding. There is neither a location cue nor is the position of the relevant item specified in advance. Only a criterion attribute is specified in advance, e.g., the colour 'red' or the form 'square'. Subjects are instructed to select for responding the item carrying this criterion attribute, e.g., 'name the red letter (not the blue ones)' or 'name the colour of the square (not of the triangles)'. Again, the main result observed is efficient selection. As in partial-report bar-probe tasks 'location' errors are often observed (see, e.g., Snyder, 1972, and Frykland, 1975). In RSVP tasks often

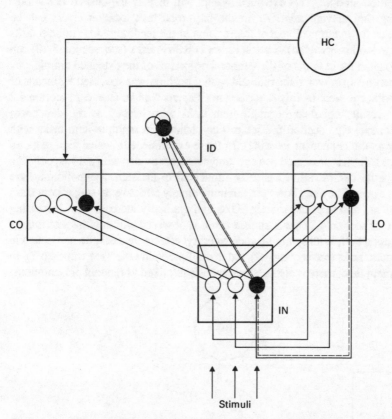

Figure 8.5.2 Extended independent processing model adapted for selection tasks with a criterion attribute. CO stands for colour module.

'timing' errors are observed (see section 3.10). In our view, the most parsimonious way to account for selective performance in this type of task starts from the assumption that the verbal instruction, by means of the criterion attribute, ultimately has the same effect as a location cue. Figure 8.5.2 is intended as an example. It serves to illustrate this assumption for the 'name the red letter' instruction. The figure is in all respects the same as the earlier ones except that now a colour module is inserted. The additional assumption is that the verbal instruction with regard to the criterion attribute gives rise to an *effective* advance *expectation* in this colour module: the positions where red can appear are prepared or preactivated. If the colour red indeed activates one of these positions, this position in the colour module activates its corresponding position in the location module. In other words, the additional magic in this case consists of a colour module that is appropriately prepared by the verbal instruction, plus connections from positions in this colour module to corresponding positions in the location module. This extended system will display the desired behaviour: selecting the relevant item. As in the bar-probe task location errors can be accounted for in terms of spatial imprecision of the feedback loop (in both tasks the same loop is involved). Timing errors in RSVP tasks (see section 3.10) can be accounted for in terms of the temporal properties of the extended circuit.

Experiments in which the relevant spatial position was specified by means of a symbolic cue were mainly described in Chapters 4 and 6 (see, e.g., section 4.2 for the results obtained in single-item tasks with latency as the dependent variable; see, e.g., section 6.7 for results obtained in multiple-item tasks with latency as the dependent variable). In these experiments a visual sign, e.g., an arrow or a digit, is presented as a cue. Subjects are provided with a rule specifying what spatial interpretation has to be 'attached' to the sign. Symbolic cues are effective cues. They are, however, not immediately effective: in single-item tasks benefits are absent at the shorter SOAs and gradually increase with increasing SOAs (see section 4.2) and a similar result is observed with multiple-item tasks (see section 5.9). With symbolic cues 'validity' effects are easily demonstrated in single-item tasks (see section 4.2) and in multiple-item tasks (see section 6.7). In single-item tasks there is also a 'strategy' effect (mixed vs random presentations;

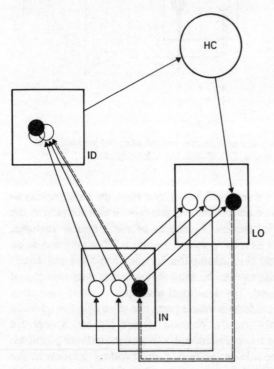

Figure 8.5.3 Extended independent processing model adapted for selection tasks with a symbolic cue.

see section 4.2). Also for this type of task the most parsimonious assumption is that the symbolic cue plus rule ultimately has an effect comparable to that of a location cue. This assumption entails that 'higher centres' are capable of 'interpreting' the symbolic cue in terms of the rule, and of transforming this interpretation into an *effective expectation* on the relevant position in the location module (see figure 8.5.3). In other words the additional magic in this case consists of 'higher centres' capable of transforming the symbolic cue plus rule into extra activation on the relevant position in the location module. It is reasonable to assume that this transformation takes some amount of time. Therefore no positive effects with short SOAs and increasing positive effects with increasing SOAs are to be expected. Moreover, it is reasonable to assume that the hypothesized 'higher centres' are also influenced by other 'signs and rules'. So validity effects and strategy effects are not really unexpected.

From the foregoing it will be clear what the essence of our explanation of selective performance in the types of tasks discussed in this section is. The essence can be summarized as follows. At the basis of selection is the circuit depicted in figures 8.3.2 and 8.4.1. An effective expectation, induced by instruction, is capable of modulating the pattern of activation in the location module. As a result, one of the positions in the location module receives extra activation. The item corresponding to that position is selected. The *expectation* involved in this process is not the 'high' level expectation implied by Deutsch and Deutsch's (1963) attention theory (see section 2.5). It is a 'low' level, partial visual-system-internal, expectation, not excluded by James's (1890/1950) view on attention (see section 2.2) and emphasized by Gibson (1941) as one of the two factors that have to be distinguished in the global concept 'Einstellung' or 'set' (see sections 2.3 and 8.1). The word *effective* is used to indicate that what is meant is not the total of a subject's expectations with regard to stimuli, task, experimenter, room, etc., but only that part of a subject's total expectations that is made effective by means of the *instruction* in the performance of the task.

The present conceptualization has one important consequence with regard to current research on selective attention in vision. In section 4.6, Symbolic cues and 'movement', we described current research concerned with the dynamics of the 'movement' of the 'spotlight' of attention in visual space. We concluded with Eriksen and Murphy (1987, p. 305) that the issue of how attention shifts from one locus to another in the visual field is still an open question. The previous and the present section start to provide an answer why this is so. In our analysis of selective attention, nowhere did a moving spotlight appear. The basic circuit introduced in section 8.3 was capable of accounting for the bulk of the results obtained in location cue experiments (see section 8.4). The circuit, complemented with additional system components that are appropriately prepared by instructions, is also capable of accounting for the main results obtained in the other types of selective attention experiments (the present section). In short, in our view no moving spotlight is involved. Attempts to document the properties of this hypothetical entity will only lead to inconsistent results. It seems that time has come to continue the work started by the Würzburg school and followed up by Gibson (1941).

8.6 Multiple simultaneous onsets

In the foregoing sections of this chapter we presented our view on how the human information processing system manages to perform one of its two major selective functions in the tachistoscopic world: the selection of the object to act upon (see section 8.1). That story is incomplete, however. It leaves lots of data unexplained. These data indicate that the smooth operation of the system as described can be severely interfered with by a very potent factor in the visual world: abrupt onsets or sudden events (see, e.g., Yantis and Jonides, 1984; Jonides and Yantis, 1988; see also sections 6.6 and 6.8). In a sense, the view as described characterizes the operation of the system in a 'silent' or 'quiet' world. But onsets severely disturb this world and seem to change it into a hectic and chaotic world.

Peculiar effects observed with multiple simultaneous onsets are not incompatible with our theoretical views developed up to now. In fact, from a scheme as depicted in figure 8.4.1 it simply follows that with multiple simultaneous onsets unique phenomena are to be expected. With multiple simultaneous onsets the input-module–location-module–input-module feedback loop is activated for several positions at the same time. In the 'orthodox' terminology: a situation is created in which attention is attracted by several new events simultaneously. In our scheme, this stimulus situation results in an ambiguous system situation: our hypothetical attentional circuit gets jammed or confused. But 'something' has to be done, and it is not surprising that the system has its own solutions for handling such a situation and that as a result unique phenomena are observed. In this section we first present a brief inventory of the attentional effects of multiple simultaneous abrupt onsets as encountered and described in previous chapters. Then we try to specify according to what rule these onsets determine the direction of attention. Last we try to integrate this factor with the view presented in the foregoing sections.

Phenomena observed with multiple simultaneous sudden events were met for cues as well as for stimulus items. For cues, the double cueing experiments of Posner and Cohen (1984) and Maylor (1985) are of importance. As stated in section 4.9 the results obtained are consistent with the view that each cue will attract attention on about 50% of the trials.

For stimulus items four phenomena, observed with multiple simultaneous onsets or events, seem of great theoretical importance.

– Firstly, attention can be captured by an irrelevant visual event, even when a highly discriminable target in a fixed and known position has to be reacted to. The main evidence was described in section 6.6 where we extensively discussed, what we called, the 'Eriksen effect' (see also section 6.8 on events).

Further supportive evidence for some kind of attentional capture by a simultaneous irrelevant event was provided by Kahneman and Chajczyk (1983) in their investigations of, what we called, the 'Kahneman effect' (see section 6.9).

- Secondly, all kinds of irrelevant abrupt visual events seem to have such an attention-capturing power, but possibly in different degrees. As described in section 6.6, interfering effects have been observed with black discs (Eriksen and Hoffman, 1972b) forms, colours and random lines (Eriksen and Schultz, 1978), neutral words (Kahneman and Chajczyk, 1983), patches of dots, clusters of coloured shapes, etc. (Kahneman et al., 1983). That different types of simultaneous visual events might have different attention-capturing powers is suggested by the results reported by Eriksen and Schultz (1978; see section 6.6) and Kahneman and Chajczyk (1983, exp. 3).

- Thirdly, the delay incurred by attentional capture increases with increasing number of irrelevant simultaneous visual events. The increase is not linear but decreases with increasing number of irrelevant events. The prime evidence here is Kahneman et al.'s (1983) study discussed in section 6.6.

- Fourthly, there is no attentional capture if the position of the impending target is precued with a location cue. The relevant data come from Kahneman et al. (1983, exp. 4) mentioned in section 6.6.

To see what happens in an experimental situation that produces an Eriksen effect it is worthwhile to analyse one set of data in detail. Table 8.6.1 presents data reported by Kahneman and Chajczyk (1983) that we can use in such an analysis; their experiment 2 (that had two conditions: noise at 2 deg and at 4 deg) and 4. These are the data from the 'dilution' experiments discussed in section 6.9 that included a 'bar alone' condition; a condition we need in our analysis. The first three rows of table 8.6.1 present the relevant Eriksen effect data. (To the data in the last two rows of the table we return in section 8.9.) The averages (X) show that adding one irrelevant neutral noise word to the coloured bar delays responding by $601 - 583 = 18$ ms. Adding a second neutral noise word gives an

Table 8.6.1 Mean RTs (ms) for a single coloured bar (Bar alone), a bar plus a neutral word (Neutral), plus two neutral words (Dual neutral), plus one incongruent colour word (Conflicting), and a bar plus an incongruent colour word and a neutral word (Conflicting-neutral). Data from Kahneman and Chajczyk (1983, Exp. 2 and Exp. 4). The column labelled X gives the means over experiments.

	Exp. 2; 2 deg	Exp. 2; 4 deg	Exp. 4	X
Bar alone	572	572	604	583
Neutral	585	581	637	601
Dual neutral	594	587	643	608
Conflicting	659	621	706	662
Conflicting-neutral	621	606	669	632

additional delay of $608 - 601 = 7$ ms. This is a typical result for the Eriksen effect (see also sections 6.6 and 6.8).

In their theoretical analysis Kahneman and Chajczyk (1983) assume that the target bar is always immediately attended to. If the bar and one neutral word are presented, the word always captures attention and is processed in parallel with the bar. If the bar and two neutral words are presented, exactly one of the two words captures attention and is processed in parallel with the target. In other words, they assume that on all word-present trials one, and only one, word captures attention and is processed in parallel with the target (see, e.g., Kahneman and Chajczyk, 1983, pp. 499, 504, 507; see also section 6.9).

For two reasons Kahneman and Chajczyk's interpretation of the Eriksen effect seems very ad hoc. First, they maintain the perfect object selection view (see also sections 6.3 and 6.9). The assumption is that on each trial attention is correctly directed to the coloured bar without delay. Capture by an irrelevant element does not prevent the immediate correct direction of attention. Second, they assume that on each trial one (of the two) word(s) captures attention. In their view there are no trials in which only the coloured bar attracts or captures attention.

Moreover, the interpretation is not only ad hoc. The interpretation is also not consistent with the data. If on each word-present trial one and only one word captures attention, identical delays have to be expected for the single neutral word condition (the word captures attention) and for the dual neutral word condition (one of the two words captures attention). So, the increase in RT from the Neutral to the Dual neutral condition is not accounted for.

The data are, however, consistent with the simpler assumption that in an Eriksen effect situation the system itself gives temporal priority to one abrupt onset from among a number of simultaneously occurring abrupt onsets. In other words, the data are consistent with the view that the attentional system depicted in figure 8.4.1 is built in such a way that 'attention is captured' by only one of the simultaneously appearing items. For Kahneman and Chajczyk's data this means that all elements presented simultaneously have a certain probability of capturing attention but that the coloured bar and the words have possibly different probabilities of attracting attention.

It is not difficult to show that Kahneman and Chajczyk's data are consistent with the assumption that on a proportion of trials the colour bar captures attention and that only on the remaining proportion of trials does one irrelevant word first capture attention. It is even possible to calculate how often the coloured bar, the single word, or one of two words presented simultaneously with a target, captures attention, i.e., it is possible to learn something about the rules that govern the Eriksen effect. This can be done by using some simple, empirically and theoretically plausible assumptions.

The assumptions we use are

- One onset at a time captures attention.
- On each trial an onset captures attention.

- The target has a potency of 1 of capturing attention.
- Each noise element has a potency a of capturing attention.
- If attention is captured by the target, it stays (there are no subsequent onsets that can capture attention).
- If attention is captured by one of the noise elements, it is subsequently 'withdrawn' and 'moves' to the target (to this assumption we return at the end of the section).

With these assumptions it is possible to use Luce's (1959) ratio rule to determine what happens in the Eriksen effect. According to this rule, the probability that an onset i captures attention, Ci, is given by

$$Ci = \frac{A_i}{\sum_{i \in L} A_i}$$

where A_i equals item i's attention-capturing potency (i.e., A_i equals 1 for the target and a for each distractor) and L is the set of all simultaneously competing onsets.

Using the average Eriksen effect data from table 8.6.1 (i.e., the data in column X), and the ratio rule, we can now write for the Bar-alone, Neutral and Dual Neutral condition, respectively,

$583 = \{1\}/\{1\}\ 583$

$601 = \{1\}/\{1+a\}\ 583\ +\ \{a\}/\{1+a\}\ X$

$608 = \{1\}/\{1+2a\}\ 583\ +\ \{2a\}/\{1+2a\}\ X$

In these equations X stands for the average reaction time on trials where attention was initially captured by a distractor and has then to be 'withdrawn' and 'move' from the distractor to the target.

The last two equations have two unknowns (a and X) and can be solved. The value obtained for X equals 624. So, the delay incurred by initially attending to an irrelevant neutral distractor word equals $624 - 583 = 41$ ms. This outcome seems perfectly reasonable and intuitively attractive. The value obtained for a equals 0.786. The probabilities that the target and the distractor capture attention when only one distractor is present, i.e., $\{1\}/\{1+a\}$ and $\{a\}/\{1+a\}$, are 0.560 and 0.440. When two distractors are present these probabilities, i.e., $\{1\}/\{1+2a\}$ and $\{a\}/\{1+2a\}$, are 0.389 and 0.306.

It is worthwhile noting that the first two probabilities are very close to 0.500 and the last two to 0.333. This suggests that, as a first approximation, the general rule characterizing the Eriksen effect is that all simultaneous onsets have about equal probabilities of capturing attention. Figure 8.6.1 shows graphically the probability that one out of N irrelevant items captures attention as specified by this general rule. The figure shows that the largest increase in probability that a distractor captures attention is between 0 and 1 distractor. Consequently also the expected increase in RTs will be largest between 0 and 1 distractor, and that is consistent with the data (see Kahneman et al., 1983).

To integrate the view on attentional capture presented in this section with the view on attention developed earlier in this chapter, two topics are of importance. The first concerns the observation that the Eriksen effect completely disappears when the position of the target is precued with a location cue. This outcome is easily understood. A location precue, as an isolated abrupt visual element, starts the attention circuit before stimulus presentation. Upon stimulus presentation, the target position is therefore already attended, and irrelevant noise elements have no opportunity to capture attention. In other words, the precue biases the attentional circuit by providing extra attentional activation to the target position only. (It is worthwhile noting that attentional selection in bar-probe tasks was accounted for in exactly the same way; see section 8.4.)

The second topic concerns the observation that in an Eriksen effect situation the subjects (nearly) always come up with the correct answer. In other words, our last assumption – 'If attention is captured by one of the noise elements, it is subsequently "withdrawn" and "moves" to the target' – deserves some further discussion. The problem, of course, is how this trick is performed. An answer to this question can be found in sections 8.4 and 8.5. At the end of section 8.4 we argued that the attention loop, if automatically activated, will not remain activated. The instruction-induced effective expectation, i.e., the top-down activation described in section 8.5, can then correct the situation. Effective expectation ultimately wins and forces attention in the correct direction. (See section 6.7 – the cue validity effect in a multiple-item task with location cues reported by Jonides, 1981 – for a similar top-down correction: the 'withdrawal' of attention.)

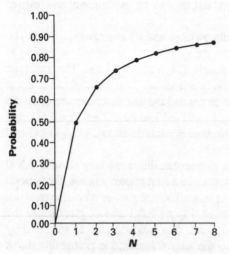

Figure 8.6.1 Probability that 1 out of N irrelevant items captures attention before attention is directed to the target.

8.7 Intention

In section 8.2 we pointed out two, for our topic, problematic aspects of Treisman's model for the perception of visual objects: a problem at the 'input' side, or, a problem with regard to attention, and a problem at the 'output' side, or, a problem with regard to action. In the previous sections of this chapter we tried to take care of the 'input' side problem. Attention, conceived as a kind of appendix, was replaced by a system-internal form of attention: a feedback loop from a location module to an input module. Instead of 'attention directed at position' we used 'position directed at attention'. And it appeared that this form of attention, in cooperation with and guided by effective expectations, was capable of accounting for the major part of, what can be called, the selective attention phenomena reported in the empirical part of our study.

To stop theorizing at this point, however, creates an unwanted situation. This is not only because important phenomena, like response competition, remain still unexplained. It is mainly so because attention, as now conceived, itself introduces a major problem. To see this, it is worthwhile to return for a moment to figure 8.2.1: Treisman's model. What we basically did in our foregoing excursions was only a kind of reshuffling of modules. Treisman's basic idea – attention addresses a great number of modules simultaneously via one or another 'master map of locations' – was simply taken over. In other words, also in our conception attentional selection is object selection: attention selects all dimensions – colour, form, orientation, etc. – of an object simultaneously. So, up to now, only object selection is adequately accounted for. And it is exactly this attentional object selection that creates a problem.

The important point is, of course, that for the *execution of an action* not the whole object selected by attention, but only a subset of the object's properties, is of relevance. This becomes immediately clear if we take a simple goal-directed action and have a closer look at it. *Picking apples* is the standard example. (Also see Neumann, 1985; 1987; Allport, 1987.) Apples have many properties that can be translated into a particular action. The colour can be named, its location pointed at, or its shape can be drawn. Only a limited number of these properties is important for and determined by the act of picking. The property location-in-space must be translated into distance and direction of the arm movement, the properties shape and size into the precise hand movement. Furthermore, the property location-in-space must not influence the precise hand movement or the 'manipulation component' of the movement (whether the apple is far or near, the ultimate finger grip has to be exactly the same) and the properties shape and size must not influence the distance travelled or the 'transportation component' of the movement (whether the apple is round or square, the hand has to move the same distance). Still other properties, for example the colour of the apple, must not influence the action at all. They must be temporarily completely blocked from influencing the action systems (whether the apple is red, green, black, blue, pink or purple must not influence the performance of the action). So, for task execution one or another form of property selection is necessary; some properties have to be translated into action, or in components of an action, other properties have to be prevented from affecting the action systems.

That not the whole object, but only a subset of its properties, is relevant for task execution is less clear, but equally true, for the laboratory tasks discussed in the previous sections (see also Chapter 2). For a letter naming task, for instance, only the shape of the object is relevant. Size, colour and brightness are irrelevant. But one can also ask the subject to name, for instance, the colour or the size of the letter. And then the form of the letter is irrelevant. So, also for these laboratory tasks, attentional object selection brings too much. For task execution, in addition, property selection is necessary (see also Kahneman and Treisman, 1984, p. 31).

So, the problem we have to face now, is, how to conceive this additional property selection. Fortunately it appears that the visual system is built in such a way that exactly this property selection is easily possible. In section 8.2 we already stated that the visual system is not just for 'perceiving' or 'seeing', but for action. Creutzfeldt (1979; 1985) has repeatedly emphasized this function for the visual system in general and for the different visual modules (see sections 1.10 and 7.1) in particular. His observations indicated that the various modules not only differ with regard to the *origin* of the signals they are working on, but also with regard to the *destination* of the products of their computations. Neurons within each visual area may not only be characterized by their trigger features (e.g., colour or motion), but also by their typical behavioural responses to stimuli. In this view, each visual area becomes (part of) a different link, or channel, between the eye and the motor-apparatus. Allport (1987) and Jeannerod (1981a, b) defend exactly the same position. In Jeannerod's view, the different properties of visual objects (e.g., their shape, colour, etc.) are matched by specific mechanisms which generate motor commands appropriate for each property. Responses to external events are mediated by separate channels each of which is characterized by a given input–output relation or production.

For the answer to the question of how to conceive the additional property selection, it is of importance to note that the choice of an action determines the relevance of properties. If an action is chosen, the set of properties that is relevant for response is fixed. As stated in section 8.1, in our laboratory tasks the instruction artificially determines the action choice. In Gibson's (1941) terminology, the instruction to the subject induces an intention to act. This intention to act can be equated with property selection. It can be conceived as an (advance) preparation in the task-relevant modules or an (advance) setting of the task-relevant perceptuo-motor channels. Then the intention to act picks out the response properties when attentional selection presents all properties of the object to be acted upon.

So, in our conceptualization, attention (in cooperation with expectation) performs object selection (see the previous sections). This object selection might possibly be sufficient for 'perceiving' or 'seeing' the selected object, as Treisman suggests (see section 8.2). However, for adequate 'task performance' or 'behaviour', attentional selection is not sufficient. In addition one or another form of property selection is needed. In our proposal a specific intention to act is at the basis of this second form of selection. Both attention (guided by effective expectation) and intention are involved in the execution of a task (see also section 8.1).

That for adequate task performance at least two selective mechanisms are required was recently also nicely demonstrated with a connectionist model developed by Phaf (1986; see also Phaf, Van der Heijden and Hudson, 1990). In fact, the model is a simple 'human' subject, named SLAM. Because we need aspects of the model in subsequent sections we introduce it here in some detail.

SLAM stands for SeLective Attention Model. It is a connectionist model for attention in visual selection tasks, inspired by the McClelland and Rumelhart (1981) model for word recognition. (There is, however, also considerable neurophysiological and psychological evidence supporting the general principles embodied in SLAM; see Phaf et al., 1990.) The model essentially consists of a structured set of interconnected nodes in which activation passes. Implemented as a computer program it is able to simulate the performance of a typical subject in a number of selective attention tasks.

SLAM was initially designed to perform in a simple 'filtering' task with equivalent stimuli (see, e.g., section 6.2). In such a task a typical stimulus may consist of a red disc on the left and a blue square on the right. Given these six attributes – red, blue, disc, square, left, right – and two objects per stimulus a total of 16 different stimuli can be constructed. The subject is asked to name one attribute of one of the two objects (the response attribute) while the object is specified by another attribute (the criterion attribute). Some examples: Name the colour on the left, name the form of the red one, or, name the position of the square.

Figure 8.7.1 shows a part of SLAM's processing network involved in this type of task. As in the McClelland and Rumelhart model three levels are distinguished: (a) a mapping level with three relatively independent modules containing nodes for all combinations of features in two dimensions; a colour × position module (containing nodes for blue-left, blue-right, red-left, and red-right), a colour × form module (with nodes for blue-disc, blue-square, etc.) and a form × position module (disc-left, etc.), (b) a feature level with three relatively independent modules containing nodes representing single features; a colour module (containing nodes for red and blue), a position module (left, right) and a form module (disc, square), and (c) a motor programme level with nodes representing the six possible answers in our simple filtering task (e.g., 'red', 'blue', 'left', etc.).

There are two groups of connections via which activation passes: between-level and within-level connections. The between-level or vertical connections in SLAM are determined by the 'connectivity by compatibility' principle: the nature and strength of these connections is determined by the compatibility of the representations of the nodes. (For instance, the 'blue-left' node at the mapping

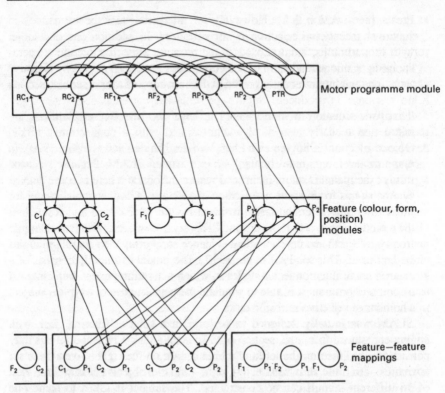

Figure 8.7.1 Part of Phaf's (1986) selective attention model for performing filtering tasks: SLAM.

level contributes to the activation of the compatible 'blue' node and 'left' node at the feature level but hinders the activation of the incompatible 'red' node and 'right' node.) There are both bottom-up and top-down connections. Via these connections, a stimulus, introduced as activations in the mapping level, activates its corresponding nodes in subsequent levels. Ultimately, response nodes are activated and a response can be generated (see Phaf et al., 1990, for the details).

The within-level or horizontal connections are all inhibitory. There are only within-module inhibitory connections, so only 'equivalent' units can inhibit each other (e.g., colour nodes inhibit colour nodes but not position nodes). This feature of SLAM is, of course, consistent with our theoretical elaborations in Chapter 7. In fact, the inhibition between the letters in a row of letters can be regarded as inhibition between the equivalent units in a 'letter × position' module.

In the context of this section the important aspect of SLAM is that it shows in its operation that besides attention (and effective expectation) for object selection, also intention for property selection is needed for adequate performance in selective attention tasks. The demonstration that both forms of selection are needed proceeds in essence as follows.

1. Presenting SLAM with a stimulus only – e.g., a red disc on the left and a blue square on the right – i.e., activating all mapping-level nodes which correspond with this stimulus, results in a symmetric state of activation and a corresponding random responding. The responses 'red', 'blue', 'disc', 'square', 'left', and 'right' are equally probable. Moreover, on a large number of trials no response is produced. Such a presentation corresponds to the rather unrealistic situation in which a subject performs a naming task without any instruction at all.

2. Object selection is implemented by providing one of the two objects at the mapping level, e.g., red disc left, with extra 'attentional' activation. (To how this is exactly done I return in the next section.) This extra activation breaks the symmetry in favour of the attended object. The stimulus plus this attentional input will result in simulations in which one of the three responses activated by the selected object – 'red', 'disc', and 'left' – will be produced with about equal frequency. Furthermore, on a relatively large number of trials no response will be produced. This kind of presentation corresponds to the rather unrealistic experimental situation in which a subject is required to select and name an object, without being instructed what attribute of the object has to be named. The outcome of the simulation shows that it is impossible to produce regular and predictable *behaviour* with 'object selection' only (see also section 2.7).

3 Property selection can be implemented by providing all nodes in one module, e.g., for the intention to name colours all nodes in the colour module, with extra continuous activation. This extra activation breaks the symmetry in favour of the intended class of responses. The stimulus plus only this response property activation will result in about equal proportions of 'red' and 'blue' responses. On a large number of trials no response will be produced. This simulation corresponds to the rather unrealistic situation in which the subject is instructed to name the colour, without any indication about the object whose colour has to be named. The outcome of this simulation demonstrates the impossibility of producing adequate *behaviour* with property selection only (see also section 2.7).

4. In SLAM, only the combination of stimulus-induced activation, object selection (i.e., attention, guided by effective expectation, favouring one object representation; 'red', 'disc', 'left') and property selection (i.e., intention, favouring one class of attributes: 'red', 'blue') leads to the required selective behaviour. In our example then almost only the response 'red' is produced (a few errors are made) and there are no trials without responses.

So, as asserted, also in SLAM only the cooperation and intersection of the effects of attentional object selection and intentional property selection produce the correct behaviour. The intention to act in a specific way solves the problem created by attention: selecting and emphasizing far too much. Let us now leave the topic 'selection' and have a brief look at the phenomenon 'response competition'.

8.8 Response competition: equivalent response attributes

In Chapter 4 we introduced our view with regard to the function of attention. Attention has a function in the time domain. By assigning priorities in time to positions in space, attention is capable of speeding up responding (see section 4.7). The theoretical elaborations presented in Chapter 7 and the present chapter are consistent with this point of view and merely make it more explicit. In Chapter 6, however, we encountered a completely different view with regard to the function of attention. Theorists conceived attention as a spotlight or a zoom lens involved in the processing of information. The experimental results seemed to indicate that the spotlight was much too large and processed far too much. In these views attention has an effect opposite to the one we hypothesized. It is responsible for slowing down responding by causing response competition (see, e.g., sections 6.3, 6.4 and 6.5).

We are now in a position to have a closer look at where response competition comes from and how it is ultimately resolved. To really see what is going on, however, a number of distinctions has to be made. The first concerns equivalent attributes (see, e.g., section 6.2) and non-equivalent attributes (see, e.g., section 6.1). The second distinction is only relevant with non-equivalent attributes and concerns integral combinations (see, e.g., section 4.10) and spatially separate presentations of attributes (see, e.g., section 6.1). This section is concerned with response competition observed with equivalent attributes. Section 8.9 deals with response competition observed with non-equivalent attributes.

With, what are generally regarded as, word–word, colour–colour and letter–letter variants of the Stroop task (see, e.g., Van der Heijden, 1981; Hagenaar and Van der Heijden, 1986; Glaser and Glaser, 1982; Eriksen and Eriksen, 1974; Eriksen and Schultz, 1979; see also section 6.2) interfering effects of, what can be called, the *response* attribute of irrelevant objects are obtained, i.e., from the colour of an irrelevant object in a colour naming task and from the shape of an irrelevant object in a letter naming task. Substantial response competition is only observed from colours and letters with names used for naming the relevant colours or letters. 'Neutral' colours (see, e.g., Van der Heijden, 1981; Hagenaar and Van der Heijden, 1986) and 'neutral' letters (see, e.g., Eriksen and Eriksen, 1974; Eriksen and Schultz, 1979) cause virtually no competition. And irrelevant dimensions of relevant and irrelevant objects such as brightness, position and size, seem to produce no response competition. How to explain this pattern of results?

SLAM can provide at least the beginning of an answer. SLAM is not only capable of producing qualitative results as described in the foregoing section. Besides producing correct responses and incorrect responses in acceptable proportions, its response selection and evaluation mechanism also allows for the generation of responses in time. Therefore also its behaviour in time, i.e., its pattern of RTs, could be investigated. A variety of different experiments with RT as the dependent variable – filtering tasks and 'Stroop' tasks – reported by different authors was simulated (see Phaf, 1986; Phaf et al., 1990, for the details). In this way response competition could be studied in great detail.

The important point is now that, while in SLAM attentional selection is perfect object selection, with 'object' referring to the conjunction of attributes (e.g., colour, form, and size) occupying a restricted area of visual space, realistic patterns of 'response competition' were observed in all relevant multiple-item simulations. So, in SLAM, response competition with equivalent items is not the result of imperfect attentional selection, as proposed by spotlight and zoom lens views. Of course, perfect attentional object selection can also not be responsible for this result. So, in this situation, attention is not responsible for the response competition observed! SLAM's parallelism (restricted by intramodular inhibition) together with the implementation of intention (addressing all possible relevant response properties), must be at the basis of this result. It is worthwhile to consider in detail how, in the type of task under discussion, this response competition arises and how it is ultimately resolved. So, let us have a closer look at what happens in SLAM, for instance, in the colour–colour variant of the Stroop task described at the end of the previous section: a red disc on the left and a blue square on the right and colour naming as the task.

In the simulations either the effect of a visual selection cue or the effect of a verbal selection cue was implemented. The visual selection cue, a barmarker indicating one of the objects, was a location cue, not a symbolic cue. Because a location cue is visually presented, just as the stimuli, it was consistently treated as a form on a position in the form × position module in the mapping level or first level. Because a location cue is very close to the position of the relevant stimulus, it was presented at the position of the object whose response property had to be named. The verbal selection cue, representing a spoken advance instruction, e.g., to name the colour at the left, was implemented as extra activation, coming from a not further specified source, directly to the node representing the position of the relevant object in the position module at the feature level or second level.

The two types of cues have as a first result in common an extra increase of activation of the position node at the second level representing the position of the relevant object. A very fast, subsequent effect is that, via recurrent or top-down excitatory connections, all nodes at the mapping level representing a feature on the relevant position receive an extra activation. This activation represents attention. So in SLAM attending starts at the position of the relevant object. It has as a result that the activity level in the nodes in the mapping level representing the whole relevant object with all its features is increased. (Notice that, despite differences in details, in SLAM our major theoretical views with regard to attention, presented in the foregoing sections, are implemented. In SLAM attentional selection is object selection. This selection is clearly early selection. Position information is at the basis of this early object selection process. Attention essentially consists of position information that is fed back via top-down connections. Therefore attentional object selection is very fast but not immediate.)

What subsequently happens in SLAM can be described in a number of ways. In the following I prefer clarity over precision (see Phaf, 1986; Phaf et al., 1990, for exact descriptions). The increased activation in the nodes representing the attended object at the mapping level proceeds upwards in the network. At the feature level, it has to break the stimulation-caused symmetry in activation and has to ensure that in all feature modules the nodes representing the features of the relevant object have ultimately the highest level of activation. There are two different aspects to this. First, the extra attentional activation counteracts the intramodular inhibition and causes the relevant nodes to win. Second, via the intramodular inhibitory connections, this extra activation exerts a strong inhibitory action on the nodes representing the features of the irrelevant object. This causes these nodes to lose. So besides attentional-relevant-object enhancement there is a simultaneous hard-wired indirect attentional-irrelevant-object suppression in SLAM. (Such a simultaneous enhancement–suppression effect of attention was already suggested by Keele and Neill, 1978, p. 42; see also Van der Heijden, 1990, and Chapter 7.) After some period of time the relevant object really stands out in terms of level and duration of activation.

The foregoing story applies to all feature modules on the second level. For response competition, the important point now is that breaking the symmetry is especially difficult in the module containing the nodes representing the response attribute. In this module the activations of all nodes are strongly amplified by activation coming from a not-further-specified source. This extra activation implements intention. As a result of this amplification all the nodes in this module start with a relatively high level of activation. Consequently, there is much more to win (and to lose) in the intramodular inhibition battle in this module. And it is exactly the time needed to break the symmetry in this module that shows up as response competition.

As a result of object oriented attention, however, the node representing the response attribute of the relevant object ultimately wins this war. And because in exactly this node all activations that can cooperate converge and 'summate', i.e., because exactly this node is the intersection of the positive effects of stimulation, attention and intention, it has, after a period of time, the highest level of activation from all nodes at the second level. In SLAM this node has therefore also the highest chance of picking out the response. So, in SLAM, in this situation response competition is neither the result of attentional involvement nor of one or another kind of 'horse race' between equivalent attributes. What is of importance is the inhibition within modules and the time needed by attention to resolve the intramodular competition. With equivalent stimuli the response competition problem is produced by stimulation and intention and has to be solved by attention.

In section 6.10 we addressed the question of whether the response competition logic was logically and empirically tenable. We indicated that the reasoning can only be valid if 'being processed' is a sufficient condition for response competition to show up. For equivalent items we are now in a position to answer the question:

Is 'being processed' really a sufficient condition? It appears that being processed is not a sufficient condition for response competition to show up. Response competition, as a negative sign that irrelevant information is processed in parallel with relevant information, only shows up when that information is processed *and* fits in with the task requirements. The evidence presented suggests that it is 'intention' that determines whether interference is observed. The most parsimonious assumption is that all information is processed in parallel (see Chapter 7) and that intention, by amplifying task-relevant properties, determines whether signs of parallel processing of information are observed. Of course, this view is completely at variance with the 'reading' hypothesis. Because the response competition logic is based upon that hypothesis, this view also takes away the basis of the response competition logic and casts serious doubts upon its products such as spotlights and zoom lenses. There is, however, one factor that appreciably complicates issues. That factor is, indeed, attentional capture.

As stated, in SLAM attentional selection is perfect object selection. Attentional selection in SLAM is also perfect, in the sense that SLAM always immediately selects the relevant object. As we have seen in several places, however, with real subjects sometimes erroneous selections precede the correct selection (see especially section 8.6: multiple simultaneous onsets). In the present conceptualization, such an initial erroneous attentional selection must result in severe response competition (or even erroneous responding), because, in terms of SLAM, the activations in all nodes representing properties of an irrelevant object are initially boosted by attentional activation. So, here we have a case in which response competition can be seen as being caused by erroneous attentional involvement (and subsequently resolved by correct attentional involvement; see section 8.6). In section 6.9, however, we saw that also without such erroneous selections response competition is still also observed. Remember that in situations where the Eriksen effect disappears, response competition is still found. Therefore SLAM can be regarded as producing only the response competition as observed with correct selections. For real subjects, however, an additional source of response competition has to be recognized: response competition as a result of erroneous attentional capture. To this additional source of response competition we briefly return at the end of the next section.

8.9 Response competition: non-equivalent response attributes

With regard to the response competition paradigm with non-equivalent attributes, i.e., with regard to the Stroop task proper, two experimental situations have to be distinguished. In the orthodox Stroop task and in the single-response variant an interfering effect of an irrelevant attribute (the word) of the *relevant* object is observed (see, e.g., Dalrymple-Alford and Budayr, 1966; see also section 4.10). With separate (bilateral) presentation of colour and word, however, a delaying effect of an irrelevant attribute of an *irrelevant* object is found (see, e.g., Dyer, 1973b; Gatti and Egeth, 1978; Merikle and Gorewich, 1979; see also section 6.1).

In both tasks only colour words that are also used to name the colours produce substantial competition. Other words produce appreciably less or no competition (see, e.g., Klein, 1964, and Kahneman and Chajczyk, 1983). There is, however, an important difference between the results obtained with the orthodox Stroop task and the task with separate (bilateral) presentations. Response competition is much larger with integral Stroop stimuli than with separated Stroop stimuli (see sections 6.1 and 6.3). Moreover, up to now, only with separated Stroop stimuli has 'dilution' been reported (see section 6.9). How to understand this pattern of results?

To understand what is going on in this type of task SLAM was extended so that it could also perform in tasks with non-equivalent stimuli, i.e., with Stroop stimuli. Figure 8.9.1 gives the complete model with schematized connections between modules. 'Wordness' is simply regarded as a fourth independent feature. Therefore three modules are added at the mapping level: a word-colour module (containing nodes for the word 'RED' in red, 'RED' in blue, 'BLUE' in red and 'BLUE' in blue), a word-form module and a word-position module.

Words have a special status in SLAM. Their high stimulus–response compatibility is implemented as direct connections between the mapping level and the response level (see for similar proposals, e.g., Van der Heijden, 1981, Warren and Morton, 1982, and McLeod and Posner, 1984). These 'privileged

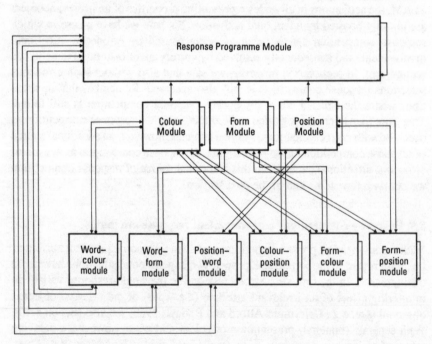

Figure 8.9.1 SLAM complete, with schematized representation of excitatory and inhibitory connections.

links' between word modules and motor program module are responsible for creating the asymmetry in Stroop interference mentioned in section 4.10 (see Van der Heijden, 1981; Phaf, 1986; Phaf et al., 1990, for further details).

A number of Stroop tasks with integral Stroop stimuli and with separated Stroop stimuli were simulated. These simulations clearly showed the difference in response competition: large with integral and small with separate (bilateral) Stroop stimuli. Given the model depicted in figure 8.9.1 and object selection as specified earlier, the difference in results obtained is easily understood. With separate presentations, the 'privileged loop' for words creates some interference. Attention, however, only boosts the activity in the nodes representing the properties of the object carrying the colour, not the activity in the nodes representing the properties of the colour word. The intention to name colours, implemented as extra activation in the colour module, in cooperation with attention can easily cope with this interference. So, not much response competition is observed. With integral Stroop stimuli the situation is completely different. Because colour and word are united in one object, attentional object selection not only boosts the colour activation, but also the colour word activation. In other words attention now creates a large part of the problem. Only the intention to name the colour is left for solving this problem. Therefore in this situation severe response competition is observed.

Of course, also in this type of task SLAM operated with perfect object selection. However, just as with equivalent stimuli, also with spatially separate Stroop stimuli, real subjects might sometimes initially select the irrelevant object. On a proportion of the trials this attentional capture might give rise to considerable response competition, caused by attention (see section 8.8). Exactly in this context one spectacular phenomenon observed with separate Stroop stimuli is easily explained: 'dilution', or, what we called, the 'Kahneman effect' (see section 6.9).

Kahneman and Chajczyk (1983) relate, in my view correctly, the Kahneman effect to the Eriksen effect (i.e., to 'cognitive masking' or 'filtering costs'). For this reason we presented the Kahneman effect data together with the corresponding Eriksen effect data in table 8.6.1 (see the last two rows in this table). Our interpretation, in terms of the Eriksen effect, of these data is summarized in the following equations (we use the average RTs in the column labeled X in table 8.6.1).

Conflicting: $662 = X + 0.50C$ (A)
Conflicting/neutral: $632 = X + 0.33C + 0.33N$ (B)
'Dilution': $30 =   0.17C - 0.33N$ (A − B)

In these equations X stands for the time needed to select and respond to the coloured bar. C stands for the additional amount of time needed when the incongruent colour word initially attracted or captured attention, i.e., for the additional response competition as a result of an initial wrong selection. N stands for the additional amount of time when the neutral word initially captured attention, i.e., for the delay observed in the Eriksen effect. The values 0.50 and 0.33 are the values given by the rule governing the Eriksen effect as specified in section 8.6. The row labelled 'dilution' gives the difference between the row 'Conflicting' and the row 'Conflicting/neutral'. This difference shows that a Kahneman effect is already to be expected if C is about twice as large as N. Because an attended neutral word produces little interference (about 40 ms; see section 8.6), it is reasonable to assume that C is appreciably larger than N. So, it is reasonable to assume that the Kahneman effect is simply a consequence of the Eriksen effect.

One last remark with regard to response competition is in order. In the literature, the generally accepted view is that all variants of the Stroop task involve essentially the same processing and selecting operations (see, e.g., Van der Heijden, 1981). However, the conceptualization presented in this chapter is completely at variance with this view. In the different types of tasks we distinguished in sections 8.8 and 8.9, there are different causes for the response competition and the competition is solved in different ways. In the Stroop variant with equivalent stimuli (see section 8.8), parallel processing of the information together with intention causes the problem. Attention has to solve the problem. With separate Stroop stimuli parallel processing (and the 'privileged loop') causes the problem. Attention in cooperation with intention solves the problem. With integral Stroop stimuli parallel processing (and the 'privileged loop') and attention cause the problem. Intention has to solve the problem. So, the different response competition paradigms have to be clearly distinguished. Treating them all as the same obscures a lot of relevant and theoretically intriguing differences.

8.10 Conclusion

Writing a study like the present one is like travelling in a foreign country. Lots of what one sees is more or less expected from information received earlier. Then, details get filled in and relevant distinctions become clearer; accuracy–latency, single-item–multiple-item, location-cue–symbolic-cue, identification–selection, identity–position, attention–eye-movements, attention-as-selection–response-competition, etc., etc. One also gets brief glimpses of promising regions that one cannot enter because of limited resources. But it is tempting to evaluate critically, with the model presented in this chapter as a starting point, topics like visual (feature, conjunction, etc.) search, visual (metacontrast, backward, etc.) masking, further aspects of location information functioning as attention, the relation between location information and global form information, 'pre-attentive' analysis, unit formation, aspects of action control, etc., etc. And, last but not least, one also encounters real surprises. Events that force one to alter one's paths. For me there was an event that really surprised me. I conclude this study by describing what it was.

As stated in Chapter 2, attention is an ambiguous and elusive concept. A number of notions, in shifting compositions, are involved. Well aware of this problem we first investigated what notions of attention take part in these shifting compositions. A brief review of the earlier literature in Chapter 2 taught us that at least three relevant notions have to be distinguished: attention, expectation and intention. Armed with this knowledge it was possible to review the information processing literature on effects of attention proper. The strategy followed was to look for the operation of attention under conditions with effects of expectation and intention fixed. And, because 'In practice, the *observable* criterion for successful "attention" to (or awareness of) an environmental event invariably turns on the ability of the subject to *act* voluntarily, or, arbitrarily, in response to that event ...' (Allport, 1987, p. 408), as a devoted information processing psychologist, I especially looked for the effects of voluntary attention. But, and for me quite unexpected, still two different notions seemed to be involved in shifting compositions: two separate modes of control over the allocation of attention. Often not the subject, but the visual world seemed in control.

Of course, we could and should have known this from the outset. Descartes already recognized two notions of attention. He used the term 'attention' to refer to a voluntary, controlled, intentional, process of paying attention to an object, and the term 'admiration' for the case where an object attracts attention without intention. Also in early introspective and experimental psychology two notions of attention were clearly distinguished: involuntary or passive attention where the world has the initiative and voluntary or active attention where the actor or perceiver has the initiative (see, e.g., Von Helmholtz and James in Chapter 2). The same distinction was made by the Gestalt psychologists. Wertheimer (1923) distinguished between subjectively controlled concentration of attention, and attention resulting from structural properties of perceptual figures. Koffka (1935) defined voluntary and involuntary attention as 'forces' going respectively from the self to an object and from an object to the self.

For obvious reasons – remember the event–event laws of the standard philosophy of science – during and at the end of the behaviouristic era, the main emphasis was on passive, involuntary, attention, and active, voluntary, attention was nearly neglected. Not the subject, but the world was in control. Berlyne's and McDonnell's research forms a good example (see, e.g., Berlyne, 1950; 1951; 1960; McDonnell, 1970). These investigators were interested in the power of a stimulus to attract attention, or, in the factors determining the outcome of competition among several stimuli for the control of overt behaviour. The impact of stimulus factors like luminous intensity, contrast with the background, change, albedo, and novelty was investigated.

Also for obvious reasons – remember the causal properties of the realist philosophy of science – in information processing psychology (and in cognitive psychology) the main emphasis is on active, voluntary, attention. Not the world, but the subject is in control. Especially at the start of these movements but also still nowadays, passive involuntary attention is nearly completely neglected. (One noticeable exception is found in the work of Jonides and associates.) In most experiments subjects receive an instruction. Then a stimulus is presented.

Subjects are expected to be completely in control and to behave as specified in the instructions.

In Chapter 1 we already saw that the bottom-up or world-driven approach only will never really work (see also James, 1890/1950, Hebb, 1949, and Neisser, 1967, quoted in section 1.4). In the course of this study we were more and more confronted with the fact that a top-down or subject-controlled approach only will also never really work. (We collected the relevant evidence in section 8.6.) In general, only a theory that acknowledges the existence and cooperation of attention, expectation and intention and, within attention, both the contributions of involuntary and voluntary attention, will be able to elucidate the real function of attention in visual information processing tasks. Both the subject and the world have to find their proper place.

With this wisdom of hindsight chapters have to be rewritten (is it really 'benefits brought by attention' or is it 'lower costs due to capture', with which Chapter 3 mainly deals?). But the whole scientific enterprise essentially consists of a continuing rewriting of chapters. Therefore, as a conclusion, I simply summarize the main theses that I submit as guidelines for further journeys and rewritings. Visual spatial selective attention

- consists of (late) position information joining, and interacting with, (early) identity information,
- and provides temporal order or temporal structure in a spatially structured visual world.
- It performs its job in close cooperation and interaction with expectations and intentions,
- and is controlled by both the subject and the world.

References

Allport, D.A. (1980a). Patterns and actions: cognitive mechanisms are content-specific. In: G. Claxton (Ed.), *Cognitive Psychology, New Directions*. London: Routledge & Kegan Paul.

Allport, D.A. (1980b). Attention and Performance. In: G. Claxton (Ed.), *Cognitive Psychology, New Directions*. London: Routledge & Kegan Paul.

Allport, D.A. (1987). Selection for action: some behavioral and neurophysiological considerations of attention and action. In: H. Heuer and A.F. Sanders (Eds.), *Perspectives on Perception and Action*. Hillsdale, N.J.: Erlbaum.

Allport, D.A., Tipper, S.P., and Chmiel, N.R.J. (1985). Perceptual integration and post-categorical filtering. In: M. I. Posner and O.S.M. Marin (Eds.), *Mechanisms of Attention: Attention and Performance XI*. Hillsdale, N.J.: Erlbaum.

Amundsen, R. (1985). Psychology and Epistemology: The place versus response controversy. *Cognition, 20*, 127–153.

Anstis, S.M. (1974). A chart demonstrating variations in acuity with retinal position. *Vision Research, 14*, 589–592.

Atkinson, R.C., Holmgren, J.E., and Juola, J.F. (1969). Processing time as influenced by the number of elements in a multielement display. *Perception & Psychophysics, 6*, 321–326.

Averbach, E., and Coriell, A.S. (1961). Short-term memory in vision. *Bell System Technical Journal, 40*, 309–328.

Averbach, E., and Sperling, G. (1961). Short-term storage of information in vision. In: C. Cherry (Ed.), *Information Theory*. London: Butterworth.

Babington-Smith, B. (1961). An unexpected effect of attention in peripheral vision. *Nature, 189*, 776.

Banks, W.P., Larson, D.W., and Prinzmetal, W. (1979). Asymmetry of visual interference. *Perception & Psychophysics, 25*, 447–456.

Barlow, H.B. (1958). Temporal and spatial summation in human vision at different background intensities. *Journal of Physiology (London), 141*, 337–350.

Barlow, H.B. (1981). Critical limiting factors in the design of the eye and visual cortex. The Ferrier Lecture. *Proceedings of the Royal Society (London) B, 212*, 1–34.

Barlow, H.B. (1985). The twelfth Bartlett memorial lecture: The role of single neurons in the psychology of perception. *Quarterly Journal of Experimental Psychology, 37A*, 121–145.

Bashinski, H.S., and Bacharach, V.R. (1980). Enhancement of perceptual sensitivity as the result of selectively attending to spatial locations. *Perception & Psychophysics, 28*, 241–248.

Bechtel, W. (1985). Contemporary connectionism: Are the new parallel distributed processing models cognitive or associationist? *Behaviorism, 13*, 53–61.

Beech, A., and Claridge, G. (1987). Individual differences in negative priming. *British Journal of Psychology, 78,* 349–356.

Berlyne, D.E. (1950). Stimulus intensity and attention in relation to learning theory. *Quarterly Journal of Experimental Psychology, 2,* 71–75.

Berlyne, D.E. (1951). Attention to change. *British Journal of Psychology, 42,* 269–275.

Berlyne, D.E. (1960). *Conflict, Arousal and Curiosity.* New York: McGraw-Hill.

Berlyne, D.E. (1966). Curiosity and exploration. *Science, 153,* 25–33.

Berlyne, D.E. (1974). Attention. In: E.C. Carterette and M.P. Friedman (Eds.), *Handbook of Perception, Vol. 1.* New York: Academic Press.

Bieri, P. (1990). Informational accounts of perception and action: sceptical reflections. In: O. Neumann and W. Prinz (Eds.), *Relationships between Perception and Action.* Berlin, Heidelberg: Springer.

Bloch, A.M. (1885). Experience sur la vision. *Comptes Rendus de Séances de la Société de Biologie (Paris), 37,* 493–495.

Boring, E.G. (1957). *A History of Experimental Psychology.* New York: Appleton-Century-Crofts (second edition).

Bouma, H. (1970). Interaction effects in parafoveal letter recognition. *Nature, 226,* 177–178.

Bouma, H. (1973). Visual interference in the parafoveal recognition of initial and final letters of words. *Vision Research, 13,* 767–782.

Brady, M. (1981). Preface – The changing shape of computer vision. *Artificial Intelligence, 17,* 1–15.

Breitmeyer, B.G., and Ganz, L. (1976). Implications of sustained and transient channels for theories of visual pattern masking, saccadic suppression, and information processing. *Psychological Review, 83,* 1–36.

Broadbent, D.E. (1958). *Perception and Communication.* London: Pergamon Press.

Broadbent, D.E. (1970). Stimulus set and response set: Two kinds of selective attention. In: D.I. Mostofsky (Ed.), *Attention: Contemporary Theory and Analysis.* New York: Appleton-Century-Crofts.

Broadbent, D.E. (1971). *Decision and Stress.* London: Academic Press.

Broadbent, D. E. (1977). Colour, localisation, and perceptual selection. In: *Psychologie Experimentale, et Comparée,* Paris: Press Universitaire de France.

Broadbent, D.E. (1982). Task combination and selective intake of information. *Acta Psychologica, 50,* 253–290.

Broadbent, D.E., and Broadbent, M.H.P. (1987). From detection to identification: response to multiple targets in rapid serial visual presentation. *Perception & Psychophysics, 42,* 105–113.

Broca, A., and Sulzer, D. (1902). La sensation lumineuse en fonction du temps. *Journal de Physiologie et de Pathologie générale, 4,* 632–640.

Bryden, M.P. (1961). The role of post-exposural eye movements in tachistoscopic perception. *Canadian Journal of Psychology, 15,* 220–225.

Bundesen, C. (1987). Visual attention: Race models for selection from multielement displays. *Psychological Research, 49,* 113–121.

Bundesen, C., Pedersen, L.F., and Larsen, A. (1984). Measuring efficiency of selection from briefly exposed visual displays: A model for partial report. *Journal of Experimental Psychology: Human Perception and Performance, 10,* 329–339.

Bundesen, C., Shibuya, H., and Larsen, A. (1985). Visual selection from multielement displays: A model for partial report. In: M.I. Posner and O.S.M. Marin (Eds.), *Attention and Performance XI.* Hillsdale, N.J.: Erlbaum.

Butler, B.E. (1980). Selective attention and stimulus localization in visual perception. *Canadian Journal of Psychology, 34,* 119–133.

Butler, B.E. (1982). Canadian studies of visual information processing: 1970–1980. *Canadian Journal of Psychology, 22,* 113–128.

Butler, B.E., and Currie, A. (1986). On the nature of perceptual limits in vision: A new look at lateral masking. *Psychological Research, 48,* 201–210.

Campbell, A.J., and Mewhort, D.J.K. (1980). On familiarity effects in visual information processing. *Canadian Journal of Psychology, 34,* 134–154.

Chambers, L., and Wolford, G. (1983). Lateral masking vertically and horizontally. *Bulletin of the Psychonomic Society, 21,* 459–461.

Chastain, G. (1982a). Violation of the retinal acuity gradient in a detection task. *Acta Psychologica, 52,* 23–31.

Chastain, G. (1982b). Nontarget detectability and interference with parafoveal target identification. *Acta Psychologica, 50,* 117–126.

Chastain, G., and Lawson, L. (1979). Identification asymmetry of parafoveal stimulus pairs. *Perception & Psychophysics, 26,* 363–368.

Cherry, E.C. (1953). Some experiments on the recognition of speech with one and two ears. *Journal of the Acoustical Society of America, 25,* 957–979.

Chow, S.L. (1986). Iconic memory, location information, and partial report. *Journal of Experimental Psychology: Human Perception and Performance, 12,* 455–465.

Clark, S.E. (1969). Retrieval of color information from preperceptual memory. *Journal of Experimental Psychology, 82,* 263–266.

Cohen, G., and Martin, M. (1975). Hemisphere differences in an auditory Stroop test. *Perception & Psychophysics, 17,* 79–83.

Colegate, R.L., Hoffman, J.E., and Eriksen, C.W. (1973). Selective encoding from multielement visual displays. *Perception & Psychophysics, 14,* 217–224.

Coltheart, M. (1972). Visual information processing. In P.C. Dodwell (Ed.), *New Horizons in Psychology* 2. Harmondsworth: Penguin.

Coltheart, M. (1975). Iconic memory: a reply to Professor Holding. *Memory & Cognition, 3,* 42–48.

Coltheart, M. (1980a). Iconic memory and visible persistence. *Perception & Psychophysics, 27,* 183–228.

Coltheart, M. (1980b). The persistences of vision. *Phil. Trans. R. Soc. London, B290,* 57–69.

Coltheart, M. (1983). Ecological necessity of iconic memory. *The Behavioral and Brain Sciences, 6,* 17–18.

Coltheart, M. (1984). Sensory Memory – A tutorial review. In: H. Bouma and D.G. Bouwhuis (Eds.), *Attention and Performance X, Control of language processes.* Hillsdale, N.J.: Erlbaum.

Coltheart, M., Lea, C.D., and Thompson, K. (1974). In defense of iconic memory. *Quarterly Journal of Experimental Psychology, 26,* 633–641.

Cornsweet, T.N. (1970). *Visual Perception.* New York: Academic Press.

Cowey, A. (1979). Cortical maps and visual perception; the Grindley memorial lecture. *Quarterly Journal of Experimental Psychology, 31,* 1–17.

Cowey, A. (1981). Why are there so many visual areas? In: F.O. Schmitt, F.G. Worden, G. Adelman and S.G. Dennis (Eds.), *The Organisation of the Cerebral Cortex.* Cambridge, MA: The MIT Press.

Creutzfeldt, O.D. (1979). Neurophysiological mechanisms and consciousness. *Brain and Mind, 69,* 217–253.

Creutzfeldt, O.D. (1985). Multiple visual areas: Multiple sensory-motor links. In: D. Rose and V.G. Dobson (Eds.), *Models of the Visual Cortex.* New York: Wiley.

Crick, F.H.C. (1984). Function of the thalamic reticular complex: The searchlight hypothesis. *Proc. Natl. Acad. Sci. USA, 81,* 4586–4590.

Cummins, R. (1983). *The Nature of Psychological Explanation*. Cambridge, MA: The MIT Press.

Dalrymple-Alford, E.C., and Budayr, B. (1966). Examination of some aspects of the Stroop color-word test. *Perceptual and Motor Skills, 23*, 1211–1214.

Dennett, D.C. (1978). *Brainstorms. Philosophical essays on mind and psychology*. Brighton: Harvester.

Dennett, D.C. (1984). Computer models and the mind – a view from the East Pole. *Psychology and Artificial Intelligence*. TLS, December 14, 1453–1454.

Deutsch, J.A., and Deutsch, D. (1963). Attention: some theoretical considerations. *Psychological Review, 70*, 80–90.

DeYoe, E.A., and Van Essen, D.C. (1988). Concurrent processing streams in monkey visual cortex. *Trends in Neurosciences, 11*, 219–226.

Dick, A.O. (1969). Relations between the sensory register and short-term storage in tachistoscopic recognition. *Journal of Experimental Psychology, 82*, 279–284.

Dick, A.O. (1971). On the problem of selection in short-term visual (iconic) memory. *Canadian Journal of Psychology, 25*, 250–263.

Dick, A.O. (1974). Iconic memory and its relation to perceptual processing and other memory mechanisms. *Perception & Psychophysics, 16*, 575–596.

Di Lollo, V. (1977). Temporal characteristics of iconic memory. *Nature, 267*, 241–243.

Di Lollo, V. (1980). Temporal integration in visual memory. *Journal of Experimental Psychology: General, 109*, 75–97.

Ditchburn, R.W., and Ginsburg, B.L. (1952). Vision with a stabilized retinal image. *Nature, 170*, 36–37.

Downing, C.J., and Pinker, S. (1985). The spatial structure of visual attention. In: M.I. Posner and O.S.M. Marin (Eds.), *Mechanisms of Attention: Attention and Performance XI*. Hillsdale, N.J.: Erlbaum.

Driver, J., and Tipper, S.P. (1989). On the nonselectivity of 'selective' seeing: Contrasts between interference and priming in selective attention. *Journal of Experimental Psychology: Human Perception and Performance, 15*, 304–314.

Duncan, J. (1980). The demonstration of capacity limitation. *Cognitive Psychology, 12*, 75–96.

Duncan, J. (1981). Directing attention in the visual field. *Perception & Psychophysics, 30*, 90–93.

Duncan, J. (1983). Perceptual selection based on alphanumeric class: Evidence from partial reports. *Perception & Psychophysics, 33*, 533–547.

Duncan, J. (1984). Selective attention and the organization of visual information. *Journal of Experimental Psychology: General, 113*, 501–517.

Dyer, F.N. (1973a). The Stroop phenomenon and its use in the study of perceptual, cognitive, and response processes. *Memory & Cognition, 1*, 106–120.

Dyer, F.N. (1973b). Interference and facilitation for color naming with separate bilateral presentations of the word and color. *Journal of Experimental Psychology, 99*, 314–317.

Dyer, F.N., and Severance, L.J. (1973). Stroop interference with successive presentations of separate incongruent words and colors. *Journal of Experimental Psychology, 98*, 438–439.

Egeth, H.E. (1977). Attention and preattention. In: G.H. Bower (Ed.), *The Psychology of Learning and Motivation, Vol. 11*. New York: Academic Press.

Egeth, H.E., Folk, C.L., and Mullin, P.A. (1989). Spatial parallelism in the processing of lines, letters and lexicality. In: B.E. Shepp and S. Ballesteros (Eds.), *Object Perception: Structure and Process*. Hillsdale, N.J.: Erlbaum.

Egeth, H.E., Jonides, J., and Wall, S. (1972). Parallel processing of multielement displays. *Cognitive Psychology, 3*, 674–698.

Egly, R., and Homa, D. (1984). Sensitization of the visual field. *Journal of Experimental Psychology: Human Perception and Performance, 10*, 778–793.

Einstein, A., and Infeld, L. (1938). *The Evolution of Physics.* New York: Simon and Schuster.

Engel, F.L. (1976). *Visual conspicuity as an external determinant of eye movements and selective attention.* Ph.D. Thesis, University of Eindhoven, Eindhoven, The Netherlands.

Eriksen, B.A., and Eriksen, C.W. (1974). Effects of noise letters upon the identification of a target letter in a nonsearch task. *Perception & Psychophysics, 16*, 143–149.

Eriksen, C.W. (1980). The use of a visual mask may seriously confound your experiment. *Perception & Psychophysics, 28*, 89–92.

Eriksen, C.W., and Colegate, R.L. (1971). Selective attention and serial processing in briefly presented visual displays. *Perception & Psychophysics, 10*, 321–326.

Eriksen, C.W., Coles, M.G.H., Morris, L.R., and O'Hara, W.P. (1985). An electromyographic examination of response competition. *Bulletin of the Psychonomic Society, 23*, 165–168.

Eriksen, C.W., and Collins, J.F. (1968). Sensory traces versus the psychological moment in the temporal organization of form. *Journal of Experimental Psychology, 77*, 367–382.

Eriksen, C.W., and Collins, J.F. (1969). Visual perceptual rate under two conditions of search. *Journal of Experimental Psychology, 80*, 489–492.

Eriksen, C.W., and Eriksen, B.A. (1979). Target redundancy in visual search: Do repetitions of the target within the display impair processing? *Perception & Psychophysics, 26*, 195–205.

Eriksen, C.W., and Hoffman, J.E. (1972a). Some characteristics of selective attention in visual perception determined by vocal reaction time. *Perception & Psychophysics, 11*, 169–171.

Eriksen, C.W., and Hoffman, J.E. (1972b). Temporal and spatial characteristics of selective encoding from visual displays. *Perception & Psychophysics, 12*, 201–204.

Eriksen, C.W., and Hoffman, J.E. (1973). The extent of processing of noise elements during selective encoding from visual displays. *Perception & Psychophysics, 14*, 155–160.

Eriksen, C.W., and Hoffman, J.E. (1974). Selective attention: noise suppression or signal enhancement? *Bulletin of the Psychonomic Society, 4*, 587–589.

Eriksen, C.W., and Lappin, J.S. (1967). Independence in the perception of simultaneously presented forms at brief durations. *Journal of Experimental Psychology, 73*, 468–472.

Eriksen, C.W., and Murphy, T.D. (1987). Movement of attentional focus across the visual field: A critical look at the evidence. *Perception & Psychophysics, 42*, 229–305.

Eriksen, C.W., O'Hara, W.P., and Eriksen, B. (1982). Response competition effects in same–different judgments. *Perception & Psychophysics, 32*, 261–270.

Eriksen, C.W., and Rohrbaugh, J.W. (1970). Some factors determining efficiency of selective attention. *American Journal of Psychology, 83*, 330–343.

Eriksen, C.W., and Schultz, D.W. (1977). Retinal locus and acuity in visual information processing. *Bulletin of the Psychonomic Society, 9*, 81–84.

Eriksen, C.W., and Schultz, D.W. (1978). Temporal factors in visual information processing: A tutorial review. In: J.Requin (Ed.), *Attention and Performance VII.* Hillsdale, N.J.: Erlbaum.

Eriksen, C.W., and Schultz, D.W. (1979). Information processing in visual search: a continuous flow conception and experimental results. *Perception & Psychophysics, 25*, 249–263.

Eriksen, C.W., and St. James, J.D. (1986). Visual attention within and around the field of focal attention: A zoomlens model. *Perception & Psychophysics, 40*, 225–240.

Eriksen, C.W., and Steffy, R.A. (1964). Short-term memory and retroactive interference in visual perception. *Journal of Experimental Psychology, 68*, 423–434.

Eriksen, C.W., and Yeh, Y.Y. (1985). Allocation of attention in the visual field. *Journal of Experimental Psychology: Human Perception and Performance, 5*, 583–597.

Estes, W.K. (1978). Perceptual processing in letter recognition and reading. In: E.C. Carterette and M.P. Friedman (Eds.), *Handbook of Perception, Vol IX*. New York: Academic Press.

Estes, W.K., Allmeyer, D.H., and Reder, S.M. (1976). Serial position functions for letter identification at brief and extended exposure durations. *Perception & Psychophysics, 19*, 1–15.

Estes, W.K., and Taylor, H.A. (1964). A detection method and probabilistic models for assessing information processing from brief visual displays. *Proc. Natl. Acad. Sci. USA, 52*, 46–54.

Estes, W.K., and Taylor, H.A. (1966). Visual detection in relation to display size and redundancy of critical elements. *Perception & Psychophysics, 1*, 9–16.

Flanagan, O.J. (1984). *The Science of Mind*. Cambridge, MA: The MIT Press.

Fleur, E., Lapré, L., Van der Heijden, A.H.C., and Wolters, G. (1986). *The effect of different numbers of cues and different masking patterns on letter recognition*. (Internal report, EP-86-02) Leiden, The Netherlands: University of Leiden.

Flowers, J.H., Warner, J.L., and Polansky, M.L. (1979). Response and encoding factors in "ignoring" irrelevant information. *Memory & Cognition, 7*, 86–94.

Fodor, J.A. (1981a). The mind–body problem. *Scientific American, 214* (January), 114–123.

Fodor, J.A. (1981b). *Representations*. Cambridge, MA: The MIT Press.

Fodor, J.A. (1983). *The Modularity of Mind*. Cambridge, MA: The MIT Press.

Fodor, J.A. (1985). Précis of the modularity of mind. *The Behavioral and Brain Sciences, 8*, 1–42.

Fodor, J.A., and Pylyshyn, Z.W. (1981). How direct is visual perception?: Some reflections on Gibson's "Ecological Approach". *Cognition, 9*, 139–196.

Fodor, J.A., and Pylyshyn, Z.W. (1988). Connectionism and cognitive architecture: A critical analysis. *Cognition, 28*, 3–71.

Fox, L.A., Shor, R.E., and Steinman, R.J. (1971). Semantic gradients and interference in naming color, spatial direction, and numerosity. *Journal of Experimental Psychology, 91*, 59–65.

Frykland, I. (1975). Effects of cued-set spatial arrangement and target-background similarity in the partial-report paradigm. *Perception & Psychophysics, 17*, 375–386.

Ganz, L. (1975). Temporal factors in visual perception. In: E.C. Carterette and M.P. Friedman (Eds.), *Handbook of Perception, Vol.V*. New York: Academic Press.

Garner, W.R. (1974). Attention: The processing of multiple sources of information. In: E.C. Carterette and M.P. Friedman (Eds.), *Handbook of Perception II*. New York: Academic Press.

Gathercole, S.E., and Broadbent, D.E. (1984). Combining attributes in specified and categorized target search: further evidence for strategy differences. *Memory & Cognition, 12*, 329–337.

Gatti, S.V., and Egeth, H.E. (1978). Failure of spatial selectivity in vision. *Bulletin of the Psychonomic Society, 11*, 181–184.

Gerrits, H.J.M., and Vendrik, A.J.H. (1970). Artificial movements of a stabilized image. *Vision Research, 10*, 1443–1456.

Gibson, J.J. (1941). A critical review of the concept of set in contemporary experimental psychology. *Psychological Bulletin, 38*, 781–817.

Gibson, J.J. (1960). The concept of stimulus in psychology. *American Psychologist, 15*, 1–15.

Gibson, J.J. (1979). *The Ecological Approach to Visual Perception.* Boston: Houghton Mifflin.

Glaser, M.O., and Glaser, W.R. (1982). Time course analysis of the Stroop phenomenon. *Journal of Experimental Psychology: Human Perception and Performance, 8,* 875–894.

Graham, C.H., and Kemp, E.H. (1938). Brightness discrimination as a function of the duration of the increment intensity. *Journal of General Physiology, 21,* 635–650.

Grice, G.R., Boroughs, J.M., and Canham, L. (1984a). Temporal dynamics of associative interference and facilitation produced by visual context. *Perception & Psychophysics, 36,* 499–507.

Grice, G.R., Canham, L., and Gwynne, J.W. (1984b). Absence of a redundant-signals effect in a reaction time task with divided attention. *Perception & Psychophysics, 36,* 565–570.

Grice, G.R., and Gwynne, J.W. (1985). Temporal characteristics of noise conditions producing facilitation and interference. *Perception & Psychophysics, 37,* 495–501.

Grindley, G.C., and Townsend, V. (1968). Voluntary attention in peripheral vision and its effects on acuity and differential thresholds. *Quarterly Journal of Experimental Psychology, 20,* 11–19.

Haber, R.N. (Ed.) (1969). *Information Processing Approaches to Visual Perception.* New York: Holt, Rinehart and Winston.

Haber, R.N. (1983). The impending demise of the icon: a critique of the concept of iconic storage in visual information processing. *The Behavioral and Brain Sciences, 6,* 1–54.

Haber, R.N., and Hershenson, M. (1974). *The Psychology of Visual Perception.* London: Holt, Rinehart & Winston.

Hagenaar, R. (1990). *Visual Selection in Letter Naming.* Ph.D. Thesis, University of Leiden, Leiden, The Netherlands.

Hagenaar, R. (in prep.). Pre- and postcues in a partial-report bar-probe task.

Hagenaar, R., and Van der Heijden, A.H.C. (1986). Target–noise separation in visual selective attention. *Acta Psychologica, 62,* 161–176.

Hagenzieker, M.P. (1987). *Inhibition in visual information processing: Shrink, and only shrink.* Master's Thesis, University of Leiden, Leiden, The Netherlands.

Hagenzieker, M.P., and Van der Heijden, A.H.C. (1990). Time courses in visual information processing: Some theoretical considerations. *Psychological Research, 52,* 5–12.

Hagenzieker, M.P., Van der Heijden, A.H.C., and Hagenaar, R. (1990). Time courses in visual information processing: Some empirical evidence for inhibition. *Psychological Research, 52,* 13–21.

Harter, M.R., and Aine, C.J. (1984). Brain mechanisms of visual selective attention. In: R. Parasuraman and R. Davies (Eds.), *Varieties of Attention.* New York: Academic Press.

Hawkins, M.L., Shafto, M.G., and Richardson, K. (1988). Effects of target luminance and cue validity on the latency of visual detection. *Perception & Psychophysics, 44,* 484–492.

Hebb, D.O. (1949). *The Organization of Behavior.* New York: Wiley.

Hebb, D.O. (1966). *A Textbook of Psychology.* Philadelphia: Saunders (second edition).

Hebb, D.O. (1980). A behavioral approach. In: M. Bunge, *The Mind–Body Problem, a Psychobiological Approach.* Oxford: Pergamon.

Heisser, W.J. (1988). Selecting a stimulus set with prescribed structure from empirical confusion frequencies. *British Journal of Mathematical and Statistical Psychology, 41,* 37–51.

Hilgard, E.R., and Humphreys, L.G. (1938). The effect of supporting and antagonistic voluntary instructions on conditioned discrimination. *Journal of Experimental Psychology, 22,* 291–304.

Hinton, G.E., and Anderson, J.A. (1981). *Parallel Models of Associative Memory*. Hillsdale, N.J.: Erlbaum.

Hintzman, D.L., Carre, F.A., Eskridge, V.L., Owens, A.M., Shaff, S.S., and Sparks, M.E. (1972). "Stroop" effect: Input or output phenomenon. *Journal of Experimental Psychology, 95*, 458–459.

Hoffman, J.E. (1975). Hierarchical stages in the processing of visual information. *Perception & Psychophysics, 18*, 348–354.

Hoffman, J.E., and Nelson, B. (1981). Spatial selectivity in visual search. *Perception & Psychophysics, 30*, 283–290.

Hoffman, J.E., Nelson, B., and Houck, M.R. (1983). The role of attentional resources in automatic detection. *Cognitive Psychology, 51*, 379–410.

Holmgren, J.E. (1974). The effect of a visual indicator on rate of visual search: Evidence for processing control. *Perception & Psychophysics, 15*, 544–550.

Hughes, H.C. (1984). Effects of flash luminance and positional expectancies on visual response latency. *Perception & Psychophysics, 36*, 177–184.

James, W. (1890/1950). *The Principles of Psychology (Vol. 1)*. Authorized edition, Dover Publications, Inc.

Jeannerod, M. (1981a). Intersegmental coordination during reaching at natural visual objects. In: J. Long and A. Baddeley (Eds.), *Attention and Performance, IX*. Hillsdale, N.J.: Erlbaum.

Jeannerod, M. (1981b). Specialized channels for cognitive responses. *Cognition, 10*, 135–137.

Johnston, J.A., and Dark, V.J. (1982). In defense of intraperceptual theories of attention. *Journal of Experimental Psychology: Human Perception and Performance, 8*, 407–421.

Johnston, J.A., and Dark, V.J. (1986). Selective attention. *Annual Review of Psychology, 37*, 43–75.

Jonides, J. (1980). Towards a model of the mind's eye's movement. *Canadian Journal of Psychology, 34*, 103–112.

Jonides, J. (1981). Voluntary versus automatic control over the mind's eye's movement. In: J.B. Long and A.D. Baddeley (Eds.), *Attention and Performance IX*. Hillsdale, N.J.: Erlbaum.

Jonides, J. (1983). Further toward a model of the mind's eye's movements. *Bulletin of the Psychonomic Society, 21*, 247–250.

Jonides, J., and Mack, R. (1984). On the cost and benefit of cost and benefit. *Psychological Bulletin, 96*, 29–44.

Jonides, J., and Yantis, S. (1988). Uniqueness of abrupt visual onset in capturing attention. *Perception & Psychophysics, 43*, 346–354.

Julesz, B. (1971). *Foundations of Cyclopean Perception*. Chicago: The University of Chicago Press.

Kahneman, D. (1964). Temporal summation in an acuity task at different energy levels – a study of the determinants of summation. *Vision Research, 4*, 557–566.

Kahneman, D. (1966). Time intensity reciprocity under various conditions of adaptation and backward masking. *Journal of Experimental Psychology, 71*, 543–549.

Kahneman, D. (1973). *Attention and Effort*. Englewood Cliffs, N.J.: Prentice-Hall.

Kahneman, D., and Chajczyk, D. (1983). Tests of the automaticity of reading: Dilution of Stroop effects by color-irrelevant stimuli. *Journal of Experimental Psychology: Human Perception and Performance, 9*, 497–509.

Kahneman, D., and Henik, A. (1981). Perceptual organization and attention. In: M. Kubovy and J.R. Pomerantz (Eds.), *Perceptual Organization*. Hillsdale, N.J.: Erlbaum.

Kahneman, D., and Norman, J. (1964). The time-intensity relation in visual perception as a function of the observer's task. *Journal of Experimental Psychology, 68*, 215–220.

Kahneman, D., and Treisman, A. (1984). Changing views of attention and automaticity. In: R. Parasuraman and P.R. Davies (Eds.), *Varieties of Attention*. New York: Academic Press.

Kahneman, D., Treisman, A., and Burkell, J. (1983). The cost of visual filtering. *Journal of Experimental Psychology: Human Perception and Performance, 9*, 510–522.

Kamlet, A.S., and Egeth, H.E. (1969). Note on construction of Stroop-type stimuli. *Perceptual and Motor Skills, 29*, 914.

Kandel, E.R., and Schwartz, J.H. (1985). *Principles of Neural Science*. New York: Elsevier (second edition).

Keele, S.W. (1973). *Attention and Human Performance*. Pacific Palisades, California: Goodyear.

Keele, S.W., and Chase, W.G. (1967). Short-term visual storage. *Perception & Psychophysics, 2*, 383–386.

Keele, S.W., Cohen, A., Ivry, R., Liotti, M., and Yee, P. (1988). Tests of a temporal theory of attentional binding. *Journal of Experimental Psychology: Human Perception and Performance, 14*, 444–452.

Keele, S.W., and Neill, T. (1978). Mechanisms of attention. In: E.C. Carterette and M.P. Friedman (Eds.), *Handbook of Perception, Vol. IX*. New York: Academic Press.

Keren, G. (1976). Some considerations of two alleged kinds of selective attention. *Journal of Experimental Psychology: General, 105*, 349–374.

Klein, G.S. (1964). Semantic power measured through the interference of words with color-naming. *American Journal of Psychology, 77*, 576–588.

Klein, R. (1988). Inhibitory tagging system facilitates visual search. *Nature, 334*, 430–431.

Koffka, K. (1935). *Principles of Gestalt Psychology*. New York: Harcourt Brace and Company.

Krumhansl, C.L. (1982). Abrupt changes in visual stimulation enhance processing of form and location information. *Perception & Psychophysics, 32*, 511–523.

Kuhn, T.S. (1962). *The Structure of Scientific Revolutions*. Chicago: University of Chicago.

La Berge, D. (1983). Spatial extent of attention to letters in words. *Journal of Experimental Psychology: Human Perception and Performance, 9*, 371–379.

La Berge, D., and Brown, V. (1986). Variations in size of the visual field in which targets are presented: An attentional range effect. *Perception & Psychophysics, 40*, 188–190.

La Heij, W. (1988). *Lexical context effects in reading and naming*. Ph.D. Thesis, University of Leiden, Leiden, The Netherlands.

La Heij, W., and Van der Heijden, A.H.C. (1983). Feature specific interference in letter identification. *Acta Psychologica, 53*, 37–60.

Lambert, A., Spencer, E., and Mohindra, N. (1987). Automaticity and the capture of attention by a peripheral display change. *Current Psychological Research and Reviews, 6*, 136–147.

Larochelle, S., McClelland, J.L., and Rodriguez, E. (1980). Context and the allocation of resources in word recognition. *Journal of Experimental Psychology: Human Perception and Performance, 6*, 686–694.

Lawrence, D.H. (1971). Two studies of visual search for word targets with controlled rates of presentation. *Perception & Psychophysics, 10*, 85–89.

Lefton, L.A., and Haber, R.N. (1974). Information extraction from different retinal locations. *Journal of Experimental Psychology, 102*, 975–980.

Lindsay, P.H., and Norman, D.A. (1977). *Human Information Processing*. New York: Academic Press (second edition).

Livingstone, M., and Hubel, D. (1988). Segregation of form, color, movement, and depth: anatomy, physiology, and perception. *Science, 240*, 740–749.

Lovie A.D. (1983). Attention and behaviourism – fact and fiction. *British Journal of Psychology*, *74*, 301–310.

Luce, R.D. (1959). *Individual Choice Behavior*. New York: Wiley.

Lupker, S.J., and Massaro, D.W. (1979). Selective perception without confounding contribution of decision and memory. *Perception & Psychophysics*, *25*, 60–69.

Mackworth, J.F. (1962). The visual image and the memory trace. *Canadian Journal of Psychology*, *16*, 55–59.

Mackworth, J.F. (1963a). The relation between the visual image and post-perceptual immediate memory. *Journal of Verbal Learning and Verbal Behavior*, *2*, 75–85.

Mackworth, J.F. (1963b). The duration of the visual image. *Canadian Journal of Psychology*, *17*, 62–81.

Manicas, P.T., and Secord, P.F. (1983). Implications for psychology of the new philosophy of science. *American Psychologist*, *38*, 399–413.

Manicas, P.T., and Secord, P.F. (1984). Reply to comments. *American Psychologist*, August, 922–926.

Marcel, A.J. (1983). Conscious and unconscious perception: An approach to the relations between phenomenal experience and perceptual processes. *Cognitive Psychology*, *15*, 238–300.

Marr, D. (1980). Visual information processing: The structure and creation of visual representations. *Phil. Trans. R. Soc. Lond.*, *B290*, 199–218.

Marshall, J.C. (1984). Multiple perspectives on modularity. *Cognition*, *17*, 209–242.

Massaro, D.W. (1975). *Experimental Psychology and Information Processing*. Chicago: Rand McNally.

Massaro, D.W. (1983). Icons and iconoclasts. *The Behavioral and Brain Sciences*, *6*, 31.

Massaro, D.W. (1986). The computer as a metaphor for psychological inquiry: considerations and recommendations. *Behavior, Research Methods, Instruments & Computers*, *18*, 73–92.

Massaro, D.W. (1987). Information processing theory and strong inference: a paradigm for psychological inquiry. In: A.F. Sanders and H. Heuer (Eds.), *Perspectives on Perception and Action*. Hillsdale, N.J.: Erlbaum.

Matthews, M.L. (1973). Locus of presentation and the selective masking effect. *Canadian Journal of Psychology*, *27*, 343–349.

Maylor, E.A. (1985). Facilitatory and inhibitory components of orienting in visual space. In: M.I. Posner and O.S.M. Marin (Eds.), *Mechanisms of Attention: Attention and Performance XI*. Hillsdale, N.J.: Erlbaum.

Maylor, E.A., and Hockey, R. (1985). Inhibitory component of externally controlled covert orienting in visual space. *Journal of Experimental Psychology: Human Perception and Performance*, *11*, 777–787.

McClean, J.P., Broadbent, D.E., and Broadbent, M.H.P. (1982). Combining attributes in rapid serial visual presentation tasks. *Quarterly Journal of Experimental Psychology*, *35A*, 171–186.

McClelland, J.L. (1979). On the time relations of mental processes: An examination of systems of processes in cascade. *Psychological Review*, *86*, 287–330.

McClelland, J.L., and Rumelhart, D.E. (1981). An interactive activation model of context effects in letter perception: I. An account of basic findings. *Psychological Review*, *88*, 375–407.

McClelland, J.L., and Rumelhart, D.E. (1986). *Parallel Distributed Processing. Vol 2: Psychological and biological models*. Cambridge, MA: The MIT Press.

McDonnell, P.M. (1970). The role of albedo and contrast in a test of selective attention. *Perception & Psychophysics*, *8*, 270–272.

McLeod, P., and Posner, M.I. (1984). Privileged loops from percept to act. In: H. Bouma and D. Bouwhuis (Eds.), *Attention and Performance X: Control of language processes*. Hillsdale, N.J.: Erlbaum.

Merikle, P.M. (1980). Selection from visual persistence by perceptual groups and category membership. *Journal of Experimental Psychology: General, 109,* 279–295.

Merikle, P.M., and Gorewich, N.J. (1979). Spatial selectivity in vision: field size depends on noise size. *Bulletin of the Psychonomic Society, 14,* 343–346.

Mertens, J.J. (1956). Influence of knowledge of target location upon the probability of observation of peripherally observable test flashes. *Journal of the Optical Society of America, 46,* 1069–1070.

Mewhort, D.J.K. (1987). Information stores and mechanisms: Early stages of visual processing. In: H. Heuer and A.F. Sanders (Eds.), *Perspectives on Perception and Action.* Hillsdale, N.J.: Erlbaum.

Mewhort, D.J.K., and Butler, B.E. (1983). On the nature of brief visual storage: there was never an icon. *The Behavioral and Brain Sciences, 6,* 31–33.

Mewhort, D.J.K., Butler, B.E., Feldman-Stewart, D., and Tramer, S. (1988). "Iconic memory", location information, and the bar-probe task: A reply to Chow (1986). *Journal of Experimental Psychology: Human Perception and Performance, 14,* 729–737.

Mewhort, D.J.K., and Campbell, A.J. (1978). Processing spatial information and the selective-masking effect. *Perception & Psychophysics, 24,* 93–101.

Mewhort, D.J.K., and Campbell, A.J. (1981). Toward a model of skilled reading: an analysis of performance in tachistoscopic tasks. *Reading Research: Advances in Theory and Practice, 3,* 39–118.

Mewhort, D.J.K., Campbell, A.J., Marchetti, F.M., and Campbell, J.I.D. (1981). Identification, localisation, and "iconic memory": an evaluation of the bar-probe task. *Memory & Cognition, 9,* 50–67.

Mewhort, D.J.K., Johns, E.E., and Coble, S. (in press). Early and late selection in partial report: Evidence from degraded displays. *Perception & Psychophysics.*

Mewhort, D.J.K., and Leppmann, K.P. (1985). Information persistence: Testing spatial and identity information with a voice probe. *Psychological Research, 47,* 51–58.

Mewhort, D.J.K., Marchetti, F.M., Gurnsey, R., and Campbell, A.J. (1984). Information persistence: A dual-buffer model for initial visual processing. In: H. Bouma and D.G. Bouwhuis (Eds.), *Attention and Performance X, Control of language processes.* Hillsdale, N.J.: Erlbaum.

Minsky, M. (1985). *The Society of Mind.* New York: Simon & Schuster.

Mishkin, M., Unerleider, L.G., and Macko, K.A. (1983). Object vision and spatial vision: two cortical pathways. *Trends in Neurosciences, 6,* 414–417.

Moray, N. (1967). Where is capacity limited? A survey and a model. *Acta Psychologica, 27,* 84–92.

Moray, N. (1969). *Attention: Selective processes in vision and hearing.* London: Hutchinson Educational.

Morton, J. (1969). Interaction of information in word recognition. *Psychological Review, 76,* 165–178.

Mowrer, O.H., Rayman, N.N., and Bliss, E.L. (1940). Preparatory set (expectancy) – an experimental demonstration of its 'central' locus. *Journal of Experimental Psychology, 26,* 357–372.

Mullin, P.A., and Egeth, H.E. (1989). Capacity limitations in visual word processing. *Journal of Experimental Psychology: Human Perception and Performance, 15,* 111–123.

Müller, H.J., and Findlay, J.M. (1987). Sensitivity and criterion effects in the spatial cuing of visual attention. *Perception & Psychophysics, 42,* 383–399.

Müller, H.J., and Rabbit, P.M.A. (1989a). Spatial cueing and the relation between the accuracy of "Where" and "What" decisions in visual search. *Quarterly Journal of Experimental Psychology, 41A*, 747–773.

Müller, H.J., and Rabbit, P.M.A. (1989b). Reflexive and voluntary orienting of visual attention: Time course of activation and resistance to interruption. *Journal of Experimental Psychology: Human Perception and Performance, 15*, 315–330.

Murphy, T.D., and Eriksen, C.W. (1987). Temporal changes in the distribution of attention in the visual field in response to precues. *Perception & Psychophysics, 42*, 576–586.

Navon, D., and Gopher, D. (1980). Task difficulty, resources, and dual-task performance. In: R.S. Nickerson (Ed.), *Attention and Performance VIII*. Hillsdale, N.J.: Erlbaum.

Neill, W.T. (1977). Inhibition and facilitation processes in selective attention. *Journal of Experimental Psychology: Human Perception and Performance, 3*, 444–450.

Neill, W.T. (1979). Switching attention within and between categories: evidence for intracategory inhibition. *Memory & Cognition, 7*, 283–290.

Neill, W.T., and Westberry, R.L. (1987). Selective attention and the suppression of cognitive noise. *Journal of Experimental Psychology: Learning, Memory, and Cognition, 13*, 327–334.

Neisser, U. (1967). *Cognitive Psychology*. New York: Appleton-Century-Crofts.

Neisser, U. (1976). *Cognition and Reality*. San Francisco: Freeman.

Neumann, O. (1980). *Informationsselektion und Handlungssteuerung*. Dissertation, Bochum.

Neumann, O. (1984). Automatic processing: A review of recent findings, and a plea for an old theory. In: W. Prinz and A.F. Sanders (Eds.), *Cognition and Motor Processes*. Heidelberg, Berlin: Springer.

Neumann, O. (1985). Die Hypothese begrenzter Kapazität und die Funktionen der Aufmerksamkeit. In: O. Neumann (Ed.), *Perspektiven der Kognitionspsychologie*. Heidelberg, Berlin: Springer.

Neumann, O., (1987). Beyond capacity: a functional view of attention. In: H. Heuer and A.F. Sanders (Eds.), *Perspectives on Perception and Action*. Hillsdale, N.J.: Erlbaum.

Neumann, O. (in prep.). *Konzepte der Aufmerksamkeit*. Bielefeld University.

Neumann, O., Van der Heijden, A.H.C., and Allport, D.A. (1986). Visual selective attention: Introductory remarks. *Psychological Research, 48*, 185–188.

Nissen, M.J. (1985). Accessing features and objects: is location special? In: M.I. Posner and O.S.M. Marin (Eds.), *Attention and Performance XI*. Hillsdale, N.J.: Erlbaum.

Norman, D.A. (1968). Towards a theory of memory and attention. *Psychological Review, 75*, 522–536.

Norman, D.A., and Bobrow, D.S. (1975). On data-limited and resource-limited processes. *Cognitive Psychology, 7*, 44-64.

Palef, S.R., and Olson, D.R. (1975). Spatial and verbal rivalry in a Stroop-like task. *Canadian Journal of Psychology, 29*, 201–209.

Palmer, S.E., and Kimchi, R. (1986). The information processing approach to cognition. In: R.J. Knapp and L.C. Robertson (Eds.), *Approaches to Cognition: Contrasts and controversies*. Hillsdale, N.J.: Erlbaum.

Paschal, F.C. (1941). The trend in theories of attention. *Psychological Review, 48*, 383–403.

Pashler, H. (1984). Evidence against late selection: Stimulus quality effects in previewed displays. *Journal of Experimental Psychology: Human Perception and Performance, 10*, 429–448.

Phaf, R.H. (1986). *A connectionist model for attention, restricting parallel processing through modularity*. Master's thesis, University of Leiden, Leiden, The Netherlands.

Phaf, R.H., Van der Heijden, A.H.C., and Hudson, P.T.W. (1990). SLAM: A connectionist model for attention in visual selection tasks. *Cognitive Psychology*, 22, 273–341.

Popper, K. (1959). *The Logic of Scientific Discovery*. New York: Basic Books.

Posner, M.I. (1975). Psychobiology of attention. In: M. Gazzaniga and C. Blakemore (Eds.), *Handbook of Psychobiology*. New York: Academic Press.

Posner, M.I. (1978). *Chronometric Exploration of the Mind*. Hillsdale, N.J.: Erlbaum.

Posner, M.I. (1980). Orienting of attention. The VIIth Sir Frederic Bartlett Lecture. *Quarterly Journal of Experimental Psychology*, 32, 3–25.

Posner, M.I., and Boies, S.J. (1971). Components of attention. *Psychological Review*, 78, 391–408.

Posner, M.I., and Cohen, Y. (1984). Components of visual orienting. In: H. Bouma and D.G. Bouwhuis (Eds.), *Attention and Performance X*. Hillsdale, N.J.: Erlbaum.

Posner, M.I., Cohen, Y., Choate, L., Hockey, G.R.J. and Maylor, E., (1984). Sustained concentration: Passive filtering or active orienting? In: S. Kornblum and J. Requin (Eds.), *Preparatory States and Processes*. Hillsdale, N.J.: Erlbaum.

Posner, M.I., Cohen, Y., and Rafal, R.D. (1982). Neural system control of spatial orienting. *Phil. Trans. R. Society, London, B298*, 187–198.

Posner, M.I., Nissen, M.J., and Ogden, W.C. (1978). Attended and unattended processing modes: The role of set for spatial location. In: H.L. Pick and I.J. Saltzman (Eds.), *Modes of Perceiving and Processing Information*. Hillsdale, N.J.: Erlbaum.

Posner, M.I., and Snyder, C.R.R. (1975). Facilitation and inhibition in the processing of signals. In: P.M.A. Rabbit and S. Dornic (Eds.), *Attention and Performance V*. New York: Academic Press.

Posner, M.I., Snyder, C.R.R., and Davidson, B.J. (1980). Attention and the detection of signals. *Journal of Experimental Psychology: General, 109*, 160–174.

Posner, M.I., Walker, J.A., Friedrich, F.A., and Rafal, R.D. (1984). Effects of parietal lobe injury on covert orienting of visual attention. *Journal of Neuroscience, 4*, 1863–1874.

Possamai, C.A. (1986). Relationship between inhibition and facilitation following a visual cue. *Acta Psychologica, 61*, 243–258.

Proctor, R.W. (1978). Sources of color-word interference in the Stroop color-naming task. *Perception & Psychophysics, 23*, 413–419.

Pylyshyn, Z.W. (1981). Psychological explanations and knowledge-dependent processes. *Cognition, 10*, 267–274.

Ratliff, F. (1952). The role of physiological nystagmus in monocular acuity. *Journal of Experimental Psychology, 43*, 163–172.

Rayner, K. (1977). Visual attention in reading: Eye movements reflect cognitive processes. *Memory & Cognition, 4*, 443–448.

Rayner, K., Inhoff, A.W., Morrison, P.E., Slowiaczek, M.L., and Bertera, J.H. (1981). Masking of foveal and parafoveal vision during eye fixations in reading. *Journal of Experimental Psychology: Human Perception and Performance, 7*, 167–179.

Rayner, K., McConkie, G.W., and Zola, D. (1980). Integrating information across eye movements. *Cognitive Psychology, 12*, 206–226

Rayner, K., Slowiaczek, M.L., Clifton, C., and Bertera, J.H. (1983). Latency of sequential eye movements: implications for reading. *Journal of Experimental Psychology: Human Perception and Performance, 9*, 912–922.

Reeves, A., and Sperling, G. (1980). Attentional gating in short-term visual memory. *Psychological Review, 93*, 180–206.

Regan, J. (1978). Involuntary automatic processing in color-naming tasks. *Perception & Psychophysics, 24*, 130–136.

Remington, R., and Pierce, L. (1984). Moving attention: Evidence for time-invariant shifts of visual selective attention. *Perception & Psychophysics, 35*, 393–399.

Rose, S.P.R. (1980). Can the neurosciences explain the mind? *Trends in Neurosciences, 3*, May 1980, I–IV.

Roufs, J.A.J. (1972). Dynamic properties of vision. I. Experimental relationships between flicker and flash thresholds. *Vision Research, 12*, 261–278.

Rumelhart, D.E. (1970). A multicomponent theory of the perception of briefly exposed visual displays. *Journal of Mathematical Psychology, 7*, 191–218.

Rumelhart, D.E., and McClelland, J.L. (1986). *Parallel Distributed Processing. Vol. 1: Foundations*. Cambridge, MA: The MIT Press.

Sanders, A.F. (1983). Towards a model of stress and human performance. *Acta Psychologica, 53*, 61–97.

Schneider, W., and Shiffrin, R.M. (1977). Controlled and automatic human information processing: I. Detection, search, and attention. *Psychological Review, 84*, 1–66.

Seymour, P.H.K. (1977). Conceptual encoding and locus of the Stroop effect. *Quarterly Journal of Experimental Psychology, 29*, 245–265.

Shapiro, R.G., and Krueger, L.E. (1983). Effect of similarity of surround on target-letter processing. *Journal of Experimental Psychology: Human Perception and Performance, 9*, 547–559.

Shaw, M.L. (1978). A capacity allocation model for reaction time. *Journal of Experimental Psychology: Human Perception and Performance, 4*, 586–598.

Shaw, M.L. (1980). Identifying attentional and decision-making components in information processing. In: R.S. Nickerson (Ed.), *Attention and Performance VIII*. Hillsdale, N.J.: Erlbaum.

Shaw, M.L. (1984). Division of attention among spatial locations: A fundamental difference between detection of letters and detection of luminance increments. In: H. Bouma and D.G. Bouwhuis (Eds.), *Attention and Performance X: Control of language processes*. Hillsdale, N.J.: Erlbaum.

Shaw, M.L., and Shaw, P. (1977). Optimal allocation of cognitive resources to spatial locations. *Journal of Experimental Psychology: Human Perception and Performance, 3*, 201–211.

Shepherd, M., Findlay, J.M., and Hockey, R.J. (1986). The relationship between eye movements and spatial attention. *Quarterly Journal of Experimental Psychology, 38*, 475–491.

Shevrin, H., and Dickman, S. (1980). The psychological unconscious: a necessary assumption for all psychological theory? *American Psychologist, 35*, 421–434.

Shibuya, H., and Bundesen, C. (1988). Visual selection from multielement displays: Measuring and modeling effects of exposure duration. *Journal of Experimental Psychology: Human Perception and Performance, 14*, 591–600.

Shiffrin, R.M., and Atkinson, R.C. (1969). Storage and retrieval processes in long-term memory. *Psychological Review, 76*, 179–193.

Shiffrin, R.M., and Schneider, W. (1977). Controlled and automatic human information processing: II. Perceptual learning, automatic attending, and a general theory. *Psychological Review, 84*, 127–190.

Shor, R.E. (1970). The processing of conceptual information on spatial directions from pictorial and linguistic symbols. *Acta Psychologica, 32*, 346–365.

Shulman, G.L. (1984). An asymmetry in the control of eye movements and shifts of attention. *Acta Psychologica, 55*, 53–69.

Shulman, G.L., Remington, R.W., and McClean, J.P. (1979). Moving attention through visual space. *Journal of Experimental Psychology: Human Perception and Performance, 5*, 522–526.

Shulman, G.L., Sheehy, J.B., and Wilson, J. (1986). Gradients of spatial attention. *Acta Psychologica, 61*, 167–181.

Shulman, G.L., Wilson, J., and Sheehy, J.B. (1985). Spatial determinants of the distribution of attention. *Perception & Psychophysics, 37*, 59–65.

Sichel, J.L., and Chandler, K.A. (1969). The color-word interference test: The effects of varied color-word combinations upon verbal response latency. *The Journal of Psychology, 72*, 219–231.

Skelton, J.M., and Eriksen, C.W. (1976). Spatial characteristics of selective attention in letter matching. *Bulletin of the Psychonomic Society, 7*, 136–138.

Skinner, B.F. (1977). Why I am not a cognitive psychologist. *Behaviorism, 5*, 1–10.

Skinner, B.F. (1985). Cognitive science and behaviourism. *British Journal of Psychology, 76*, 291–301.

Snyder, C.R.R. (1972). Selection, inspection and naming in visual search. *Journal of Experimental Psychology, 92*, 428–431.

Solso, R.L. (1979). *Cognitive Psychology*. New York: Harcourt Brace Jovanovich.

Sperling, G. (1960). The information available in brief visual presentations. *Psychological Monograph, 74(11)* (whole no. 498).

Sperling, G. (1963). A model for visual memory tasks. *Human Factors, 5*, 19–31.

Sperling, G. (1984). A unified theory of attention and signal detection. In: R. Parasuraman and D.R. Davies (Eds.), *Varieties of Attention*. New York: Academic Press.

Sperling, G., and Reeves, A. (1980). Measuring the reaction time of an unobservable response: A shift of visual attention. In: R.S. Nickerson (Ed.), *Attention and Performance VIII*. Hillsdale, N.J.: Erlbaum.

Stelmach, L.B. (1984). Does rate of processing determine ease of target detection? *Journal of Experimental Psychology: Human Perception and Performance, 10*, 108–118.

Stone, J., and Dreher, B. (1982). Parallel processing of information in the visual pathways: A general principle of sensory coding? *Trends in Neurosciences, 5*, 441–446.

Strangert, B., and Brännström, L. (1975). Spatial interaction effects in letter processing. *Perception & Psychophysics, 17*, 268–272.

Stroop, J.R. (1935). Studies of interference in serial verbal reactions. *Journal of Experimental Psychology, 18*, 643–662.

Styles, E.A., and Allport, D.A. (1986). Perceptual integration of identity, location and colour. *Psychological Research, 48*, 189–200.

Szentagothai, J. (1975). The "module-concept" in cerebral cortex architecture. *Brain Research, 95*, 475–496.

Taylor, S.G., and Brown, D.R. (1972). Lateral visual masking: Supraretinal effects when viewing linear arrays with unlimited viewing time. *Perception & Psychophysics, 12*, 97–99.

Tipper, S.P. (1985). The negative priming effect: Inhibitory priming by ignored objects. *Quarterly Journal of Experimental Psychology, 37A*, 571–590.

Tipper, S.P., and Cranston, M. (1985). Selective attention and priming: Inhibitory and facilitatory effects of ignored primes. *Quarterly Journal of Experimental Psychology, 37A*, 591–611.

Titchener, E.B. (1908). *Lectures on the Elementary Psychology of Feeling and Attention*. New York: Macmillan.

Todd, J.T., and Van Gelder, P. (1979). Implications of a sustained–transient dichotomy for the measurement of human performance. *Journal of Experimental Psychology: Human Perception and Performance, 5*, 625–638.

Townsend, V.M. (1973). Loss of spatial and identity information following a tachistoscopic exposure. *Journal of Experimental Psychology, 98*, 113–118.

Townsend, J.T., Taylor, S.G., and Brown, D.R. (1971). Lateral masking for letters with unlimited viewing time. *Perception & Psychophysics, 10*, 375–378.

Tramer, S. (1981). *Data versus probe errors in the bar-probe task: A re-evaluation of the dual-buffer model*. Unpublished M.A. Thesis, Queen's University at Kingston.

Treisman, A.M. (1960). Contextual cues in selective listening. *Quarterly Journal of Experimental Psychology, 12*, 242–248.

Treisman, A.M. (1964). Verbal cues, language, and meaning in selective attention. *American Journal of Psychology, 77*, 206–219.

Treisman, A.M. (1969). Strategies and models of selective attention. *Psychological Review, 76*, 282–299.

Treisman, A.M. (1977). Focussed attention in the perception and retrieval of multidimensional stimuli. *Perception & Psychophysics, 22*, 1–11.

Treisman, A.M. (1988). Features and objects: The fourteenth Bartlett memorial lecture. *Quarterly Journal of Experimental Psychology, 40A*, 201–237.

Treisman, A.M., and Gelade, G. (1980). A feature integration theory of attention. *Cognitive Psychology, 12*, 97–136.

Treisman, A.M., and Gormican, S. (1988). Feature analysis in early vision: Evidence from search asymmetries. *Psychological Review, 95*, 15–48.

Treisman, A.M., Kahneman, D., and Burkell, J. (1983). Perceptual objects and the cost of filtering. *Perception & Psychophysics, 33*, 527–532.

Treisman, A.M., and Paterson, R. (1984). Emergent features, attention and object perception. *Journal of Experimental Psychology: Human Perception and Performance, 10*, 12–31.

Treisman, A.M., and Schmidt, H. (1982). Illusory conjunctions in the perception of objects. *Cognitive Psychology, 14*, 107–141.

Treisman, A.M., and Souther, J. (1985). Search asymmetry: A diagnostic for preattentive processing of separable features. *Journal of Experimental Psychology: General, 114*, 285–310.

Tsal, Y. (1983). Movements of attention across the visual field. *Journal of Experimental Psychology: Human Perception and Performance, 9*, 523–530.

Turvey, M.T. (1977). Contrasting orientations to the theory of visual information processing. *Psychological Review, 84*, 67–88.

Turvey, M.T., and Kravetz, S. (1970). Retrieval from iconic memory with shape as the selection criterion. *Perception & Psychophysics, 8*, 171–172.

Ungerleider, L.G., and Mishkin, M. (1982). Two cortical visual systems. In: D.J. Ingle, M.A. Goodale and R.W.J. Mansfield (Eds.), *Analysis of Visual Behaviour*. Cambridge, MA: The MIT Press.

Van Essen, D.C. (1979). Visual areas of the mammalian cerebral cortex. *Annual Review of Neurosciences, 2*, 227–263.

Van Essen, D.C., and Maunsell, J.H.R. (1983). Hierarchical organization and functional streams in the visual cortex. *Trends in Neurosciences, 6*, 370–375.

Van der Heijden, A.H.C. (1975). Some evidence for a limited capacity parallel selfterminating process in simple visual search tasks. *Acta Psychologica, 39*, 21–41.

Van der Heijden, A.H.C. (1978). *Short-term visual information forgetting*. Ph.D. Thesis, University of Leiden, Leiden, The Netherlands.

Van der Heijden, A.H.C. (1981). *Short-term visual information forgetting*. London: Routledge & Kegan Paul.

Van der Heijden, A.H.C. (1984). Postcategorical filtering in a bar-probe task. *Memory & Cognition, 12*, 446–457.

Van der Heijden, A.H.C. (1986). On selection in vision. *Psychological Research, 48*, 211–219.

Van der Heijden, A.H.C. (1987). Central selection in vision. In: H.Heuer and A.F.Sanders (Eds.), *Perspectives on Perception and Action*. Hillsdale, N.J.: Erlbaum.

Van der Heijden, A.H.C. (1989). Probability matching in visual selective attention. *Canadian Journal of Psychology, 43*, 45–52.

Van der Heijden, A.H.C. (1990). Visual information processing and selection. In: W. Prinz and O. Neumann (Eds.), *Relationships between Perception and Action*. Berlin, Heidelberg: Springer.

Van der Heijden, A.H.C., and Eerland, E. (1973). The effects of cueing in a visual signal detection task. *Quarterly Journal of Experimental Psychology, 25*, 496–503.

Van der Heijden, A.H.C., Hagenaar, R., and Bloem, W. (1984). Two stages in postcategorical filtering and selection. *Memory & Cognition, 12*, 458–469.

Van der Heijden, A.H.C., La Heij, W., and Boer, J.P.A. (1983). Parallel processing of redundant targets in simple visual search tasks. *Psychological Research, 45*, 235–254.

Van der Heijden, A.H.C., La Heij, W., Phaf, R.H., Buys, D.A.C.H., and Van Vliet, E.C. (1988). Response competition and condition competition in visual selective attention. *Acta Psychologica, 67*, 259–277.

Van der Heijden, A.H.C., Malhas, M.S.M., and Van den Roovaart, B.P. (1984). An empirical interletter confusion matrix for continuous-line capitals. *Perception & Psychophysics, 35*, 85–88.

Van der Heijden, A.H.C., Neerincx, M., and Wolters, G. (1989). Location cuing benefits with exposure duration variations. *Bulletin of the Psychonomic Society, 27*, 35–38.

Van der Heijden, A.H.C., Schreuder, R., De Loor, M., and Hagenzieker, M. (1987). Early and late selection: Visual letter confusions in a bar-probe task. *Acta Psychologica, 65*, 75–89.

Van der Heijden, A.H.C., Schreuder, R., Maris, L., and Neerincx, M. (1984). Some evidence for correlated separate activation in a simple letter-detection task. *Perception and Psychophysics, 36*, 577–585.

Van der Heijden, A.H.C., Schreuder, R., and Wolters, G. (1985). Enhancing single-item recognition accuracy by cueing spatial locations in vision. *Quarterly Journal of Experimental Psychology, 37A*, 427–434.

Van der Heijden, A.H.C., and Stebbins, S. (1990). The information processing approach. *Psychological Research, 52*, 197–206.

Van der Heijden, A.H.C., Van Gelder, I., Vermeulen, M., and Winkel, C. (in prep.). Dilution: The Kahneman effect.

Van der Heijden, A.H.C., Wolters, G., and Enkeling, M. (1988). The effects of advance location cueing on latencies in a single-letter recognition task. *Psychological Research, 50*, 94–102.

Van der Heijden, A.H.C., Wolters, G., Fleur, E., and Hommels, J.G.M. (in prep.). Single-letter recognition accuracy benefits and position information.

Van der Heijden, A.H.C., Wolters, G., Groep, J.C., and Hagenaar, R. (1987). Single-letter recognition accuracy benefits from advance cueing of location. *Perception & Psychophysics, 42*, 503–509.

Van Hoorn, W. (1972). *Ancient and Modern Theories of Visual Perception*. Amsterdam: University Press Amsterdam.

Van Werkhoven, S., Wolters, G., and Van der Heijden, A.H.C. (1986). *The influence of masking on recognition of cued letters*. (Internal report, EP-86-01). Leiden, The Netherlands: University of Leiden.

Vaughan, J. (1984). Saccades directed at previously attended locations in space. In: A.G. Gale and F. Johnson (Eds.), *Theoretical and Applied Aspects of Eye Movement Research*. Amsterdam: North-Holland.

Von Helmholtz, H. (1871). Ueber die Zeit welche nötig ist, damit ein Gesichtseindruck zum Bewusstsein kommt. *Berliner Monatsberichte*, June 8, 333–337.

Von Helmholtz, H. (1894). *Handbuch der physiologischen Optik*. Hamburg, Leipzig: L. Vos.

Von Helmholtz, H. (1924). *Treatise on Physiological Optics*. Rochester, New York: Optical Society of America.

Von Wright, J.M. (1968). Selection in visual immediate memory. *Quarterly Journal of Experimental Psychology, 20,* 62–68.

Von Wright, J.M. (1970). On selection in visual immediate memory. *Acta Psychologica, 33,* 280–292.

Von Wright, J.M. (1972). On the problem of selection in iconic memory. *Scandinavian Journal of Psychology, 13,* 159–171.

Warren, C., and Morton, J. (1982). The effects of priming on picture recognition. *British Journal of Psychology, 75,* 117–129.

Warren, R.M., and Warren, R.P. (1968). *Helmholtz on Perception: Its physiology and development.* New York: John Wiley & Sons.

Watson, J.B. (1913). Psychology as the behaviorist views it. *Psychological Review, 20,* 158–177.

Watson, J.B. (1919). *Psychology from the Standpoint of a Behaviorist.* Philadelphia: Lippincott.

Weichselgartner, E., and Sperling, G. (1987). Dynamics of automatic and controlled visual attention. *Science, 238,* 778–780.

Wertheimer, M. (1923). Untersuchungen zur Lehre von der Gestalt II. *Psychologische Forschung, 4,* 301–350.

White, B.W. (1969). Interference in identifying attributes and attribute names. *Perception & Psychophysics, 6,* 166–168.

Wolff, P. (1987). Perceptual learning by saccades: A cognitive approach. In: H. Heuer and A.F. Sanders (Eds.), *Perspectives on Perception and Action.* Hillsdale, N.J.: Erlbaum.

Wolford, G., and Chambers, L. (1983). Lateral masking as a function of spacing. *Perception & Psychophysics, 33,* 129–138.

Wolford, G., and Hollingsworth, S. (1974). Lateral masking in visual information processing. *Perception & Psychophysics, 16,* 315–320.

Wundt, W. (1874). *Grundzüge der physiologische Psychologie.* Leipzig: Engelman.

Wundt, W. (1912). *An Introduction to Psychology.* London: Allen & Unwin.

Yantis, S. (1988). On analog movements of visual attention. *Perception & Psychophysics, 43,* 203–206.

Yantis, S., and Jonides, J. (1984). Abrupt visual onsets and selective attention: Evidence from visual search. *Journal of Experimental Psychology: Human Perception and Performance, 10,* 601–621.

Zeki, S. (1978). Functional specialization in the visual cortex of the rhesus monkey. *Nature, 274,* 423–428.

Zeki, S., and Shipp, S. (1988). The functional logic of cortical connections. *Nature, 355,* 311–317.

Name index

Aine, C.J. 87
Allmeyer, D.H. 231
Allport, D.A. 15, 20, 26, 30, 32, 50, 51, 59, 130, 210, 247–8, 249–51; on attention and action 32, 244–6, 269, 270, 281; on attentional 'spotlight' 92, 251; on limited vs unlimited capacity processing 60, 167, 237, 242; on 'perfect selection' 176; on selective cueing 167, 248, 249–50
Amundsen, R. 5, 11
Anderson, J.A. 30
Anstis, S.M. 56–7
Atkinson, R.C. 199, 211
Averbach, E. 53, 132, 134–6, 138, 139, 145, 162

Babington-Smith, B. 123–4, 126
Bacharach, V.R. 66, 68, 70, 71, 72, 88, 89, 100
Banks, W.P. 231
Barlow, H.B. 16, 26, 216
Bashinski, H.S. 66, 68, 70, 71, 72, 88, 89, 100
Bechtel, W. 30
Beech, A. 130
Berlyne, D.E. 32, 61, 89, 281
Bertera, J.H. 59, 222
Bidloo, Prof. 117
Bieri, P. 20, 24
Bliss, E.L. 40
Bloch, A.M. 216
Bloem, W. 51, 91, 172
Bobrow, D.S. 60, 238
Boer, J.P.A. 191, 237
Boies, S.J. 99
Boring, E.G. 37, 40, 245
Boroughs, J.M. 219

Bouma, H. 231
Brady, M. 27
Brännström, L. 231
Breitmeyer, B.G. 89, 112, 198
Broadbent, D.E. 9, 20, 22, 26, 47–50, 55, 59–60, 63, 127, 165, 182, 184; on early selection 51, 64, 138, 139; filter theory of attention 41–4, 49, 64, 139, 167, 238; on limited capacity processing 60, 64, 238, 242, 243; on rapid serial visual presentation (RSVP) 93–6; on serial processing 170; split-span experiments 42, 48; on stimulus set and response set 52
Broadbent, M.H.P. 93–5
Broca, A. 223–6
Brown, D.R. 231
Brown, V. 108, 113, 115
Bryden, M.P. 123
Budayr, B. 127, 130, 171, 277
Bundesen, C. 132, 133
Burkell, J. 189
Butler, B.E. 87, 141, 142, 143, 247
Buys, D.A.C.H. 50

Campbell, A.J. 51, 136, 141–3, 145, 148
Campbell, J.I.D. 51, 136
Canham, L. 219
Chajczyk, D. 172, 176–7, 179, 182, 183, 184, 190, 201–4, 265–6, 278, 279
Chambers, L. 231
Chandler, K.A. 127, 171
Chase, W.G. 158
Chastain, G. 231
Cherry, E.C. 42
Chmiel, N.R.J. 130
Choate, L. 124
Chow, S.L. 51, 142

Subject index